Visions of Violence

German Avant-Gardes

After Fascism

RICHARD LANGSTON

Northwestern

University Press

Evanston

Illinois

Northwestern University Press

www.nupress.northwestern.edu

Copyright © 2008 by Northwestern University Press. Published 2008. All rights reserved.

Printed in the United States of America

10 9 8 7 6 5 4 3 2 1

Library of Congress Cataloging-in-Publication Data

Langston, Richard, 1970–

    Visions of violence : German avant-gardes after fascism / Richard Langston.

        p. cm. — (Avant-garde & modernism studies)

        Includes bibliographical references and index.

        ISBN-13: 978-0-8101-2471-4 (pbk. : alk. paper)

        ISBN-10: 0-8101-2471-8 (pbk. : alk. paper)

        ISBN-13: 978-0-8101-2466-0 (cloth : alk. paper)

        ISBN-10: 0-8101-2466-1 (cloth : alk. paper)

        1. Avant-garde (Aesthetics)—Germany. 2. German literature—20th century—History and criticism. 3. Violence in literature. 4. Violence in art. 5. Fascism in literature. I. Title. II. Series: Avant-garde and modernism studies.

PT405.L3118   2007

830.9'1109045—dc22

                                    2007028620

♾ The paper used in this publication meets the minimum requirements of the American National Standard for Information Sciences—Permanence of Paper for Printed Library Materials, ANSI Z39.48-1992.

For John

Contents

Figures

Acknowledgments

This book would have been impossible without the support of a vast network of people and institutions made available to me over a lengthy period of time. Washington University in St. Louis provided me with financial support as a graduate student to conduct preliminary research in Munich, Germany. More recently, the University of North Carolina at Chapel Hill has provided me with invaluable financial support, without which this project would never have been possible. I am grateful for support from UNC's Research Council, Small Research Grant, and the Spray-Randleigh Foundation. I am also indebted to the former dean of the School of Arts and Science, Bernadette Gray-Little, for securing for me the precious time and the financial support necessary to complete the research and writing of *Visions of Violence*.

I am extremely appreciative of the generosity of the following public and private research centers that opened their doors to me over the course of many years: the Nachlaß Peter Weiss at the Akademie der Künste in Berlin; Raphael Vostell at the Galerie Vostell Berlin; Mercedes Guardado Vostell, David Vostell, and José Antonio Agúndez García of the Museo Vostell in Malpartida de Cáceres, Spain; Ilona Lütken at the Archiv Sohm, Staatsgalerie, Stuttgart; Reiner Ziegler of the Haus des Dokumentarfilms, Stuttgart; and Günther Hörmann of the Hochschule für Gestaltung in Schwäbisch Gmünd. The following individuals have also made films available to me: Alexander Kluge, Lutz Koepnick, Danette Pachtner, Chris Pavsek, Paul Poet, and Florian Vogel.

I have had the good fortune to talk with and learn from a great many scholars ever since this project first saw the light of day during my graduate studies. In some cases, the shortest of conversations have been tremendously inspiring and productive for my work on the avant-garde. In other instances, I have profited enormously from a sustained intellectual exchange. As all of these interactions have shaped my thinking about the avant-garde, I can only acknowledge them, in fairness, alphabetically: Claudia Breger, Tina Campt, Rich Cante, Tyler Curtin, Diedrich Diederichsen, Dorothea Dietrich, Bill Donahue, Eric Downing, Sabine Eckmann, Kai Evers, Gregg Flaxman, Boris Groys, Randall Halle, Jonathan Hess, Ken Hillis, Gerald Izenberg, Martin Jay, Claudia Koonz, Juliet Koss, Alice Kuzniar, Paul Michael Lützeler, Peter McIsaac, Claudia Mesch, Bill Rasch, Ann Marie Rassmussen, Mark Rectanus, Katrin Sieg, Kathryn

Starkey, Reinhild Steingröver, Kristine Stiles, Kris Thomas Vander Lugt, and Robert Weninger. Brigitte Rossbacher deserves special attention, for she has been a great mentor, friend, and colleague without whom I would never have found the time amidst my many professional duties to finish this book. Lutz Koepnick stands out above the rest. He saw me through my intellectual training, pushed me in my thinking about the avant-garde, shared with me his own work on the topic, and gave me opportunities to talk with others about my scholarship. This book would simply not exist were it not for him.

Graduate students at Duke University, Indiana University, and the University of North Carolina at Chapel Hill have provided me with valuable opportunities to spin out my ideas. Their insights have been most productive for the development of my work. Cyrus Shahan has been exceptional in this respect.

Portions of chapters 2, 3, and 7 first saw the light of day at conferences, in particular those of the Modern Language Association and the German Studies Association. Similarly, an excerpt of chapter 2 on Peter Weiss was previously published in *Modernism/modernity* 14, no. 2 (2007), 273–90. I am grateful to the Johns Hopkins University Press for granting me permission to reprint this work as part of *Visions of Violence*.

I am most grateful to the staff at Northwestern University Press and series editor Rainer Rumold, as well as the anonymous readers who provided me with invaluable feedback. My copy editor deserves the highest praise, too.

Many others have been my even keel over the many years I spent completing this project. Friends in St. Louis, the Triangle, and Berlin have kept me sane and plied me with much-needed diversions. My family watched from afar as I reinvented the wheel; their long-distance support has been a solid foundation in my early professional life.

Abbreviations

"AAG"   Hans Magnus Enzensberger, "The Aporias of the Avant-Garde," in *Zig Zag: The Politics of Culture and Vice Versa*, 235–64 (New York: New Press, 1997).

AP   Walter Benjamin, *The Arcades Project*, trans. Howard Eiland and Kevin McLaughlin (Cambridge, Mass.: Belknap, 1999).

BB   Miriam Hansen, *Babel and Babylon: Spectatorship in American Silent Film* (Cambridge, Mass.: Harvard University Press, 1991).

BH   Rolf Dieter Brinkmann, *Briefe an Hartmut 1974–1975* (Reinbek bei Hamburg: Rowohlt, 1999).

BT   Martin Heidegger, *Being and Time*, trans. John Macquarrie and Edward Robinson (San Francisco: Harper, 1962).

"CH"   Walter Benjamin, "On the Concept of History," in *Selected Writings, Vol. 4: 1938–1940*, ed. Howard Eiland and Michael Jennings, 389–400 (Cambridge, Mass.: Belknap, 2003).

DE   Max Horkheimer and Theodor W. Adorno, *Dialectic of Enlightenment: Philosophical Fragments*, ed. Gunzelin Schmid Noerr, trans. Edmund Jephcott (Stanford, Calif.: Stanford University Press, 2002).

"DMB" Alexander Kluge, "Die Macht der Bewußtseinsindustrie und das Schicksal unserer Öffentlichkeit," in *Industrialisierung des Bewußtseins*, ed. Klaus von Bismarck et al., 51–129 (Munich: Piper, 1985).

DP   Gottfried Benn, *Der Ptolemäer*, in *Gesammelte Werke*, ed. Dieter Wellershoff, vol. 2, 1377–1429 (Frankfurt am Main: Zweitausendeins, 2003).

E   Rolf Dieter Brinkmann, "In der Grube," in *Erzählungen*, 7–67 (Reinbek bei Hamburg: Rowohlt, 1985).

EP   Rolf Dieter Brinkmann, *Erkundungen für die Präzisierung des Gefühls für einen Aufstand: Träume Aufstände/Gewalt/Morde REISE ZEIT MAGAZIN Die Story ist schnell erzählt (Tagebuch)* (Reinbek bei Hamburg: Rowohlt, 1987).

"FP"   Dieter Wellershoff, "Fiktion und Praxis," in *Literatur und Veränderung: Versuche zu einer Metakritik der Literatur,* 9–32 (Cologne: Kiepenheuer und Witsch, 1969).

FSS   Wolfgang Kraushaar, ed., *Frankfurter Schule und Studentenbewegung: Von der Flaschenpost zum Molotowcocktail 1946–1995,* vol. 2: *Dokumente* (Frankfurt am Main: Rogner und Bernhard bei Zweitausendeins, 1998).

GB   Dieter Wellershoff, *Gottfried Benn: Phänotyp dieser Stunde: Eine Studie über den Problemgehalt seines Werkes* (Cologne: Kiepenheuer und Witsch, 1958).

GE   Oskar Negt and Alexander Kluge, *Geschichte und Eigensinn,* vol. 2, *Der unterschätzte Mensch: Gemeinsame Philosophie in zwei Bänden* (Frankfurt am Main: Zweitausendeins, 2001).

HF   Jürgen Beck and Wolf Vostell, ed., *Happenings, Fluxus, Pop art, Nouveau réalisme: Eine Dokumentation* (Reinbek bei Hamburg: Rowohlt, 1965).

"HK"   Alexander Kluge, "Heidegger auf der Krim," in *Chronik der Gefühle,* vol. 1, 417–34 (Frankfurt am Main: Suhrkamp, 2000).

HL   Wolf Vostell, *Happening und Leben* (Neuwied: Hermann Luchterhand, 1970).

HS   Giorgio Agamben, *Homo Sacer: Sovereign Power and Bare Life,* trans. Daniel Heller-Roazen (Stanford: Stanford University Press, 1998).

"IG"   William S. Burroughs, "the invisible generation," in *The Ticket That Exploded,* 205–17 (New York: Grove, 1967).

JK   Ulrich Enzensberger, *Die Jahre der Kommune I: Berlin 1967–1969* (Cologne: Kiepenheuer und Witsch, 2004).

KM   Rainer Langhans and Fritz Teufel, *Klau mich!* ed. Bernward Vesper (Frankfurt am Main: edition Voltaire, 1968).

"MB"   Walter Benjamin, "On Some Motifs in Baudelaire," in *Selected Writings, Vol. 4: 1938–1940,* ed. Howard Eiland and Michael Jennings, 313–55 (Cambridge, Mass.: Belknap, 2003).

MM   Theodor W. Adorno, *Minima Moralia: Reflections on a Damaged Life,* trans. E. F. N. Jephcott (London: Verso, 1974).

"NB"   Rolf Dieter Brinkmann, "Notizen und Beobachtungen vor dem Schrieben eines zweiten Romans," in *Der Film in Worten: Prosa, Erzählungen, Essays, Hörspiele, Fotos, Collagen 1965–1974,* 275–95 (Reinbek bei Hamburg: Rowohlt, 1982).

ND   Theodor W. Adorno, *Negative Dialectics,* trans. E. B. Ashton (New York: Continuum, 1973).

ODM   Herbert Marcuse, *One-Dimensional Man: Studies in the Ideologies of Advanced Industrial Society* (Boston: Beacon, 1964).

"OL"   Roland Barthes, "Objective Literature," in *Critical Essays,* trans. Richard Howard, 13–24 (Evanston: Northwestern University Press, 1972).

OM   Fredric Jameson, foreword to *On Meaning: Selected Writings in Semiotic Theory,* by Algirdas Julien Greimas, trans. Paul J. Perron and Frank H. Collins, vi–xxii (London: Frances Pinter, 1987).

"PCH"   Walter Benjamin, "Paralipomena to 'On the Concept of History,'" in *Selected Writings, Vol. 4: 1938–1940,* ed. Howard Eiland and Michael Jennings, 401–11 (Cambridge, Mass.: Belknap, 2003).

PU   Fredric Jameson, *The Political Unconscious: Narrative as a Socially Symbolic Act* (Ithaca: Cornell University Press, 1981).

RB   Rolf Dieter Brinkmann, *Rom, Blicke* (Reinbek bei Hamburg: Rowohlt, 1979).

"RT"   Dominick LaCapra, "Reflections on Trauma, Absence, and Loss," in *Whose Freud? The Place of Psychoanalysis in Contemporary Culture,* ed. Peter Brooks and Alex Woloch, 178–204 (New Haven: Yale University Press, 2000).

RTV   Mark Andrejevic, *Reality TV: The Work of Being Watched* (Lanham: Rowman and Littlefield, 2004).

S   Rolf Dieter Brinkmann, *SCHNITTE* (Reinbek bei Hamburg: Rowohlt, 1988).

SAR   Matthias Lilienthal and Claus Philipp, ed., *Schlingensiefs AUSLÄNDER RAUS* (Frankfurt am Main: Suhrkamp, 2000).

SB   Alexander Kluge, *Schlachtbeschreibung* (Olten: Walter, 1964); Alexander Kluge, *Schlachtbeschreibung: Ein Roman* (Frankfurt am Main: Suhrkamp, 1983).

SBC   Peter Weiss, *The Shadow of the Body of the Coachman,* trans. E. B. Garside, in *Marat/Sade, The Investigation, and The Shadow of the Body of the Coachman,* ed. Robert Cohen, 1–39 (New York: Continuum, 1998).

"SLS"   Walter Benjamin, "Surrealism: The Last Snapshot of the European Intelligentsia," in *Selected Writings, Vol. 2: 1927–1934,* ed. Michael W. Jennings et al., 207–21 (Cambridge, Mass.: Belknap, 1999).

"ST"   Andreas Huyssen, "The Search for Tradition: Avantgarde and Postmodernism in the 1970s," in *After the Great Divide: Modernism, Mass Culture, Postmodernism,* 160–77 (Bloomington: Indiana University Press, 1986).

TAG   Peter Bürger, *Theory of the Avant-Garde,* trans. Michael Shaw (Minneapolis: University of Minnesota Press, 1984).

TB   Avital Ronell, *The Telephone Book: Technology, Schizophrenia, Electric Speech* (Lincoln: University of Nebraska Press, 1989).

"UN"   Rolf Dieter Brinkmann, "Ein unkontrolliertes Nachwort zu meinen Gedichten," *Literaturmagazin* 5 (1976): 228–48.

"WMP" Hans Magnus Enzensberger, "Weltsprache der modernen Poesie," in *Einzelheiten II: Poesie und Politik,* 7–28 (Frankfurt am Main: Suhrkamp, 1984).

Visions of Violence

Only exaggerations per se today can be the medium of truth.
—Theodor Adorno, "The Meaning of Working Through the
Past," in *Critical Models: Interventions and Catchwords*

We are not postmodernists. I believe in the avant-garde.
—Alexander Kluge[1]

Introduction: Visions of Violence

Violence and Fantasy

What became of the avant-garde in Germany after the Second World
War and the Holocaust? Some have dismissed this question outright,
claiming that the avant-garde was dead well before Hitler came to power
and that postwar attempts to resurrect it only produced hollow imitations.
On the contrary, not only did the avant-garde rematerialize in Germany
after fascism, but it also found a new purpose.

Nazi Germany's book burnings, its campaign against degenerate art,
and its persecution of experimental artists pushed the avant-garde—that
extreme faction of aesthetic modernity intent on bulldozing affirmative
culture—to the brink of extinction. Out of exile and inner emigration,
from the battlefields and concentrations camps, disciples of the avant-
garde returned to postwar Germany. Yet the avant-garde they restored
instantly found itself in a radically different world. Decimated Germany
had little left to destroy, and in the shadow of unparalleled war and genocide, the avant-garde's aesthetic violence—shocking montages of irrationality, madness, primitivism, war, and the apocalypse—had lost its force.
The avant-garde anti-aesthetic had become aesthetic reality.

The story of these two metamorphoses—the violent transformation
of European reality and the concomitant reconfiguration of the avant-
garde—is best told from the perspective of violence: what was the original
use of avant-garde violence, and what became of it after 1945? In the first
three decades of the twentieth century, avant-garde movements regularly

3

concocted vivid visions of violence as either the cause or the effect of their push for societal and cultural renewal. Italian futurism, for example, glorified war and championed an art committed to nationalist rejuvenation through "violence, cruelty, and injustice."[2] German expressionism regularly spun imminent doomsdays, deadly Oedipal revolts, and social revolutions into its eschatology. Fueled by the chaos of world war, nationalistic militarism, and the cacophony of urban experience, Dada appointed chaos as the cornerstone of its anti-aesthetic assault on European bourgeois society. Surrealism unleashed the maelstrom of the unconscious as the secret weapon in its "war" on rationality and the latter's anesthesia of everyday perception and experience.[3]

While each of these avant-garde movements incorporated and signified mayhem differently, the common denominator among all of them was a conviction that folding violence into art emancipated art from the shackles of the dominant cultural institutions that it otherwise aided and abetted. Violence shattered those venerable qualities like the beautiful that ensured art's status as art. Violence also sought to transform art into a raw force capable of reshaping people's perceptions of themselves, their place in society, and even the very composition of the societies in which they lived. Attention to historical context shows that the purpose of the early avant-gardes' violence corresponded in large part to their temporal relationship to the Great War. Fin-de-siècle incarnations prior to World War I (like futurism and early expressionism) turned to violence in much the same ways that emergent groups in Germany (like anarchists, revolutionaries, aestheticists, and anti-Semites) did in order to generate a sense of a national public sphere. With the outbreak of unprecedented modern warfare in 1914, these disparate and often opposing appeals to violence congealed in the name of national renewal.[4] In the wake of the horrors of war, ensuing avant-gardes like Dada and surrealism distanced themselves from the violence of nationalism and instead wielded their own brand of violence to expose the falseness of national regeneration and wholeness.[5]

Violence unquestionably propelled the aesthetic and social objectives of these early avant-gardes. Its physics—how violent effects traveled from the avant-garde's anti-aesthetics to the sociopolitical arena—remain, however, a point of scholarly contention. In the interwar period, intellectual debates hypothesized whether violence was solely an aesthetic effect with ideological implications or an actual stimulus capable of assaulting the psychology of the mind or even the physiology of the brain. As for the first of these two positions, avant-garde violence frequently found itself linked to an aesthetic of mimesis. For detractors of the avant-garde like Georg Lukács, the fragmentation so common among much avant-garde work represented an assault on art's ability to unveil the invisible social forces that shape the circumstances of lived reality. Conversely, avant-garde proponents like Ernst Bloch contended that montage accurately captured the splintered nature of modern experience, something that quotidian perception failed to discover. The principle consequence of these foundational "expressionism debates" from the 1930s—the antithetical relationship between realism and avant-gardism—continues today to shape scholarly discourse about avant-garde aesthetics.[6] The avant-garde exists either to bankrupt or to fulfill art's mimetic promise. The French literary scholar Vincent Kaufmann, for example, echoing seminal thinkers like Bloch, Herbert Marcuse, and Peter Bürger before him, recently declared that the avant-garde sought *"to realize art in life"* and hence was intimately bound up with capturing authentic experience by not availing itself of the key constituents of art, namely "representation, spectacle, and fantasy."[7] For Kaufmann, the avant-garde smashes the illusions endemic to realism. As faithful as he is to both Lukács' and Bloch's positions, he nonetheless goes too far by absolutizing this dichotomy at the price of eliding a crucial middle ground, one that even Bloch and Lukács were remiss in acknowledging. Kaufmann's insistence on the avant-garde's loathing of any and all "fantasmatic contamination" is hasty. The avant-garde teemed with violent fantasies. They can be found in futurist founder F. T. Marinetti's allegory of winged marauders who extinguish the light of the moon, in expressionist painter Ludwig Meidner's hallucinations of millenarian earthquakes in the modern metropolis, in Dada filmmaker Hans Richter's enchanted, herky-jerky world of unruly objects, and in surrealist ringleader André Breton's obsession with the illogic of dreams.

If fantasy was indeed at work in the violent visions of the avant-garde, can theoretical models explain this "fantasmatic contamination"? On the whole, the avant-garde does not conspire with the popular genre of fantasy and its engrossing, self-coherent tales about impossible worlds.[8] Likewise, Sigmund Freud's psychoanalytic idea of fantasy as the distorted sign of repressed taboo desires misses the explicit intentionality of avant-garde violence. Not escapism, veiled critique, or an unconscious defense mechanism, avant-garde fantasy acted as a vehicle for its textual and extra-textual politics. As much as the avant-garde evoked verisimilitude, it also violently rejected it. Violence was what much of the avant-garde injected into its perceptions of everyday life in order to imagine and herald that life's imminent overthrow. To this end, the realm of fantasy facilitated aesthetically the avant-garde's attack on the status quo by envisioning the destruction of the world as a real possibility.[9] The force of its fantasies arose, therefore, out of the irresolvable tension between the imagination and reality. This is why surrealists themselves never executed the "simplest surrealist act," namely firing a pistol blindly into a crowded street.[10] To do so, as fascist Germany had, would have abandoned the aesthetic matrix from which the avant-garde derived its power.

In the aftermath of World War II, all this changed irrevocably. As philosopher Theodor Adorno remarked in 1956, the violent visions from the golden age of the avant-garde lost their shock value.[11] In the shadow of war and genocide, it was clear to him that the avant-garde's fantasies had become historical reality. In spite of Adorno's bleak assessment of surrealism, the transformed relationship between avant-garde violence and the violent realities of postwar Germany did not signal the avant-garde's deactivation. Although the gulf between the avant-garde and realism dwindled, the avant-garde's newfound mimetic capacity apropos the disasters of Germany's past did not evince a Lukácsian realism. On the contrary, the avant-garde after fascism continued to instrumentalize fantasy as a means with which to envision the destruction of the world as a historical reality. Instead of forging ahead with the pre-fascist avant-garde's original quest to blast with fantasy a path toward utopia, the post-fascist avant-garde evoked the bygone horrors of Nazism as fantasies more real than any realism could convey. The exclusive province of neither memory nor historiography, the post-fascist avant-garde in West Germany discarded the sober rules of historicity. In so doing, it concocted visions of the past more penetrating than any mimetic claim to truth. What these visions of violence sought to achieve is the subject of this book.

Theory as History: Conceptualizing the Avant-Garde After Fascism

Critical thinking about the avant-garde after fascism is divided into two major camps. On one side, adherents contend that the avant-garde persisted over the course of the twentieth century. Typical of these assessments is a categorization of essential traits endemic to every manifestation of the avant-garde. In Renato Poggioli's anatomy of the avant-garde originally published in 1962, he characterized a still-thriving postwar avant-garde that positioned activism and antagonism as two of its defining features.[12] One of West Germany's first chroniclers of twentieth-century vanguard aesthetics, Helmut Heißenbüttel, contended in a 1963 essay on the history of visual poetry that after fascism a German avant-garde continued to strive toward a new stage of human expression by traversing traditional media boundaries.[13] Decades later, Greil Marcus, like Poggioli before him, assembled an international cast of avant-garde characters, located in different historical moments and places, all of whom spoke the same avant-garde language; the common denominator among Marcus's specimens—"a critique of modern society"—captured the transhistorical ethos of the avant-garde.[14] Yvonne Spielmann identified contemporary German avant-gardes as having inherited from their nineteenth- and twentieth-century precursors the twin characteristics of transformational critique and futurity.[15] In their case for an avant-garde within contemporary German literature, Bettina Clausen and Karsten Singelmann distilled the avant-garde down to its essential structure, namely the antagonistic divide between its sociopolitical and aesthetic strategies and the constitution of dominant society.[16] And art historian Kristine Stiles maintained most recently that the name *avant-garde* cannot be reduced to a brief chapter in history but rather applies to every aesthetic intervention in the social status quo that exhibits "radical probity." [17] Regardless of whether its scope is international or purely German, each of these instances illustrates the centrality of an essentializing typology for the advocacy of an avant-garde after fascism.

Unlike this first camp with its insistence on the resilience of the avant-garde's oppositionality, the opposing faction insists that the avant-garde died. The most extreme of these accounts pinpoints its demise well before Hitler's rise to power in 1933, and insists that it never again arose from its own ashes. Peter Bürger's seminal essay from 1974, *Theory of the Avant-Garde,* represents the most sophisticated incarnation of this approach. Primarily concerned with the avant-garde's place in the history of modern European aesthetics, Bürger defines the avant-garde as having sought the "destruction of art as an institution set off from the praxis of life." [18] Although the avant-garde failed by the middle of the twenties to disable those social institutions responsible for banishing art from everyday experience, it nevertheless succeeded in exposing the fact that it was no longer possible to herald one aesthetic mode as more advanced than another. "The historical succession of techniques and styles," Bürger claims, "has been transformed into a simultaneity of the radically disparate" such that both realism and montage could coexist peacefully alongside one another

(*TAG*, 63, 87). With aesthetic norms vanquished, the demise of the avant-garde subsequently heralded the advent of the postmodern condition in the arts.[19] Accordingly, any and all attempts to resurrect the avant-garde and reiterate its attacks on institutionalized art invariably suffer from an ignorance of the historical consequences of its ancestors. For Bürger, the "neo-avant-garde" of the postwar period merely generated autonomous art in spite of its revolutionary intentions.

Far less drastic and in some cases even disapproving of Bürger's sweeping conclusions, other representatives from this second camp assent to the avant-garde's death, but only as the precondition for its later renaissance. This more moderate wing has called attention to the avant-garde's new cultural contexts in postwar Western societies, citing the emergence of new political blocs and cold war ideologies, cybernetics, communication technologies, expanded forms of commodification, and intellectual currents like post-structuralism.[20] Focused less on the fate of aesthetics than on the new social functions of the avant-garde, these arguments differ from Bürger's above all in their location of postmodernity vis-à-vis the avant-garde. While Bürger heralds the avant-garde's demise as the advent of aesthetic postmodernism (e.g., an "anything-goes" pastiche), these disparate voices argue that postmodernity is not of the avant-garde's own making. A sociocultural late-capitalist phenomenon that first materialized in the second half of the twentieth century, postmodernity, according to these accounts, instigated the rejuvenation of the avant-garde, which for decades had fallen into disrepair, by becoming the new target of its attacks. In short, this position contends that precisely because times have changed the original idea of the avant-garde accrued new potency. Common to all of this camp's proponents is a dilemma over this renewed avant-garde's name. Should the addition of a prefix (like Bürger's *neo-* and *post-*) signal its historical transformation? Does an entirely different designation (like *experimental*) better describe the new historical context? Or is the original title still accurate?

For all their keen insights, the conceptual histories of the European avant-garde from both camps are not without their shortcomings and pitfalls. Oblivious to historical context, the first camp fails entirely to consider how German fascism sent the avant-garde underground and into exile. Thirteen years in the avant-garde's long history in Germany are missing, and in these accounts the gap apparently left not even the slightest scar upon its return. With respect to the second camp, Benjamin Buchloh, the most vehement critic of Bürger's influential push to rehistoricize the avant-garde, has rightly challenged his simplification of art history and his vulgar definition of postmodernism, as well as his undertheorized indictment of neo-avant-garde plagiarism.[21] The less extreme variant of Bürger's thanatophilic perspective, while attentive to historical shifts, often replicates the essentialism of the first camp by scripting narratives of avant-garde permanence amidst social change. While the context is new, the avant-garde's "critique of modern society" is not. Absent again in a great many of these accounts is the consideration of fascism's immediate effects on the reemergence of the European avant-garde. It should come then as no surprise that none of these conceptual histories takes into account the centrality of violence in movements like Dada and surrealism, movements that Bürger calls the "historical avant-garde." Similarly, these accounts neither mine critically the functional differences between avant-garde violence and fascist violence, nor do they assess at all the transformed value of the avant-garde's violent fantasies after fascism.[22] In order to remedy these shortcomings and blind spots, *Visions of Violence* steers clear of the transnational and transhistorical essentialisms of the first camp as well as the second camp's disregard of the avant-garde's nationally bound transformations after 1945. Comprehending accurately the avant-garde after 1945 requires grasping how context and text functioned as two countervailing forces: the social and aesthetic repercussions of world war and mass murder at work in the aesthetic transformation and articulation of the historical avant-garde, and, conversely, the post-fascist avant-garde's inspection and intervention into the effects of mass death and genocide on a population of perpetrators, victims, and their children. To this end, this book identifies the imagined spectral effects of violence from the past as *the* defining feature of Germany's avant-gardes after World War II and the Holocaust.

Positioning German Avant-Gardes

Elucidating Nazism's impact on the constitution of the postwar European avant-garde in general, and the West German avant-garde in particular, raises the question of the role of the nation-state in ways that conform to and break with many of these aforementioned theory-driven histories. As previously established, historical avant-gardes like Italian futurism and German expressionism assumed defiant stances vis-à-vis dominant national identities. Through their shared commitment to negating the dominant idea of nation, the culturally distinct avant-gardes strewn about pre–World War I and interwar Europe assumed similar poses that facilitated transnational dialogues and international alliances. Buchloh contends, however, that the avant-garde's geographic imagination changed radically after 1945. The growing influence of global culture industries in the postwar period invited neo-avant-gardes to identify national and regional identities as potentially subversive.[23] Globalized capital was, however, not the sole factor in determining the postwar permutation of this long-standing dialectical tension between internationalism and nationalism. Precisely because of its culpability for the crimes of fascism, the Federal Republic of Germany has contributed arguably more than any other Western country to reframing the avant-garde as a preeminently national and post-fascist concern.[24] Conversely, reinscribing the nation and thereby obscuring its disastrous history became a prominent concern in every sphere of West German life after 1945. Westward-leaning internationalism and democracy have and continue to be contested sites of redemption in that country's endless reconstruction. This rebuilding of the nation proceeded, however, at the cost of diminishing the historical consciousness of Germany's violent past. If, as historian Michael Geyer insists, Germans fell silent about the integral role of violence in the historical construction of postwar German modernity, was not the profiteer—the new nation—also subject to this reticence?[25] In an essay from 1964 aptly titled "Am I German?" writer Hans Magnus Enzensberger concurred that "for Germans, the extinction of *Nationalität* as an objective, socially galvanizing force is comparatively near at hand."[26] Consequently, this silence—Geyer calls it postwar Germany's "stigma of violence"—soon became a prime target for that country's avant-garde insurrections.

Examining this silence as a function of West German avant-gardes after fascism necessitates the consideration of patently German questions, ones that might appear at first sight to complicate the applicability of a German model for other European contexts. Although it wrestles only with West German avant-gardes, *Visions of Violence* nonetheless hypothesizes that the translatability of its underlying assertions about the avant-garde's turn to national history after 1945 is a matter of degree and not of kind. While the history of Nazism was a uniquely German burden in the second half of the twentieth century, the ways in which the Federal Republic's avant-gardes intervened in postwar modernity's push away from the past was not. Tracking down and explicating German post-fascist avant-gardes must therefore begin by navigating this first of many forks in the road. Do the internationalist strains of West Germany's avant-garde—like concrete poetry, existentialism, abstract expressionism, absurdism, the Situationist

International, Fluxus, and pop—draw attention to this silence through their inverse proportionality to the nation? Do more explicit national engagements with the "stigma of violence" exude international overtones? If so, does this second internationalist register enhance or detract from the force of its critique? To position the fascist past as a decisive motor in postfascist avant-gardes also necessitates untangling and unmasking the ways in which dominant German discourses on the avant-garde confused the idea of the avant-garde as a synonym for modernity. In his cultural history of the German avant-garde, for example, Jost Hermand notes that by the sixties the dedifferentiation of the avant-garde had advanced in Germany to the point that the avant-garde, like modernity, applied to anything new in the last 150 years of European aesthetic history.[27] The ensuing theoretical confusion over the frequent conflation of the avant-garde with postmodernism would soon make this conundrum doubly difficult.

A great many West German thinkers greeted postmodernism with suspicion, if not outright animus. The grounds for this cold reception lie primarily in the ramifications of postmodernity's afterwardness, the implication that modernity died, and the belief that its prefix would undermine the redemptive potential of *post-* in Germany's post-fascist place in time. Nevertheless, delineating the postmodern from the modern and the avant-garde proved tricky. With respect to the first West German squabble over postmodernism from 1968, Andreas Huyssen noted that the hoopla was a case of mistaken identity. Prompted by Canadian scholar Leslie Fiedler's lecture "The Case for Post-Modernism" held at the University of Freiburg, German intellectuals initially mistook Fiedler's celebration of postwar avant-garde attacks on modernity and the artificial divide between high and popular culture as the end of modernity itself.[28] Far more telling are the historical grounds cited in the German defense of modernism. The idea of the modern emerged in the wake of the Third Reich as the preeminent West German bulwark against the fascist past and the communist occupation of the East.[29] Accordingly, the false impressions generated by Fiedler's celebration of the avant-garde, impressions that hastily concluded that he eulogized modernity, derived their force from a shared sense that modernity's end would foster the "newest form of fascism."[30] Of particular concern to Fiedler's critics were his disregard for fascism's appeal to mass culture; his high estimation of the very same hallucinatory dreams, visions, and ecstasies that led Gottfried Benn into fascism; and his overall contempt for the Enlightenment tradition.[31] One member of Fiedler's audience went so far as to declare, "only we who still must wrestle with the phenomenon of National Socialism can understand at all just how dangerous your talk is."[32] This perceived danger, which Fiedler unknowingly generated with the postmodern label and which obscured his actual affirmation of the avant-garde, did not arise due to a German unfamiliarity with the avant-garde. On the contrary, the idea of the avant-garde reemerged immediately after 1945 and German intellectuals' command of its history quickly became unparalleled.[33] Nevertheless, these early discourses conflated the avant-garde more often than not with modernity, the operative term in the Federal Republic for progress away from the shameful fascist past and toward a prosperous democratic future.

The skirmish over Fiedler's essay from 1968 exposed just how entrenched the West German conviction was that modernity could cordon off the fascist past from the democratic, post-fascist present. On the surface, the avant-garde had seemingly nothing to contribute to the quarantining of history. In a sequel to these debates in the eighties, the avant-garde ostensibly vanished altogether, while the threat of the fascist past loomed even larger. Spawned by postmodernist architect James Stirling's new wing for Stuttgart's Staatsgalerie, completed in 1984—a building that embodied key characteristics that Robert Venturi originally associated with Las Vegas's playful pastiche—this second skirmish initially cited postmodernity with threatening Germany's tradition of modernist architecture. Beneath this case of defending a national tradition lurked suspicions more grave: Stirling's recycling of historical forms signaled the resurrection of a proto-fascist aesthetic bedazzled by the monumentality of classicism (as was the case with Albert Speer).[34] In effect, postmodernism's play with history compromised modernity's containment of fascism as a piece of history receding into the past. Postmodernity, as exemplified by Stirling's architecture, also invited fascism once again to take hold of the German cityscape. This fear of the postmodern Trojan horse was hardly limited to imported British architecture. Like Jürgen Habermas before him, Manfred Frank derided French post-structuralist philosophy in 1984 for its "fascistically colored neo-vitalisms" rooted in the reactionary ideas of "Gobineau, Nietzsche, and Chamberlain."[35] In 1987, Hanns-Josef Ortheil declared a postmodern turn in German literature but to this end mollified Fiedler's sixties radicalism by insisting that postmodernism "does not depart from the aesthetic project of modernism."[36] In effect, conceptualizing German postmodernism was only feasible by transforming threats to modernity's existence into promises of its perpetuity. As was the case with the avant-garde, postmodernism eventually became tenable in Germany on the condition that it, like the avant-garde, became just another aspect of modernity.

These two "postmodern" quarrels (circa 1968 and 1984) expose a fundamental spatiotemporal crisis underlying Germany's trouble with the avant-garde. If the avant-garde, as Bürger and many others rightly claim, is a category independent from modernity, the German discourse on progress away from fascism (commonly associated with the modern) versus regression backward into fascism (the usual indictment against the postmodern) left no obvious place for a sui generis avant-garde to reside. When the avant-garde reemerged nominally after 1945, it was categorized as just another name for German modernity committed to the present and future and inimical to the past. When the avant-garde reemerged in the guise of the postmodern, it was decried as fascism redux. And when the postmodern aesthetic finally matured in the eighties not just in word but also in deed, the avant-garde ostensibly vanished from view, leaving modernity to fend off the onslaught of Germany's fascist specters. The actors in these debates neither perceived the avant-garde's transformation due to fascism nor did they grasp the intricacies of its new position in postwar Germany. While the 1968 debates corrected previous assumptions that the avant-garde—like the affirmative modernity under Adenauer—bracketed off the past, they nevertheless concluded erroneously that this backward glance was amoral. In the renewed dialogues over a decade later, silence about the avant-garde, which implied both its obsolescence as well as its surrender to postmodernism, wrongly disqualified it as a contender in the postwar German struggle over the construction of temporal consciousness after world war and mass genocide.

In contradistinction to all these ideologically charged positions, the German avant-gardes presented in *Visions of Violence* demonstrate an allegiance to their forerunners' critique of affirmative modernity. In particular, these avant-gardes targeted modernity's continued faith in technological, social, and economic progress away from the fascist past. Postwar modernity, Geyer maintains, was predicated on falling silent about the violence with which fascist modernity engineered German society according to its fantasies of imperialist expansion and racial purity.[37] Conversely, post-fascist avant-gardes not only discerned, but also worked against, this derealization of the Nazi past. These avant-gardes seek out a markedly different temporal consciousness than the radical futurity that so many postwar aesthetic histories and theories ascribed to the avant-garde from before World War II. To be sure, the historical avant-garde never limited its employment of violence to bring about only utopian time. As discussed further in chapter 1, the time of the historical avant-garde was always paradoxical, for its desired futurity was predicated on both its covert study of the past as well as its intent on progressing away from the present. In contradistinction, post-fascist avant-gardes—the product of a paradigm shift—jettison their forerunner's feigned disavowal of the past and instead engage the violence that once was as the negative blueprint for what could be. This turn to the past is, however, not postmodern. Huyssen notes, for example, that postmodernism "relegate[d] history to the dustbin of an obsolete epistémè, arguing gleefully that history does not exist except as text, i.e., as historiography" ("ST," 172). Rather than eliminating the referent of historiography, as is the case with the postmodern, these avant-gardes materialize history to the extreme, deploying exaggerations, distortions, and fragmentations so as to explode the modernist myths of the Bonn (and later the Berlin) Republic's claims to radical democratic reform. Just as postmodernism fails to describe accurately these avant-gardes' investment in history, renaming them *arrière*-gardes" would overemphasize their attention to the past. The post-fascist avant-garde exhibits a dialectical awareness of the past's importance in navigating the modernist present toward a better future, when all modalities of time—the past, the present, the future, and what Walter Benjamin calls the ethical dimension of messianic time—are brought to bear on lived experience. Similarly, to call them "neo-avant-gardes" would imply a repetition that simply was not the case precisely because of the immediate impact fascism had on both the constitution of postwar West German society and, by extension, the avant-garde. The avant-garde did indeed change after 1945. This temporal transformation was necessary for it to intercede effectively in the ways in which postwar modernity inhibited the consciousness of its violent origins in fascism. *Visions of Violence* thus argues that these avant-gardes require no unique designation. Like their precursors they, too, are invested in radically disrupting and altering modern experience.

Mind Versus Matter: The Medium of Realism

Much ink has been spilled over Germany's coming to terms with its Nazi past. Well before the fuzzy neologism *Vergangenheitsbewältigung* (coming to terms with the past) came to light in the mid-fifties, the postwar West German public sphere was consumed by questions of guilt and suffering.[38] Where philosophers, theologians, and politicians were quick to muse early on about the ethical viability of collective guilt, West Germans latched onto the stories of expellees from eastern Germany and Eastern Europe and of German prisoners of war in order to craft their own narratives of German suffering and victimhood.[39] Assigning culpability and jettisoning blame were flip sides of the same psychological dilemma, namely forgetting (i.e., remembering selectively) the past. According to the ever-dialectical philosopher Theodor Adorno, the erasure of memories of the violent past was "an achievement of an all too alert consciousness."[40] Psychoanalyst Alexander Mitscherlich later countered that the psychic defense mechanisms responsible for the repression, denial, and derealization of the Nazi past eluded the realm of consciousness entirely.[41] Be they conscious or unconscious, the processes underlying Germans' inability to mourn the crimes of Nazism and, by extension, to secure the democratic foundations of the fledgling Federal Republic were widely recognized as the result of a defective collective psyche.

Adorno's call for the institution of a "democratic pedagogy" grounded in psychoanalysis and sociology made clear in 1959 that it was entirely in Germany's power to correct this inhibited psychology. Whether and, if so, when this condition changed for the better over time is not entirely clear. In spite of the commotion caused by the Auschwitz trials in the first half of the sixties and the student rebellions in the later sixties, each of which decried the fascist specters throughout West Germany, many concur that it took the German broadcast of the American TV miniseries *Holocaust* in 1979 to initiate a noticeable engagement with German guilt.[42] Alas, others like Eric Santner doubt this psychological evolution, citing the explosion of paternal biographies in the late seventies and eighties as evidence of the second and third generations' assimilation of their parents' stunted psychic structures. The infamous "historians' debate" (*Historikerstreit*) that erupted in 1986, in which a small handful of German historians experimented with relativizing National Socialism and the Holocaust, was yet another signal that, at the brink of reunification, German culture was still prone to the narcissism and forgetting that Adorno warned against almost three decades earlier. To be sure, exceptions abound. Santner has, for example, drawn attention to Anselm Kiefer's early photographic portraits from 1969, in which the artist carved out "a breathing space where the work of decathexis might unfold."[43] Elsewhere, Santner identifies the eighties cinema of Edgar Reitz and Hans Jürgen Syberberg as having intervened successfully in dominant patterns of and discourses on memory, mourning, and melancholy.[44] Santner's evidence does suggest that the realm of cultural representation has been adroit at identifying and unveiling this psychic lack that has continued to befall Germans. However, important follow-up questions like when cinema, art, and literature first mastered their role as analyst of the German mind, which documents other than Santner's examples belong to this roster, and whether they actually had an effect on the collective mental life of German society remain unanswered. In short, an evolutionary history of the aesthetics of *Vergangenheitsbewältigung* has yet to be written.

There are good reasons why such a history has not and perhaps should not materialize. For one, it is arguable that the central term— *Vergangenheitsbewältigung*—is too imprecise and is better replaced by established Freudian concepts like mourning and melancholy, working-through and acting-out. Second, assessing the inroads of memory and mourning diachronically would need to consider a complex array of unruly variables like mass versus individual psychology, the transmission of lived and conveyed experience, and the sociology of postwar generations and cohorts, factors that thwart the adoption of a simple comparative control. Third, if working through the past entails articulating historical knowledge with a conscientious national identity, such a history would need to account for the messy and highly contentious ways in which identity politics have complicated Germanness according to nationality, gender, ethnicity, religion, class, and even affect. Fourth, in Germany's late-capitalist "society of the spectacle," remembering is no longer what it used to be; within the last three decades of the twentieth century, it has developed into an imaginative construct that has less to do with incorporating memories of past violence than with externalizing history as a set of consumable images that exonerate the mind from actual coping.[45] Fifth, the recent arrival of trauma as a critical heuristic with which to explain the involuntary incapacitation of the German mind suggests that any such evolutionary history cannot ferret out a slow progression of conscious acts of atonement; instead, it must acknowledge how perpetrators' dormant self-inflicted wounds emerge belatedly but without necessarily divulging the secrets of their origins. Sixth, an evolutionary historiography of *Vergangenheitsbewältigung* would install the teleology of modern progress as its motor without ever questioning whether such concomitant psychic processes actually follow other nonlinear and noncumulative temporalities. Above all, working through the past, regardless of whether the mechanism in question describes either conscious or unconscious processes (or even both), excludes the body entirely from the equation. Discourses of coping have privileged the (damaged) German psyche without considering adequately the ways in which bodies have persisted as thresholds to the German past.

Amidst the body boom in North American cultural studies, a handful of German studies scholars have sought to balance out these Cartesian discourses by casting light on historically contingent forms of embodied being. In *Sex After Fascism: Memory and Morality in Twentieth-Century Germany*, historian Dagmar Herzog demonstrates how the evolving postwar imaginary of the fascist's sexual body not only framed the ways in which Germans remembered fascism but also determined their own postfascist body politics. Julia Hell's *Post-Fascist Fantasies: Psychoanalysis, History, and the Literature of East Germany* attends to literary fantasies about the paternal communist body that produced a historical and ideological space distinct from that which the condemned fascist body was imagined to have occupied. And Leslie Adelson's *Making Bodies, Making History: Feminism and German Identity* illustrates how images of bodies in contemporary German prose—no longer an object of or allegory for history, as was the case in postwar literature—reflect the active ways subjects construct and position their contested and conflicted identities and knowledge apropos German history. What these three contributions counteract, above all, is a pervasive Cartesian rift between the dominant moralizing theorization of memory and mourning and the largely neglected corporeal empiricism nonetheless prevalent in cultural representations of postwar and contemporary Germany.[46] In spite of each of their unique foci and methodological approaches, all three concur that the body in post-fascist culture occupies a decisive role in mediating and framing the historical experience of fascism, an experience otherwise inaccessible to cognition alone. Additionally, they make clear that the body's role in remembering the past changes over time, reflecting the sociopolitical and cultural junctures of postwar and contemporary German history. Regardless of whether the exclusion of the body they seek to remedy is a function of the dialectic of reason, an epistemological black hole attributable to trauma, an unconscious defense mechanism like displacement, or even a gendered division of postwar mental labor, works like those of Herzog, Hell, and Adelson show that bodies have long been decisive constituents all too easily overlooked in the complex processes of reckoning with the German past.

Visions of Violence follows in the footsteps of these formative studies. West Germany's post-fascist avant-gardes also identify the body as the primary matrix of historical experience. As in the case of Hell's and Adelson's literary studies, the bodies in the avant-gardes presented here function as vital fantastic conduits between the deficiencies of cognition and the vanished historical experiences of German fascism. For these avant-gardes, to know the past is to fantasize about, configure, and conjoin forms of embodiment both past and present. To be sure, the various bodies under inspection in *Visions of Violence* are aesthetic phenomena, projections of the lingering effects that the violence of fascism were believed to have either left or continue to leave on bodies. They are as much representations of something lived and real as they are visions of something missed and imagined. As will be seen, the claim to historical authenticity that these avant-gardes pin to representations of the material body changes over time. When juxtaposed alongside one another, the six case studies in *Visions of Violence* suggest this transformation is attributable, in part, to avant-garde alliances with technologies of representation, alliances that promise but then inevitably fail to close in on the real of historical experience by virtue of their putative ability to materialize fantasies and thus bridge the past and present. In the course of this book's narrative of West German avant-gardes, as the horrors of fascism recede backward into the space of experience, the technological mediation of an imagined historical violence eventually morphs into pure mediation. Originally a medium for representation, technologies utilized for conjuring the past eventually become the return of the repressed, historical violence itself.

Post-fascist avant-gardes make, however, crucial departures from the bodies featured in the narrative prose studied by both Hell and Adelson. For one, these avant-gardes position violence at the nexus of their representational strategies. In the ensuing case studies, bodies are torn asunder; physically assaulted and polluted; stripped bare and smothered; tortured, infected, and paralyzed; blinded, vivisected, and frozen; and dematerialized entirely. While the brutalities these avant-gardes mete out cast a multitude of different bodies both past and present as *the* object of history, these bodies represent anything but pure passivity. For every destructive act attributed to the violence of fascism, the bodies in these avant-gardes either replicate this violence or produce a counter-violence intended to usurp both the consciousness and conscience that undergird dominant modes of surviving, remembering, and commemorating the past.[47] Furthermore, this violence to and by bodies—frequently rendered using montage—eschews narrative. These bodies neither tell stories, nor are they the means with which to tell stories. Instead, they lay bare corporeal conditions, ontological states attributed to the past and rematerialized for the sake of expanding the epistemological limits of the present. In this respect, West Germany's post-fascist avant-gardes undertake a fantastic archaeology of violated and violent bodies in order to substantiate those episodes from Germany's past that have eluded the empires of epistemology and historiography.

Broken, bloodied, and dismembered bodies are certainly nothing new to the avant-garde. In his chronicle of the avant-garde from 1920, Richard Huelsenbeck championed, for example, Dada's vanguardism because of its macabre exhibitionism. "The highest art," he insisted, "will be . . . the art which has been visibly shattered by the explosions of the last week, which is forever trying to collect its limbs after yesterday's crash." Lest one conclude that Huelsenbeck anthropomorphized this art as a damaged body, he continues with the qualification that Dada's art is the butchered body itself: "The best and most extraordinary artists will be those who every hour snatch the tatters of their bodies out of the frenzied cataract of life." [48] The realist intent underlying Huelsenbeck's account is unmistakable. The dismemberment he attributes to the explosions and crashes of urban life—a corporeal translation of Georg Simmel's sociological assessment of the mental price of cosmopolitan living—are real signs of the damage that modern experience putatively inflicts on bodies. This realism, which Bloch chalked up to the avant-garde's conviction in fragmented reality, must not, however, be conflated with the corporeal realism characteristic of post-fascist avant-gardes. After 1945, the historical reality ascribed to obliterated bodies is not reducible to conceptual debates about whether authentic reality under modernity corresponds to either closed models of objective totality or open models based on subjective fragmentation. To be sure, this pivotal facet of the aforementioned expressionism debates has not lost its relevancy in postwar and contemporary German culture. In fact, it has become increasingly more complicated and therefore that much more pressing since the growing influence of postmodernity in Germany, the imbrication of hyperinflated fragmentation with universalizing claims to wholeness, and the frustration of any and all claims to authenticity. Nonetheless, the historical origins and ethical imperatives that post-fascist avant-gardes ascribe to the categories of totality and fragmentation are the decisive factors that demarcate their claims to reality from those of the historical avant-garde. For these avant-gardes, corporeal wholeness after 1945 is as much a symptom of the illusions of post-fascist modernity as it is a sign of the forgetting, amnesia, and denial that blanketed German society in the wake of fascism's violence. Conversely, violated and fractured bodies, both past and present, are flagged as the loci of real historical violence. The authority that these avant-gardes assigned to fascism's violent excesses is, in part, a claim to historical realism. This violence is also intent on achieving a higher order of totality, one in which visions of violated bodies cultivate an expansive temporal consciousness of the past's influence on the present. Similiarly, it petitions for a conscience about the necessity of seeking out conditions for a redemptive future, one in which the violent fascist past reveals potential ways out of the very modern progress that once begot and still threatens to beget that violence.

Six Historical Stations, 1938–2002

The following reconceptualization of the idea of the avant-garde presents not a singular avant-garde but rather a multiplicity of avant-gardes. The common denominator among them all is their use of visions of bodies in order to explode the strictures of postwar temporal experience. In spite of their shared politics of time, the post-fascist avant-gardes that comprise this history do not emulate the trajectory of the historical avant-garde with its succession of waxing and waning movements. The course underlying this study's design reflects neither a fragile mortality nor a tenaciousness for reinvention and resurrection. To the contrary, the forward push toward the twenty-first century depicted here belongs to a dominant conception of West German time, one for which the fascist past necessarily recedes into oblivion. The temporal sequence of avant-gardes in *Visions of Violence* attests to the necessity to account for and counteract evolving forms of obfuscating consciousness. In every instance, the motor of this evolution of obliviousness as well as the basis for its deactivation by the avant-garde lies in the promises and failures of both new and old technologies of representation, from literature to cinema to virtual reality. In every instance the media are, on the one hand, held accountable for the paralysis of the German mind and, on the other hand, imbued with the power to make perceptible past realities through the body. Likewise, these avant-gardes are largely singular in nature. Although the avant-garde collective along with the concomitant genre of the manifesto did resurface after 1945, Germany's post-fascist avant-gardes are more often than not the labor of unaffiliated individuals. Some scholars have attributed the disappearance of the avant-garde collective after fascism to the cold war as well as the West's ideological investment in neo-humanist individualism.[49] This study maintains that the predominance of independent avant-garde practitioners after National Socialism has as much, if not more, to do with the imagined historical significance of the individual body with respect to the collective German body. In the examples discussed in *Visions of Violence,* envisioning the past ethically takes place primarily through individual bodies. The past itself is, however, an imagined dimension populated by legions of bodies, either disciplined or decimated.

Visions of Violence brings together six cross-sections of Germany's post-fascist avant-garde from the last sixty years. Its primary documents are both canonical and noncanonical and include examples from literature, the visual and performing arts, film, television, audio recordings, and theater. These case studies are not intended as an exhaustive roster of the artifacts or the practitioners of Germany's post-fascist avant-gardes. On the contrary, each episode chosen for this book illuminates diachronically and synchronically the ways in which these avant-gardes envision bodies from the past as corporeal conditions to be either incorporated into, if possible, or to simply affront an interminably deficient historical consciousness. Each chapter also demonstrates how these visions of the embodied past morph according to shifting ontological certitudes and epistemological blind spots throughout postwar and contemporary German history. Furthermore, the identity of the bodies in *Visions of Violence* changes with each case study. This story thus begins with the exile's homecoming to postwar Germany, moves on to Germans and Jews who came of age during West Germany's reconstruction, and closes with a younger generation intent on making sense of the postmodern disintegration of the German nation, its history, and the material body. Along the way, these post-fascist avant-gardes wrestle with the problem of how to represent their violent fantasies, to make knowable the past, such that the experiences they mediate do not succumb to normative discourses of *Vergangenheitsbewältigung.* Before embarking on this story about Germany's post-fascist avant-gardes, *Visions of Violence* returns to the theory-history problem addressed at the outset of this introduction. Can a theory of the avant-garde explain this reconfiguration of avant-garde practice after fascism? Far from designating abstract thought as the ultimate validation of the existence of these avant-gardes, the first chapter explicates how theories of the historical avant-garde from the thirties anticipated this new post-fascist paradigm after 1945, and how, in hindsight, post-fascist avant-garde theory from the eighties exposes the fundamental ways in which fascism transformed the historical avant-garde. A foundation for each and every case study, this preliminary treatise thus establishes the important legacies of the historical avant-garde as well as the decisive breaks endemic to the post-fascist avant-gardes.

The first two case studies underscore the dearth of indigenous models for an avant-garde after 1945 and the need to appropriate and modify foreign prototypes. Chapter 2 illuminates how painter, writer, and filmmaker Peter Weiss inverted French surrealism in the fifties in order to make perceptible the exilic experience of corporeal displacement and fragmentation that fascism engendered. Chapter 3 turns from fascism's exiles to writer Dieter Wellershoff's coterie of "new realists," some of whose members found it impossible to produce bona fide facsimiles of the French *nouveau roman* surfacing in the fifties and early sixties; neither new French avant-gardes nor old German ones proved effective for containing the spectral return of fascist embodiment. Chapter 4 shifts to the rebellious sixties and investigates how artist Wolf Vostell's happenings envisaged historical spaces of mass murder (Auschwitz) without ever conflating those highly politicized spaces of contemporary suffering (Vietnam), as was the case among a cadre of student rebels. Chapter 5 returns to the darling among Wellershoff's new realists, Rolf Dieter Brinkmann, and illustrates just how far the initial promises of new realism had deteriorated; by the seventies, reality had fallen prey to mass media so completely that it became the sole product of a technologically mediated return of fascist violence. A counterpoint to Brinkmann's extreme anti-postmodern stance, chapter 6 explores Alexander Kluge's long-standing efforts to refunctionalize and articulate new and old media in order to open historical spaces in which it becomes possible to speak with the dead. Chapter 7 crosses the threshold of reunification by inspecting dramatists Christoph Schlingensief's and René Pollesch's performative engagements with virtual reality and the normalization of violence from Germany's divided and fascist pasts. In the concluding remarks to this final chapter, *Visions of Violence* takes stock of these six stations of Germany's post-fascist avant-gardes and shows how this one historical trajectory among many possible trajectories comes full circle. From Weiss to Pollesch and back again to Weiss, *Visions of Violence* argues that the reemergence of the exile at the millennium suggests that the unique space once occupied by West Germany's post-fascist avant-gardes—a space distinct from modern progress and postmodern pastiche and one where an ethics of time assumed central importance—has begun to falter. But first things first: *Visions of Violence* maps how these avant-gardes fortified themselves against the forces of modernism and postmodernity.

The avant-garde is that which, in the flash of the dialectical image, disrupts the linear time-consciousness of progress in such a way as to enable . . . the possibility of a better future.
—Peter Osborne, *The Politics of Time: Modernity and Avant-Garde*

Only when the horror of annihilation is raised fully into consciousness are we placed in the proper relationship to the dead: that of unity with them, since we, like them, are victims of the same conditions and of the same disappointed hope.
—Max Horkheimer and Theodor Adorno, *Dialectic of Enlightenment*

1. Deaths and Reconfigurations
Avant-Garde Time After Fascism

On the Futurity of the Historical Avant-Garde

When is the avant-garde? Students and scholars of the avant-garde are wise to separate this awkward little question from its imperfect variant, *When was the avant-garde?* An inveterate preoccupation among countless thinkers, this second query has produced countless biographies that, in retrospect, double as obituaries. Historicizing the avant-garde is fraught with peril. Because the avant-garde is so frequently unintelligible, the signification that accompanies historiography has certainly helped to secure the avant-garde its rightful place in the annals of Western aesthetic and cultural history. Conversely, dating it and rendering it transparent has very often resulted in the declaration of its death. To name the avant-garde is at once to kill it off. This double bind has especially been the case in German aesthetic theory and intellectual history after fascism. By suspending the avant-garde in the present tense, the initial question does not imply that any and all obituaries are premature or that the avant-garde prevails in an interminable present as an immutable entity unscathed since its beginnings. On the contrary, asking *When is the avant-garde?* presupposes that the avant-garde possesses a unique temporal consciousness that departs from modernity's axis of linear, irreversible time with its three fundamental stations: the past, present, and future. As its name implies, the avant-garde occupies a place in time at the forefront of the present. Diagnosing the avant-garde's temporal ontology in greater detail is nevertheless methodologically tricky. Above all, choosing which or whose avant-garde to inspect surfaces immediately. The boundary between "When is" and "When was" begins to collapse, for does not every concrete manifestation of the avant-garde eventually expire? In things avant-garde, the question of mortality is unavoidable. As much as this first chapter wishes to forestall this slippage from the synchronic to the diachronic, the diachronic dimension of the avant-garde requires inspection, too, if only to throw into relief the temporal particularities of German avant-garde consciousness as it developed throughout the second half of the twentieth century.

This tack is absolutely necessary for studying German avant-gardes after fascism. For one, it refutes the innumerable declarations of its premature death well before the rise of fascism. *Visions of Violence* contends that in spite of Nazi prohibitions and the hardships many avant-gardists experienced in exile, the avant-garde persisted in Germany well into the second half of the twentieth century without necessarily degenerating into modernism or morphing into postmodernism. Pursuing the question *When is the avant-garde?* is indispensable insofar as it pinpoints a paradigm shift at the halfway point in the continuum of the German avant-garde's past one hundred years. By querying the avant-garde's temporal consciousness, *Visions of Violence* contends that German avant-gardes after 1945 did indeed continue their forerunners' quest for alternative modes of experiencing modern time. Yet this quest after German fascism embarked on a markedly different path than its forerunners. Illuminating these transgenerational links and innovative breaks cannot proceed philologically, however. What the avant-garde in Germany became was that which interwar thinkers like Walter Benjamin had initially hoped the first generation of avant-gardes would have realized prior to the catastrophes of fascism.[1] Asking *When is the avant-garde?* thus illustrates a vital initial link between pre-fascist avant-garde theorizing and post-fascist praxis. What emerged as avant-garde after Hitler had, in part, already been articulated in terms of a patently German theoretical intervention into the inadequacies of the historical avant-garde in light of fascism's imminent dominion over Germany. Hardly a lofty vocation unto itself, retheorizing the avant-garde in the shadow of National Socialism was both a political charge in its own day and a message in a bottle of what and when the avant-garde should be in the future. After fascism, this message languished for decades before one exceptional post-fascist theoretical moment not only acknowledged its receipt but also confirmed its relevance for a culture in which the forward march of modern time functioned in large part as an escape from the horrors of its recent past.

Conceiving Germany's post-fascist avant-garde as the inheritor of a decades-old theoretical modification of the historical avant-garde must come with several caveats. If Benjamin's message, for example, did indeed arrive in the future, it did not describe precisely the historical demands that would be placed on the post-fascist avant-garde. The interim realities of fascist violence necessitated yet another modification of the theory of the avant-garde. The theoretical message in a bottle—a blueprint of the ideal avant-garde capable of transforming West German culture—would only become useful in the postwar present if it intervened in the dominant temporal consciousness that arose out of fascism's defeat. Second, this second modification was steeped in an ethical imperative born out of fascism's mass-produced death, world war, and mass destruction. To evoke the avant-garde after 1945 was at once to question the possibility of German time ever moving forward again after the murder of millions. Accordingly, avant-garde time after 1945 found itself shuttling between the poles of repetition, progress out of, and regression back into the urban ruins, mountains of corpses, and battlefields that National Socialism left in its wake. And third, modifying Benjamin's prescient theory of a better avant-garde from the years of exile had to revise the intimate relationship between the body and time that galvanized under fascism and that has haunted Germany ever since. After 1945, a great many German avant-gardes identified the human body as a material basis upon which to realize this new yet not-so-new paradigm for intervening in the course of modern time. Pursuing the genesis and nature of this original message, tracking its voyage into the future, and ascertaining its reconfiguration after fascism; all this sleuthing requires a set of circuitous time travels. Starting in the European sixties—the height of avant-garde memorializing—the ensuing story first journeys backward to the twenties of the Weimar Republic and the exilic thirties—the heyday of (German) theory's confrontation with the (French) avant-garde—and then jumps forward again into the West German fifties and sixties, that point in history when theory began to acknowledge the traumatic implications of the Holocaust for German time. The voyage concludes with a final leap forward into the eighties, a moment when the sign of postmodernity began making substantial inroads into West German art and philosophy. More importantly, it marks that point when avant-garde theory finally grasped the implications of a message in a bottle that the Frankfurt School thinkers had dispatched some forty years earlier.

When then is the avant-garde? According to Renato Poggioli's compendium *The Theory of the Avant-Garde,* Italian futurism captured in name what would become the temporal rule for all other avant-gardes to come. Futurism, not the movement that began in 1909 but rather the inner logic of all avant-gardes, describes the avant-garde's self-designated position outside and ahead of present time. A harbinger of an imminent revolution, the avant-garde anticipates utopia. It is the most extreme incarnation of modernity's irreversible march of progress into the future. This hardly answers the original question, though. Poggioli is quick to note that the futurist moment of the avant-garde is not without its complexities and contradictions.[2] How is it now possible, he writes, to anticipate something that has yet to happen and about which one can know nothing? Neither of the present nor of the future, the avant-garde occupies (under its self-appointed guise as predecessor) an intermediate stage in time somewhere between the present, the past, and a potential future that has yet to be actualized. Where Poggioli legitimizes the temporal paradoxes of the avant-garde as imparting a mythical force essential for its raison d'être, the much more sober Hans Magnus Enzensberger suggests in his essay "The Aporias of the Avant-Garde" that these paradoxes do not just invalidate its claims to futurity but also deem it entirely "nonsensical and unusable."[3] Although the avant-garde construes itself as being of the future, the avant-garde's temporal translation of the spatial metaphor *en avant* can, ironically enough, only be confirmed a posteriori. In spite of its desire to escape the present and arrive at some unknown future, the avant-garde can only materialize through careful reflection on what *was* avant-garde. With the ascent of the consciousness industry in the postwar period, avant-garde futurity lost any and all credibility. Futurity became the algebra of consumer trends whereby capital junks the very thing it anticipates at the moment it is reified. In Enzensberger's mind, there was little doubt that the idea of the avant-garde was an irreconcilable oxymoron whose inflated postwar currency warranted a healthy dose of skepticism.

Published in the same year, Poggioli's and Enzensberger's assessments of avant-garde temporality are identical in terms of how they both punctuate the essential nature of its futurity. Yet the question *When is the avant-garde?* is not the paramount question they seek to answer, nor does it lead to the same conclusion. At the core of Poggioli's and Enzensberger's arguments lies a greater concern for that other question of the avant-garde: Is it *dead* yet? In both instances, the avant-garde's forward displacement in time validates, on the one hand, its inexorable capacity to reemerge again and again like a phoenix (Poggioli) or, on the other hand, the need for its interment (Enzensberger). Poggioli's optimistic outlook acknowledges the diachronic persistence of futurity in all avant-gardes. Conversely, Enzensberger contends that from his post-apocalyptic position—where modernity has begun to show signs of exhaustion—historical investigation reveals that the avant-garde was in fact always obsessed with the past.[4] Surpassing the traditions of yesterday, destroying legacies, negating historical narratives, and trailblazing into the future were the manifest flip sides of the avant-garde's surreptitious yet intensive engagement with the past. What the avant-garde called revolt was actually the result of careful study of modernity's masters, the absorption of their established ideas, and most importantly, the effacement of all traces of any retrograde reflection. Nothing less than a smuggling and laundering ring, the avant-garde looked backward into aesthetic modernity's past in order to envision and promote a future it proclaimed as opposing everything that was and is. Enzensberger clearly complicates Poggioli's response to the question *When is the avant-garde?* From his vantage point, the avant-garde is not the most extreme manifestation of the "horizon of expectation." Instead, the historical avant-garde operated as a clandestine courier that secretly articulated each side of the temporal divide of modernity—the split between the past and future—by disingenuously passing off its engagement with modernity's history as something new. For Enzensberger, the reincarnation of the avant-garde after fascism was crucial for exposing its forerunner's longstanding preoccupation with avowing and disavowing the past. "Every avant-garde today spells repetition," Enzensberger exclaims, because "it keeps the back doors open for itself" without ever acknowledging critically its indebtedness to history ("AAG," 264).

The grounds for Poggioli's and Enzensberger's differences lie in their relationship to modernity. While Poggioli equates the avant-garde with modernity, Enzensberger disqualifies all avant-gardes past and present because of their antipathy to modernity. Not only does Enzensberger differentiate modernity from the avant-garde, but he also insists that this divide has widened in the wake of the twentieth century's world wars, fascism, and genocide. Auschwitz and Hiroshima, he maintains, mark the end of an era ("WMP," 27). Accordingly, post-apocalyptic modernity has been divested of its nebulous futurist moment. In the postwar period, modernity's lifeblood lies in interrogating the excesses and errors of its own past. Far from promoting nostalgia or eschewing such essentially modern concepts as progress, innovation, or the new, Enzensberger contends that visitors to the museum of modernity must liberate its modern and avant-garde artifacts from musealization. To do so, one must first destroy the museum's contents in the name of "historical critique." One must then read in these ashes insights into the aporias hidden within the avant-garde's history. Only through the lessons gleaned by historical critique can the modern impulse transcend the threat of repetition evinced by what others have both derided and celebrated as the "neo-avant-garde." The continued career of modernity after fascism is contingent upon a dialectics of time that arrives at a horizon of expectation through the space of experience. In spite of its appearance of extremism, Enzensberger's prescription for sustaining the spirit of modernity on the carcass of the avant-garde is unquestionably one of moderation. Although his proposed method of "productive incinerating" (*produktiv verbrennen*) echoes the violent posturing of bygone avant-gardes, in actuality it is a meticulous process whereby poetry emerges from the spirit of critique ("WMP," 9). Similarly, the temporal consciousness of this post-apocalyptic modernity inhabits concurrently the past and the present in its commitment to the new ("WMP," 9, 28). The new, however, no longer refers to an unknown future. In an effort to sidestep the pitfalls of the avant-garde's futurity, Enzensberger translates *en avant* from its forced temporal designation back into its original spatial denotation. He thereby suggests that the new must manifest itself in the creation of a world language of poetry, a linguistic space international in scope yet nevertheless attentive to the peculiarities of German history. Futurity, Enzensberger suggests in "The Aporias of the Avant-Garde," has no place in modern consciousness.

Revising Benjamin's Revisions

Enzensberger leaves little doubt that Theodor Adorno's dictum—poetry after Auschwitz is barbaric—inspired his vision of post-apocalyptic modernity. In the wake of Auschwitz, Enzensberger insists that genocide not only marked the passing of the avant-garde, but also necessitated a careful reevaluation of and a turn away from vanguard modernity's futurist myth.[5] His seemingly proto-postmodern valuation of past time was not, however, the first to charge modernity with the task of looking backward into history. Captivated by surrealism since the second half of the twenties, Walter Benjamin petitioned that the idea of the avant-garde was not antithetical to historical reflection. In the course of conceptualizing *The Arcades Project,* he uncovered the aporias of surrealism and imagined a retooled avant-garde capable of unleashing what Susan Buck-Morss deftly describes as "a politically empowering knowledge of the collective's own unconscious past."[6] Thus, it was not in spite of but rather because of the past that Benjamin's idea of avant-garde experience could derive its revolutionary force. Unlike both Adorno and Enzensberger—who disparaged surrealism because of its overemphasis on the irrational dream and its overindulgent dogmatism, respectively—Benjamin contended that surrealists like Louis Aragon forfeited a decisive appreciation of modern time due to their celebration of chance. Because the surrealists gambled their fate away, they failed to exhaust the revolutionary potential encapsulated in their techniques. For Benjamin, surrealism's advances neither outweighed its shortcomings nor hampered its potential modification. For example, in Convolute N, the methodological backbone of *The Arcades Project,* Benjamin wrote that "whereas Aragon persists within the realm of dream, here the concern is to find the constellation of awakening."[7] For Benjamin, sleeping, dreaming, and waking were essential metaphors for disparate modes of temporal consciousness. If sleeping and dreaming described surrealism's overindulgences, then Benjamin's time of awakening stood for a politically charged epistemology, a moment of revolutionary consciousness. To be sure, the time of awakening is much more complicated than just getting out of bed. Tracing the contours of Benjamin's temporal typology and expounding upon his politics of time necessitates pinning down a myriad of concepts deployed throughout his oeuvre. In addition to seemingly unambiguous designations like the past, present, future, progress, and utopia, Benjamin also erects his thought on philosophically rich ideas like fulfilled time, now-time (*Jetztzeit*), the time kernel (*Zeitkern*), messianic time, cyclical time, historical time, and empty time. Add to this list his vocabulary for various forms and degrees of historical consciousness—history, historicism, memory, forgetting, reminiscence (*Gedächtnis*), remembering (*Eingedenken*), repetition (*Wiederholung*), and belatedness (*Nachträglichkeit*)—and the temporal complexities in Benjamin's thinking begin to come into view. This evidence alone leaves little doubt that the question *When is the avant-garde?* ran to the core of Benjamin's thinking about modern aesthetics and politics.

Grasping Benjamin's classification of time first requires establishing his overall intentions.[8] How was surrealism a precursor to Benjamin's own theoretical reworking of the avant-garde? Why did the state of interwar surrealism necessitate amendment? What could an improved surrealism realize? The point of departure for Benjamin was surrealism's fascination with everyday experience. Of particular interest to him were those quotidian spaces in which surrealists engaged in otherwise suspect activities like dreaming, intoxication, and urban loitering. As Benjamin saw it, surrealism sought to transform the everyday into a political experience, for such practices—subsumed under the title of profane illumination—brought about a "loosing of the self" that enabled individuals "to step outside the charmed space" of modern capitalism replete with its endless sea of commodities.[9] Alluded to by André Breton though never fully realized, this critical distance from the present contained within itself the potential to open up the historical dimensions of everyday experience as well.[10] Herein lies the "trick" that Benjamin strove to develop in *The Arcades Project*, a "trick by which this world of things is mastered" through adopting "a historical view of the past" that is politically explosive ("SLS," 210). Far from merely making room for the past in surrealism's interrogations of the present, Benjamin's call for a "Copernican revolution in historical perception" arose from his conviction that modern capitalism had been inducing dreamlike states of existence since the nineteenth century (*AP*, K1, 2). Consequently, commodity fetishism had transformed the experience of modern linear time into empty cyclical time, whereby the present was solely measured according to perennial newness. The temporal consciousness of bourgeois modernity had incurred an amnesia—thanks to the plague of phantasmagorias—that left it entirely without a critical sense of history or the capacity for collective agency. Awakening thus refers to Benjamin's conviction that it was the task of the avant-garde literally to shock the masses with such traumatic force that they depose the enduring dream of modern capitalism. This awakening was to facilitate a different, commemoratory order of remembering—Benjamin calls it *Eingedenken*— and to mobilize historical objects such that the prevailing illusions of present cyclical time crumbled.[11] Committed to exhuming the detritus from nineteenth-century Paris, *The Arcades Project* intended to show how yesterday's oneiric commodities could be mobilized in such a way as to unlock the empowering knowledge of the unconscious past that had always been entombed within them. Equipped with historical knowledge about the truth of capitalism and its preservation of the status quo, the waking collective stood poised to experience the temporality of the "now" (*Jetztzeit*), an instantaneous moment described by Peter Osborne as the gathering up of the past in the present.[12]

With all its vitriol for the nineteenth century's false idea of progress, Benjamin's philosophy of time was nevertheless heavily invested in what lay beyond the present. On the one hand, he harshly criticized progressive social forces like the Weimar Republic's Social Democrats for placing false hopes in the future while having divested themselves entirely of their own history of class struggle.[13] As if to provide a model for his "cultural historical dialectics" that was diametrically opposed to the failures of the political left, Benjamin evoked Judaism's prohibition against "inquir[ing] into the future" as the necessary corrective for modernity's soothsayers and their enchantment with the future ("CH," 397). Similarly, in the paralipomena to his "On the Concept of History," he reminded himself to incorporate into the foundation of *The Arcades Project* a description of the historical materialist as a seeing prophet who must turn away from the future and instead kindle his gaze on "the rapidly receding past."[14] On the other hand, at the core of Benjamin's intricate constellation of phenomenal and existential temporal modalities lay a desire to sow, as Osborne notes, "the seeds of a new futurity," to "perceive . . . the contours of the future in the fading light of the past," and to actualize modernity's original yet unfulfilled promise of social progress ("PCH," 407). For Benjamin, there existed two mutually imbricated sites of future time. For one, the discarded trash of the past contained within it a future life—Benjamin called it culture's "after-history"—that only emanated from the dustbins of history with the intervention of Benjamin's historical materialist method of remembrance (*AP*, N7a, 1). The after-history of an object was, however, not merely its return to the present. That would have only amounted to blind repetition. Instead, it entailed an act of destruction necessary for wrenching it out of the continuum of history, linking with it Benjamin's theological-materialist notion of a universal redeemed history (also known as messianic time), and capturing in the present a fleeting transcendent moment of possibility, *Jetztzeit*.[15] The second order of futurity in Benjamin's thinking arose from this dialectic of empirical history with the messianic. According to Osborne's reading of Benjamin, another more ethical futurity, one distinct from the tautology of conventional modern progress, emerged if the now—a dialectical snapshot of the past and the messianic—interrupted the dream of the present.[16]

Benjamin's philosophy of surrealism was much more than a conceptual precursor or even a counterpoint to Enzensberger's post-apocalyptic tally of the avant-garde's excesses. In contradistinction to Enzensberger's model that squelches future time and therewith the very possibility of a post-war avant-garde, Benjamin's thought expanded the temporal boundaries of the avant-garde by incorporating precisely that which Enzensberger would later claim to have been its contraband, the past. By accommodating not just all three dimensions of modernity's temporal spectrum (past, present, and future) but also the extra-historical millenarian realm of the messianic, Benjamin trumped the temporal limitations of Enzensberger's theory well before it was ever written. Where Enzensberger's "critical history" merely seeks lessons for the present from the mistakes of the past, Benjamin described avant-garde temporality as encompassing the *arrière* (rear) to the *après* (after).[17] In order to steer the progression of time toward a redemptive future, his idea of avant-garde time as a force with which to intervene in the experience of the everyday also jettisoned linear time for a disjointed, nonlinear temporality that jumped backward and forward. Most importantly, Benjamin countered the central enigma of avant-garde futurism—anticipating the unknowable—by elevating the theological dimension of the end of history—the day of judgment—as a yardstick against which to conceive a truer experience of progress. With this broad palette of temporal concepts, Benjamin sought to erect a better model of the avant-garde than the surrealists themselves had drafted and practiced. In spite of Enzensberger's wholesale censure of the avant-garde after Hitler, Benjamin's modification of surrealism—his vision for an avant-garde politics of time—became after the Holocaust a prototype for Germany's innumerable avant-gardes' own quests for redemption. Imagining this heritage requires grafting Benjamin's work onto a time which he and his work knew nothing about. As Irving Wohlfahrt pointed out after the initial scholarly swell that emerged with the posthumous publication of *The Arcades Project* in 1982, anyone casting Benjamin's unfinished project in their own future present must decide whether or not his historically bound framework still applies in spite of the cataclysmic historical events that transpired in the interim.[18] If Benjamin's faith in surrealism was indeed not misplaced, it is essential to ask whether such an endeavor need refract through Benjamin's program Adorno's treatises on philosophy and culture after Auschwitz. Appropriating Benjamin for the postwar West German context necessitates squaring his idea of the redemptive beyond with the wake of guilt and suffering that followed Nazi Germany's unimaginably violent will to power. Evoking Adorno will show how the disruptions to modern linear time engendered by avant-garde temporality after fascism and the Holocaust have less to do with serving socialism's utopian narratives and more to do with visualizing the traumatic effects of those events on Jews and Germans alike. Amending Benjamin's theory of avant-garde time must first, however, work through the difficulties Adorno had with Benjamin's work, reservations that emerged already due to Benjamin's faith in the avant-garde, reservations that solidified after Adorno realized in disbelief that he himself had somehow managed to live through the Holocaust.

Reading Benjamin Through Adorno

Of all the border patrols that Benjamin's work would have to pass in order for it to see the light of day after his own demise, it was that of his friend and colleague Theodor Adorno which proved to be the most critically unrelenting. Any attempt to resurrect Benjamin's philosophy of avant-garde temporality for the postwar period cannot avoid contending with Adorno's critique of Benjamin's intellectual trajectory in general and his appreciation of the French avant-garde in particular. In transplanting Benjamin into the future, we must first assess Adorno's misgivings about Benjamin's *Arcades Project,* account for the ways the Holocaust impacted traumatically on Adorno's thought, and reflect on how to resolve the differences between Adorno's and Benjamin's conceptualizations of trauma and time. Entering into the fray of trauma is absolutely essential to haul Benjamin's ideas of fulfilled time beyond the Holocaust. Adorno's thinking would eventually insist that the systematic killing of millions called into question the feasibility of afterwardness after Auschwitz. How is the redemption of history possible when the forward march of time proved so unimaginably murderous and unstoppable? Well before Adorno ruminated on the limitations on time after the death camps, he had already produced in the mid-thirties an extensive laundry list of shortcomings in Benjamin's surrealist-inspired theory of time. With respect to Benjamin's reverence for surrealism, Adorno asserted that surrealism failed, because of its love for the world of objects, to transcend the commodity fetishism already so central in the false consciousness of everyday life. By appropriating surrealism's profane illumination, Benjamin's version of historical materialism would merely replicate the epistemological delusions already at work in capitalism's phantasmagoria. Furthermore, Adorno found Benjamin's path toward *The Arcades Project* too Brechtian, too Jungian, too mystical, too affirmative in its embrace of a premodern golden age, too under-dialecticized, and thus too deficient philosophically.[19] In light of all the fundamental conceptual and methodological differences between them—the acme certainly being Benjamin's celebration of a revolutionary potential within mass culture versus Adorno's veneration of the autonomous artwork—Adorno nevertheless reminded Benjamin that his intervention into the homogenous progression of modern time was the common bond that tied their projects together. The underpinnings of Benjamin's first book on baroque tragedy formulated for Adorno a blueprint for their shared investment in philosophizing the intrusion into modern time. Consequently, it also represented a beacon toward which Benjamin's misguided project on nineteenth-century Paris must return. For all his good will, Adorno's estimation of Benjamin's veneration for and incorporation of surrealism into his theoretical method never transcended his original misgivings. Where Benjamin had sought to move philosophy into the experiential and epistemological realms of surrealism, Adorno continued to fortify philosophy until his death against the growing metastasis of culture of which he believed surrealism was a part. The crux of this contention manifested itself in the degree to which each believed critical thought could intervene in the passing of time.

In spite of his contentions, Adorno did not dismiss Benjamin's temporal model out of hand, nor did he discount surrealism's interventionist potency altogether. In fact, the anthropological character of Benjamin's art of brushing "history against the grain" found its partial confirmation in the work that Adorno completed in the shadow of the Holocaust ("CH," 392). In *Minima Moralia* he reiterated Benjamin's call to write history anew from the perspective "of the vanquished" and therewith underscored the importance of dredging up into the present history's "waste products and blind spots" that "outwitted the historical dynamic."[20] At the book's close, he insisted that the practice of philosophy must seek out messianic perspectives that could provide a redemptive relief to the state of despair that determines the state of modernity. Adorno even cited surrealism therein as having successfully interceded in the name of the truth into the false sheen of happiness, the *"promesse de bonheur"* (*MM*, 223).[21] His concessions notwithstanding, Adorno left little doubt in *Minima Moralia* that Benjamin's appropriation of surrealism was ultimately not far removed from philosophical satanism. Benjamin's wish to "discover the new anew"—to wrestle the utopian quotient of the new away from the rotten ideology of progress—struck Adorno as being thoroughly delusional, for the epistemological faculties of modern man had also succumbed to the logic of the commodity (*AP*, K1a, 3).[22] How, Adorno conjectures, can one see the new anew when seeing and knowing are already implicated within the logic of the phantasmagoria? What Benjamin thought to be a means of breaking out into true progress, Adorno dismissed as merely the replication of the temporality of traumatic neuroses whereby the return of the old is nothing more than what it always was (*MM*, 236).[23] In effect, Benjamin's surrealist philosophy merely regurgitated the phantasmagorias of yesterday. Adorno's inference that Benjamin naively assimilated the temporality of trauma modeled after the idea of the return (*Rückkehr*) was, in part, the upshot of a fundamental objection to Benjamin's emplacement of the messianic. For Benjamin, the constellation composed of "splinters of messianic time" shot through the present was conceived as an exoteric phenomenon like the physical shock effects of avant-garde cinema, as described in his "Work of Art" essay, for example ("CH," 397). The transitory revelation of messianic shards would guarantee that the return of the new was in fact unique (and thus revolutionary) in the present. Convinced that the messianic must remain radically other for it to retain its promise of redemption, Adorno insisted that this millenarian dimension was an "utterly impossible thing" precisely because it "presupposes a standpoint removed" (*MM*, 247). At best, it is possible only when imagined esoterically as an impossibility. For Adorno, the messianic could never intercede in the return of the new. When reified, the new was always damned to sameness. Adorno's criticism that Benjamin duplicated the temporal pattern of traumatic neurosis without ever successfully transcending the sameness in repetition (*Wiederholung*) implied that the supplement required for what Sigmund Freud called working-through (*Durcharbeiten*)—a penetrating and critical form of memory—was entirely absent.[24]

Adorno was, however, certainly not one to dismiss either the validity of traumatic temporality—the unconscious intrusion and reworking of the past in the present—or its relevance to the historical moment of his thinking. The famous opening to his *Negative Dialectics* on the belatedness of philosophy—he writes, "Philosophy lives on because the moment to realize it was missed"—assumed concrete historical contours in his final meditations on metaphysics, where he returned to his fifteen-year-old rumination on the chronotope of art and life "after Auschwitz."[25] Here Adorno grounds philosophy's missed moment in Judeocide, a limit event that resisted all efforts to "squeez[e] any kind of sense" out of it, "defie[d] human imagination as it distills a real hell from human evil," paralyzed the "metaphysical faculty," and generated something akin to survivor guilt with its recurring nightmares of the ovens (*ND*, 361–63). On the role of a "temporality of Auschwitz" in Adorno's philosophy, Fredric Jameson suggests that these symptoms arose from Adorno's own personal experiences. Jameson writes, "He himself proved unexpectedly to have outlived those who were herded into the gas chamber."[26] And as Sigrid Weigel has aptly pointed out, the last of the aforementioned symptoms assumed particular importance for coupling this "unexpected survivorhood" with philosophy's own belatedness. The guilt of living after Auschwitz, which reoccurred precisely because it could not "be made fully, presently conscious," was not just traumatic but also delineated the limits of Adorno's consciousness-raising philosophy (*ND*, 364).[27] In effect, Auschwitz was a traumatic event, a black hole receding into the past that persisted on by reverberating into the present. Philosophy's obligatory relationship to this historical trauma resided in its resolute refusal to fill this void. Against the backdrop of the Holocaust, negative dialectics was to emerge as a traumatizing philosophy for traumatized living. Adorno's insistence on philosophy's necessity to turn against itself was, however, not the most explosive assertion at work in his book's concluding pages. For all his insistence on Auschwitz's status as an "actual event" with discernibly indiscernible repercussions on critical thought, the slippage he purposefully advanced between the historical event and the transhistorical domain of modern existence was far more provocative. Ultimately, Auschwitz was for Adorno as much a rupture in time as it was a point along a continuum of sameness.

As was the case with many other West German writers and critics, Enzensberger inferred from Adorno's initial declaration on poetry after the Holocaust from 1951—"To write poetry after Auschwitz is barbaric"—a radical historical juncture, one that smacked not just of prohibition but also of finitude.[28] Yet when read within the larger context of Adorno's philosophy, the impossibility of art's afterwardness after Auschwitz did not mark a historical paradigm shift, as his early critics inferred. Contrary to Enzensberger and others who considered Adorno as having blown the twentieth century in two, Adorno's enigmatic edict illustrated preeminently what he had already established with Horkheimer in the *Dialectic of Enlightenment*, namely the heinous "dialectic of culture and barbarism" fostered under the sign of modernity.[29] In other words, Auschwitz was not only a continuation but also a crystallization of the life-dream as hell that Benjamin sought to unearth anthropologically amidst the garbage of the nineteenth century. Read in tandem with the seventh thesis from the theoretical introduction to *The Arcades Project,* Adorno's voice sounds strikingly similar to that of his deceased friend and mentor: "There is no document of civilization which is not at the same time a document of barbarism," Benjamin declared. "And just as such a document is never free of barbarism, so barbarism taints the manner in which it was transmitted from one hand to another. The historical materialist therefore dissociates himself from this process of transmission as far as possible" ("CH," 392). If, according to Adorno, Auschwitz was the culmination of modern progress that he, Benjamin, and the rest of the Frankfurt School identified as the bull's-eye of their theoretical interventions, general public knowledge of this genocide a posteriori in no way generated a shift in the social conditions that would have prevented its resurrection. "That fascism lives on," Adorno insisted in his famous 1959 essay on the myth of *Vergangenheitsbewältigung* (coming to terms with the past), "is due to the fact that the objective conditions of society that engendered fascism continue to exist."[30] The temporal delineation inferred by Adorno's declaration referred, therefore, less to what others designated, for good or for bad, as Germany's zero hour in 1945, and more to a much larger block of modern time in which human life unknowingly persisted under conditions "like a concentration camp" (*ND*, 380).[31] Adorno's chronotope "after Auschwitz" thus signified a time that already *was* well before *it*—the Holocaust—happened and it continued to *be* well on into the present.

The homology that Adorno fleshed out in his move from the personal and micro-historical to the structural and macro-historical grew out of a necessary dialectical constellation of the temporal specificity of loss (in Auschwitz) and the transhistorical character of absence (as generated by capitalism). Adorno was of course not advocating ahistoricism in doing so. On the contrary, his mistrust of most post-Holocaust culture on account of its unthinking complicity with barbarism led him to seek out structures of absence within loss. In so doing, he foreclosed the possibility of debasing the specific traumatic event of loss through narrative representation. Unlike loss, absence, as Dominick LaCapra notes, "is not an event and does not imply tenses," it could not be rendered as a narrative unless it were conflated with or converted into an actual historical loss.[32] This shift explains why, for example, Adorno celebrated the work of Samuel Beckett, "a novelist of absence." On Beckett and absence, LaCapra remarks that his writing "works [to] deploy ways of both acting out and working through absence" ("RT," 190). Acting out and working through absence, as Beckett does, are markedly different than performing the same compensatory work with respect to a loss. At best, they can only foster a greater sense of tolerance for the impossibility of an ultimate solution for something that is foundationally absent ("RT," 187). By pushing Auschwitz into the ontological realm of absence, Adorno thus fortified its traumatic character by quarantining the very things that could lead to its trivialization: history and the instrumentalization of memory. Seen in this light, Adorno's objections to Benjamin's project could be recast entirely in terms of how Adorno's ethically grounded conceptualization of and relationship to trauma necessitated bracketing off Benjamin's original quest to break out of time. This ethical dimension in Adorno's thought became most pronounced in his philosophical and experiential interface with loss.

In Adorno's *Negative Dialectics,* Auschwitz is both a moment of loss and a state of absence. "The guilt of a life," he wrote, "which purely as a face will strangle other life . . . is irreconcilable with living. And the guilt does not cease to reproduce itself, because not for an instant can it be made fully, presently conscious" (*ND,* 364). Guilt, patterns of repetition, epistemological black holes, these are, as Weigel rightly notes, classic Freudian symptoms of loss (*ND,* 167). Unquestionably aware of his allusion to trauma, Adorno designated philosophy as the therapeutic tool with which to work through these unconscious compulsions. Like early twentieth-century psychoanalysis's wartime use of shock therapy as well as Benjamin's appropriation of avant-garde shocks, Adorno claimed that philosophy after Auschwitz administered a counter-shock to the survivor, one that could presumably penetrate deeper and more vigorously into the melancholy that cannot "be made fully, presently conscious." Here Adorno exchanged his terms abruptly. Instead of overcoming the repressed elements of the Holocaust that instigated mechanisms like repetition, this working-through unveiled fundamental ontological and epistemological categories (essence, truth, consciousness, happiness) that were absent from everyday life. Working through the trauma of Auschwitz philosophically was automatically a reckoning with the long-standing violent effects of modernity on the individual, a treatment whose efficacy Adorno implied as barely exceeding the impulsive reiterations of acting-out. While Adorno preserved the historical specificity of loss only to amplify its applicability for working through absence, Benjamin never sublimated his thinking about loss into the realm of absence. Although Benjamin did not live to know the history of the Holocaust, traumatic loss had consumed his thinking ever since his materialist turn. His initial interest in the shocks of surrealist literary montage, which he later aligned with Baudelaire's, Dada's, and Dziga Vertov's own brand of traumatophilia, grew out of his preoccupation with the profane and particular and his conviction that working through the condition of modernity was possible. Shock was absolutely necessary to wake the masses from the dream of the phantasmagoria. To be sure, the loss that shock induced was profitable, for it unbound energies, whereby individuals could attain corporeally a level of temporal experience (and thus go beyond the reaches of the consciousness) otherwise veiled by capitalism. In other words, Benjamin's shock therapy located absence within loss such that every historical moment encapsulated the potential to retrieve absence as a loss. In this case, working-through was not only feasible but also effectual. A perfect inversion, Adorno's negative dialectics situated loss within absence and therewith insisted that a definitive solution is dubious. For him, working-through could become conscious of acting-out but could never culminate into a counterforce against it. The suffering, guilt, and trauma of surviving Auschwitz were deemed interminable. Herein lay the key to Adorno's ethics of time after the Holocaust, the grounds for shoring up his critique of Benjamin, as well as the hurdle that Benjamin's politics of time would have to surmount.

In many respects, Adorno's postwar reproach of Benjamin revolved around their divergent notions of trauma. For Adorno, trauma referred to an excess of stimuli that incapacitated the cogito such that the original traumatizing event remained unknowable. Symptoms attributed to a trauma arose, however, not from the violence itself but rather from the elaboration that internal psychic processes ascribed to this irresolvable gap in consciousness. Conversely, Benjamin's position on trauma awarded greater force to the mechanistic, insofar as it preserved the distinction between the external stimulus, the "stimulus barrier" within the consciousness of the traumatized person, and other systems of memory beyond the reach of consciousness. As for these "other systems," knowledge of the original traumatic event was not erased, as was the case with Adorno and his survivor guilt. Instead it "becomes a component of *mémoire involontaire*," a psychic realm where individual and collective pasts collided while remaining entirely dissociated from the domain of consciousness ("MB," 317).[33] Linked up with Marcel Proust's idea of *mémoire de l'intelligence,* Benjamin's model of trauma insisted that external stimuli pierced the mind's defense mechanisms and left memory traces. These shards could later become serviceable, producing forms of experience steeped in the fullness of historical time. These differences apropos the etiology of trauma are neither misunderstandings of Freud nor are they antithetical. As Ruth Leys makes clear in her genealogy of trauma studies, Freud failed over the many years of writing about hysteria, neurosis, and anxiety to resolve the tension between these two trauma paradigms, the first being Adorno's psychical model and the second Benjamin's mechanical model. These divergent poles delineated the conceptual boundaries of trauma theory that would follow in Freud's wake.[34] Building upon Leys's work by reiterating his own hybridized model of trauma, LaCapra contends that rather than citing one or the other as more credible, both positions can and must be credited as coexisting within the traumatic condition precisely because of the paradoxical nature of actual traumatic experience.[35] LaCapra exemplifies this synthesis in terms of the interdependency between repetitive psychic processes and active forms of remembering:

> Acting out may be a requirement or precondition of working through problems. Acting-out and working-through are in general intimately linked but analytically distinguishable processes, and it may be argued that a basis of desirable practice is to create conditions in which working-through, while never fully transcending, may nonetheless counteract the force of acting-out and the repetition-compulsion in order to generate different possibilities . . . in thought and life. ("RT," 191–92)

To be sure, Adorno and Benjamin did not exemplify either of these trauma paradigms perfectly, nor did they ever arrive at a synthesis as envisioned by Leys and LaCapra. In fact, both Benjamin and Adorno advanced criteria that were counterintuitive to the contrastive positions they incorporated into their negotiations on absence and loss. For example, the idea of *Nachträglichkeit* or "deferred action"—so central to the psychic antipode of Freud's thinking on trauma—assumed central importance in Benjamin's schema of avant-garde temporal consciousness, whereby the retranscription of the past as a shock in the present was elevated from its Freudian status of unconscious repetition to that of historical materialist method. Such overlaps and appropriations notwithstanding, framing Adorno's difference with Benjamin according to the distinct core of their notions of traumatic temporality, especially when cast within more comprehensive and inclusive models like those of Leys and LaCapra, shows how both belong to one single, comprehensive system of temporal thinking. Instead of suffering from a deficiency, Benjamin's work occupies one pole in the conceptualization of trauma that Adorno could not and would not give credence to precisely because of the weight that Auschwitz bestowed upon his previous thinking about art, philosophy, and life.

By expanding upon the implications of Adorno's and Benjamin's distinctly divergent incorporations of traumatic time, a detour around the border control that blocked Benjamin's passage into the postwar becomes possible. The long-standing irreconcilability of Adorno's and Benjamin's positions—most succinctly described by Jürgen Habermas as the former's relegation to consciousness-raising and the latter's utopian quest for redemption—morphs into countervailing processes that simultaneously undercut and supplement one another. Far from disposing with the nuclei of their respective works, the heuristic of trauma, with all its internal and irresolvable tensions, allows for the acknowledgment and preservation of those key concepts that fuel the opposing moments within Benjamin's and Adorno's philosophies. Their treatises on the location of the messianic as the moment of redemption—their crucial difference over the exoteric and the esoteric—assume striking affinities to the tensions endemic to historical traumas. The irresolvable pull between Freudian binaries like unconscious repetition and conscious interpretation, working-through and acting-out, and mourning and melancholy illustrate this homology perfectly.[36] As is the case with these imbricated and antagonistic processes of trauma, Benjamin does bring to Adorno's overriding despair over the immutable sameness of modern temporality a means with which to reconstitute the full dimensionality of modern time. Conversely, Adorno curtails the efficacy of Benjamin's operative use of shock and the expansion of time backward and forward by foreclosing the possibility of breaking out from within the traumatic condition of modernity (ND, 406). In other words, Benjamin grants the imagination the power to re-cathect life after Auschwitz, while Adorno illuminates the resistances that impede any such fantastic operation's full success. By morphing their mutually exclusive arguments about temporality and agency into a combinatory field, the bleakness of Adorno's "missed time" and his philosophy's proximity to and its distinctness from acting-out enter into an interminable to-and-fro between its hopelessness and the hopefulness of Benjamin's "exploded time" and its correspondences to and departures from working-through. Although coterminous and oppositional, Adorno and Benjamin inadvertently implicate one another by virtue of the exclusivity of their notions of absence or loss. They thus instigate and retract in varying degrees new beginnings and lingering endings. Furthermore, Adorno's resistances to Benjamin, far from diminishing the potency of his theory of avant-garde temporality, open up a far richer basis with which to conceptualize the passing of and intervention into time in the postwar period. While Benjamin insists on conjoining the beyond with the past in order to blast the present into another future, Adorno suggests that the trauma-induced disjointedness between present and past, along with the paralysis of metaphysical transcendence, necessitate a self-reflective holding pattern: the finitude of negative dialectics that turns on itself. In effect, out of the friction between them a multiplicity of temporalities arises, competing regimes of time that anticipate and resist the coming emergence of the postmodern, about which *Visions of Violence* has much more to say.

Benjamin's Message in a Bottle

Who discovered Benjamin's message after fascism? Who managed to see it through Adorno's eyes? Who succeeded in synthesizing their antinomies? Ever since the early twentieth century, a great many avant-garde manifestations have crafted their politics in terms of a need to break out and jump ahead of the flow of modern, forward-marching time. Furthermore, the directionality, degree of success, and shelf life of these temporal intrusions into time have been a source of discord, especially when the idea of the avant-garde underwent thorough scrutiny after 1945. Benjamin was unrivaled by other thinkers in terms of the temporal reach of his philosophy of surrealism, and his blueprint for an avant-garde experience of temporal fullness not only departed from the early twentieth-century avant-garde's principal emphasis on futurity, but also foreshadowed the post-fascist German avant-garde's focus on Germany's past. Just as Benjamin accredited his notion of surrealism with "the substitution of a political for a historical view of the past," so too were individual recuperations of the avant-garde after 1945 committed to exhuming graves, conjuring spirits, and reanimating corpses in order to blow the avant-garde's own apolitical present into smithereens ("SLS," 210–11). And yet Benjamin's philosophical augmentation of the avant-garde, for it to illuminate accurately post-fascist avant-garde conditions, cannot account in its unaltered form for the historical, ethical, and philosophical sea change that Adorno pinpoints in Auschwitz and that calls into question the viability of any such politics of time. Reframing the long-standing debate between Benjamin and Adorno in terms of a dialectically irresolvable tension between the desire to change the course of history and the foreclosure of its fulfillment resolves but a fraction of the transplantation necessary to actualize

Benjamin's model of avant-garde temporality after its own historical moment. In addition to heeding Adorno's epistemological and metaphysical objections, a revision of Benjamin's and Adorno's theories, especially if it is to apply to the framework of postwar German cultural history, must also account for the ways in which theorizing both the object of forgetful sleep and the rationale for waking must transcend their mutual focus on the commodity. As each of the case studies of *Visions of Violence* will demonstrate, the core of many post-fascist avant-gardes surpasses its forerunners' concerns for the commodity and, for that matter, their disdain for the category of the work of art. After fascism and the Holocaust, a great many avant-garde practitioners in West Germany no longer sought to unleash the lost fullness of time through the commodity. Instead, they looked back at their own bodies as the bearers of secret cargo from the past. To conceptualize this shift, to grasp fully the unique temporal ontology of the post-fascist avant-garde as it plays itself out within the confines of West German cultural history, escaping the gravitational field of Adorno's influence on postwar thought as well as his critique of Benjamin is crucial. Though thoroughly indebted to Adorno and Benjamin alike, Oskar Negt and Alexander Kluge's colossal *Geschichte und Eigensinn* transcends the philosophical quagmire between Adorno and Benjamin and typifies the temporal interventions characteristic of so many postwar West German avant-gardes.

The title of Negt and Kluge's untranslated magnum opus, roughly *History and Obstinacy* in English, immediately discloses its interest in problems with time and history, problems not unlike those mined by Adorno and Benjamin. Ironically, the uneven reception of the book has suggested that it inhabited its own obstinate relationship to temporality ever since its debut in 1981.[37] Although specialists heralded it as a major landmark in its own day, *Geschichte und Eigensinn* appeared to a great many, especially given its substantial Marxist lexicon, to be a belated postscript to the bygone days of orthodox Marxist thinking from the West German sixties and mid-seventies. For others, the three-volume work was an uncanny anticipation of post-Marxist, post-structuralist thinking in France that would eventually gain ascendancy among the rest of Germany's intellectuals by the nineties. Even within the field of critical theory, their book was seemingly out of step. In spite of their respective tutelages under Adorno, Negt and Kluge followed their mentor's footsteps enough to make clear both their indebtedness as well as their unmistakable departure from his hermetic language and its esoteric implications. *Geschichte und Eigensinn* is unquestionably a product of its own time. A sequel to their first collaboration nine years earlier, *The Public Sphere and Experience,* their second collaboration identifies the fallout of the West German student movement, the rise of decentralized social movements in the seventies, the consolidation and privatization of the media, and, above all, the acme of German terrorism in 1977 as influential factors for its inception.[38] Yet among the second generation of Frankfurt School theorists—Jürgen Habermas having had the most prominent voice—Negt and Kluge struck out in an opposing direction that did not consider the avant-garde impulse an antiquated mistake. The disparity within the critical reception of Negt and Kluge's hefty tome—the uncertainty over its status as anachronism, contemporary zeitgeist, or prophecy—sheds little light on the work's interest in history, the enigmatic role of obstinacy therein, or its illumination of avant-garde temporal consciousness after fascism. In order to address these basic questions, one would do well to reflect further on Jameson's aside that Negt and Kluge's book is a direct descendant of Benjamin's unfinished *Arcades Project.*[39] If this is so, then how do Negt and Kluge instantiate Benjamin's idea of fulfilled time in the postwar period?

At the outset of *Geschichte und Eigensinn,* Negt and Kluge liken history to the problem of sleeping. In a note that echoes Benjamin's own interest in surrealism, dreams, the spell of the phantasmagoria, and the revolutionary potential in awakening, they write: "The 'sleep of reason' is not reason that dozed off, reason that sleeps for a while, but rather sleep in the form of reason. . . . Such reason guards its sleep against awakening from violent dreams."[40] Negt and Kluge go on to explicate the metaphor "sleep of reason" by turning to the topic of secrets—Benjamin himself wrote of the past's "secret index" ("CH," 390)—as it relates to Marx's illumination of the logic of capital. Borrowing directly from Marx's *Grundrisse,* Negt and Kluge maintain that history under the reign of capital, which exhibits the false appearance of a totality, is actually maintained by keeping secret not only its constitutive processes but also those elements of historical experience that elude or exceed the requirements of capitalist production. In other words, reality is nothing other than a fiction, for the history that constitutes it, unbeknownst to the subjects of that reality, is in truth as fragmentary as it is self-perpetuating. Essential for the maintenance of this secret of capital are two systemic controls. The first is the permanent repetition of those processes that engender the fragmentation of historical experience, and the second is the expropriation of the cognitive abilities that individuals require to rouse themselves from the sleep of capitalist reason. In much the same way that Benjamin (and Adorno for that matter) wrote of the present as the interminably always-the-same (*das Immergleiche*), Negt and Kluge cite capital as having successfully dehistoricized its employment of human labor as a historical phenomenon. Against this loss of historical consciousness—homologous with the loss of reality, language, corporeal senses, and (as will be explicated below) nation—Negt and Kluge (once again in close affiliation with Benjamin's own language) insist that the only productive response available to the expropriated is a dialectical jump over into *erfüllte Zeit*, "fulfilled time" (*GE*, 44).

Negt and Kluge's preliminary diagnosis of and prescription for waking up from the dream of *Kapitallogik* is unmistakably akin to Benjamin's own forty-year-old quest to break out of the never-ending dream of historical time (*Geschichtszeit*). As many commentators on *Geschichte und Eigensinn* have pointed out, Negt and Kluge present their overall intentions most clearly in the third programmatic chapter of their three-volume book, where they draft guidelines for a politics of engagement with the political economy of capital (*GE*, 88). Theirs is the theory of resistance to capital that Marx never wrote, a "positive dialectic" to match, if not trump altogether, the reign of Adorno's negativity.[41] And like Benjamin, they too cite time as one of several crucial variables in the constitution of their political theory. On the one hand, their politics necessitates escaping the riptides of modern alienated time. They write, for example: "The revolutionary process—when it is emancipatory—does not manufacture revolutionary results but rather works on the required spaces and times. It builds protective spheres" (*GE*, 71). This construction of an autonomous temporal zone is unquestionably homologous to what Benjamin initially sought to achieve with his hashish experiments and his notion of profane illumination, which he later folded into his theory of the dialectical image.[42] On the other hand, from within this "time sluice" (*Zeitschleuse*) Negt and Kluge see it possible to reconstitute the fullness of lived time. Within this temporal dimension, it becomes possible to articulate dialectically the relationality (*Zusammenhang*) between the past, present, and future that capitalist processes of division splinter apart (*GE*, 212). The objective of their own "Copernican revolution" thus entails uncovering the missing pieces of present experience by restoring their nature prior to capitalistic fragmentation. Such a move involves unearthing the original motives of experience prior to their incorporation by capital and then "project[ing] their original relationality, which belongs to the past, into the future" (*GE*, 213). This projection, they add, must not be mistaken for the future itself. Instead, it entails a formal transformation of the past into a relationality between what was and what should have been, about which a collective would become conscious and that could go on to orientate future, less fragmented collective energies. Equally reminiscent of Benjamin's nonlinear temporal geometry, Negt and Kluge's time travels through the present, past, and into the future are intended to counteract the deletion of time by producing more of it. The relationality generated "will not resemble sleep for an entire society," but rather will resemble a state somewhere between wakefulness and alertness (*Wachsein*) (*GE*, 1145).

In light of the striking similarities with the temporal politics in Benjamin's *Arcades Project*, Jameson's conjecture about *Geschichte und Eigensinn* is remarkably insightful. It would be premature, however, to conclude that Negt and Kluge simply pilfer Benjamin's temporal glossary or, for that matter, submerge the sign of Adorno and his critique of the inexorable *Rückkehr* (return). Of the many departures from Benjamin's project at work in Negt and Kluge's thinking, the most significant and far-reaching is their deliberate relocation of messianic time.[43] According to Benjamin's eschatological framework, the redemption (*Erlösung*) of historical time was to occur with the coming of the messiah at the end of history. While Negt and Kluge acknowledge Benjamin's well-known allegory of the messianic by incorporating both his description of "the angel of history" and a facsimile of Paul Klee's painting *Angelus Novus* on which it was based, there are no angels in Negt and Kluge's theory (*GE*, 282–83). Their notion of redemption is nevertheless still to be found beyond the reach of historical time. Instead of jettisoning the category of the beyond to the ends of time, they bury it so deep within the human body's cells that no force can tap it directly. And like Benjamin's angel, their notion of redemption entails fostering a form of memory along the lines of Benjamin's idea of *Eingedenken*. Redemption is then stripped of its theological connotations and is left to denote a process whereby something lost is regained through an even exchange (in the sense of *einlösen*): those who achieve the redemption of history (*die Einlösung der Geschichte*) would have exchanged one set of memories for another set trapped within the nether reaches of the body (*GE*, 362).[44]

In order to explicate the murky chasm between memory and the body, Negt and Kluge reconfigure Karl Marx's early ruminations on alienated and unalienated labor.[45] For Marx, alienated labor was what commodity production demanded of its workers and, more importantly, what undermined the possibility of any organic relationship between the labor expended and the laborer's personal investment in the commodity produced. Negt and Kluge expand Marx's idea through the logic of analogy to apply to the labor employed for the social production of a nation's history. They also maintain that, while the hegemony of alienated labor has certainly been responsible for the disastrous course of history—World War II and the Holocaust being two primary examples—the labor capacity within a given society can never be tapped completely. From below the purview of capital there is always a surplus of labor power that will escape and resist the mandates of production. It indubitably fails to enter into the annals of history because of unfavorable proportions between it and the growing mass of alienated labor. Herein lie the seeds of Negt and Kluge's redemptive memory. Appropriating the concept of diaspora to illustrate the dissociation of this minor history of labor within a nation like Germany, they claim that "there must be a partial German diaspora in German history between the result of history, **this** Germany, and that **other** Germany, on which work has been done but without having produced results" (*GE,* 392).[46] In other words, Negt and Kluge's redemption consists of charging *dominant* memories with the task of recovering *other* discarded memories locked within the body.

Were this the extent of Negt and Kluge's blueprint for their brand of redemption, Adorno's original criticisms of Benjamin's positivism would ring doubly true. The archaeological-like recovery of diasporic histories of living labor would rely on cognitive faculties that themselves would require the sovereignty of perception and consciousness that Adorno swiftly condemned in Benjamin's own project. Adorno's reproaches necessitate only slight alteration in order to imagine the potential problem at hand: If you transpose the minor history of living labor into consciousness . . . you not only take the magic out of the concept . . . but you also deprive it of that objective liberating power.[47] Negt and Kluge do not overlook, however, the implications of Adorno's pronouncement: modernity— especially now that it stands in the shadow of its apocalyptic apogee in Auschwitz—delineates the boundaries of epistemological inquiry and paralyzed metaphysics. For one, Negt and Kluge insist that "we can know nothing of the locus of historical processes," an assertion they substantiate by adding that the language with which to retell history is implicated in the very hegemony it seeks to counter (*GE,* 542–43). Second, they reiterate that capital's processes of division and separation have expropriated the cognitive abilities necessary for entering knowledge of Germany's other lost history into consciousness. Third, they apply the rule of exception to their own work; *Geschichte und Eigensinn* neither makes any claim to transcendental truth nor does it seek to reflect merely the status quo of historical time. The validity of their theory rests therefore in its obstinate incongruence with praxis. An unmistakably Adornean nonidentical relationship, this tension between theory and praxis provides the orientation necessary for the construction of redemptive memories (*GE*, 482). Negt and Kluge also assert that "historical knowledge has no bearing on" the successful manufacture of this relationality (*GE*, 597). The challenge they see in this networking is ultimately a corporeal one. Sensory perception, the five senses in particular, cannot penetrate Germany's other history. The senses are not only sociohistorically determined but are also barred de facto from ever accessing actual historical experience; that is the exclusive province of the deceased. Redemption, they insist, is entirely contingent on the ability to speak with dead people.

Negt and Kluge fulfill this impossible task by circumventing the usual windows to the mind. "Experiences," they profess, "must not only pass through the head, but rather through the body" (*GE*, 777). Unlike the empirical capacities of social organs like the eye, for example, the organ's individual cells possess an overlooked propensity to work according to their own inner logic. In other words, mental perception must not be conflated with what the eye actually sees. This elementary nature of cells—their conservative unwillingness to cooperate, especially when forced from above, to the brink of their physical abilities—corresponds to a fundamental condition of resistance and rebellion that capital triggers when it seeks to expropriate one's own senses: *Eigen-sinn,* or "obstinacy." Again and again, Negt and Kluge remind their readers that this cellular obstinacy, like unalienated labor, has prevailed for two thousand years unaltered. And yet obstinacy, the most rudimentary of senses—Marx called it the most humane sense—continues to prevail well into the present as the epicenter of opposition to historical progress. Alas, it fails to link up within a social collective into one single associative relationality. Doing so, compiling the sum total of all cellular resistances in not just one individual but rather in an entire society, is not only the precondition for emancipatory resistance but also the recipe for engaging in redemptive memory work. The sole trick lies in establishing sensory (*sinnlichen*) contact between "today's social nerves and the nerves of deceased people" (*GE*, 596). Alas, this operation is difficult at best. Negt and Kluge explain the problem as one of underdeveloped remote senses (*Fernsinne*) capable of tapping deep into "long memory" (*GE*, 679):

The deeper sensory organs are developed only privately and deal almost exclusively with immediate conditions. Many have Tel Zatar or Vietnam in their head, but no one cares to feel them with their nerves. Within this sphere of concrete senses there is a lack of unfragmented, humane labor capable of performing the translation between [historical] situations. **The immediate senses operate, while no work is performed on the remote senses. Above all, they do not shape society. That is the political problem of the present.** (GE, 597)

Extant, virtually inaccessible, and routinely ignored, this other corpus of historical experiences—meant quite literally, Negt and Kluge call it "subcutaneous" history—proves accessible in only the most exceptional of circumstances (GE, 678). One such moment, the corporeal immediacy of mourning, would need to stir the public so violently as to bring forth "oceans of tears" (GE, 1146).

In Germany, the testing ground for Negt and Kluge's theory, the establishment of subcutaneous contact with the past has continually failed to materialize. Citing the seminal assertions by psychoanalyst Alexander Mitscherlich in his study *The Inability to Mourn,* Negt and Kluge suggest that the conditions in Germany for building the corporal basis for redemptive memory have remained deficient throughout the twentieth century. While the capacity to mourn certainly prevails in individuals' non-public lives, Germans have yet to collectively bury Hitler, mourn the downfall of Nazi Germany, or acknowledge the dashed hopes for redeeming German history in 1945 and starting anew. Additionally, they have not tackled any of the other aforementioned systemic losses incurred throughout their long-standing communal efforts to produce one catastrophe after the next. The obstacle is not merely the universal deficiency within all human bodies of sensory organs capable of remembering the "nerves of deceased people." Germans, say Negt and Kluge, have repeatedly invested excessive amounts of energy in the production of regional and national identities, investments facilitated by processes of fragmentation (and accumulation) that conjure up the all-consuming illusion of *this* murderous Germany while obscuring entirely any and all traces of *that* other, better Germany about which only the dead know. In effect, Negt and Kluge posit that Germans can jump-start acts of collective mourning with a post-Cartesian insurrection of *res extensa* over *res cogitans.* This shift would establish a new economy of embodiment whereby bodies then and now fill in the mnemonic gaps that the subservient mind smoothed over because of its compliance with historical time. Negt and Kluge do not bestow, however, upon individual or collective bodies any such power to reverse the status quo, nor do they risk courting positivism by submitting a simple formula for such a revolt of bodies. With the German mind arrested by the demands of "German empiricism" and the German body's emancipatory secrets left unorganized and untapped, the last remaining hope for unmasking the fictitious nature of the reality principle resides in the work of fantasy (*GE*, 368). Psychoanalysis, they argued almost a decade earlier, must not have the final word on fantasy as that repressed defense mechanism intended to compensate for the unbearable expropriations endemic to the political economy of capital. Hidden within fantasy also lie the seeds for a "practical critique of the alienated conditions" of modern existence that, when sown correctly, can prove volatile enough to trigger collective forms of resistance and emancipation.[48] In other words, the subjects of history could feasibly experience through fantasy a temporality that borders on the dimensions of fulfilled time. In an intolerable moment in time, fantasy can give rise to a past wish as well as its future fulfillment. Fantasy is the spark that could trigger the very same revolt the body wished it could achieve. What remains to be seen, however, is how fantasy pertains directly to German cultural history after 1945 in general; how it informs West German avant-garde production in particular; and how, if at all, the body assumes a role in its articulation of a redemptive time in the German context.

Fantasies of Suffering, Death, and Destruction

For fantasy to contribute successfully to the intervention in the interminable course of historical time, it must, in Negt and Kluge's mind, follow several substantive and formal requirements. For one, fantasy cannot be forced to reconstruct a historical totality. Instead, it must inspect specific temporal differences. These differences may involve fissures engendered by historical processes (like alienated labor) or the disparities between those processes and historical narratives laced with obstinacy. In other words, fantasy probes the "breaks and consequences" of history and therewith hypothesizes missing connections and contexts—the relationality—that neither congeal into a unified whole nor present themselves as entirely intelligible (*GE*, 542). Second, fantasy is not a finished product, the work of art itself, but rather a process that emanates from the imagination's engagement with disparate, fragmentary forms. Fantasy draws attention to the undervalued work of the "remote senses" that perform the translational work between the disparate spatial and temporal situations normally hampered by the productive forces of history. Herein lies the aesthetic kernel underpinning Negt and Kluge's theory of relationality, for the work of fantasy is originally facilitated by the handicraft of the *monteur* who "juxtaposes, ruptures, collects, pursues strewn arrangements, samples" (*GE,* 222). Third, fantasy is a multifarious thing that assumes numerous guises and functions. Of greatest importance are two constitutive dimensions of fantasy that are essential for opposing and altering the state of reality; Negt and Kluge call them fantasy's irrational and revolutionary coordinates.[49] While the irrational designates the critical realm of protest—the dimension of anti-realism—where the five senses retract from the oppressive dictates of reality, the revolutionary (the most unclear but omnipresent dimension of all) corresponds to visions of utopian transformation.[50] Similarly, fantasy is only potent when those organizational structures of everyday consciousness—what Negt and Kluge call the horizontal and vertical axes of empiricism—are disabled. Otherwise, fantasy has no chance of ever making a difference. Kluge writes, for example, that fantasy should produce a "surprise . . . that one suddenly understands something—according to a non-contemporaneous concept—in its depth and then from this deepened perspective directs their fantasy at a real event."[51] This moment of comprehension—what Negt and Kluge repeatedly call a learning process (*Lernprozeß*)—is not, as Jameson rightly points out, conscious, rational, or voluntary.[52] Fantasy obliquely addresses the voiceless body's capacity for *Eigensinn* in spite of its inculcation by the dead labor of history.

By nominating fantasy as the proxy for the obstinate body, Negt and Kluge continue an essential line of thinking about the primacy of embodiment that coursed through both Benjamin's and Adorno's thinking. In Benjamin's earliest rumination on surrealism, the short essay "Dream Kitsch" from 1927, he contended that its ingenuity lay in its penetration of the body; surrealism functioned exclusively within the body's interior. In his revised essay on the subject two years later, he shifted from the singular body to collective embodiment and asserted that a revolutionary moment emerged when "all the bodily innervations of the collective" discharged in concert with one another ("SLS," 217–18). Later, in his "Work of Art" essay, he implied that the shock effects induced by radical film montage led to a heightened sensory perception that transcended the realm of contemplation. And in the theoretical aphorisms intended to introduce *The Ar-*

cades Project, he charged his materialist historiography with the power to incapacitate the mind with a shock that, in turn, would allow the materialist to behold shards of messianic time in the dialectical image. Although it never prominently emerged in the core of his dialectical materialism, the body (and conversely the trouble with cognition) nonetheless figured in Adorno's writing as well. In his most sustained engagement composed with Horkheimer, he charged modernity with maiming the wholeness of the human body, insofar as civilization "repressed and distorted" its "instincts and passions" in the name of erecting and maintaining class differences. As a result, the living body had long been rendered a corpse (*DE,* 192). Conversely, he identified the body as embodying the potential for freedom and resistance.[53] The most pronounced instance of this is found in *Negative Dialectics* when, after driving home the dismal fate of metaphysics, Adorno inferred that any hope of restarting it anew lay in the ability of negative dialectics not only to "think . . . against itself" but also to deliver a "shock" that could bring about the "transfigured body" (*ND,* 364–406). Common to both Benjamin's interest in aesthetic shock and Adorno's rumination on philosophical shock was a desire to make the body enunciate directly what the domesticated senses mediate and mollify. Because the body guards its secrets all too well, Negt and Kluge employ one of those "other systems of the psyche" ("MB," 317). Fantasy is not the body's unfettered voice, but rather a symptom of its alienation, the negative reversal of what the body would say if it could.

What can and must be said, then, on behalf of the body and the unbearableness of its inclusion in historical time, especially assuming that it underlies a great many avant-garde manifestations in Germany after 1945? According to Adorno, the single most important message after Auschwitz emanated from and pertained to the body's destruction in the death camps. A categorical imperative never to allow genocide to repeat itself, this message transcended the limits of discourse by conveying directly to the body a feeling of the past that assumed the form of an ethical guideline for the future. "The new imperative," he wrote, "gives us a bodily sensation of the moral addendum—bodily, because it is now the practical abhorrence of the unbearable physical agony to which individuals are exposed" (*ND,* 365). Adorno's sensation of abhorrence was unquestionably rooted in the experience of being confronted phantasmically by the suffering of the Nazis' victims through, for example, images of their physical remains. When Adorno wrote of genocide as "absolute integration" and immediately thereafter contemplated "whether after Auschwitz you can go on living," the invisible term that made this extrapolation between past events and the present plausible was this feeling of horror (*ND*, 362–63). Yet Adorno's abhorrence, like Julia Kristeva's idea of abjection, carried with it an ethical imperative to prevent the return of the abject.[54] Like fantasy, it also functioned as a defense mechanism to fortify the borders and integrity of one's own body from the death of absolute integration. In other words, the past suffering of victims engendered fantasies of suffering among the descendants of perpetrators. Certainly prone to conflate the historicity of the suffering body with the systemic function of abjection for all living bodies, these fantasies anchored in the victim's suffering comprise, however, only one half of Negt and Kluge's prescription for bestowing fantasy with the power to expose the falseness of historical time as well as the possible return of the Holocaust. To do so, fantasy would have to account for the relationality between suffering and the historical conditions that caused it. In order for fantasy to transcend its normative status as a mere expression of alienation, it must also probe the gap between the victim's suffering body and the perpetrators who are culpable for that suffering. For any such constellation of fantasies to assume the gravity required to instigate an intercession in the course of historical time, it would also need to captivate an entire collective such that the phantasmatic work invested would measure up quantitatively to the collective alienated labor that was to be redeemed. In sum, the case studies compiled in this book demonstrate how West German avant-gardes sought to intertwine their mutual desire to break out of the burdens of German time with a penchant for fantasizing about bodies—both the victims' and perpetrators'—and the secrets they conceal. Yet the fulfillment of all these criteria is, in any one example, exceptional at best. Any given fantasy's corporeal object, the breadth of the relationalities it unveils, and the use to which its revelations are put are all, in large part, a function of that avant-garde's temporal distance from the crimes of fascism. As will be seen, the many reconfigurations of the avant-garde after 1945 repeatedly fall short of accruing the necessary influence to organize collective forms of work (e.g., the work of mourning) required for supplanting the dominion of historical time over an entire nation. At best, fulfilled time is something achieved individually within the span of a fleeting moment and, at worst, remains trapped within the confines of its conceptual fantasies.

When is the avant-garde? Benjamin's original design to reconfigure the avant-garde into an emancipatory time machine was exceptionally prophetic for postwar West Germany. Indeed, the Federal Republic of Germany indulged in a myth of a national caesura that kept the past at arm's length from the future. Not only did this containment blur entirely the continued dominance of modern cyclical time, but it also blocked the possibility of speaking with the dead from Germany's recent history. In line with the core of Benjamin's avant-garde template, post-fascist avant-gardes—in particular those in the West German context—strove to intercede in the perennial fragmentation of time by suturing the Nazi past and the post-fascist present with an ethically bound vision of a redeemable future. The key to their success lay in the task of remembering what the mind cannot. Partial heirs to Benjamin's avant-garde project, Negt and Kluge locate the site of this memory within the material body, only to foreclose its immediate access. Only fantastic visions of violence can acknowledge the existence of the body's sequestered memories, and only through their careful articulation can they ever make a difference for future time. Yet Negt and Kluge leave ample evidence that they tend not only to the utopian élan of Benjamin's project but also to the strictures that Adorno laid out. While they certainly retain Benjamin's original intention to improve upon surrealism by expanding the temporal reach of its revolutionary claims, they also uphold Adorno's insistence on an exhaustive dialectical approach that dares not fail to scrutinize redemptive solutions for their possible entanglement in the wheels of progress. By elevating the position of the body to the forefront of their own theory, Negt and Kluge insist on another material basis for facilitating a shift in the experience of time, one that locates the messianic beyond the oppressive realm of the commodity.[55] So close, the body's secrets, as well as its potential for effecting the desired temporal change, prove, however, nearly impossible to materialize. Because of this, it is arguable that the ingenuity of *Geschichte und Eigensinn* lies in its ability to accommodate within one system of thought both the exoteric and esoteric modalities of their mentors. Negt and Kluge's work also bridges the disagreement over agency that separates their intimations of trauma. While they conflate, like Benjamin, structural absences (e.g., Marx's notion of "primitive accumulation") with the historical specificity of loss—they write explicitly of loss and never of absence—they nonetheless refrain from implying that working through these losses is a simple matter of translating their theory into praxis or, for that matter, of rewiring the body and mind so as to thwart their further absorption into the production processes of a national history like Germany's. In effect, the mourning they seek to initiate is inevitably plagued by recurring bouts of acting-out. To be sure, the theoretical message in a bottle that Negt and Kluge received from Benjamin and tempered according to Adorno's admonitions remains just that, theoretical. Whether and to what degree Negt and Kluge's theoretical reconfiguration of Benjamin put down roots in the realm of the aesthetic are questions which the remainder of *Visions of Violence* seeks to answer.

Do we not also know that we must first pass through surrealism's fields of rubble in order to be able to begin anew?
—Wolfdietrich Schnurre, "Theater der Zeit," *Der Skorpion*

Every intellectual in emigration is, without exception, mutilated.
—Theodor Adorno, *Minima Moralia: Reflections on a
Damaged Life*

2. Peter Weiss and the Exilic Body

Surrealism After 1945

"The destructive character," Walter Benjamin wrote in 1931, "knows
only one watchword: make room. And only one activity: clearing away."[1]
A crystallization of his political-philosophical engagement with the dire
social and cultural politics of the Weimar Republic, Benjamin's essay on
progressive violence—in large part a manifesto for escaping the quagmire of the present—echoed his earliest veneration for surrealism.[2] Like
Benjamin's destructive character, surrealism, with its penchant for razing,
clearing, and moving forward, aimed to explode ossified cultural forms
and institutions, unleash experience from the confines of the affirmative aesthetic, destabilize subjectivity, topple bourgeois politics, and eject
"sclerotic" liberal ideals of freedom. The overriding spatial aspect in the
destructive character, the production of an "empty space" devoid of images, foreshadowed what Benjamin would later see in surrealism, namely
its evisceration of the ideological space of society's dominant order—the
world of images (*Bildwelt*)—in order to make possible a messianic "image
space" (*Bildraum*).[3] By demolishing the bourgeois space of the *Bildwelt*,
the destructive character within surrealism facilitated a "poetic politics,"
a moment when art would transition into action. Indeed, surrealism and
the destructive character belong to Benjamin's evolving political commitment to envisioning the revitalization of a Left in crisis. In the second
draft of his seminal 1936 essay, "The Work of Art in the Age of Mechanical
Reproduction," Benjamin reformulated his political theory of the destruc-

tive character of surrealism as the politicization of art, the antipode of fascism's propagandistic aestheticization of politics. As Irving Wohlfahrt points out, Benjamin saw the imminent rise of National Socialism and accordingly insisted (albeit obliquely) that, in the face of growing reactionary cults of violence, any successful opposition would have to wield its own brand of counter-violence.[4]

At the close of his essay on the destructive character, Benjamin underscored once again the progressive impetus underlying his appropriation of violence. He wrote: "What exists he reduces to rubble—not for the sake of the rubble, but for that of the way leading through it."[5] Benjamin's brand of destruction was to be understood as a means to an end and not an end unto itself. Jump forward roughly fifteen years to the immediate postwar period, a time Benjamin himself would never experience, and his call to break down barriers and scout out lines of flight suddenly seems pointless. Fascism's political machinery had not only crumbled, but swaths of Germany's landscape had also been reduced to mountains of actual rubble. While the post-fascist wasteland encompassed a very different order of destruction than what Benjamin invoked in his essay, there was, nevertheless, no need to destroy, for many of the political, social, and cultural spaces of Germany had already been bombed away. As countless stories, reports, photographs, documentaries, and feature films of Germany's obliterated urban topography made clear, the serpentine paths through the rubble, a vast network of footpaths and makeshift roads, were immeasurable. But most important of all, in the immediate aftermath of World War II the productive gradient between the vistas of French surrealism and the valleys of the German intelligentsia in crisis, which Benjamin had identified in his 1929 surrealism essay, evaporated. With fascism deposed, surrealism's intoxications for the sake of revolution were unnecessary, for there appeared, at least at first, to be no "walls or mountains" to bulldoze. Nevertheless, surrealism resurfaced in war-torn Germany, especially within the literary arena.

Karl Krolow's first poems from 1943, written during his inner emigration in Nazi Germany, exhibited, for example, an early propensity for surrealist metaphor, one that Krolow would continue to foster well after his first postwar collection, *Gedichte* (*Poems*) in 1948. In his reading of Krolow's *Die Zeichen der Welt* (*The Signs of the World*), literary critic Hans Egon Holthusen praised the poet for masterfully folding the earliest manifestations of French surrealism (à la Paul Eluard) into German nature poetry (à la Wilhelm Lehmann) and therewith arriving at German

Romanticism's idea of "progressive universal poetry."[6] In early September 1947, at the first meeting of what would become West Germany's leading literary salon, Gruppe 47, hostess Ilse Schneider-Lengyel was invited to read "her surrealist poems and with them introduced a peculiar element into the working group."[7] Quickly forgotten and never published, the "peculiar" poems that Schneider-Lengyel read aloud certainly arose out of her conviction that "surrealism meant a break with a bygone era" and that it would prove effective in the creation of a post-nationalistic humanism.[8] Two months later, Alfred Andersch declared at the group's second meeting that Germany's young generation of postwar writers stood before a clean slate, a tabula rasa, and must therefore rise to the occasion by seeking out new and original literary forms for which there exist no formal rules. Surrealism (among a handful of other aesthetic programs) had proven capable, albeit with varying degrees of success, of paving the way for a German literature intimately committed to freedom.[9] Quite aware of the existentialist fervor in the aftermath of the war, the Berlin surrealist poet Johannes Hübner took stock in 1948 of surrealism's and existentialism's contributions to the arts in the pages of the culture magazine *Athena*. He concluded that only surrealism adequately captured the paradoxes at work in the concept of the beautiful in the atomic age.[10] A select few who summoned French surrealism from the twenties and thirties into the barren valleys of postwar Germany, Krolow, Schneider-Lengyel, Andersch, and Hübner all fell silent on those qualities of surrealism that had captivated Benjamin's imagination.[11] Common to each of their fascinations with surrealism was a constructive impulse, a desire to fill in what was lost or missing—for Krolow it was the rejuvenation of a transhistorical poetics, for Schneider-Lengyel humanism, for Andersch freedom, and for Hübner historically relevant aesthetics—because of fascist violence. Consequently, none of them sensed in their postwar embrace of surrealism even a trace of the progressive destructive character that Benjamin had diagnosed as having been its center of gravity.

Grand historical narratives of the twentieth-century avant-garde have usually disqualified this first wave of interest after fascism in what had been avant-garde before fascism as "superficial revival," recycling, or recovery.[12] The absence of any and all appreciation for the destructive character in the four aforementioned postwar recuperations of surrealism would seem to substantiate these charges of inauthenticity. With surrealism's destructive core preempted by Allied bombings, the balancing act between representation and politics that Benjamin had identified as having been so central to the historical avant-garde suddenly tilted toward the former. With their world already unmade, the artist and poet were much more disposed to assembling rather than disassembling new forms of existence with and in the work of art. And except for a few early enfants terribles like Rainer Maria Gerhardt and Werner Rieger, literary aesthetics after Hitler would have little if anything to do with unmitigated political commitment, especially since Germany owed its near annihilation in the war to the unbridled excesses of ideology.[13] In spite of this radical shift in historical conditions, a modicum of interest in surrealism persisted throughout the second half of the forties and well into the fifties. While they certainly forged temporal and spatial links to what was surrealism and what claimed to be its postwar international legacy, small literary and art journals like Karl Otto Götz's *META,* Max Hölzer and Edgar Jené's *Surrealistische Publikationen,* and Rudolph Wittkopf's *Profile* as well as Dieter Wyss's primer *Der Surrealismus* left, however, scant influence on the postwar cultural landscape. Ultimately, the surrealist impulse, unspeakably too "peculiar" for German readers and writers alike, failed to take root in the Federal Republic of Germany. Some would even go on to lambast it as a "curse of morbid decadence."[14]

There are several historically grounded explanations for this failure. According to Jost Hermand, the concept of the avant-garde was subsumed under the sign of modernism as soon as it became apparent from the currency reform in the Western occupied zones in 1948 and the establishment of an East German state in 1949 that the antagonisms between East and West were turning into a war of ideologies.[15] Modernism's cult of the alienated subject as well as its indulgence in nonrepresentation became rallying cries against the ideologically brazen realism deployed in the totalitarian Soviet bloc. While the poet Franz Mon confirmed Hermand's thesis when he ruminated on the rampant "disgust [among writers] for any kind of indoctrination" in the immediate postwar period, he also insisted that the surrealist avant-garde had simply reached its endgame.[16] Particularly effective at challenging dogmatic ideologies in its heyday, surrealism's somnambulist approach to creating text and image—its illogical metaphors, the blurring of dream with image, and its fascination with the temporal logic of chance—became asocial and noncommunicative.[17] Jettisoning the volatile realm of the unconscious that orthodox surrealism had exalted, much of German poetry (more so than any other literary genre) ventured forth under the twin titles of experimentalism and concretism. With publication titles like *artikulationen, Konstellationen,* and

Kombinationen, the overall constructive thrust in experimental literature was unmistakable.[18]

In an era in which the vestiges of the historical avant-garde were downgraded in West Germany into abstract idioms anchored in an apolitical aesthetic modernism, the persistence of surrealist techniques throughout the fifties was met with confusion and rejection. Paul Celan, Unica Zürn, and Peter Weiss, three now-canonized writers who continued to engage surrealism throughout the fifties, were received with varying degrees of suspicion within the Federal Republic of Germany. While each of their biographies is as markedly different as is their contact with and incorporation of surrealism, what binds them together is the centrality of displacement in their personal and textual relationship to surrealism. For the Romanian native Celan, surrealism initially grabbed his attention during his curtailed studies at medical school in Tours, France, in 1938. Following a brief exposure to Romanian surrealism while residing in Bucharest between 1945 and 1947, Celan would interface in Vienna with German surrealist artist Jené before relocating to Paris permanently. After three years of involvement in Berlin artistic circles, Zürn abruptly followed artist Hans Bellmer to Paris in 1953, where as an expatriate she soon found herself immersed in postwar French surrealist circles. An exile himself who fled National Socialism in 1938 because of his surrealist work, Bellmer would continue to influence Zürn's surrealist output until her suicide in 1970. Though initially exposed to cubism, expressionism, and New Objectivity around 1932, Weiss overlooked the fervent reception of German, Austrian, and French modernist and avant-garde works during his studies at the Academy of the Arts in Prague from 1937 to 1938. The German-Jewish Weiss would finally encounter surrealism in 1940 in Sweden through exiled painter Endre Nemes and again three years later in the Swedish artists' collective Fyrtiolisterna while undergoing psychoanalytic self-analysis. Surrealism belonged in each of these instances to an experience of being elsewhere, as an exile, an émigré, or somewhere in between. Without delving into their work, it is apparent that spatial displacement from home—the impossibility of returning home—plays a central role in these protracted explorations of surrealism after fascism. Furthermore, each of these surrealist encounters after 1945 stands in stark opposition to those invocations of surrealism from within Germany that insisted on heralding a new era. For all three of these writers, fascist violence not only shaped the experience of displacement (lived or fantasized) but also influenced their appropriation of surrealism. The surrealist moment in this small body of work illuminates the post-fascist exilic legacy of Germany's (and then France's) historical avant-garde that found itself without a home between 1933 and 1945.[19] With displacement as the defining moment in their life and work, these writers crafted surrealism to illuminate the violent origins of being elsewhere and gave voice to its spectral effects on the present and future.

Surrealism and Existentialism

Examining the state of surrealism in Germany after 1945 might seem like an exercise in futility, especially in light of the countless obituaries calling it yet another avant-garde death. Dieter Wyss, for example, insisted in his surrealism primer from 1949–50 that the 1947 Parisian surrealism retrospective confirmed his suspicions that "surrealism is practically dead, at least in its homeland." "This is not surprising," he continued, "for it anticipated that which became horrifically real between the years 1933 and 1945."[20] Wyss's comments notwithstanding, whether and when surrealism died remains uncertain. Did it expire in France with its political turn in 1929, the German invasion of western Europe in 1940, Breton's American exile that same year, the end of the war and the surrealist revival in Paris in 1945, or Breton's death in 1966? Posed solely within the German context, the question assumes entirely different dimensions. Did surrealism ever establish itself firmly enough within Germany before National Socialism eradicated so-called degenerate art such that a postwar appearance could be called a return? Was the negligible interest in surrealism in war-torn Germany the result of a second failed attempt to transplant foreign goods into German soil? Above all, was surrealism, over twenty years old, not dead on arrival? In 1956 Theodor Adorno answered the last of these questions in the affirmative: "After the European catastrophe," he insisted, "the Surrealist shocks lost their force."[21] Adorno's focus on the mitigated shocks of surrealism overlooked the fact that the postwar challenge to a surrealist avatar in Germany was equally, if not more, attributable to the success of another French export: existentialism.[22] Inspecting the existentialism boom in postwar Germany is essential to understanding postwar German surrealism in exile. The grounds for existentialism's quick rise to dominance illuminates why surrealism could only succeed in isolation and when practiced in protracted exile. By first interrogating the embrace of existentialism within Germany, this query throws into relief the grounds for why and how practitioners of surrealism (like Peter Weiss) advanced a unique and important reconfiguration of the avant-garde, especially at a time when the very notion of a distinct avant-garde was fading due to the rapid ascent of modernism.

For Andersch, the tabula rasa of postwar Germany was an opportunity to rejuvenate the German spirit in one single creative act. Taking his cue from Jean-Paul Sartre's preface to the play *The Flies* (*Les mouches*), Andersch identified in 1948 a chance in existentialism to break free from the burdens of Germany's past and embrace a future committed to freedom. As many scholars have already established, however, this promise of a new beginning, also known as the infamous *Stunde Null* (zero hour), was at best a myth. In fact, Andersch unknowingly gave credence to this when he exclaimed in the very same essay, "The significance of existentialism is self-evident from the fact that it has worked its way throughout every camp [of thought]."[23] Just as atheists and Christians alike rallied around existentialism, so too was an imminent Marxist variant already imaginable in 1947. Freedom, Andersch insisted, transcended partisan concerns. Although postwar existentialism's roots reach back to a myriad of French and German sources predating the end of German fascism, its broad appeal among writers in the immediate postwar period—certainly a function of its suspicion toward every ideological stripe—overlooked its earlier career among writers in exile during the war.[24] Whereas existentialism after fascism endorsed a radical individualism borne out of "temporary nihilism," existentialism during the exilic experience was steeped in isolation, exclusion, and despair. In this respect, French existentialism's cast of aliens, outsiders, strangers, and exiles who strove in vain to retrieve a sense of belongingness was curiously reminiscent of those protagonists (in exile novels by writers like Hermann Bloch, Klaus Mann, Stefan Zweig, and others) for whom seclusion and futility were cornerstones of existence.[25] The question as to just how far the exilic experience (as precipitated by fascism) can and should be articulated with the many philosophical and literary permutations of existentialism must for now remain unanswered. These tentative homologies are nevertheless reason enough to reevaluate the uniqueness of the existentialist discourse in war-torn Germany. More importantly, the potential continuity of this discourse between the periods of exile and reconstruction points toward a dangerous conflation whereby the exilic moment within the existentialist sensibility was elevated to a normative ontological position in postwar Germany. Said differently, the German Sartre boom—a phenomenon quickly propelled forward by German literary journals, newspapers, theatrical productions, philosophical and theological discourses, literature, and translations of Sartre—exchanged home for exile and thereby installed displacement from one's own history as the point of departure for a new postwar beginning. At Sartre's invitation, Andersch indulged in this elision when he equated the postwar predicament of German intellectuals with that of the French *résistance,* of which Sartre played a part.[26]

Of the many contemporary criticisms leveled at existentialism (the French media scandal from 1945–46 about Sartre's affiliation with Heidegger, Georg Lukács' scathing anti-existentialism essay from 1951, and Jürgen Habermas's memoir from 1959 being three prime examples), none addressed the potential colonization after 1945 of the exilic condition before 1945.[27] In fact, Sartre himself categorically dismissed both exile and surrealism when, taking stock in 1947 of the latter's relevance after German occupation, he wrote: "[Surrealists] who have returned [from exile] are exiled among us. They were the proclaimers of catastrophe in the time of the fat cows; in the time of the lean cows they have nothing more to say."[28] A decadent prophet of war in the interwar years, not only did surrealism prove in hindsight to be a failure in the battle against fascism, but its postwar reincarnation was deemed theoretically misguided and politically futile when sized up against existentialism. This futility, Sartre insisted, was attributable, above all, to surrealism's insistence on blurring the boundaries between consciousness and unconsciousness, perception and representation, as well as the imaginary and the real. By maintaining the distinctness of these binaries, it became possible to realize a politics capable of real change. For Sartre, exile and surrealism—the former an indication of the latter's irrelevance, and conversely, the latter an invalidation of the former's usefulness—had nothing to offer a post-apocalyptic world. However, the crass distinctions that Sartre drew between existentialism and surrealism (a position he would later amend slightly), as well as existentialism's eclipse of the exilic condition, were not clear-cut in Germany.[29] The existentialist discourse in Germany was not impervious to lingering vestiges of surrealism. Similarly, German exiles who remained abroad after 1945 were influenced by both the legacies of surrealism and the international existentialist explosion. This was especially the case with Peter Weiss. Certainly aware of the many different existentialist dramas by Sartre, Albert Camus, and Jean Anouilh produced in Sweden between 1945 and 1950, Weiss invoked at the close of his autobiographical novel, *Fluchtpunkt* (*Vanishing Point*), scenes from Sartre's play *Morts sans sepultures* (*Men Without Shadows*) performed in Göteborg, Sweden, in 1946 in order to illustrate his own past experiences in exile. Likewise, while sorting through his library in 1947, Weiss's autobiographical voice picks out surrealists Hans Arp, Max Ernst, Antonin Artaud, the comte de Lautréamont, and André Breton as having stood the test of time, especially in light of existentialism's ascendancy.[30] Weiss scholarship to date has not yet firmly delineated clear breaks between the surrealist and existentialist moments in his work, a distinction that Sartre thought to be night and day. Otto Best, for example, insists that Sartre's notion of existence-as-hell shaped Weiss's entire output beginning in 1948. Others petition that surrealism remained a constant in his work beginning with his very first publication in Swedish, a series of thirty prose poems titled *Från ö till ö* (*From Island to Island*).[31] In exception, Alfons Söllner suggests that with Weiss's first drama, *Der Turm* (*The Tower*), he folded his prior surrealist affinities into the existentialist idiom that dominated theater at the time.[32] Weiss, however, destabilized this genre-specific containment of existentialism's influence on his output when he classified his oeuvre from the late forties to the late fifties as having begun with a distinct surrealist period and concluded under the spell of Sartre, Jean Genet, Eugène Ionesco, and Samuel Beckett.[33]

Whether and to what degree Weiss "sartrefied" surrealism (as was the case among some amnesiac proponents of surrealism in postwar Germany) or whether Weiss's long-standing fascination with surrealism appropriated the language of existentialism, these two paths should not deflect attention from the central concern in Weiss's artistic output since 1938.[34] While a genealogy or conceptual topography of Weiss's early works drawn up according to their existentialist or surrealist affinities is certainly possible, both avenues of inquiry would indubitably foreground concept over history and thereby obscure the problem at hand, namely how to grapple with exile as an interminable condition, as the point of departure for Weiss's explorations of surrealism and existentialism. Unlike those contemporaries who appropriated the conceptual space of exile either to smother history or to deny it altogether, exile remained for Weiss, especially after 1945, a central theme both in his work and his personal life. In an interview from 1979, Weiss recollected that "the '50s were in large part more exilic for me than the years during fascism."[35] If existentialism left an imprint on Weiss's work, it eclipsed neither the impact of exile on Weiss nor the centrality of surrealism for its articulation. Sorting out this entanglement and determining how Weiss retooled the historical avant-garde in order to address his postwar predicament necessitates taking a step backward in time to that point in Weiss's biography when fascism transformed his status as voluntary émigré into that of forced exile. Reaching back before Weiss's engagement with surrealist strategies in writing (and later in film), this chapter lays bare the fragmentation of the exilic body and the subsequent quest for wholeness as the central topi in his early oeuvre. Weiss's search explored a variety of media before evolving into a new form of surrealism that sought to stave off exile's lingering violent effects by lending it a voice.

Backward Glances: Peter Weiss the Painter

On the experience of exile, Susan Rubin Suleiman writes, "Those who leave home with no thought of return and succeed, well or badly, in settling elsewhere, occasionally cast backward glances at what they left behind."[36] Turning one's back on and then later glancing backward at the viewer are crucial motifs in the paintings and drawings that Weiss completed at a most critical juncture in his biography, his emigration to Sweden in early 1939. The first prominent treatment of figures glancing backward is the painting *Jüngling am Stadtrand* (*Youth at the City Limits*) from 1938 (fig. 1), which Weiss painted during his second pilgrimage to his mentor Hermann Hesse in Tessin, Switzerland.[37] Weiss repeated this subject in the ink illustrations to his story "Traktat von der ausgestorbenen Welt" ("Tractate from the Extinct World") written during his forced migration from Zurich via Berlin to Alingsås, Sweden. Paintings in which Weiss captures figures who turn their backs to the viewer include *Flußlandschaft* (*River Landscape*), *Der Hausierer* (*The Peddler*), *Jahrmarkt am Stadtrand* (*Annual Fair at the City Limits*), and *Gartenlandschaft mit Figuren* (*Garden Landscape with Figuren*).[38] With respect to the first of these images, *Jüngling am Stadtrand*, Weiss himself described it twenty-four years later in conjunction with a dream about his longtime friend Hermann Levin Goldschmidt, to whom he sold the painting in January 1939 in order to afford his passage to Alingsås:

In the middle of a level courtyard filled with black trees, their leaves sparse and trunks enclosed by circular railings, stood a man, his left foot slightly forward, his back turned to the viewer. To the right, stairs led up to an iron arch bridge. In front of a freight locomotive atop the red walls of a railway embankment, a set of barriers rose up at an angle. The sky was a cool, greenish blue. The foliage of the trees stared into

Figure 1
Peter Weiss, *Jüngling am Stadtrand*, 1938. Oil on wood. 26 x 23 inches.

metallic motionlessness. The atmosphere was captivated by resignation and departure. [That was] back then, when the old world finally came to an end and we were thrown entirely into exile.[39]

In a letter to his brother, Goldschmidt described this painting in terms of an existential choice of freedom: the man "must decide where he wants to go. The path of the walls & the stairs, toward which he is turned, lead to the city, . . . an ugly & technical city—and a railway yard. There is, however, a green gate in the one wall, the gate to freedom, so to speak."[40] Weiss, too, emphasized the personal significance of the green gate in the composition in his first letter to Goldschmidt written from Sweden: "Oh Hermann, if I could just find the green door again. I've tangled myself up in a few things, must fight against the city, and feel like I'm in a dream. Everything is completely unreal."[41] Read in tandem, Weiss's recollection from 1962 and the letters from 1938 and 1939 throw into relief a tension within the painting that transcends the site of redemption. With his hands tucked in his trousers, the nearly flattened black figure positioned at the focal point of the canvas turns his head slightly to the right and gazes toward the stairs and bridge, while his left foot points toward the green gate. While the canvas's scene clearly sets up a tension between two lines of flight (the gate versus stairs), the vectors of this tension trace themselves back to the man's body where visual perception and corporeal movement infer a Cartesian split. The splitting of the body, the body falling apart into pieces, runs, however, much deeper than initially intimated by this step to the left and look to the right.

The delineation of pictorial space as suggested by Weiss and Goldschmidt divides the canvas into quadrants, the axes of which bisect the central figure horizontally and vertically. While the longitudinal axis locates the figure as a site of tension between the diametrically opposed lines of flight, the latitudinal axis, which cordons off the figure's head along with the lines of flight from his torso and limbs, infers that the body and the seeing mind are entirely out of step with one another. There exists, in addition to these two axes, a third plane in *Jüngling am Stadtrand* that splits the figure's body yet again. Much more than a mere act of turning his back on the viewer, the figure's stance engenders a crucial separation between front and back that elevates the aforementioned disagreement between foot and eye into a phenomenological deconstruction of the body. That part of the human anatomy that eludes the empire of one's own gaze, the back exists as an invisible presence, a corporeal site located behind the nodal point of visual perception. Far more radical than the Cartesian dualism between the head and torso, the back—by virtue of its status as the structurally absent body part par excellence—not only exposes the sovereignty of the omniscient eye as a falsehood, but also underscores the primacy of fractured embodiment. This is precisely what phenomenologist Maurice Merleau-Ponty proposed when he wrote, "My body as given to me by sight is broken."[42] Engendered by the fragmentation inherent to perspectival embodiment, the overlooked fault lines between individual parts of the body and, by extension, between the visible and invisible run to the core of *Jüngling am Stadtrand*. Instead of deploying the canvas as a field of mediation with which to transcend the limitations of the eye and therewith assemble the fragmented body into a whole spectacular image, Weiss resolutely puts on display the emblem of corporeal fragmentation, the otherwise invisible back.[43] Although the figure's nearly flattened body is certainly longitudinally intact from head to toe, the posterior view of the gazing figure engenders a division along the body's *plana frontalia* that inverts the economies of vision and corporeality entirely.

This reversal escapes Weiss's and Goldschmidt's readings of the painting entirely; for them, the figuration of the back serves as a metaphor with which the epistemological process of looking forward is represented. Cast in the Romantic tradition of Caspar David Friedrich's looking subjects who turn their backs in favor of a sublime nature, their appraisals neither account for the absence of any sublime horizon nor do they recognize the body as a space within space. When considered within the painting's greater depth of field, the figure's back acts as a threshold between the barren foreground and the urban background. Given his implied mobility, the figure's passage through this bifurcated space also marks time. The distance between his back and the lower edge of the canvas represents traversed space. The figured space between him and the rear courtyard wall awaits him in his narrative future. More importantly, this plane divides the dorsal from the ventral side of the body, leaving it phenomenally an impossible whole comprised of parts that invariably evade the eye. Read from this perspective, Weiss's painting inverts the customary corporeal blind spot. The back, that body part facing the past, becomes visible, while the front, pointed into the future, is veiled. Contrary to his own viewing position, the figure's corporeal space in front of the frontal plane, his future, vanishes, while the space that stretches from behind it, his past, is fully discernible. Although the difference between the green door and the iron arch bridge may appear as obvious choices to the figure, the viewer sees a body whose own corporeal future is not only obscured but also distinctly partitioned off from its corporeal past. In sum, *Jüngling am Stadtrand* portrays exile as a radical temporal and spatial break that transpires entirely within the body.

Subsequent reworkings of the back motif, especially in Weiss's large-format oil paintings reminiscent of the magic realist style, continue to transcend, with varying degrees of success, this phenomenal splitting of the body engendered by being "thrown entirely into exile." In *Der Hausierer (The Peddler)*, the central figure, whom biographers have frequently conflated with the struggling artist Weiss, has turned slightly to the left so that he can glance backward over his shoulder and toward the picture plane of the canvas. While the front of his body remains hidden from view, the wandering salesman's backward glance signals not only a new awareness of his location in time and space but also a mastery over the corporeal dissociation engendered by exile. Suggestive of Mannerism's torqued *figura serpentinata*, the peddler, however, must twist his body to look into his past, albeit momentarily, for, as the largely obscured vendor's tray that juts out forward from his chest intimates, his goal lies before him; the circus tent located at the distant city's edge is presumably that place where the peddler hopes to sell his wares and establish himself in the city in which he has just arrived. As if to imply that this corporeal torsion and the ocular and temporal wholeness it affords is too much to handle, the backward glance disappears in Weiss's subsequent work. Nevertheless, the question of the interrelatedness of the split body, the eye's *punctum cecum* (blind spot), and the spatio-historical sense of time linger. The re-occurring central figure in the aforementioned works vanishes in *Jahrmarkt am Stadtrand* (*Annual Fair at the City Limits;* fig. 2), Weiss's largest canvas, painted in 1940. Taking once again the urban periphery as its milieu, the painting employs the same magic realist style from before to depict a mass of circus visitors, most of whom have their backs turned to the viewer. The three notable exceptions located at the bottom of the canvas—a young girl, an amputee, and a blind man—all gaze directly and resolutely back at the picture plane. While the symbolic richness of the entire painting—the work's epic proportions evoke Hieronymus Bosch and Pieter Breugel the Elder—certainly exceeds the action limited to this corner of the canvas, these three characters refer directly back to the aforementioned problem in *Jüngling am Stadtrand* and *Der Hausierer.* The young girl (without question an allusion to Weiss's deceased younger sister, who frequently appears in his early paintings as an enduring ego ideal) shares with the legless and sightless men an uncanny ability to stare directly into the extraterritorial space previously marked by the youth's and peddler's bodies as the exilic past.[44] The identity of these characters has an immediate bearing on the direction and force of their gaze. Either the traumatic past comes to haunt the present, as is the case with the young girl, or corporeal disability affords one the otherwise foreclosed ability to look back unrelentingly. In the case of the blind man, it is his inability to see that radically undoes the dominant phenomenal economies that articulate front with back, part with whole, and future with past. Looking back is for him the equivalent of looking straight ahead.[45] In the case of the amputee, the body has been physically dismembered, albeit along an entirely different plane and more explicitly than the one at work in the previous painting. Of particular importance here, however, is the inverse proportionality of his look "backward" to his corporeal integrity. In effect a physical realization of the phe-

Copyright Gunilla Palmstierna-Weiss. Courtesy of Jürgen Schutte, Berlin.

Figure 2
Peter Weiss, *Jahrmarkt am Stadtrand*, 1940. Oil on canvas. 52 x 40 inches.

nomenal split portrayed in *Jüngling am Stadtrand*, the amputee beholds
the space of the past precisely because he is no longer whole.

Weiss's interest in the unmaking of bodies persisted throughout the
forties. He offset his Picasso-inspired studies of whole fleshy bodies (e.g.,
Die Kartoffelesser [*The Potato Eaters*]) begun in 1942 with subsequent images of cannibals hacking human limbs from the same year (*Die Kan-
nibalenküche* [*The Cannibals' Kitchen*]), as well as a mortician dissecting a
cadaver (*Obduktion* [*Dissection*]). In spite of this thematic thread, Weiss's
style and the grounds for his attention to the body in pieces had shifted

Figure 3
Peter Weiss, *Die Gefangenen,* 1946. Ink on paper. 9 x 17 inches.

significantly by 1945. The sketch *Die Gefangenen* (*The Prisoners*) from a series of images titled "Konzentrationslager" ("Concentration Camp") portrays, for example, three emaciated nude male figures crouched around
and drinking from a small pond, in which a human head, two feet, a
knee, and a forearm (none of which are anatomically in relation to one
another) float (see fig. 3). Where before Weiss had employed a variant of
realism "that arose out of dreams" in order to capture the oneiric quality of the exilic existence, this later work uses allegory to cast reality as
nothing less than a macabre dream.[46] An unmistakable engagement with
the revelation of genocide within Nazi Germany's camps, *Die Gefangenen*
shifts the origin of dismemberment from displacement to barbarism, all
the while implying a complementarity between the two fates. The fragmentation prompted by exile and the dismemberment of bodies in extermination camps were but opposing sides of the same historical event, fascism. Even more gruesome than *Die Gefangenen,* an untitled sketch from
1946 (fig. 4) contains detailed studies of bloodied bodies torn asunder and
broken limbs grafted onto fantastic prostheses. Most noteworthy is an upper torso whose forearms have been replaced by wooden and crystalline
caps affixed to the upper arm by metal braces, as well as the study of a
hand, its digits replaced by an assortment of tools (a hammer, a corkscrew,
clippers, and a knife). What both sketches share and what Weiss had not
explicitly displayed prior to these images is the inference of a retrievable
wholeness after a previous dissociation of the body. In the former instance,
the men who drink from the pool—their bodies are folded such that their

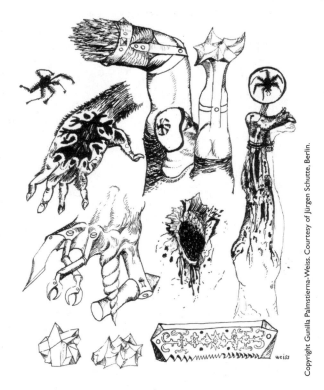

Figure 4
Peter Weiss, untitled sketch, 1946. Ink on paper.
9.5 x 7.5 inches.

face, front, and back are simultaneously visible—have clearly survived as a whole when others, whose remains they practically feed off of, have not. In the latter image, the fantastic prostheses, in particular the hand, verge on science fiction in terms of their incorporated and enhanced functionalization. In effect an extreme in his visual engagement with the dissociation of the body, Weiss's turn to artificial limbs, which shifts from substitution to augmentation, implies that wholeness was indeed retrievable. Without question a prelude to Weiss's later engagement with surrealism, the material body and fantasy converge in this image to form an amalgam that exceeds normal human capacities. Read diachronically vis-à-vis Weiss's earlier depictions of the body, these younger images intimate that Weiss's initial quest "to find the green door again" operated according to a teleology which presumed that the body was originally whole prior to its exilic dissociation and that this lost wholeness was reversible.[47] As Weiss's unsuccessful request to retrieve the painting *Jüngling am Stadtrand* for a Swedish exhibition in March 1941 made clear, however, retrieving the past into the present, reeling in the image of the "green door" from its provenance in Switzerland to Scandinavia, reconstituting a seamless continuum between Weiss's "back" and "front," were impossible.[48]

Exactly at this moment Weiss began to call into question his vocation as painter. In hindsight he confessed that painting failed to represent forcefully "the shattered world" of which his body was an integral part.[49] As many of his last images make clear, Weiss minimized the crisis between the fractured body and the visual perception that exile generated.[50] In effect, the absence of representations of perspective and perception vis-à-vis exile denoted Weiss's inability in the visual field to transcend the corporeal dilemma of displacement. Far from abandoning these problems altogether, Weiss continued throughout the fifties to explore through literature and film the possibilities of mending the exilic body back together. Hardly a failure, though, Weiss's paintings established the experience of exile and embodiment as imbricated phenomenal problems. In a manner strikingly reminiscent of Merleau-Ponty's most fundamental claims in post-Cartesian philosophy, Weiss identified the exiled body as possessing a fixed ocular perspective through which it orients itself with respect to time and space and gives meaning to the objective world. Neither an exclusive subject nor an exclusive object, Weiss's painted bodies were, moreover, spaces passing through larger spatial and temporal terrains such that the interrelationality of both influence the perception and phenomenal constitution of each other. Due to its embodied point of view, the exiled body—a sum of parts—was also never capable of accessing itself as an entire entity. On this point, Weiss diverged from Merleau-Ponty. For Merleau-Ponty, the body assembled, in spite of the *punctum cecum* and the concomitant corporeal fragmentation, a phantasmatic sense of itself—a body image—as an "inter-sensory" and "sensori-motor" totality.[51] For Weiss, this unity was something lost and to be regained, a trauma first conceived as something having compromised the eye and later characterized as having literally cleaved the body into parts. The year 1947 was a critical juncture in Weiss's work, when his explicit traumatic representations gave way to his appropriation of surrealist sensibilities. Reversals in his economy of representation abounded. Reality assumed the guise of dreams and the fantastic superseded the phenomenal. If, as Benjamin insisted, ur-surrealism's efficacy as an avant-garde rested in its destructive character—he writes of the technologically facilitated "interpenetration" of the body and image space—surrealism for Weiss was to be anything but a tool with which to enact such traumatophilia.[52] For Weiss, surrealism would have to undergo a reversal of its own in order to articulate the trauma of exile.

The Trauma of Displacement: Weiss's Literary Turn

In his essay "Reflections on Exile," Edward Said insists that the exilic experience—a hallmark of the twentieth century's world wars, totalitarian regimes, deportations, and ethnic cleansing campaigns—resembles that of trauma. Exile, he writes, "is the unhealable rift between a human being and a native place, between the self and its true home." It is "a condition of terminal loss," "a discontinuous state of being," and a "broken" being that is "neither aesthetically nor humanistically comprehensible."[53] Festering wounds, forced departures and impossible homecomings, the incomprehensible and interminable sense of loss and, above all, melancholy, these topi are as much the province of exile as they are of trauma. Defining trauma as "any violent shock and its consequences to the personality," psychoanalysts León and Rebeca Grinberg reinforce this convergence in their work on migration. Trauma is not an unexpected physical blow to the nervous system as Freud and others once described it but rather manifests itself in exile, the Grinbergs argue, in the form of an "accumulation of several partially traumatic events." This trauma commences prior to the moment of separation and its effects "run deep and last long" after the moment of displacement.[54] Of all the traumatic symptoms of exile the Grinbergs enumerate—the insecurity of uprootedness; feelings of defeat and nostalgia, skepticism and hatred, persecution and survival guilt; forestalled spatial demarcations, farewells, and temporal closures—it is "ego disintegration and dissolution and a blurring of boundaries" that characterize its most extreme symptoms.[55] In spite of its longevity, exile trauma, the Grinbergs insinuate, in no way forecloses the possibility of working through its lingering causes and effects. According to Said, literature plays a pivotal role in the exile's never-ending quest to "overcome" what he describes as "the crippling sorrow of estrangement." The writer oftentimes strives to reconstitute the brokenness of his exilic condition by piecing together with language a semblance of the wholeness of that lost and irretrievable existence before exile.[56] Said leaves, however, the matter of form entirely unresolved. Reminiscent of Cathy Caruth's proposition that trauma persists as an ineluctable enigma, Said's insistence on the incomprehensibility of exile could be taken to suggest, as Caruth does, that the traumatic traces of exile manifest themselves as textual gaps (i.e., epistemological voids) that literature can best throw into relief.[57] On the contrary, neither the imaginary worlds captured within fiction, which Georg Lukács champions in *Theory of the Novel,* nor Adorno's "disconnected and non-binding" aphorisms from *Minima Moralia* gain precedence in Said's argument as forms with which to master the traumatic event.[58] As with Said, Weiss's continued exploration of the predicament of exile in literature espouses hope for exile's termination while questioning nonetheless the feasibility of any such ultimate solution.

Scholarship has devoted scant attention to the place of trauma in Weiss's early literary work.[59] An exception is Alfons Söllner's monograph *Peter Weiss und die Deutschen (Peter Weiss and the Germans),* which preceded the rise of Anglo-American scholarship on trauma by roughly half a decade. Although he never defines the *terminus technicus* "trauma," Söllner begins his study with the claim that twentieth-century German history is riddled with "traumatic experiences" of failed democracy, fascism and war, occupation, and geopolitical division. Söllner is initially concerned with the psychic mechanisms that prevented the German collective from integrating the unmastered phantoms of its past into the rational present, and he implies, without ever stating it directly, that a pandemic traumatic neurosis throughout postwar Germany, the principal symptom of which was silence, left German identity in a prolonged state of crisis. In contradistinction to this German perpetrator trauma, Söllner presents Peter Weiss as having endured his own set of traumatic experiences, which stood in diametrical opposition to those of Germans. Forced emigration because of his Jewish parentage, writes Söllner, was for Weiss "an experience of shock" that culminated in the artist's exclusion from postwar West Germany's institution of art and its public sphere as well.[60] Of greatest concern to Söllner are the discrepancies between German trauma and Weiss's exilic trauma. When read against the larger historical backdrop, Weiss's early literary works stand out as a counterpoint to a German inability to mourn, for Weiss's protagonists seek to overcome the trauma of being rendered silent by engaging in a "battle for a new language." Conversely, Germans not only fell silent about their past but also derealized it such that they became immune to feelings of guilt and melancholy.[61] Within this greater psychohistorical context, Söllner contends that the linguistic realization of Weiss's struggle out of silence encompassed roughly seven years of literary output (1946–52) that terminated with the most radical language experiment he would ever craft, the so-called micro-novel (*Mikro-Roman*) *The Shadow of the Body of the Coachman*. In his reading of the novel as a story about a failed writer, Söllner maintains that it, in almost allegorical fashion, exposes how silence about and repression of a traumatic past can only lead to failure.[62] Söllner's emphasis on the centrality of language in the text's admonition is hardly misguided. Weiss himself asserted on several occasions that this book, his official German literary debut, was a linguistic exercise meant to facilitate the reacquisition of German, not as a mother tongue but rather as a foreign language.[63] Indeed, the relationship between language, perception, and representation has been a thread that consistently runs throughout the critical reception of Weiss's novel. While a few scholars have given credence to Weiss's insistence that language problems are inextricably grounded in the exilic condition, only a couple have delved directly into the nexus of the novel's title and content—the body. Of these, none have ferreted out the preexisting links between the body, exile, and vision. To establish these links and access the exilic logic of Weiss's appropriation of surrealism, the overarching crisis of the body in the micro-novel requires initial elucidation.

Rejected in 1952 and then accepted eight years later for publication, *The Shadow of the Body of the Coachman* was originally printed in a limited run of one thousand copies and became a critical sensation overnight. Comprised of eleven loosely connected vignettes and seven collages carefully interspersed throughout, the micro-novel centers around a nameless first-person narrator. The narrator is one of eleven guests rooming in a desolate country boarding house, and he meticulously records the events he sees and hears over the course of three days. Though seemingly worlds away from the formal and substantive problems raised in the painting *Jüngling am Stadtrand,* the micro-novel's eleven scenes revolve around the very same spatial, temporal, and corporeal crises of exile. Space is already prominent at the work's outset when the narrator surveys the visual terrain surrounding the boarding house's privy. "Through the half-open door I see the muddy, trampled path and the rotten planks around the pigsty. The snout of the pig sniffs along the wide crevice whenever it isn't rooting in the mud, snorting and grunting."[64] With little to see while perched on the toilet, he abandons the visual and resorts to the acoustic in order to record his environs: the sound of pigs, the wind, crows, dripping rainwater, a saw, and the humming of a hired man. After defecating, he emerges from the house and confirms visually the spatial relationships that are only partially imaginable aurally. The spatial orientation of the self and the constitution of the self's identity assume primary importance. Enclosed inside a box with a narrow aperture, a camera obscura of sorts, the narrator—he announces his task on the toilet to be that of "concentration" and "observation"—establishes a teleology between "I see," "I hear," and "I can imagine." The shift affords him the ability to assemble the outside world out of its perceived parts. His vantage point ultimately brings him to declare at the beginning of vignette 2, "I am now . . . "[65]

This slippage between epistemological wholeness and ontological certitude at the novel's opening is not as stable as it might seem. Of the eleven other bodies that fall within the narrator's line of sight, he perceives none as being whole in spite of his thoroughness. Mr. Schnee, fellow boarder and avid rock collector, appears in the second vignette solely in terms of his hands. Heightening this fragmentation, the narrator sees Mr. Schnee's face framed in a windowpane. He then crosses paths with the tailor, a man whose patched clothes intimate his own corporeal fragmentation. Finally, he spies through another window a *tableau vivant* of a young family:

> I noticed the father, the mother, the infant, and the son in the following distribution and relation to each other: the mother sitting on the edge of the bed at the back of the room, half in the dark, her breast bared, and the infant at her breast; the father standing at the table in the middle of the room, his fists propped on the tabletop in front of him, the light from the window full on him, outlining the face thrust forward with the mouth wide open; and opposite him, not sitting but squatting on his heels, the son, his chin pressed against the edge of the table, his shoulders pulled up to his ears, staring into the father's open mouth. (*SBC*, 4)

A master of depth of field, the narrator captures not only the contours of the room but also the spatial relationship of the bodies fixed in that space: mother's breast vis-à-vis her infant and the father's fist, face, and mouth vis-à-vis his son's chin, shoulders, and ears. The narrator never evokes the family's bodies as being whole. Phenomenally, he segments their bodies and frames select parts for exhaustive inspection. This metonymic displacement of the whole to its parts is anything but arbitrary. Concentration on the family's organs, limbs, and orifices draws attention to those somatic sites with the greatest symbolic potency in the family's Oedipal conflict. It also conveys an illusory sense of symbolic wholeness where materially there is none. All in all, this attention to body parts—the narrator's underlying desire to "give an outline to what I've seen"—hardly comes to fruition (*SBC*, 18). His fixation on body parts, their features, and movements continues throughout the remainder of the novel. In his most severe phenomenal dismemberment of other bodies, the narrator erases the subject entirely and implies that limbs are fully automated and independent unto themselves. The meal in vignette 4 includes a handful of salient passages that employ the passive voice to illustrate this shift: "Hands holding spoons are now lifted toward the pots from all sides"; "the mouths open"; "the tin mugs are occasionally grabbed by the other hands"; and "the liquid penetrates into the mouths" (*SBC*, 8–9). This fervor to document every microscopic detail throughout the day accomplishes the opposite of total omniscience. Body fragmentation assumes its most literal manifestation in the person of the doctor, incorrectly described in the dinner scene as a "whole body." In actuality, the doctor is an assemblage whose individual parts are sutured together by stitches and bandages from head to legs (*SBC*, 8). He later implies in a litany of whispered sentence fragments that he has performed nothing less than a vivisection on himself. The numerous invasive incisions, lacerations, biopsies, and drainages undertaken in his bedroom—all brought about because of a mysterious and enduring pain he wishes to excise surgically—result in total disorientation: "arm all slashed, lose direction, lose the door, the table, wrong door, don't know upstairs, downstairs, up or down, sit in the dark, don't know arm or leg, pain the same" (*SBC*, 22). In this vertiginous state, he removes his black sunglasses to reveal his "empty, whitish" eyes and concludes in sentence fragments that there is "nothing more to see, even the strongest light, all in the dark" (*SBC*, 22). The doctor's body occupies a crucial position in the novel's corporeal economy, for it illustrates a radical divide between feelings of pain (whose origins are as nebulous as those of the boarders themselves), the corporeal fragmentation it generates, and the ability to perceive these symptoms with the naked eye.

The exceptional status of the doctor's self-mutilated body sheds light on the narrator's complicated relationship to his own body. Where the doctor suffers from debilitating pain that severs, disorients, and blinds, the narrator is committed to the exact opposite: assembling, orienting, and seeing. Unlike all the other boarders, he perceives in his painstakingly detailed protocols a path away from what he calls the "new, short, and broken-off" and toward a position of sustained clarity and wholeness (*SBC*, 6). His one-point perspective is a quest for power over the subjects who populate his line of vision; while their bodies fail to heed his phenomenal pursuit of wholeness, his body initially seems entirely intact, a whole body subsumed by authority of the "I" that accordingly disappears behind the eye. In contradistinction to his ability to record acts of perceiving other bodies in pieces, he is repeatedly unable to document the minute actions undertaken by his own body parts: "I, I hardly notice how I eat," he admits during the meal with the other boarders (*SBC,* 10). This looking beyond the self such that the lived body disappears from view follows normative patterns of perceptual embodiment. According to philosopher Drew Leder, "The body conceals itself precisely in the act of revealing what is Other."[66] But although the narrator indeed refrains from engaging in the self-mutilation practiced by the doctor, his being-in-the-world is not as exceptional as it first seems. In spite of his conviction that he is an intact subject fixed in time and space—"I am now . . . "—devoid of the phenomenal dissociation, metonymic condensation, or surgical segmentation that plague the other body-objects, his body also succumbs to fragmentation and thereby reveals its own rightful place among partial objects. As is the case with the other boarders, his limbs revolt against his absent whole self so that they, too, become the motor that propels him through time and space. This first occurs in vignette 2 when he recalls his passage from the outhouse to his attic room: "My hands pulled me, and my feet under which the steps were creaking pushed me higher and higher" (*SBC,* 5). It is no coincidence that the ascendancy of the narrator's body parts occurs at exactly that moment when he surveys his environment while in motion. Drifting through the kitchen, he remarks how its objects glided by (*vorüberglitten*) him. Gliding (*gleiten*), phenomenologist Erwin Straus asserts, can on the one hand be pleasurable, for it affords one the sense of overcoming space. It also frightens, for it not only prevents the perceiving individual from differentiating space into discrete units but also continually "threaten[s] to become falling."[67] Gliding not only preempts one's ability to perceive and therefore know oneself in the world but also modifies this relationship insofar as the body is perceived as belonging "to both 'bodily space' and 'external space.'"[68] The narrator's hands that pull and feet that push unquestionably signal a shift whereby his body, which was otherwise an absent whole, becomes visible as a few select parts that join the object realm of other automated limbs. No longer an exclusive subject, he becomes aware of his own corporeal instability precisely because he is gliding. Motion deprives him of his mastery so that his body is perceived as being asunder from itself.[69] This fall from totality lasts only a moment, for the narrator restricts his movements throughout his three-day chronicle to an absolute minimum; his corporeal wholeness is in large part contingent upon remaining still. Returning to the narrator's unique, inversely proportional relationship with the doctor, it is clear that for both of them the body is a point of departure. Unlike the doctor, however, whose pain has brought about a blindness that prevents him from experiencing anything beyond his own disfigured body, the narrator's distance from the events and bodies he observes aids and abets his overall quest to perceive an intact world from his insides out. Approached then in terms of a crisis of the body, *The Shadow of the Body of the Coachman*—frequently misconstrued as a deviation in Weiss's oeuvre—upholds the very same theme of corporeal fragmentation developed in the paintings completed at the outset of his exile. Grasped in terms of this long-standing theme of traumatic displacement, the micronovel exhibits in the ocular obsession of its own mysteriously displaced narrator a self-awareness of the lost whole body and proceeds accordingly to recover it. In effect, the sought-after green door painted in 1938 has become in 1952 the body itself.

The Shadows of Bodies

The instability of the narrator's whole body and his mania for microscopic descriptions of other bodies point toward an overriding phenomenal and corporeal economy in the text, a discursive flow that continually pushes from part to whole. The desire to make a whole body out of its parts is most forcefully underscored in vignette 3, when the narrator reports that when alone in his room he dedicates himself to the art of *erdenken von Bildern,* literally the "conceiving of images."[70] It is here where surrealist ways of seeing intrude into the narrator's phenomenological obsessions. "For this," he reports, "I lie stretched out on the bed; within reach, beside me, on the table, there is a plate full of salt from which I occasionally take a few grains to put in my eyes. The function of the salt is to stimulate the tear glands and thus blur my vision" (*SBC*, 6). Far from merely blurring his vision, these experiments in visual perception dissolve the narrator's spatial confines and conjure up illusions of unmitigated wholeness:

> Directly below me . . . there gleamed a face as if in moonlight, yet there was no moon nor any stars, a face with thin cheekbones, a full, dark mouth, dark shaded eyes, and under the face a slim throat against the flowing hair, and under the edge of the throat the sharply outlined collar bone with the bare straight shoulders, and under the shoulders the

bare breasts circumscribed by lines of shadows, with the black centers of the nipples, and under the breasts the ribs. (*SBC,* 7)

After seeing the rest of this female apparition, the narrator admits that he "felt her nearness so strongly" that he "took the mirage for reality and made a hasty movement with [his] arms which immediately tore the image" (*SBC,* 7). Something deeply desired, this whole woman is a construct, a whole body carefully sutured together piece by piece, a metonymic string of signifiers that begins with the head and arrives at closure with the toe. Several scholars like Otto Best have insisted that this first of several visions is nothing less than the narrator's exploration of surrealist techniques for augmenting perception. Where Best describes this as a visual equivalent of surrealism's *écriture automatique,* others chalk the experiments up to the narrator's flight from reality, his escape into the dream, and a path toward wish fulfillment by the unconscious.[71] Indeed, the narrator's use of salt does evoke surrealism's pharmacokinetic methods for inducing what Benjamin called "profane illumination," intoxications of thought to which hallucinogenic drugs could provide an "introductory lesson." There exist crucial differences between the narrator's salt and Benjamin's hashish, the most salient of which is the former's inability to rupture psychochemically the rigid borders between "dreaming and waking states."[72] Compared to one of André Breton's earliest trancelike experiences in which he perceived "a man walking cut half way up by a window perpendicular to the axis of his body," Weiss's narrator employs salt to accomplish the exact opposite.[73] Instead of closing his eyes and activating the realm of the unconscious to disclose a forbidden world of fantastic and random assemblages, he achieves with eyes wide open what he otherwise cannot: capturing the spectacle of a whole body.

Compared to his Sisyphean task of assembling quotidian reality into a whole, these solitary salt experiments are hardly a triumph. This failure to make "seeing into an occupation" comes to light in the novel's collages (*SBC,* 18). Ignored by scholars until very recently, the micro-novel's collages, which Weiss created five years after completing the text, exist in a twilight space between the ocularcentrism within the text and the extratextual realm of images.[74] If images, as Weiss would later declare in his cosmology of language, simultaneously convey all their components as a single totality, then the gridlike collages that the text juxtaposes with particular narrative scenes announce that the totality seen is actually a collection of fragments.[75] Totality, like absolute transparency, is a fiction. In

Figure 5

Peter Weiss, first collage in *The Shadow of the Body of the Coach-man,* 1959. 10 × 7 inches.

the lower left-hand corner of the very first collage (fig. 5) inserted just one page after the description of the apparition of a woman, a man in profile gazes through an optical device. By virtue of two other related images positioned in his line of sight in the collage's far-right column, it is suggested that both of these apparatuses unveil what otherwise eludes the eye; as suggested by the prism in the lower right-hand corner and a camera lucida above it, both optical aids expose the individual elements that comprise larger natural phenomena (i.e., the dispersal of light into a spectrum).

Like the rigid block grid that determines the relation between the collage's individual parts, these scientific instruments of reason reveal the hidden order in the visible world by unveiling the interdependency between part and whole.[76] As much as the collage invokes by way of metaphor the salt experiments from vignette 3, it nevertheless questions the wholeness that the narrator mistakenly takes to be real. Whereas the woman recounted in the text appears as a string of signifiers that begins with her head and face, she appears decapitated in the collage. With her abdomen and headless body positioned at the same implied depth of field (or column) as the prism and light projector, the collage infers the male gaze—unlike the scientific instruments—to be capable of divining a whole from the sum of a woman's parts. Similarly, her head, although directly in the crosshairs of the male gaze, loses both detail and definition the farther the man's eye penetrates until it finally eclipses the head altogether. As his gaze travels from left to right, the collage establishes the male gaze as wielding a violence that severs the female body along the Cartesian divide such that the remainder is only her *res extensa*. Unlike the unified whole spied in the salt vision, he beholds through his looking glass a headless female body, her abdomen singled out in the top-right corner but not yet penetrated by his eye.

Recognizing this discord between text and collage is crucial, for not only does it make clear that the latter is not a mimetic illustration of the events unfurled in the former, but it also attests to the unresolved intermedial tensions in Weiss's avant-garde output throughout the fifties. With respect to the collage's status as image, it is arguable that as a metanarrative agent it, and not the narrator, taps into the anatomy lessons of surrealism, the most important of which is the fundamental nature of misrecognition in the identification with images. As surrealist film scholar Linda Williams points out, Jacques Lacan's linguistic revision of Freudian psychoanalysis—in particular his theory of the mirror stage—encapsulated and expounded upon the very same surrealist concerns about the purity of "nonverbal image-discourse" that culminated in surrealist writings like those of Antonin Artaud. Just as Artaud exposed "the image of the Other" as "a seductive illusion of wholeness," so too did Lacan insist that the narcissistic desire to equate the specular image of the Other with the self was a fiction. This misrecognition arises because the imaginary order in which such identifications transpire systemically denies the a priori presence of the symbolic.[77] Misrecognition is thus an inherent unawareness of Lacan's proposition that "the unconscious is structured like a language."[78] Once the illusion is eventually smashed, the subject—with only the linguistic structures of the symbolic at its disposal—desires to regain an originary sense of totality by literally stringing signifiers together "word to word and from line to line" in an interminable chain (*SBC*, 17). By throwing salt into his eyes, Weiss's narrator not only testifies to the centrality of misrecognition in his "attempts at writing" but also short-circuits the nostalgic logic of metonymic desire, as if to suggest that it can attain fulfillment once and for all. Although firmly rooted in the visual registers of the pre-linguistic imaginary, Weiss's collage, on the other hand, counters this misrecognition by rupturing the myth of wholeness. Far from merely repeating surrealism's proto-psychoanalytic exercises, or even reconciling the body in pieces as a normative transhistorical condition, Weiss's collages deploy instances of the imaginary that are situated outside the false perceptions of the narrator in order to establish a basis on which to think through the limited binarism of fragmentation-versus-wholeness. Consumed by his desire to access the imaginary, the narrator fails to recognize at the micro-novel's close the proto-cinematic solution to his dilemma.

First mentioned in vignette 2 as someone heard and not seen, the coachman of the micro-novel's title is marked as an absence until the final vignette. The climax of the novel, the penultimate scene in which the narrator sees shadows of the coachman and the housekeeper engaged in intercourse in the kitchen, stands out as an exceptional moment in the narrative in which bodies become whole:

> Only the shadow of the raised hand of the housekeeper holding the coffeepot stuck out from the shapeless, condensed joining of the shadows of the bodies. The shadow of the coffeepot swayed back and forth, the shadow of the bodies also swayed back and forth; and now and then the shadow of the heads in profile, sticking close together, rose above the clump of bodies. (*SBC*, 37)

Though frequently interpreted as a spectacle that traumatizes the narrator, the sex scene actually leaves the narrator feeling "absolute[ly] indifferent" (*SBC*, 35).[79] This indifference, which brings him to consider terminating his writerly quest to transcend the "short, broken off," arises from the fact that this "visual game" does not resemble the illusory outcome of his salt-induced visions, nor does it allow for the perpetual quest for wholeness through metonymy.[80] Said differently, the shadows of the alien bodies he surveils do not correspond to his own desired specular image; while the bodies' shadows intermittently appear to have appendages, they fuse to form a corporeal mass discernible only as a blob that rocks back and forth. Indivisible and anatomically foreign, the "clump of bodies" exhibits a shadowy mass (*Schattenmasse*) solely in terms of its optical unity and forestalls any and all identification.[81] This short circuit is all the more astonishing given the fact that this spectacle, a mere projection of silhou-ettes, is nothing less than a pre-cinematic experience, a makeshift shadow play: "I could see . . . the shadows falling from the kitchen window onto the ground in the yard while I was leaning out of my window inhaling the night air" (*SBC,* 37). Reading this rough replication of cinema as a manifestation of the imaginary, as Christian Metz might, is problematic. This screen does not reflect the ego ideal as does a mirror but rather dis-torts it. Similar to surrealist film in terms of its disruption of identification with the screen, this proto-filmic moment in vignette 11 departs, however, from surrealism's disinclination to distort the perceived image.[82] Ironi-cally, it also contradicts Weiss's own assessment of surrealist film's greatest contribution to avant-garde cinema, which he articulated in 1956 in his study on the history of avant-garde film. Unlike Luis Buñuel's surrealist films, which turned "away from the aestheticizing character" of earlier vanguard cinema that merely played "with light and shadows" and exag-gerated photographic "effects and technical finesse," the light show that closes *The Shadow of the Body of the Coachman* does exactly that.[83] As if to suggest that the imaginary signifier must be jettisoned, the play of shad-ows proposes another sur-reality for identification, one that transcends the fiction of (lost) wholeness as instantiated by the virtual woman in the salt hallucinations as well as the misrecognition that accompanies her. In place of these visions, the light show infers that non-totalizing forms of embodi-ment can be rectified by smashing the mirror and, with it, the blueprint for an ideal anatomy. Although the narrator fails to acknowledge the les-sons embedded in this accidental film—he leaves his last sentence without any closing punctuation as if to suggest that it must be continued—Weiss made non-totalizing corporeal assemblages comprised of non-contiguous body parts the centerpiece of his first mature avant-garde film.

Weiss's Realist Cinema

Filmed while he wrote *The Shadow of the Body of the Coachman,* Weiss's second film, *Studie II (Hallucinationer),* is comprised of twelve scenes, each of which contains disparate nude male and female body parts positioned so that they rock, tilt, walk, wave, grasp, hoist, rotate, and quiver. Filmed with a static camera, each of the *tableaux vivants* sets a markedly different assemblage of body fragments against a black background that reduces the depth of field to the limited space occupied by the bodies. While they evoke in name the salt experiments from the micro-novel, the twelve hallucinations in the six-minute black-and-white film have little in common with the narrator's forced instrumentalization of a dreamlike state. According to Weiss's own critical assessment of his film, each mise-en-scène was pieced together to create deformed "figures" that were meant to evoke "strong erotically-tinged feelings."[84] In an interview with Harun Farocki many years later, Weiss insisted that the basis for the film was a series of ink sketches of deformed and anatomically disproportionate bodies that "dealt with the exile situation," which he described to be "dreamlike" and "traumatic."[85] Weiss's thumbnail readings of the film, in which he underscores the themes of desire, deformed bodies, and the trauma of exile, intimate that his development from painter to writer to filmmaker traveled full circle. As was the case with both the painting *Jüngling am Stradtrand* and the micro-novel, the film displays Weiss's recurring predicament of bodies torn asunder. Unlike the painting, which encodes loss corporeally and identifies its recovery through time-space displacement, the film conceives of loss as an interminable and irreversible condition. Taking the misrecognition at the close of the micro-novel as its point of departure, the film also moves beyond the text's embrace of the imaginary as a visual means to recover linguistically the lost whole body. If both painting and text represent the effects of exilic trauma on the body along with the drive to master, albeit unsuccessfully, its concomitant fragmentation, the film marks a breakthrough for Weiss insofar as it radically subverts the foregoing object of desire. *Studie II* represents the apogee of Weiss's engagement with the broken body during his second exile in the fifties, because it gives voice to an immaterial traumatic force whose effects his works cannot escape.

The film's initial scene establishes vision and desire as the points of departure for the remaining eleven scenes. This mise-en-scène is comprised of three distinct body formations, the most prominent being a male torso and head lying face-up, its right arm raised in the air with a glass ball in hand (see fig. 6). With a pair of legs atop his chest—its feet point toward his head—the man stares at the ball, which he carefully twirls in his hand. Intersecting his line of sight is an arm that protrudes from the right-hand

Figure 6

Peter Weiss, first scene from *Studie II (Hallucinationer),* 1952.

perimeter of the frame, its hand opening and closing slowly. Behind the male's torso on the left-hand side of the frame, a nude female in profile gazes into a mirror such that her visage is reflected toward the camera. A self-reflective acknowledgment of the imaginary and the illusion of the specular image, the woman-mirror arrangement echoes itself in the male head/torso-glass ball constellation insofar as both involve a scopic drive. Whereas the mirror illustrates the illusory constitution of an ego ideal, the glass ball—a perfect complete form unto itself—embodies wholeness a priori. The glass ball makes corporeal unity radically other. The close proximity of the ball to the arm fragment is highly significant in this tableau, for their stereoscopic juxtaposition in the male's line of sight suggests a relation; the ball the man twirls is inversely proportional to the spherical empty space outlined by the arm's flexing fingers. Called by Weiss the film's "tranquil mode," this scene establishes the falsity of the mirror and the absence of corporeal unity; the totality of the glass ball cannot be reproduced by what must remain fragmentary, the body in pieces.

If scene 1 expresses solace derived from literally foregrounding a fragmented ontology, scene 2, an expression of "inner disquietude," operates as a counterpoint (see fig. 7). Here the theme of the aforementioned glass ball's integrity is developed further with soap bubbles blown by a shadowy figure in the frame's lower left corner. Behind a gently bending leg that

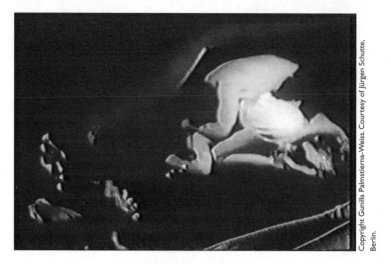

Figure 7
Peter Weiss, second scene from *Studie II (Hallucinationer)*, 1952.

juts out from the top boundary of the frame lies a pair of clumped bodies rocking together, a scenario not unlike the one that closes *The Shadow of the Body of the Coachman*. Unlike the previous scene, this constellation invites an equivalency between the spherical mass of bodies and bubbles. Inner turmoil finds its expression in the leg that slices the depth of field in half so that the bubbles are divided from the clumped bodies. As if to delineate the perfect, inorganic, and geometrical from its futile replication using human bodies, the leg is, like the arm fragment from before, the body fragment that disrupts the hallucinated dream of wholeness from offscreen. Scene 3, in which two legs frame a face toward which one of two hands raises and lowers a goblet full of water, punctuates the foregoing idea of unfulfilled desire (see fig. 8). An allusion to the glass ball and bubbles, the goblet and the water it holds have become the object of desire. The water never reaches the mouth and the face is left to behold the spectacle of four limbs, none of which are anatomically related to each other. The conceptual trajectory of *Studie II* reaches an initial plateau with scene 4, in which four sets of body parts exist independently of one another (see fig. 9). Peering downward into the frame from above, a face looks but does not tend to a second face positioned in the opposite corner of the frame. This other face, set back farther into the depth of field than

Figure 8

Peter Weiss, third scene from *Studie II (Hallucinationer)*, 1952.

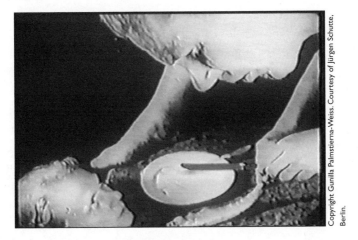

Figure 9

Peter Weiss, fourth scene from *Studie II (Hallucinationer)*, 1952.

the first, looks above and beyond a pair of hands that protrude from the right side of the frame and cut a herring on a plate with fork and knife. A foot rests on the geographical plane behind the plate. Situated in their own distinct position in the frame's three-dimensional composition, these body parts refrain from interpellating one another. The libidinal vectors from the frame's gazes have no target, and the potential objects of desire

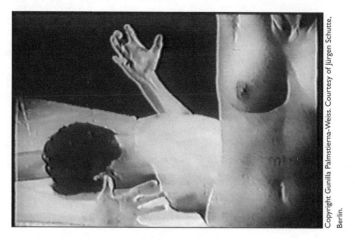

Copyright Gunilla Palmstierna-Weiss. Courtesy of Jürgen Schutte. Berlin.

Figure 10

Peter Weiss, ninth scene from *Studie II (Hallucinationer)*, 1952.

within the frame persevere unnoticed and unclaimed. The idea of *Unlust* that Weiss identified in this constellation must be taken literally as a negation of desire by arresting it with and in space. From the falseness of the initial mirror, *Studie II* progresses toward the suspension of desire altogether and deems fractured embodiment an unalterable condition.

Studie II continues with eight more configurations, four of which (numbers 5, 6, 8, and 10) document the reemergence of desire as an intrusion of the symbolic order into the initial dream of arrested desire. Scene 9, described by Weiss as a figuration of "maturity and inner resistance," reiterates the previous suspension of desire in scenes 2 through 4, particularly with its fists that clench at nothingness (see fig. 10). Scenes 7, 11, and 12 overlap in their preoccupation with sleeping figures, the overriding topos of a film whose subtitle announces the coming of dreamlike hallucinations. Particularly striking because of their juxtaposition, scenes 11 and 12 reveal the nature of the screen in Weiss's film. If each individual mise-en-scène represents a dreamlike hallucination, and if the composition and trajectory of all the scenes rupture—in the tradition of surrealist film—the illusions of the imaginary signifier so that fulfillment of desire is frozen, are these final scenes not also a hallucinatory assault on the desire to sleep? If the dream, as Freud contends, is the fulfillment of the desire to sleep, are these surrealist-like dream-images of sleepers (dreaming) not a self-effacing move to disrupt the dream, a dream against dreaming? Scene 11, labeled by Weiss a "lullaby," provides an answer (see

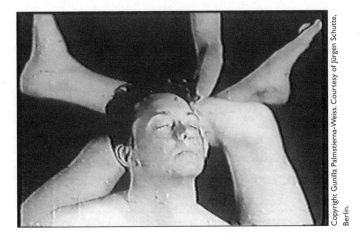

Figure 11

Peter Weiss, eleventh scene from *Studie II (Hallucinationer)*, 1952.

fig. 11). Comprised of two body assemblages, the tableaux depicts an arm protruding downward from the upper perimeter of the frame, the palm of its hand affixed to the left temple of a tightly framed man's head with eyes closed. Together they gyrate clockwise, while behind them a pair of legs rotates in the opposite direction. Inducing sleep, the title and composition suggest, assumes serene, machine-like rhythms. As with the previous scenes, however, the assemblage of body parts must not be conflated as comprising a single composite form. The opposing directionality of the leg assemblage vis-à-vis the sleeping torso-arm aggregate makes clear that the sought-after dream of wholeness (which is induced by the fragmented body) cannot mask, let alone reverse, the unrelenting intrusion of bodily fragmentation. Not the cause but rather the symptom of what Lacan calls "something quite primary," the film's automatic limbs once again pit their on-screen dream against the body's desire for wholeness. In effect, the film functionalizes traumatic symptoms—body parts—in order to approximate surrealist disruptions within the imaginary screen. The culmination of this is the twelfth and final scene, the sole mise-en-scène in which just the symptom appears: atop a headless torso lies another legless and headless trunk with its back facing the camera (see fig. 12). From underneath the torsos, two legs jut out to the left of the frame and from the bottom edge an arm rests, its fingers moving ever so slightly atop the torsos. Literally a pile of mostly lifeless body parts, this scene elevates the screen as the exclusive subject of the dream. Described by Weiss as "drowning in

Peter Weiss and the Exilic Body 91

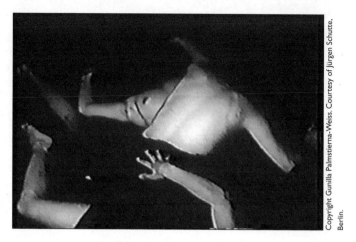

Figure 12
Peter Weiss, twelfth scene from *Studie II (Hallucinationer)*, 1952.

loneliness and sleep," it infers this condition of the fragmented body to be a state of finitude.

The prominence of the human back within the final scene once again suggests that Weiss ends *Studie II* just as he began his painterly engagement with exile around 1938. Yet this return of the back—the body's phenomenal locus of fragmentation—in this film is more than an inconsequential shift in the medium of representation. Lacan contends that, just as the image screen conceals the real, it also points toward its existence. Indeed, along with the repetition of the back as the symptom of a lost corporeal wholeness *Studie II* incorporates the return of the traumatic real as something "unassimilable" that persists beyond the fragmented body as well as the frame of representation. In his seminar on the gaze, Lacan speaks of the "stain" as the visible mark through which the traumatic real gazes and thereby blinds the subject. In *Studie II* this stain exists exclusively within the realm of the audible. Performed and recorded by Weiss, the film's soundtrack is his first "experiment with the possibilities of a new acoustic world . . . of screeching, scratching, and clanking."[86] The originality of Weiss's "noise of hallucinations" lies neither in its approximation of Pierre Schaeffer's *musique concrète,* for example, nor in its use in nonnarrative film. Weiss's soundtrack is original because of its "acousmatic presence" and the lack that it signifies. Defined by Michel Chion as an offscreen sound that a film never traces visually back to its cause or source, the acousmatic in *Studie II* initially assumes a relation-

Figure 13

Peter Weiss, title shot from *Studie II (Hallucinationer)*, 1952.

ship with the bodies on screen.[87] The title scene (fig. 13), in which two sets of hands scratch away at the top of the frame, infers that this sound emanates from the frenetic digits, but this reciprocity quickly destabilizes as subsequent scenes refrain from suturing image with sonic space. At one moment sounding from within the frame and at another from without it, the film's acousmatic noise ultimately originates from elsewhere, passes through the black voids in the open frame long enough to imply, briefly, a plausible correspondence with the image, and then moves on, reassuming sovereignty. The soundtrack's spatial voids—a simultaneous transcendence and omniscience—point to another space beyond, yet coterminous with, the visible frame and afford it a voice. That this acousmatic sound in *Studie II* says nothing with language is crucial, for the message's high pitch and eerie timbre convey pure affect, a sense of the uncanny, if not horrific, that haunts the image. The "new acoustic world" in *Studie II* is nothing less than the return of the real, the missed traumatic encounter that eludes the symbolic chain of meaning but nevertheless returns from beyond the image screen.[88] This is the "stain" of exile, the original violence that tore the body asunder.

Accordingly, the subtitle for *Studie II* accrues greater significance. Like Freud, Weiss conflated the visual distortions of dream work with the symptoms of psychoneuroses as homologous forms of regression from reality. Hallucinations, as defined by Lacan (as well as Merleau-Ponty and Straus), belong, however, to the dominion of psychoses and express themselves primarily acoustically. For Lacan, the verbal hallucinations of the madman—voices that emanate from no one and nowhere—result when the barrier between reality and the real crumbles such that the latter overflows the former. In this respect, the prefix *sur* in Weiss's surrealism is a poor fit. Surrealism's quest to disrupt and transcend reality, along with its dialectical resolution of the boundaries between dreaming and waking, the conscious and unconscious, rationality and irrationality, misses Weiss's filmic project entirely. *Studie II* abandons surrealism's dialectics of representation. Just as the psychotic sees no difference between reality and the real, the film envisions a world in which Benjamin's destructive character has become the reality principle. Weiss's post-fascist surrealist project is more realist than surrealist, for its dreams of fragmented bodies are entirely the product of historical traumas precipitated by fascism's violence. This is especially evident in the final tableau, in which the pile of bodies evokes unmistakable associations with the gruesome iconography of the Holocaust. (In fact, Weiss's reference to drowning [*Ertrinken*] in his description of this scene echoes his aforementioned sketch from 1946 [fig. 3] in which prisoners drink from a pool full of floating limbs and heads.) Given Weiss's prevailing preoccupation with exile, this conflation of psycho-phenomenal body fragmentation (as precipitated by displacement) and the savagery practiced in Nazi extermination camps might appear excessive or, worse, seem to lapse into the "quietism of despair" common among zealous existentialists of the time. On the contrary, as Weiss established in his 1965 essay "Meine Ortschaft" ("My Place"), the cities and towns through which he passed as an exile all stood in singular opposition to the one place for which he, a European Jew, was meant: Auschwitz. "The living person who comes here from another world," he wrote of his visit to Auschwitz in late 1964, "possesses nothing other than his knowledge of facts, written reports, testimonies from witnesses. They are a part of his life, something he bears, but he can only apprehend that which befalls him."[89] A foil with which to imagine the devastation of the Holocaust and, conversely, an image with which to summate the corporeal fragmentation caused by forced displacement, exile and genocide together are the recto and verso of a historical consciousness that Weiss would continue to designate as the core of his work. Unlike his later literary and theatrical masterpieces that envisage historical narratives unfolding with respect to biographies, places, and events, Weiss's early avant-garde work, in particular *Studie II,* conceives of history visually in terms of its bodily effects. History, those originary forces that precipitated the dissociation of the human body in the first place, eludes the ocular empire entirely. If the real is indeed the diachronic dimension of History that transcends individual experience, the acousmatic presence in *Studie II* operates as a term limit in the film's engagement with the body. Not only does it accentuate the symptoms of trauma, but it also gives voice to the missing cause of that trauma, History.[90] *Studie II* thus imagines the conditions for working through this trauma without ever realizing them. Locked into the repetitive forms of acting-out (to which both the desire for wholeness and the fragmentation of the body belong), the film nevertheless acknowledges a dimension beyond the synchronic realm of melancholy, a temporal space related to yet different from it.

Coda: Impossible Returns

In the eight years spent finding a publisher for *The Shadow of the Body of the Coachman,* Weiss completed seven nonnarrative films, five documentary films, and one feature film. In the late fifties he began making collages, which have often been thought to be the final chapter of his early engagement with surrealism and the visual arts. With the publication of his micro-novel in West Germany, the loneliness of exile putatively came to a close. However, Weiss's literary return to Germany was anything but a homecoming. Initially published in 1960 in Franz Mon's compendium of postwar modernism, *movens,* vignettes 7 and 8 from the micro-novel, which peak with the narrator's visit to the self-mutilating doctor, were to illustrate what Mon heralded as modernism's postwar "dialectic between the whole and the singular." Mon insisted that the works sampled in his collection illustrated how the "artistic articulation" of symbol and reality can approach and approximate epistemologically the transcendental wholeness of the "thing itself" otherwise beyond the realm of quotidian perception.[91] Yet Weiss's micro-novel, especially this excerpt about the radical self-induced segmentation of the body, does not exemplify any such dialectical resolution. On the contrary, the novel fails to acknowledge a dialectical wholeness that Weiss's avant-garde film would later debunk. In a similar misappropriation, Suhrkamp editor Walter Höllerer incorporated Weiss in a double issue of *Akzente* from November 1964. The volume purported to bring together works by writers whom Höllerer considered the contemporary heirs to the historical avant-garde.[92] Grouped under the rubric "change" (*Veränderung*), Weiss was included to illustrate a new breed of writing, one that disposed with the perception and memory of an increasingly specious everyday reality. The volume's motley roster of international writers was to demonstrate the power to negate the trivial, and construct absolute modes of perception. Ironically, the progress Höllerer ascribes to Weiss's language, its supposed twin aspirations to destroy and create, does echo Benjamin's destructive character and even retains it as the exclusive province of the artist. Weiss's reinvention of surrealism was, however, worlds apart from Höllerer's vision of a renewed avant-garde. The original violent moment that brought Weiss's project into being existed from without. Given its traumatic constitution, this impulse prevented any such constructive impulse. As *Studie II* makes clear, the value of the legacies of surrealism after fascism lies in its ability to interrogate and arrest the desire for wholeness, to imagine the traumatic dissociation of the body as interminable, and to begin to grasp the body in pieces vis-à-vis the inexorable history that violated it.

That "realistic" and "avant-gardiste" art exist side by side today
is a fact that can no longer be objected to legitimately.
—Peter Bürger, *Theory of the Avant-Garde*[1]

Realism is a moral concept.
—Roland Barthes, "Probleme des literarischen Realismus,"
Akzente

3. Nouveau Realismus

The Male Body and the Space of History

Realism Along the Rhine

In 1956, literary realism seemed possible on only one side of the Rhine. In April of that year the Parisian journal *Documents* arranged a conference in Vézelay, France, titled "The Writer Before Reality" to which fourteen German and eight French poets, authors, and critics were invited. According to the German proceedings published later that year, the French were thoroughly delusional. Critic Roland Barthes insisted on the possibility of a dialectical resolution of nineteenth-century bourgeois and twentieth-century socialist realisms, something he called "total realism." Poet and novelist Luc Estang insisted on the viability of a "critical realism" intent on intervening in dominant semiotic systems that undergird and mediate everyday experience. And novelist Alain Robbe-Grillet called for a post-metaphysical realism skeptical of all forms of anthropomorphic significa-tion. Reality, he declared, is what always already is: the world of concrete presence, indifferent things, and impenetrable surfaces. While the French sought ways of reinvigorating realism, the Germans in attendance were in absolute agreement that realism is an utterly impossible thing. Even the most optimistic German writer in attendance, Karl Korn, confessed that realism can be mimetic in postwar societies only if it lends credence to the abstractions endemic to technological bureaucracies. According to this logic, Franz Kafka's *The Castle* was far more realistic than *Stalingrad*,

Theodor Plievier's best-selling 1945 novel based on eyewitness accounts of Nazi Germany's deadliest battle. By far the most skeptical of the bunch, poet Günter Eich exclaimed that he did not know what reality was. Because the brain is limited in its capacity to perceive all of reality, because the passing of time unseats every writerly attempt to capture a moment comprehensively, and because language is hampered by its limited descriptive powers, reality can, at best, only be that which the poet claims it is. Capturing reality can therefore only amount to fiction.[2] *Documents* editors falsely concluded that realism had reached its end stage in postwar Europe; anyone could espouse their own definition of the real. In truth, a crass national divide revealed itself in 1956. While the French insisted on reinvigorating literature's relationship to "objective reality," the Germans indulged in "subjective idealism."[3] This divide served as a powerful differential that eventually enabled one episode of West Germany's post-fascist avant-gardes to reclaim realism as a tool for constituting a historical consciousness through the body.

The German animus toward realism and reality had nothing to do with mere contrariness. Scholars attribute this refusal to myriad factors. The persistence of German idealism with its drive to transcend the common world, a suspicion toward the ideological thrust in East German realism, and an inability to engage the recent German past politically all played significant roles in the pervasiveness of symbolism, allegory, metaphor, and abstraction in West German literature of the fifties.[4] As influential as these individual philosophical, geopolitical, and psychological factors were, the need to reestablish a modern German tradition after fascism was equally decisive. In fact, ensconcing a tradition absorbed any and all other individual factors. No single writer fulfilled this quest for tradition more than Gottfried Benn, for whom empirical reality had long been in an irreparable crisis. Reflecting over four decades after his own debut as one of German expressionism's foremost practitioners, Benn claimed in 1955, amidst a flurry of postwar misunderstandings, that all variants of expressionism shared a conviction in the disintegration of reality. "It no longer existed at all," he wrote of reality around the fin de siècle.[5] With reality shattered, the most fundamental coordinates of social experience— nature and the materiality of life, power and history, time and space—all vanished. Trapped within this chaos, literary realism had but one course of action, namely to lend credence to the interior landscapes of the unfettered mind. Benn captured the initial shock that the dissolution of reality induced through the figure of Dr. Rönne, a young doctor for whom the exacting empiricism of the medical sciences gave way to debilitating hallucinations. Over the course of time, from before World War I to West German reconstruction, the shock of this radical divorce of self from world faded. Instead, Benn's postwar comeback elevated this decay of reality as a cornerstone of social consciousness. Considered then from the vantage point of Benn's unparalleled impact on postwar literary aesthetics under Chancellor Konrad Adenauer, the German rebuke of literary realism in France in 1956 was indicative of the institutionalization of one German historical avant-garde as the paradigm of postwar modernity. In effect, German expressionism's erstwhile rebuke of reality—its realignment of realism with *l'art pour l'art*—became the dominant weltanschauung in the Federal Republic of Germany.

Benn died almost two months to the day after Eich had professed in France that his world was composed entirely of language. While certainly no disciple of Benn, Eich's absolute discursivization of the world was unquestionably an epigone of Benn's own idea of *Ausdruckswelt* (world of expression), which he advanced in his most influential postwar credo.[6] That same month, Robbe-Grillet published his programmatic remarks from Vézelay in expanded format under the title "A Future for the Novel," in which he called for literature's restoration of objective realism. At this little-noticed intersection of national literatures in the summer of 1956, the aesthetic divide between Germany and France could not have been wider. With time, however, news of France's investment in realism migrated eastward across the Rhine. Two years later the French journal *L'Express* heralded, albeit belatedly, the official debut of the *nouveau roman* and Robbe-Grillet quickly found himself as one of its primary theoreticians. That same year Walter Höllerer's and Hans Bender's *Akzente* made Robbe-Grillet's and Nathalie Sarraute's programmatic statements on French new realism accessible to a broad German audience. And perhaps most significantly, the young Germanist Dieter Wellershoff published a sweeping monograph that, while unquestionably awestruck by Benn's aesthetic genius, nevertheless exposed the disastrous political consequences of his solipsistic phenomenology for postwar West Germany. Wellershoff's critique certainly did not unseat once and for all Benn's spell over the anti-realist impulse underlying much of West Germany's literature.[7] Nevertheless, his study marked an important initial incursion into the popularity of Benn's atomized reality and internalized realism. While the West German adoption of the *nouveau roman* had to wait several more years before seeing the light of day—Günter Grass's and Heinrich Böll's enormously popular and symbolically rich novels from 1959 took Germany by storm—the emergence of a German new realism in the early sixties was not a simple case of replicating Robbe-Grillet's model on German soil. On the contrary, employing Robbe-Grillet's ocularcentric realism—Barthes had already dubbed it in 1954 as an heir to Europe's prewar historical avant-garde—did not always amount to a perfect copy.[8] Bits of Benn's early and late poetics infiltrated the translation. Far from diminishing the severity of its attack on German anti-realism, the hybrid end product betrayed both Benn's and Robbe-Grillet's standpoints to produce a remarkably critical and historically cognizant new realism that was especially attuned to the derealization of West Germany's Nazi past in its democratic present. This breach was nowhere more manifest than in the work of German new realism's youngest practitioner, Rolf Dieter Brinkmann. By paying attention to the depiction of bodies in Brinkmann's 1962 debut closely, this chapter illuminates how Brinkmann incorporates Benn's and Robbe-Grillet's divergent poetics in order to disrupt the affirmative course of time after fascism. The male body plays a crucial role in this incursion, for in it and through it the German past is violently invoked and revoked. But before delving into Brinkmann, who held Benn in high esteem, Benn's prescient relationship to postmodernism first requires elucidation.[9]

The Late Benn and Postwar German Cynicism

In the mid-nineties Dieter Wellershoff encapsulated his four-decade-long engagement with Gottfried Benn in a word: Benn was postmodern. In fact, Benn was putatively one of Europe's first postmodern thinkers, a forerunner to Jean-François Lyotard, who first proclaimed the end of modernity's grand narratives in 1979. Wellershoff pointed out in his 1995–96 Frankfurt Lectures that Benn, too, best heralded the advent of the postmodern in his 1949 Berlin novella *Der Ptolemäer* (*The Ptolemaist*). "The comprehensive gaze, total control, the unity of life, harmony—I rejected that," exclaimed the protagonist and proprietor of war-torn Berlin's beauty institute "Lotusland" in Benn's novella.[10] For Wellershoff, the beautician's rejection of universalisms and syntheses (in favor of what would become Lyotard's "particular perspectives," "immeasurable diversity," and "reality-experiments") was irrefutable proof of Benn's postmodern convictions.[11] Yet Wellershoff's emplacement of Benn's *Der Ptolemäer* within the intrinsically ambiguous field of the postmodern said nothing about the grounds for why Benn warranted this privileged status. Whereas Lyotard cited in his seminal essay on postmodernity the technological transformation of scientific knowledge as the historical agent for precipitating the atomization of social relations, Wellershoff provided no such explanation for Benn's farsightedness. Furthermore, Wellershoff's induction of Benn into the ranks of postmodernism rang curiously congratulatory, curious insofar as Wellershoff's original ruminations from the fifties were equally awestruck as they were critical of Benn. If Benn was indeed a postmodern on a par with Lyotard, Wellershoff's confession from the nineties omitted one vital qualification. Benn's insistence on the fragmentary nature of reality did not evince his postmodern affinities. Rather, it was the consequence of his absolute embrace of this fragmentary condition that foreshadowed Lyotard's model for postmodernism.[12] Wellershoff's recent synthesis of French postmodern theory and German post-expressionist prose thus glossed over a crucial distinction not only in Benn's own oeuvre but also between postwar France and Germany, a distinction that Wellershoff himself happened upon in 1958.

Wellershoff began his 1958 monograph on Benn with the proviso that the breaks in Benn's career—his scandalous passage from exemplary expressionist to Nazi mouthpiece to inner immigrant to postwar sensation—should not obfuscate the "impressive continuity, indeed the coerciveness" of his thought throughout his lifetime.[13] Constant throughout Benn's oeuvre was the abstract, unmanageable, and impenetrable condition of modern reality (*GB*, 39–40). Yet in spite of this constant conviction of the obliteration of a unified world, there existed one crucial break in Benn's career, a break that emanated from his contretemps with fascism. Wellershoff explained this divide primarily in terms of shock: "The loss of reality, the alienation of self and world that impinges on consciousness in the Rönne phase, is accepted in the Ptolemaic phase and is converted into the comfort of indifference" (*GB*, 33). This Rönne phase corresponded to Benn's early expressionist beginnings that repeatedly featured Dr. Werff Rönne and that peaked in the midst of World War I. In the first of his eight Rönne novellas, *Gehirne* (*Brains*) from 1915, Benn's doctor appears as an overwhelmed and psychologically unstable pathologist who is commissioned to substitute for the head physician at a hospital. After two years and two thousand autopsies, Rönne's consciousness has vanished through his fingers. He assumes responsibility for a clinic when he is thoroughly "exhausted" and disorientated, overloaded by an ungovernable objective world, alienated from his own past, no longer in control of the borders of his body, and haunted by distant voices.[14] Rönne's psychological constitution borders on psychosis, something akin to shell shock; referring to his own experiences as a military physician, Benn wrote in 1934: "In war and peace, on the front and on base, as an officer and as a doctor . . . the trance never forsook me that this reality does not exist."[15] The entirely incapacitated Rönne thus performs only the most rudimentary of his duties, as if they were an out-of-body experience. According to Wellershoff's reading, Rönne's near-phenomenological paralysis and self-imposed isolation culminate in an irrationality that borders on insanity; fantasies from within compensate for the shocking horrors from without (*GB*, 16, 26).

Whereas Dr. Rönne falls prey to the shocks that consume his professional and private life, Benn's postwar beautician adopts a comprehensive array of defensive strategies to protect himself from the shock of a vanished reality. Instead of adhering to the rationality of modern medicine as Rönne does, he chooses a profession that is solely concerned with the external appearance of a few select body parts. He names his salon after the lotus-eaters in Homer's *Odyssey*—men "who ate from the fruits, needed no other bread, [and] could hope and forget"—and therewith encapsulates his entire indifferent postwar worldview. "In a world in which such iniquities happened and that is based on such iniquitous principles . . . it was really immaterial [*gleichgültig*] whether some people lived a few days longer or slept a few nights more" (*DP*, 1378). The attainment of beauty encapsulates a "selective attitude"—"a conceptual limitation"—focusing solely on the superficial concerns of varicose veins, shampoos, and haircuts. Mindlessly servicing the vanity of others is but a modern analog to ingesting the fruits of the lotus, a path to "reclusiveness, convention, and avoidance of customs" (*DP*, 1395). In opposition to the bogus myths of rationality that infect the entirety of reality, the beautician exclaims that only the realm of the dream can promise any freedom. Within the space of his inner dream life he experiences infinity, a boundless mode of thinking entirely incompatible with the most fundamental tenets established by the fathers of modern rational cognition: Euclid, Kepler, Galileo, Hume, and Descartes, among others. His waking life can only advance toward the "autistic reality" evoked in his dreams, which primitive peoples once established as the cornerstone of their existence, by extinguishing the temporal and spatial quadrants of the rational experience (*DP*, 1395). He collapses the past and future into an all-encompassing, solipsistic present. "In a stupidly composed *Tat tvan asi* (thou art that) . . . the unification of self with the lost world of things will be fulfilled" (*DP*, 1395). According to Wellershoff, the beautician's split identity—his Janus face of superficial conformity and interior nonconformity—is nothing less than a cynical model of being (*GB*, 238). Benn's beautician even admits as much. Cynicism and pessimism are the recto and verso of "his gravity and bond to earth" (*DP*, 1393). All in all, nothing shocks the beautician. He has seen the horrors of humanity. Not only does he withdraw himself from the post-apocalyptic world that he disdains, but he also buffers himself when forced to interact with the outer world through pure superficiality.

On the historical career of the modern cynic, Peter Sloterdijk states that "there have been mass numbers of them in Germany since the First World War—[they] are no longer outsiders."[16] Wellershoff, too, acknowledged the wide appeal of cynicism in Benn's day. "In Germany," he explained, "dictatorship, war, collapse, postwar misery, the conflict between East and West were essential obstetricians" for the birth of a social-psychological condition he called Germans' "without-me mentality" (*GB*, 216). Symptomatic of this pandemic malaise among Germans were feelings of exhaustion, an inability to engage the world, an inward retreat to the private sphere, ruminations on life's barest essentials, the will to resist all politics and ideological appeals, an apathy toward collective political processes, and a conviction in conformity as a form of self-extrication. This disposition was especially formidable immediately after 1945, when the war's catastrophes were fresh in German minds. Instead of dissipating over time, this cynicism established itself as a normative condition during the restorative economic miracle. This evolution of German cynicism, what Sloterdijk calls "enlightened false consciousness," is reflected perfectly in the literary career of Benn. Wellershoff claimed that Benn was the most representative index of the German spirit, especially in the fifties. As for when Benn first encapsulated this condition, Wellershoff claimed, "After the abrupt fall in 1934 . . . one can read the state of today's phenotype" (*GB*, 217). The decisive moment for Benn in the summer of 1934 was the Night of the Long Knives, when Hitler liquidated potential rivals (like Ernst Röhm) from his storm troopers. In response to what he called a "gruesome tragedy," Benn broke with National Socialism, which he had fervently hoped in 1933 would facilitate the transformation of Friedrich Nietzsche's will to power into the will to art (*GB*, 195, 194). The utopian hopes that Benn placed on Nazism prior to this shock, and his exceptional turn to fascist politics as the harbinger of an aesthetic transcendence previously exemplified by Rönne's expressionist hallucinations, were smashed. Thoroughly disillusioned, Benn's subsequent return to literature entailed a thorough disavowal of expressionism's praise for the early Nietzsche, any and all political ideologies, the belief in the progression of history, the existence of a rational telos, and the social utility of the aesthetic, all values that National Socialism employed in its own mythmaking.[17] What remained for Benn was a Spenglerian cultural pessimism so severe that art could now only claim validity when absolute in its negativity vis-à-vis the outside world of social experience. Rönne's visions reemerged not as a symptom of shock but rather as an essential strategy for surviving postwar modernity.

According to Wellershoff, fascism played a central role in the genesis of Benn's post-fascist cynicism. In contradistinction to Sloterdijk, however, Wellershoff reads Benn's cynicism not as "the logical locus of German fascism," but rather as its traumatic symptom, the logical consequence of fascist violence for those who stood on the side of the perpetrators.[18] The fact that Benn's worldview ensconced itself as the paradigmatic zeitgeist in postwar West Germany comprises therefore the "hidden" critical core of Wellershoff's reading of Benn, a critique that targeted Benn's emblematic flight from reality.[19] Accordingly, the late Benn's cynicism was the point of departure for Wellershoff's critical reflection on a pandemic intellectual and cultural problem, namely the cynical mode endemic to postwar modernity in West Germany (*GB*, 12). In light of the trajectory of Benn's responses to the fragmentation of reality from 1915 to 1949, the crucial distinction that warranted his ranking among the late twentieth century's postmodernists was the denigration of shock into quietism, a shift that Wellershoff underplayed entirely in his 1995–96 lectures. While Wellershoff celebrated at the close of the millennium the aesthetic consequences of Benn's atomized worldview as a prescient postmodernism, this in no way lessens his sociopolitical critique of Benn's symptomatic asceticism, a reclusiveness that Wellershoff had already deemed reprehensible in 1958 and that Sloterdijk would indict again twenty-five years later as the cornerstone of postmodern culture. Yet over the course of time, this double bind in Wellershoff's early reckoning with Benn—Benn's revolutionary negation of a cohesive reality and his reprehensible indifference toward a fragmented social world—came undone. In addition to editing the complete works of Benn, Wellershoff penned a dissertation in 1952, the 1958 monograph, three newspaper articles, three essays, and then finally his lecture in 1962–63, all on various facets of Benn's career. And then Wellershoff burned all the poetic bits and prosaic pieces he had written to date. Benn, the indifferent one (*der Gleichgültige*), was a deficient template for Wellershoff's own literary aspirations.[20] Benn's cynicism proved politically disastrous. With Benn out of the spotlight, Wellershoff looked westward across the Rhine toward Paris.

Nouveau Spaces and the Time of Things

Wellershoff first engaged creatively the *nouveau roman* in a vignette from 1960 titled "Während" ("During"), an early text that survived his literary immolation. Hardly a forgery of any single practitioner of French new realism, Wellershoff's short scene of a vacation on the Dutch coast applied the early Robbe-Grillet's optical precision to multiple synchronous narrative strands and points of view.[21] Before publishing his first new realist novel six years later, Wellershoff read portions of his manuscript before West Germany's premier literary salon, Gruppe 47, and published excerpts in prominent literary journals like Walter Höllerer's *Akzente* and Karl Heinz Bohrer's *Merkur*. During this lengthy incubation period, Wellershoff fostered (in his capacity as the new acquisitions editor at Cologne's theretofore conservative publisher Kiepenheuer and Witsch) other emergent writers to help advance his highly unorthodox interest in advancing a new realism. While the contours of Wellershoff's coterie of new realists first began to materialize in 1962, the first concrete deliberation on Neuen Realismus only arrived in 1965. In a brief tract published in a Kiepenheuer and Witsch marketing brochure in 1965, Wellershoff announced the emergence of a new realism that stood in direct opposition to the fantastic, grotesque, stylistically sophisticated, and abstruse idioms of postwar modernism in West Germany spearheaded by Grass.[22] In place of modernism's penchant for metaphysical transcendence and the universalization of a singular human ontology, Wellershoff petitioned for a critical realism steeped in the sensual and concrete, the quotidian and present-day. The substantive focus of what had quickly ballooned (thanks to critic Heinrich Vormweg's commentaries) into Wellershoff's "Cologne School of New Realism" was "disruptions, deviations, the inconspicuous, the detours, and thus the resistance of reality against the hasty need for meaning." Reality was captured as something chaotic, dynamic, incomprehensible, unfinished, and elusive. Formally, this new realism modeled itself after cinema. Shuttling between the literary approximation of cinema's close-ups and panoramic shots, slow motion and time-lapse photography, and thick and thin narrative details, Wellershoff's new realism was to convey "subjective, delimited, momentary, and animated perspectives."[23] In a follow-up essay published four years later, Wellershoff elucidated precisely the components that comprised what he insisted was the true modern novel: French novelist Claude Simon's penchant for slow-motion techniques and blurry snapshots; Robbe-Grillet's sharp and detailed study of objects and incomprehensible details; and Nathalie Sarraute's excavation of hidden psychological states of mind.[24] German new realism was, in other words, the product of eclecticism, a synthesis of what had been theretofore anything but a coherent school. Wellershoff called for the compression of the *nouveau roman*'s divergent instantiations into a German whole.

There is no mistaking Benn's underlying influence on Wellershoff's thinking. Just as with Rönne and the Ptolemaic beautician, reality for Wellershoff was no longer something coherent or comprehensive. Elsewhere Wellershoff explained that the pervasiveness of institutional imperatives under late capitalism had atomized the relations between every sector of society such that no writer could ever encapsulate all the far-flung, circuitous, and abstract particles of reality. Once the fundamental aesthetic principle of the historical avant-garde intent on exploding art's claims to totality, collage had become the structural principle of reality itself.[25] Unlike Benn, however, Wellershoff jettisoned entirely Benn's recourse to quietism. Instead of putting on a Bennian air of indifference while reveling in a private world of unmitigated dreams, Wellershoff cited the patchwork of varying French styles as a staging area for revealing mimetically (though not comprehensively) the structural "complexity of total reality."[26] While akin to a dream on account of its "imaginary combinations," Wellershoff's new realism unmasked the unconscious conditionality of all contemporary experience ("FP," 31). German new realism was thus a thoroughly political form of writing. Wellershoff sought to attain this political potential by exposing the unmasterable qualities of reality and, conversely, by unseating any and all consoling assessments of reality's simplistic form and content. Additionally, the space of fiction was itself deemed capable of severing itself from the moment and creating a "present of non-contemporaneity" (*Gegenwart des Nicht-Gegenwärtigen*). Wellershoff designated fiction as an imaginative sphere independent from time and space where memories and images anchored in the past combine to form entirely new characters and situations, compositions entirely new and different for writer and reader alike ("FP," 30–31). In so doing, the text was to delineate possibilities of individual orientation and agency capable of transforming the field of affirmative everyday experience.

Like the *nouveaux romanciers,* Wellershoff's carefully picked coterie of new realists was anything but uniform. They neither embraced the *nouveau roman* equally nor subscribed to Wellershoff's utopian politics. Of the six writers explicitly associated with Wellershoff's 1965 programmatic statement "Neuer Realismus"—Nicolas Born, Rolf Dieter Brinkmann, Günter Herburger, Paul Pörtner, Günter Seuren, and Günter Steffens—only the first two and the last intensively engaged and embraced their French counterparts as a blueprint. Of these writers, Brinkmann was the youngest and certainly the earliest champion of French realism in Germany. In a letter dated April 1957—exactly one year after the realism conference in Vézelay—the seventeen-year-old Brinkmann illuminated for the editors of *Akzente* his poetry submissions as entirely fixated on the world of objects. "Decisive for all my work is the first impression of the singing object. It forms the meter. It determines the choice of words for the images. Of all the many impressions that arise from the same object, it is the one unsophisticated feeling. Second comes intellect. It is the mortar that is necessary for compressing the joints."[27] Given his reverence for the primacy of the object, Brinkmann's indebtedness to Robbe-Grillet's published essay from Vézelay was unmistakable to Höllerer and Bender. Consequently, the editors felt his poetics were far too derivative to merit publication. After first terminating in 1958 his high school career in the ninth grade and hitchhiking to Paris and Brussels, Brinkmann finally succeeded in 1960 in placing several of his poems in two small literary journals, an anthology of poetry, and a newspaper while apprenticing as a bookseller. Brinkmann's small beginnings caught Wellershoff's roving eye for young untapped talent, and soon thereafter Brinkmann's solicited story "In der Grube" ("In the Ditch") made the final cut for Wellershoff's 1962 anthology *Ein Tag in der Stadt* (*A Day in the City*), a book that both press and critics packaged as rigorously realist. With Wellershoff's support, Brinkmann was well on his way to challenging mainstream modernism in Germany with French contraband. Within a year, Brinkmann had advanced beyond Kiepenheuer and Witsch's legendary Böll as the press's rising star.[28]

Looking back on his literary debut twelve years later, Brinkmann confessed that of all the new French novelists it was Robbe-Grillet to whom he swore greatest allegiance. "The *nouveau roman* . . . interested me [because it contained] no plot or story but rather merely slid over the surface of things like a moving camera" (*BH*, 149). Wellershoff, too, recollected how Brinkmann was convinced early on that wrestling with Robbe-Grillet was a prerequisite for anyone writing contemporary literature.[29] Reminiscent of the desire that he had articulated in his original 1957 letter to Höllerer and Bender—a desire to convey the loneliness of his generation that came of age after fascism—Brinkmann invoked in the bio-bibliographic commentary that accompanied his major debut the philosophical core of Robbe-Grillet's realism. His contribution to "the phenomenon of the city" (the topical thread running through all six of the anthology's stories) aimed at unraveling how urban experience contributes to "the impossibility . . . of opposing oneself as an individual against [this experience in the city]." [30] As with his previous programmatic statement, Brinkmann divested his story of an eventful plot. Instead of adhering to the linearity of a conventional narrative, "In der Grube" casts its nameless protagonist into alien urban spaces full of unyielding things. Brinkmann's austere opposition of subject and object was irrefutably the product of Robbe-Grillet's influence. As Robbe-Grillet argued in his 1956 essay in *Akzente,* the world of things possesses an ontological certainty entirely independent of humans. "But the world," he insisted with the ontological phenomenology of Martin Heidegger on the brain, "is neither meaningful nor absurd. It simply *is.*" And when fiction sheds light on the fallacy of human mastery over the world and, conversely, the tenaciousness of reality, not only do all social systems of signification crumble, but humans' actual impotence vis-à-vis the world also emerges. Reality, then, lies not in the meanings awarded to things. Rather, their reality lies buried in their merely being present, "ihre Gegenwart (*présence*)." [31] Brinkmann's admiration for Robbe-Grillet's position is unmistakable. He, too, crafted his protagonist as someone entirely impotent precisely because of the city's unmasterable thingness, its "anonymity and indifference." [32]

Robbe-Grillet set out to correct what he saw as a long-standing and presumptuous influence of cultural signs on the ontological certitude of things and the phenomenological mastery of subjects. In place of a humanist world in which people project an array of anthropomorphic, metaphorical, psychological, and social significations in order to gain a sense of authority over the world, he constructed an anti-humanist view of the world in which " 'things are things, and man is only man.' " [33] To achieve both this corrective isolation of man and the liberation of objects as nothing more than things—Roland Barthes described it as driving a "rift . . . in the solidarity between man and things"—Robbe-Grillet developed a rigorous language rooted in geometrical optics. [34] In 1958 he described in much greater detail his intentions as follows:

> Suppose the eyes of . . . man rest on things without indulgence, insistently: he sees them, but he refuses to appropriate them, he refuses to

maintain any suspect understanding with them, any complicity; he asks nothing of them; toward them he feels neither agreement nor dissent of any kind. . . . his sense of sight is content to take their measurements; and his passion, similarly, rests on their surface, without attempting to penetrate them since there is nothing inside.[35]

However classically realist Robbe-Grillet's dependence on the eye and his "reliance on analogy" may at first appear, the prohibition of subjective meaning in his geometrically rigid ocularcentrism abstained entirely, as Barthes has argued, from any and all metaphor, allegory, and metaphysics. Debarring the adjective was fundamental for his poetics. Without any "naturalistic" modifiers that invite the visceral correspondence to affect, Robbe-Grillet's *nouveau roman* restricted itself to establishing only spatial and situational relationalities; his is a world entirely impervious to the psychoanalytic concerns of projection, compensation, and justification. With the roving cinematic apparatus as his model, Robbe-Grillet also pushed his reconnoitering of space even further, inasmuch as he de-Euclidized the world by proliferating the number of points of reference and figurative planes. For Barthes, all of these innovations (the estrangement of the subject, the enforcement of the object's own *Dasein,* and the explosion of classical space) were subordinate to Robbe-Grillet's incursion into modern time. Classical fiction's objects (from Balzac to Proust) always substantiated the forward march of time by submitting to an unspoken human edict of decay. The deterioration of objects functioned as literature's principal chronograph of passing time. Robbe-Grillet's objects refuted this "eschatology of matter." Instead, time in his new realism was made perceptible only through spatial displacement or concealment. In other words, time's irreversible linearity and, by extension, the progress underlying all of modernity came to a grinding halt.[36]

The most explicit temporal markers in Brinkmann's sixty-page story "In der Grube" appear at the story's beginning and ending. Traveling by train to Hamburg, the story's young male protagonist discovers to his surprise that his overnight train briefly stopped in his hometown, the very place he abruptly fled some four years previously. On a lark, he decides to disembark from the train that morning and immediately finds himself in a public restroom that the third-person narrator describes with the precision of a roaming camera. Spatial relations, the contours of surfaces, the intensity of color and light, and sounds and smells congeal into a composite portrait comprised of sentence fragments.

He stood there against the tiled wall, tiles, white, white squares, the same pattern, tiles, had buttoned his pants open and he buttoned up his pants, indifferent, heard the trickling of water, it trickled out of the nickel knobs, sprayed widely, it ran down the tiled wall, down the drain with the chunks of chlorine, urine, bright yellow, mixed with water, it flowed down into the corner, urine, his jacket was buttoned. He stepped away from the wall and went to the sink. Above it hung a mirror. He washed his hands. (*E*, 8)

In this detailed mise-en-scène the narrative eye scans the lavatory in its entirety until the point in time when the protagonist exits. After wandering aimlessly through his forsaken hometown for an entire day, he returns to the train station in the early evening, when stores closed up shop. "I had to shit," the protagonist declares at the story's close. He returns to the restroom that he visited that morning and reports, "It was still. Only the monotonous sound of water. Men stood in front of the piss wall, urine, chlorine, quiet. . . . A man stepped away from the wall, buttoned up his pants. Awash in light, the rinse water. This image that I stepped back into was right." The narrator returns once again to his point of departure (both the restroom earlier that day as well as his hometown four years ago) only to confirm that nothing had changed. Time had not passed. Because of this he must leave. "He had recouped nothing, he ventured forth again, drifted away" (*E*, 66–67). Reminiscent of Barthes' reading of Robbe-Grillet's novel *The Erasers,* Brinkmann's "In der Grube" ends where it began. The men's restroom appears just as it had that morning. As before, the narrator recounts the protagonist's waste disappearing down the drain.

Metaphors and Memories: Imperfect Translations

In spite of Brinkmann's unmistakable appropriation of Robbe-Grillet's elliptical time, "In der Grube" is hardly a perfect copy. The first of many departures from Robbe-Grillet's rigorous geometry appears already on the story's first page. Before disembarking from his train, the traveler spies a blossoming apple tree from his window and is suddenly overwhelmed by a flood of emotions: "perhaps a small sentimentality that had come over him, something he had hardly intended, to disembark here, only to tear up effortlessly the vision of the white of an apple blossom, tender and destructible, that had occurred to him" (*E*, 7).[37] The very thing

Robbe-Grillet purged from his own prose, "sensorial syncretism" between a signifying subject and anthropomorphized objects, not only intrudes in Brinkmann's narrative at its outset but also sets its protagonist in motion ("OL," 14). As constitutive as this communion is for propelling the story forward, it is equally detrimental to the replication of Robbe-Grillet's radical divorce of humans from the world. Because of this metaphor and its life-giving modifiers "tender and destructible," the narrative grants the traveler the opportunity to mask the reality of the world with subjective meanings. Consequently, objects are enforced to obey the temporal law of decay, psychology asserts its influence, transcendence appears attainable, and cyclical time gives way to linear time that stretches backward into the past. With respect to time, the apple blossoms not only instigate a nostalgic sense of the past but also mark an essential coordinate from within that past. On several occasions throughout his ramble, the protagonist recalls a blooming apple tree in his parents' yard, next to which his father would shovel a neat bed of dung and he would read adventure novels. Memory and the past come into conflict, however. The traveler insists, "But it had certainly not been that way, that he also knew" (*E,* 31, 12). Far too idyllic to be trustworthy, his childhood memories eventually collapse as nothing more than deep-seated Oedipal desires to return home and "nestle again in his mother's womb," a feat he recognizes as thoroughly impossible (*E,* 57). At the close of the story, the narrator finally establishes that the "white of the blossoms from that morning had been a mental enervation" (*E,* 67). Ultimately, the metaphor and its concomitant sentimentalities unveil themselves as a cruel lure, the narrative establishes that transcendence (through a desired coenesthesia with the ideal mother) is an illusion, and consequentially the original primacy of the object world reasserts itself at the train station ("OL," 16).[38] On board the train again, the traveler directs his attention back to the detective novel that consumed him before the unexpected intrusion of metaphors and memories. The quintessential genre for staging Robbe-Grillet's superficial cinematic eye, the detective novel—quite possibly Elmar Tophoven's 1957 German translation of *The Voyeur*—is conceivably the traveler's primer for learning how to see the world objectively.[39]

When thought of as a story about a young man's struggle to appropriate Robbe-Grillet's realist worldview, then the departures from Robbe-Grillet's *nouveau roman* in "In der Grube" result, in large part, from the irrepressible effects of what Brinkmann himself described as the "fixation of a stream of memories" (*E,* 408). Additional formal evidence of the trouble with Robbe-Grillet west of the Rhine emerges through the shuttling between the third-person narrator and the traveler's own voice, the intrusion of memories, and intermittent glimpses into his psychology. Initially, the traveler demonstrates a mastery of ocular objectivity. After exiting the restroom, he plots the world around him in the first person. "I stood before the train station. . . . silhouettes, walls, windows, in the morning light the other side of the train station plaza was distant, where the city, downtown began, the center, the loop of streets, the street cars, traffic, pedestrians, the flows, the big traffic light, that portioned the street traffic, instructed, blocked, unblocked, regulated" (*E*, 14). The traveler attains the desired effect with this detached optic. "[I] sensed everything very far away from me, without perceiving it as belonging directly to me, as if an interstice existed, a vacuum, as if I were not it, who momentarily stood there, it was removed from me, an airless space, that interposed, between eye and object and movement" (*E*, 16). This rift between the protagonist and the world quickly closes the moment he recalls his past. While heading downtown, he effortlessly associates a newspaper vendor with his dumped circle of friends. He sees a resemblance to his mother in a female washroom attendant. And Manon, the name of his ex-girlfriend, surfaces. Switching back to the omniscient third-person narrator, the story then explains that years ago Manon had stirred in him such hatred that he "would have liked to pee on her" (*E*, 19). It is arguable that this toggling between the first and third person, the intrusion of mnemonic associations and visual memories, as well as the eruption of feelings in the narrative present (indecisiveness, inaneness, ridiculousness) and from the narrative past (hatred, contempt, revulsion), all these departures from Robbe-Grillet's realist model derive from other instantiations of the *nouveau roman*. Nathalie Sarraute's exploration of the imperceptible emotions underlying all language and behavior; Michel Butor's idea of the novel as a form of self-reflective phenomenology; and Claude Simon's belief in the fallibility and confusion of memory had all traversed westward across the Rhine by 1960.[40] Yet to assume that Brinkmann's "In der Grube" explicated the synthesis of all the varying and divergent modes of French new realism that Wellershoff promoted in his manifesto of 1965 would overlook the absolutely crucial role that Benn plays in the story's increasingly messy imbrication of past with present.

With morality at a standstill and the resulting horrors of world war at his doorstep, Benn's Ptolemaic beautician disclosed his indifference toward humanity and his rationale for reclusion (*DP*, 1378). In his monograph on

Benn, Wellershoff critiqued Benn and his postwar prose as prototypes of a pandemic post-fascist German "character crisis" best described as "relativist indifference" (*GB,* 230).[41] Similarly, feelings of indifference inundate Brinkmann's story from beginning to end. The traveler first attests to the empire of his indifferent disposition when he passes the newspaper vendor on his way toward the city. He recalls how he "had never [bought a newspaper] back then, had never wanted to pick up and devour the world anymore as trumpery, that encircled us and in which I had lived back then" (*E,* 17). Indifference toward the world of the newspaper found its clearest expression in the traveler's and his friends' embrace of American popular culture: "Jazz, Thelonius [*sic*] Monk, West Coast, or Ray Charles, the hoarse singer, blues, angry, whatever was around, movies, hullabaloo, dancing, also a party at Didi's sometimes, a party at Rainer's, tight jeans, that had been enough world for us, anything else had not existed at all" (*E,* 17). However much his clique's disavowal of the world resembles "the selective posturing" and "ideational limitation" of Benn's beautician— both narratives designate, for example, the outside world as "mud"—the traveler's indifference is anything but identical to that of the Ptolemaist (*DP,* 1384, 1380; *E,* 17–18). If popular culture promised these youths an escape from the world of the newspaper, their isolationism was not a wholesale reaction against the politics, economics, or arts reported therein. On the contrary, the newspaper represents a being-in-the-world closely associated with the traveler's father. The traveler recollects, for example, how his father read the local paper every evening in his family's living room alongside his mother, who solved puzzles from a radio magazine while "operettas, tangos, waltzes, light music" droned in the background. Reading the newspaper, wondering "what all happened throughout the day" as the traveler's father had done on a daily basis, did not constitute a political engagement with the world, or, as Wellershoff wrote, "a readiness for resistance against collective processes" (*E,* 25; *GB,* 215). Within the confines of their tasteful living room, the father engaged the newspaper's reflection of a contestable public sphere as ardently as the mother perceived the fetish character in the incidental music that accompanies her digestion of dinner.[42] If the apathy that Wellershoff saw in Benn and attributed to postwar society materialized concretely in the routinized bourgeois comforts of this living room, then the youths' love for modern jazz represented an affront to this distracted world of newspapers and music. Jazz was thus a mode of indifference these youths wielded against the indifference of their parents. In other words, American popular culture afforded them the affective means with which to reject the dominant politics of the Federal Republic of Germany that Benn masterfully captured in the figure of the beautician.

On the putatively progressive character of jazz, Theodor Adorno insisted that any distinction between the "older-timer's" light music and the "younger generation's" jazz was a gross illusion.[43] Regardless of the innovative claims often associated with its quotations, syncopations, dissonances, and improvisations, mass music (regardless of specific genre) was merely the repetitive play of prescribed models that condition audiences to become regressive listeners. Before deserting his hometown, Brinkmann's traveler realized as well the fallacy of the difference he and his friends sought in jazz. Unlike his male friends who remained passionate about Art Blakey and the Jazz Messengers, he began to express indifference toward his favorite jazz vocalist, Billy Eckstine. Modern jazz, hard bop, the blues, dancing, tachism, Jackson Pollock's abstract expressionism, and poetry were no longer of concern to him, for they failed to withstand the growing culture of cynicism, against which popular culture provided a safe haven for only a short while.[44] Instead of seeking out through popular culture a distinction against the indifference of his parents, he turned to women. His first love was Elke, the girl with the short black coiffure who loved lemon sorbet. Then came Inga, Ruth, and Lisabeth. And then there was Manon with the short brown hairdo and unforgettable eyes like a deer's, the girl Rainer knew and whom the protagonist had first met at a Dave Brubeck concert. At one of Didi's parties they broke off from the other dancers. And then suddenly "her face had reverted back into indifference, it had fallen back with all the others" (*E*, 39). His final attempt to escape the purview of apathy that metastasized from his parents' living room to his teenage clique, courting Manon proved to be yet another failure. Looking back on what had happened, the traveler explains, "Manon, with whom I had initially gotten along with well, had at least fancied as much, although that had become clear to me afterward, that the thing with Manon was also just one of many indifferences" (*E*, 17). The last remaining possibility for resisting the originary indifference of his parents was to escape once and for all the ditch into which he had felt himself thrown.

As with popular culture and sex before, motion engendered another higher order of indifference against home. "[I] was still in the city, but not like back then, I did not want to think about it, wanted to leave again, it was immaterial," he thinks to himself while making his way back to the train station (*E*, 45). This indifference toward and distance from both home and the past emerge most forcefully not corporeally by walking in space, but rather phenomenologically by seeing space as a sequence of moving images. His cold roving eye that first scanned the sterile surfaces of the public restroom that morning afforded him the sole possibility of attaining distance from his bitter memories of home (*E*, 16). In spite of the impinging sentimentalities from his past, the one effective antidote is the perpetual movement achieved through sight, a cinematographic vision (to borrow Barthes' term) that sets space into motion ("OL," 18–19). Toward the close of the story, the narrator affirms the potency of his indifferent gaze. Everywhere he looks he sees indifference in the present and recalls indifference from the past. "Indifference consummated itself," the narrator later reports, such that it swallowed the air around the traveler, the city, sky, and outlying landscape, people, animals, things, and then finally the entire earth (*E*, 40, 46, 64). The objective gaze that first began shielding him in the public restroom accompanies him back to the train station. "The intermediary space, that I had before me this morning, between me and the other faces, . . . this so peculiar abstraction, the foreignness, the inconceivability of the matter, through which I had moved, that flushed me out, I felt empty" (*E*, 65). The traveler pays a visit to the restroom from that morning, scans the interior spaces, and then promptly boards the train to Hamburg. Although his train has yet to depart, the narrator assures the reader in the story's final sentence that the traveler would finish reading the detective novel that his expected layover had interrupted. If the novel in question is indeed Robbe-Grillet's *The Voyeur*, then the protagonist presumably finds in the lessons from west of the Rhine an end to a German problem that both Benn's beautician and the traveler's parents had exemplified.

Sex and Fascism: The Male Body and the Abject of History

As hopeful as this adherence to Robbe-Grillet's cinematographic eye may appear, the shards of mixed-up sentence fragments comprising "In der Grube," when strung together, tell anything but a happy story. Again and again the traveler realizes that the solution he sought by abandoning his home four years earlier turned out to be just another illusion. The pathway out of the indifference of his hometown merely led him into another ditch. On his way into the center of town he confesses, for example, "I had believed, to be able to leave the ditch forever, the adolescent, distraught misery, indifferent, in doing so I had only really crawled out of one ditch into another ditch" (*E*, 18). In a moment of extreme disillusionment, he experiences his layover in his hometown as nothing less than a fantastic wrinkle in time, "as if he had not moved away from the city, [as if] he had only had to piss and he would go straight home" (*E*, 11). The void espoused by the objective gaze only solves one half of his problems, namely the "brainwashing" induced by the irrepressibly metaphorical dimensions of the apple blossom (*E*, 67). The ocularism that locks the past out and seals him into a hermetic, indifferent present does nothing, however, to protect or disable his body from registering the past directly. The past is as much a problem in the traveler's mind as it is for his body. The past's first explicit jolt to the traveler's body occurs unexpectedly as he passes the newspaper vendor. "I recognized him," he recollects, "thrusted raw into the flesh" (*E*, 16). In this instant, human flesh registers even the most banal of memories as a sharp, immediate pain. Two far more momentous instances of corporeal memory occur, however, at either end of the homecoming when the traveler visits and revisits the restroom. These seemingly uneventful moments in fact mask past pain and violence that only becomes obvious toward the center of the story when the traveler recollects over and over again his penultimate solution to staving off the indifference of his parents. The mirrored acts of urinating (at the story's beginning) and defecating (at the story's ending) point toward a sex-gender crisis from the traveler's disavowed adolescence that, in turn, stem from a much deeper discursive dilemma, namely the impossible constitution of a post-fascist male body.

The narrator treats the second of these two episodes with excessive detail and unparalleled significance for the traveler's escape. In a foreshadowing of the actual act of defecating at the story's close, the narrator counterbalances earlier on yet another allusion to the white blossoms from the father's apple tree by linking his bowel movement with divine transcendence: "His stomach had opened itself, had emptied the intestines, he could sing hymns, closer to God, it had never conveyed anything, it floated away, nothing, simply that, floated onward, had floated forwards, had sunk, where to, immaterial, immaterial where to, sunk" (*E*, 63). This putative transcendence stands in direct opposition to that precise moment from his past when sex with a woman revealed itself to be just as ineffectual against indifference as listening to jazz. Where purging excrement out of the body evokes a sense of forward progress and metaphysical arrival, sex is associated with pollution, castration, and, worst of all, corporeal formlessness. The traveler discovered the dangers of sex to his body with the last of his girlfriends, Manon, with whom he experienced vaginal intercourse for the first time. As if to suggest the traumatic impact of this event, the narrative only alludes to it cryptically at first. After initially revealing the fact that the traveler harbors ill will toward her, the narrator adds that Manon had emasculated him with her smile. Subsequent allusions to Didi's aforementioned party and a solitary moment between the teenage boy and girl lead to further enigmatic clues: "And on that evening back then it had broken open, a quiet abscess, eczema, the hemorrhage, on that evening it had dredged him up" (*E*, 24). As if these initial innuendos were not enough, the narrator then unveils the corporeal circumstances that turned his first attempt at intercourse into a horror. Alone together in a bicycle shed, Manon purportedly incited his libido, and not long thereafter they engage in vaginal sex, an experience the narrator first describes solely in terms of Manon's bleeding, threatening body. "[A] thin stream of blood, a wave of blood, that had inundated him, dark, maelstrom, the undertow from below, sucking, the trap, the flesh trap" (*E*, 28). The threat of Manon's bleeding genitals soon advances from a wave to a full-fledged flood that consumes his body. "I went, an endless space, a vacuous space, went, I went, an escape way, the flesh gate, . . . there was permanent darkness, it had opened up on that evening, I fell into it, fell, I fell, fell endlessly, I fell endlessly, fell, became distended, was bloated, formless, misshapen, witless, walled in, consumed in darkness, incorporated, it had breached into me, flowed, flooded inward" (*E*, 38). Whether he injured Manon during intercourse or she was menstruating remains a mystery. Utterly clear, though, is just how threatening sexual intercourse is for the protagonist.

Like the early Benn's Dr. Rönne for whom "space undulated endlessly," the protagonist loses all command over his body and the world around him.[45] Unlike Dr. Rönne, however, Brinkmann's protagonist and narrator together resort to the very language that precipitated the traveler's predicament that morning. Metaphors abound through the story's recurring recollections of this sex scene. In fact, the metaphors used to zoomorphize eroticized bodies clarify just how threatening the original metaphor of the apple blossom is for the protagonist's corporeal constitution, a sentimental metaphor that had driven him to "nestle again in his mother's womb" (*E*, 57). What these metaphors connote, which the protagonist's oceanic feelings of falling into Manon's endless vagina do not, are the debilitating effects of sex and, more importantly, bodily filth on the protagonist's gender identity. In the first detailed account of the sex act, the narrator describes both teenagers as possessing "a bloodsucker, a leech" inside their bodies, a "blood-filled jellyfish, that moved, excreted, and sucked itself full again" (*E*, 28). In the final and most graphic retelling of the sex scene, the traveler recounts in the first person how his girlfriend's "jellyfish . . . had purged itself" and then "had inundated me in the shed" (*E*, 38). These metaphors are remarkable insofar as they obfuscate all differences between the figures' primary sexual characteristics. Both the protagonist and his girlfriend have blood-sucking organisms reminiscent of a phallus (the leech) and a gynocentric matrix (the jellyfish). And even in those moments when the protagonist describes his erection, he refers to a sprawling "aquatic plant," a patently feminine metaphor (*E*, 37). This combination of falling endlessly and feelings of emasculation exceed the protagonist's limits. As if to reprimand Manon for seducing him, polluting him, rendering him powerless over his own body, and unseating his masculinity, he strikes her in the face, causing her nose to bleed. "Her face," the traveler establishes after admitting to assaulting Manon, "had fallen back into indifference" (*E*, 39). This blow to her face is but one of several responses to resurrect the stability of difference. First, he regains agency by drawing blood and thereby turning Manon's flood against her. Similarly, he fantasizes inundating her with his own pollution: urine, slime, and snot. Third, he envisions himself, "in total indifference," strangling her to death, thereby annihilating the cause of this instability (*E*, 58). All this material and imagined violence emanates from a gender trouble that only metaphors can put into language. In the end, reinstating difference occurs not because of any corporeal difference. Instead, difference is contingent upon who violates whom and whether one controls one's bodily fluids. Seen in this light, the protagonist employs what Sloterdijk would later call "kynicism"—the cheeky uninhibited body—against the cynicism and indifference that Manon suddenly represented.[46]

According to Barthes, Robbe-Grillet's objective literature sets out to bankrupt the "romantic heart of things" that metaphor aids and abets, to divest humans of the control of the world through signification, and to affirm the *Dasein* of objects ("OL," 15).[47] If metaphors for Robbe-Grillet instill a false mastery over the world through signs, then for Brinkmann they accomplish the exact opposite. Metaphors trigger feelings of sentimentality that invariably lead to memories of intolerable states of corporeal destabilization. Interestingly enough, this state of formlessness into which the protagonist falls—he calls it "a void"—is linguistically identical to another "void" that the narrative's cinematographic eye engenders (*E*, 38, 16). In spite of this likeness, the voids of sexual intercourse and the objective eye are, in fact, markedly distinct. Whereas the void precipitated by genitals, blood, and sex dissolves the boundaries between his body and the world, the void afforded by the impartial eye serves as a force field separating the protagonist from the outside world. Consequently, the borders of his body remain intact. The alliance between Brinkmann's appropriation of Robbe-Grillet's narrative technique and the fortified body is nowhere more apparent than at the beginning and ending of the novel, when the traveler scans the public restroom. However, within this space corporeal rigidity also comes undone. Within the stark geometric interior of the public restroom, he purges his filth so that it "floated onward, had floated forwards, had sunk, where to, immaterial" (*E*, 63). Like the sex scene in which he drowns, corporeal orifices open to yield pollution that is, this time around, carefully expelled from the body. Although his feelings of emptiness shortly before his departure to Hamburg are rendered not just as psychological but as physical, too, this closing scene forecloses total closure of the body. In other words, this ending (like the beginning) illuminates how the ocular dispossession of a "romantic heart" in things can never fully seal off the body's boundaries. This delineation between "I and other," "inside and outside," and "conscious and unconscious" is a fundamental operation in the psychic management of a clean and proper body. Julia Kristeva calls this differentiating process "abjection."[48] Abject fluids like feces, urine, and blood not only threaten to destabilize corporeal borders, according to Kristeva, but also unseat the certitude of subjectivity. This law of abjection is, in other words, the "underside of the symbolic," a dictum intended to separate and protect the subject from materiality, animality, and even death.[49] Against the person who strictly adheres to these pollution laws stands the figure of the deject, someone who recognizes the abject within one's own body and therefore abjects himself. In so doing, the rigorous distinctions between interiority and exteriority blur. Like Brinkmann's traveler, the deject strays endlessly without ever reaching a destination. When cast in this light, Brinkmann's protagonist employs the *nouveau roman* as a literary instantiation of abjection, a phenomenological tool with which to purge filth from and reinforce the somatic boundaries of the body. However, urinating and defecating undercut the willed severity of this subject-object relationality, push his subjectivity to a borderline condition, and make obvious his body's actual status as non-object, the abject. In this respect, Brinkmann's protagonist is torn between affirming the symbolic order (which Barthes identifies as having been arrested in Robbe-Grillet's writing) and abjecting himself (which Julia Kristeva identifies as the deject's destabilization of the symbolic).

It might appear that "In der Grube" is nothing more than an account of one teenage boy's particularly traumatic rite of passage into adult heterosexuality. Far from it, consideration of the core of the story—a four-page interlude typeset in cursive script and lacking any and all punctuation—reveals how the appropriation of French objectivity plays into and off of much larger psychosocial problems endemic to post-fascist Germany's younger generation. The psychosomatic crisis of the male subject proves inextricably intertwined with the collective past. Described cryptically by Brinkmann as the protagonist's "chaotic stream of consciousness," this middle section is said to portray "the city, the moment, the people" without positive or negative bias. Everything therein finds itself "in a middle position . . . like in catalepsy" (*E*, 409). Indeed, the many fragmentary references to food, eating, hunger, and a crowded cafeteria do add up to suggest that this interlude merely recounts from within the traveler's head the rushed lunch in a hometown restaurant that he had frequented once before. Amidst the many shards of objective reality, short threads of the traveler's own impressions, reflections, and affective sensibilities surface. Scanning the restaurant, for example, he thinks, "*in view of the political situation urgent the downfall I only hope that it soon becomes better we live in the courtyard of a crematorium until everything is completely empty*" (*E*, 41).[50] Upon seeing foreign workers in the restaurant, he concludes, "*everything filthy . . . volvulus they should all go and die*" (*E*, 41). And later he muses on Germany's Nazi past only to conclude that "*what the cause of fascism was what always is kept secret*" (*E*, 44). The traveler also confesses his contempt for the others in the restaurant. He imagines himself "*pee*[ing] *in the soup pot*"; insists that "*everything is going to hell*"; and finally, referring to the entire crowd, he fumes, "*they can all kiss my ass*" (*E*, 42–43). Unlike the prose before and after this respite in the cafeteria, this unfettered window into the traveler's consciousness reveals how his departure from his small hometown did not result from superficial dissatisfactions with the indifference of parents, friends, or sex partners. On the contrary, it represents a much deeper contempt for the Federal Republic of Germany's indifferent response to the specters of its fascist past. By associating guest workers with the abject (something previously reserved for Manon), deriding Adenauer's conservative politics (especially following his party's defeats in the 1961 elections), and lambasting Germans' inability to confront their past (which Adorno had already done in 1959), all these charges against the greater German whole indicate that it is the West German nation as abject from which the traveler wishes to escape.

With this crucial link between nation and body in hand, a vast gendered dichotomy in the traveler's cosmology comes to light. He codes interiority as an utterly feminine state. His mother's womb, in which he erroneously hoped to finally find a reprieve from indifference, crumbles the moment he recollects how the abject that flowed from Manon's body endangered the integrity of his psychosomatic constitution. Bound up in the story's title, this hostile interiority merges with growing up as a teenager in his parents' small town, a ditch in which he imagines himself being buried alive. In the story's rambling interlude, this uterine-like enclosure finds its most concrete architectural equivalent in the cafeteria, the only interior space in the inner city into which he enters.[51] Lastly, he wishes upon all of Germany a violent, apocalyptic ending, one not unlike the camps in which millions perished under Nazism. Just as he had turned the tables on Manon by punching her, his fantasy of postwar Germany as crematory seeks retribution for its lingering inability to master its past crimes by annihilating every last perpetrator. In keeping with dominant postwar discourse, the traveler thus genders *Heimat* (home)—that regressive imaginary of "modern German culture's spatialized interiority"—as a woman only to desire her complete destruction.[52] If this confabulation of the abject and abjection does indeed follow the directives of the symbolic order, then what remains intact in the traveler's fantastic perception of survival after fascism is nothing less than the highly problematic law of the father that pushes him to protect the borders of his male body. When read solely in this light, Brinkmann's story eerily recalls the psychohistorical underpinnings of the fascist male body that Klaus Theweleit dissects in *Männerphantasien* (*Male Fantasies*). According to Theweleit, literal and metaphorical dirt, mud, swamps, slime, mush, and floods assumed central importance in fascist fantasies of male embodiment. Repressed for its imagined danger to the integrity of the subject, a vast feminized complex of deliquescent objects warranted both the erection of body armor and the need for real violence against the "red flood," be it woman, Jew, or communist.[53]

For all their outward similarities, Brinkmann's protagonist differs fundamentally from the psychology of the Freikorps soldiers that Theweleit lays bare. Calling the traveler a neo-fascist would overlook essential departures from the extreme subject-object psychology of the fascist male.

First and most importantly, the fits of fortification of the male body in "In der Grube" operate as a bulwark not for but rather against a post-fascist reactionary malaise called indifference. This qualification does not, however, excuse or even justify the violence against Manon. In fact, the traveler confesses just how stricken his violent outburst left him. For this reason his appropriation of Robbe-Grillet's idea of the *nouveau roman* as a phenomenological form of body armor must invariably fail, for even though its progressive intentions are different, it is nevertheless structurally identical to the fascist male body. Second, the traveler's body betrays the intentions of the appropriated French gaze by continually punctuating the superficiality of the world with metaphorical reminders of embodied experience from the past. While the body was something to protect and close off during his disastrous teenage years, this penchant for hermetic closure has matured to acknowledge the inherent ambivalence of corporeal boundaries. Repeatedly, the traveler admits that his original wish to escape the ditch merely delivered him to another. The reason for this lies not only in the shortcomings of the *nouveau roman* as model but also within his own body, for the abject he sees all around him also ends up within himself. Lending credence to his need to defecate—he establishes repeatedly in the second half of the story that "I had to shit"—the traveler finally happens upon the highest form of abjection (of self), which delivers him from the fatal errors committed earlier (*E*, 65). If shit symbolizes the "breakdown of the nation," then the closing scene in the public restroom elevates his quest to distance himself from home by entering into an in-between stage of embodiment.[54] In so doing he deploys his own body against the territorializing forces of family, home, and nation, but only insofar as he abjects himself by straying from home. Precisely for this reason he finally resorts to keep moving forward, what Gilles Deleuze and Félix Guattari call de-territorialization. Akin to the idea of the straying deject, de-territorialization entails a shift in perception that movement affords as "no longer resid[ing] in the relation between a subject and an object, but rather in the movement serving as the limit of that relation."[55] The double bind that the *nouveau roman* precipitates for the traveler—his simultaneous exclusion from and incorporation into *Heimat*—is only remedied when he remains in motion. As much as this bind applies to the traveler's difficult relationship to national identity, it also describes an ineradicable crisis of masculinity after fascism. The psychosomatic underpinnings of the fascist soldier—Theweleit boils the dilemma down to the ideological hijacking of an entire generation of men's subject-object relationality—continued to permeate gendered experience well after the end of National Socialism.

Heterogeneous Realism

In correspondence from June 1974 to April 1975 with Hartmut Schnell, a graduate student whom he met in Austin, Texas, during his first and only stay in the United States, Brinkmann counseled his new friend on his scholarship on the German expressionist Alfred Lichtenstein. Brinkmann expressed unreserved enthusiasm for Schnell's own passion to imbue the largely forgotten Lichtenstein with a fresh and invigorating reading. Warning Schnell not to fall into the trap of "small-minded academic definitions," Brinkmann nevertheless encouraged his friend to track down a few articles and book chapters, books by Michael Hamburger, Kurt Pinthus, Walter Sokel, and Kasimir Edschmid, among others (*BH*, 17). Benn's 1955 essay "Poetry of the Expressionist Decade" merited Schnell's attention, too, Brinkmann thought. After all Brinkmann's research, Schnell quickly changed his mind. With Brinkmann's blessing, he embarked on the first English translations of Brinkmann's early poems from the mid-sixties. Unsurprisingly, almost a year into their correspondence, Brinkmann returned to Benn. Intent on giving the stressed Schnell a word of encouragement, Brinkmann reminded him that "you still have an authority for your view of interpretation, namely G. Benn and the afterword by the editor, Dr. D. Wellershoff." The pressures of writing an academic essay that would do justice to his friend's poetry and its unbridled contempt for academicism proved too much for Schnell. Wellershoff's reading of Benn's poems—"the poem," Wellershoff wrote in reference to Benn's poetry, "has not a single but rather many different creators"—was, Brinkmann thought, the perfect means with which to justify Schnell's break with scholarly formulas (*BH*, 217; *GB*, 557). Yet Benn's utility was limited. Brinkmann cautioned his friend to avoid comparing his poems with Benn's. "Compared to Benn's regressive attitude, I have other perspectives—I do not want to go back, I want to be here in the present, right [*richtig*] and open." Although he was referring solely to his later poems from the mid- and late sixties, Brinkmann's revelation about a conceptual aggregate in his writing described his early prose perfectly as well. One part "defensive attitude" and another part "aggressive tone," Brinkmann's confession imbued his work with a vexing absence of alternatives. "Either-or" was never an option (*BH,* 218). Revelatory in these last letters written less than two months before Brinkmann's untimely death are both his need to distance himself from the late Benn and his near silence about the importance of the early Robbe-Grillet for his first short stories.[56]

This omission is no less conspicuous than it is revealing. Robbe-Grillet represented for Barthes the possibility of unseating modern forward-marching time. For Oskar Negt and Alexander Kluge, this temporal opening can be thought of as a time sluice, a fantastic space where, in this case, Robbe-Grillet's time of objects throws the mythical status of progress into relief.[57] On the one hand, "In der Grube" deploys this freez-ing of time in order to deprive the postwar instantiation of *Heimat* of any and all illusions of progress. The French incursion into modern time thus explodes within the German context the myth of a full recovery after fas-cism. On the other hand, however, Robbe-Grillet's "litotic time" inadver-tently facilitated the return of the repressed ("OL," 22). Borrowing Robbe-Grillet's strategies for bracketing the psychohistory of both the individual and collective fail, insofar as they reproduce forms of male embodiment endemic to the psychosomatics of fascist subjectivity. The austere begin-ning and ending to Brinkmann's story that enact Robbe-Grillet's time of things thus operate like a hard narrative shell shrouding a soft irrepressible core of memories from and fantasies about individual and collective pasts. To be sure, Brinkmann's story does not erect a facsimile of the fascist ar-mored body, nor does it parrot Benn's post-fascist beautician for whom the superficial "care of the body including varicose veins" and "fourteen-day haircut[s]" was everything (*DP,* 1384). On the contrary, "In der Grube" tags the male body as a contested and contradictory form of embodiment precisely because of its incontrovertible implication in Germany's violent past. In this respect, Brinkmann's protagonist lives up to the idea of the deject who abjects himself, insofar as his traveler strives to exclude himself and, in so doing, arrives at what Kristeva calls "excluded ground [where] forgotten time crops up suddenly."[58] Instead of jettisoning memories and histories from the past, he lends credence to the very temporality that he sees as entirely lacking in his hometown, a time zone in which his body carries with it traces of the past. If thought of as a response to the pandemic proliferation of West German indifference toward politics af-ter fascism, then Brinkmann's adaptation of French new realism—a dirty mix of Robbe-Grillet's cinematographic eye and Benn's expressionist psy-chology—does indeed push to set itself apart from the norm. That this quest comes at the price of reiterating fascist violence only shows just how bedeviled any terminal solution to escaping the ditch really is, be it home, nation, or one's own body.

Brinkmann's appropriation of Robbe-Grillet's austere *nouveau roman* certainly fulfills if not exceeds Wellershoff's call for the literary creation of "a present of non-contemporaneity," insofar as "In der Grube" networks through the male body the indifferent present with the horrific past ("FP," 30). Yet Brinkmann's turn to French new realism follows neither Robbe-Grillet's early method closely nor Wellershoff's later amalgamation of every subset of French new realism. On the one hand, the *nouveau roman* east of the Rhine inadvertently reanimates the male fascist body in the West German post-fascist context. On the other hand, it proves utterly incapable of generating a multi-perspectival aggregate of the present (à la Wellershoff) while remaining impervious to the decidedly German intrusions from the past by Benn. While "In der Grube" struggles to separate itself from the proliferation of the late Benn's strategic allegiance with indifference, the early Benn's rebuke of objective reality re-erupts at precisely those moments when transhistorical psychosomatics map themselves onto the specters of fascist embodiment. Unlike Dr. Rönne, who eventually learns to embrace formlessness as an ontological and epistemological fact of life, Brinkmann's traveler cannot do so precisely because of the past and present that he abhors. In light of these countervailing forces from and against the past, it is arguable that Brinkmann's notion of realism after fascism is not only heterogeneous but also far more encompassing than what Wellershoff had envisioned a new German realism to be in 1965. For Brinkmann, the challenge of realism resided not in lending credence to the simultaneous multiplicity of perspectives—French radical objectivity *and* German radical subjectivity—but rather in rendering the material effects that the discourses of history have on minds and bodies. Most importantly, Brinkmann's realism situates fantasy at the epicenter of this conflict, where imagined history and the abject collide and where agency against this convergence is hashed out.

Fredric Jameson has argued that the long-standing realist-modernist duality prevalent in discourses on modernism ever since the expressionism debates of the late thirties has given way to the "dialectical subversion" of modernism.[59] In the shadow of the historical avant-garde, realism was always modernism's affirmative antipode. In a move that obliquely affronts Peter Bürger's insistence on the postwar avant-garde's lack of historical consciousness, Jameson sketches with broad strokes a reinvigorated new realism, one that acknowledges modernism's subservience to the law of commodity production, especially in the second half of the twentieth century. A resuscitated realism, Jameson goes on to note, could acquire critical potential insofar as it could resist the power of reification in consumer society, reinvent the category of totality (that Barthes and Wellershoff sought, for example, in the *nouveau roman*), and articulate structural relations otherwise obscured. Although Jameson spins his vision of a new realism for another future historical moment, the general thrust of his case for realism is not without merit for Brinkmann's own critical project. To borrow from the much more precise language of Negt and Kluge, Brinkmann's realism lies somewhere between the antipodes of the antireal and the unreal, whereby the former culminates in resistance against the order of the real and the latter reflects a state not unlike the indifference that the late Benn preached.[60] Realism for Brinkmann was therefore a struggle to ward off, if not to negate altogether, the indifferent posturing in West German society that organically grew out of fascism, while acknowledging nevertheless that this desired resistance could never be impervious to the order of the unreal. In this respect, reality for Brinkmann is never simply a matter of affirming the ontological certitude of things, as Robbe-Grillet once insisted. Divorcing individual and collective histories from a timeless world of nonhuman things and spaces only contributes to the very unreal anti-historical conditions that Benn championed with his Ptolemaic view of life after fascism. Instead, Brinkmann opted for a realism open to modern irreversible time yet nevertheless critical of the past's lingering presence within the present. As will be seen in chapter 5, however, Brinkmann's faith in a hybrid realism would eventually expire, for Benn's indifference, Robbe-Grillet's cinematographic eye, as well as the drive to keep moving all succumbed to the growing empire of massmediated experience.

[The] future for us is the feasibility of history as a collectively
experienced process [that] can only be imagined by subjects
who take part in subversive, anarchistic actions.
—Dieter Kunzelmann, "Notizen zur Gründung revolutionärer
Kommunen in den Metropolen"

There can be no freedom apart from activity, and within the
spectacle all activity is banned.
—Guy Debord, *The Society of the Spectacle*

4. Holocaust Simulations
Evoking Bare Life

Adorno's Prescient Dream

On July 14, 1945, Theodor Adorno transcribed one of the many execution dreams he had dreamt since the early forties. "Execution scene.
Whether the victims were fascists or anti-fascists remained unclear. In any
case, it was a horde of naked athletic young men. They looked however
like their own metal-green sculptures. The execution occurred according to the self-service principle. Without any apparent order, everyone
approached the automated guillotine, emerged without a head, staggered
a few steps, and fell down dead."[1] Though only a fraction of his entire vision, Adorno's dream contains a gold mine of signs begging for analysis.
To be sure, the dream is not exclusively a psychic symptom of his troubled
life in exile. While this macabre vision of witnessing evokes his oblique
confession in *Negative Dialectics* that escaping the Holocaust unleashed
feelings of guilt and execution nightmares, the dream's figures also al-
lude to Adorno's critique of the Enlightenment. The automated guillotine
that lures its willing victims is particularly charged in this regard. Both a
reference to the culture industry and an allusion to the underbelly of the
Enlightenment's body politics, Adorno's dream infers that the mechaniza-
tions of modern life contribute directly to reason's regrettable disavowal
and dissociation of the body. "Being unable to escape it, one praises the
body when not allowed to hit it," Adorno and Max Horkheimer exclaimed

in the notes and drafts to *Dialectic of Enlightenment*.[2] These two interpretative tacks that mine the traumatic and philosophical origins of Adorno's dream do not exhaust its symbolic value. Two decades later, the confusion at the outset of his description of the victims' identities would become prophetic for an entire generation of young West Germans in search of corporeal differences between fascism's victims and perpetrators. Adorno's operative categories "fascists or anti-fascists" were crucial in this respect, for they straddled a line of demarcation that was paramount to the children of Nazis. What constitutes the ontological certitude of anti-fascist being? This distinction would unavoidably end up colliding with another division, one whose subsequent mystery Adorno would have easily laid to rest. The Judaic bris ensured the self-evident difference between a naked German and Jewish male body.

On June 5, 1967, three days after West Berlin police officer Karl-Heinz Kurras ignited West Germany's student movement by murdering student Benno Ohnesorg, Adorno verified this slippage. "The students have taken up a bit of the role of the Jews," he exclaimed in a seminar on aesthetics held in Frankfurt am Main.[3] Those whom Adorno targeted with his subtle admonition on their victimology were no longer interested in what their erstwhile mentor had to say. Three years prior to Ohnesorg's death, initial signs of the students' disapproval of Adorno had already emerged. The tiny Munich-based, Situationist International-leaning collective Subversive Aktion obliquely reproached him for the glaring discrepancy between his deft theory and his silence on how to practice politics.[4] In the ensuing years, various micro-cells of Subversive Aktion strived to wed Frankfurt School theory (among others) with revolutionary praxis. Of all the political forms that materialized, however, none would acquire the comprehensiveness or radicalism of West Berlin's communes. For the members of Berlin's first and most infamous commune, Kommune 1, toppling the strictures of monogamous sexuality, familial hierarchies, and bourgeois individuality was a prerequisite for concretely engaging a complex web of repression at home and abroad. The communes' larger targets included authoritarianism in West German universities, the liberal compromises of the Social Democratic Party, the inaction of the West German Sozialistischer Deutscher Studentenbund (Socialist German Students' Federation; SDS), media monopolies and their manipulation of the public sphere, the dominion of American capitalism, and, above all, the Vietnam War. Far from passing over the fascist origins of postwar German modernity in their ambitious articulation of the local and the global, these agitators wove phantasms of the Holocaust throughout their politics. In June 1967 Adorno instantly spotted the problematic equation of anti-fascism with Jewish suffering that the students had drawn.

A month after firing off his initial warning, Adorno traveled to West Berlin to present a lecture on Goethe's *Iphigenia in Tauris,* a lecture laced with allusions to what he had disparaged earlier as the students' "pure un-thinking practicisms."[5] Before Adorno took the podium, pandemonium erupted. Members of West Berlin's less promiscuous Kommune 2 circu-lated handbills chiding Adorno for his refusal to testify on behalf of two of their own, Fritz Teufel and Rainer Langhans, who had been recently arraigned for inciting arson. "Theory is afforded the freedom of fools," declared one flyer, "everyone knows it is harmless." "What should we do with this obese Teddy?" its authors asked rhetorically. "He should blather away," they countered, "in an empty auditorium and adorn-ify himself to death. Adorno is not happening, the revolution is."[6] After a brawl over the microphone and repeated calls for Adorno's allegiance, the commu-nards unfurled banners, one of which declared, "Iphigenias of the world unite!" Another announced, "Berlin's left-wing fascists welcome Teddy the classicist!" (*FSS,* 265).[7] The sarcasm in both slogans was unmistakable. The communards were as sympathetic to the humanitarian aspirations of Goethe's Iphigenia—in whom Adorno saw a premonition of the dialectic of modernity into myth—as they were earnest about identifying them-selves as fascists. Without stating it outright, these young German gentiles stood before one of Germany's most eminent German-Jewish intellectu-als to put their anti-fascism on display, albeit elliptically. For a brief mo-ment, the communards' desire to establish their anti-fascist credentials converged with their convoluted attempts to fashion themselves (using sarcasm) as the victims of West Germany's new fascist order, one of whose antecedents was the Nazi gas chamber. Having withheld his validation and defense of their victimology, Adorno, the guilt-ridden survivor of the Holocaust, was passed off as a communard foe.

Imagining Bare Life and Avant-Garde Legacies

There exists another reading of Adorno's dream and the arc that spans it and the communard theatrics from the summer of 1967, one that runs to the core of the post-fascist avant-garde's entanglement with West Germa-ny's volatile cultural politics of the 1960s. In his dream, Adorno witnesses the unveiling of what philosopher Giorgio Agamben has come to call bare life. In his philosophy-cum-history, Agamben differentiates two inextricably interwoven modalities of life that fuel modern political philosophy and politics alike. On the one hand, life is merely biological, a condition that all "animals, men, or gods" share.[8] On the other hand, life can become full, just, and good only when men lead it according to a politically qualified codex that sets humans apart from all other living things. Bare life prevails as the defining feature in the modern political constitution of the good life, for only when politics excludes bare life does full life become possible. As National Socialism's concentration camps demonstrated like never before, bare life emerged as a productive category by eugenically delineating, expelling, and eliminating purely biological bodies from the national body politic. "The separation of the Jewish body," Agamben writes of the Final Solution, "is the immediate production of the specifically German body" (HS, 174). The violent genesis of the sacred, racially pure German body was not, however, a simple matter of excluding others deemed unworthy of the good life. Fascism's biopolitics located bare life as always already existing within the good life, a kernel inherent to all biological life that can only be disavowed when displaced onto the racialized other.

As much as Agamben the conceptual historian identifies the Holocaust as a singular limit event in modern history, Agamben the philosopher is wont to insist that Nazi eugenics and the designation and manufacture of bare life constitute a paradigm for the modern.[9] The materialization of the state of exception, where bare life comes into being, informs both modern democracies and totalitarian regimes. Consequently, the binaries that the camp threw into relief (center/margin, good/evil, subject/object, interior/exterior) have since then begun to blur, Agamben contends, especially since the demise of National Socialism and the triumph of American democracy (HS, 10). In spite of the elusive distinction at work in Adorno's 1945 dream—"Whether the victims were fascists or anti-fascists"—it has no truck with Agamben's conflation. Unlike Agamben's "secret convergence" of historical and structural bare life, Adorno's dream is resolutely historical. The "zone of indistinction" in which he dreamt himself is entirely a function of experiencing German fascism's "supreme political principle" from afar and dreaming about it immediately after the fact (HS, 4, 10). What also sets Adorno's dream apart from Agamben's politico-philosophical deliberations is the unavoidable aesthetic mediation it assigns the signification of bare life. The bodies Adorno dreamt were like oxidized bronze sculptures, works of art depicting men about to be beheaded. In other words, Adorno imagined witnessing mass murder entirely as a fantastic aesthetic experience, one in which the borders between the making of inhuman life and recognizing the work of art are called into question. To be sure, Agamben does make clear elsewhere that because sacred life robs bare life of all language, the witness who survives the camp is left to render with language the impossibility of speaking of it (*HS*, 8).[10] Although an exile during the Holocaust and thus held in check by Nazi Germany's law of exception, Adorno never experienced firsthand the ontological void of the camps.[11] The historical experience of bare life assumed its most vivid contours in Adorno's dreamworld, where visions—not language—of extinguished life came into being. This experiential disconnect and the proxy of vision also shaped the communards' quest to make visible the biopolitics that made Auschwitz possible. Whether they replicated Adorno's dream of history, whether they sided with Agamben the historian or Agamben the philosopher, whether they extrapolated bare life into a structural phenomenon of postwar modernity; these questions are essential for framing the counter-politics of this eccentric wing of the West German student movement.

While Adorno's dream turned, in part, on an indistinction between imagined historical reality and aesthetic experience, the communards' later preoccupation with bare life primarily zeroed in on politicizing biopolitics while underplaying their reliance on representation; the communards strove to practice their politics through direct action and consciousness-raising. For this, art had little use. Although the student movement eventually ejected the communards from its rank and file, they both nonetheless spurned the political efficacy of pure aesthetic representation. Some four years earlier the communards' forerunners, Subversive Aktion, had already dismissed the political viability of the superstructure on the grounds that even the "artistic avant-garde . . . inevitably becomes enslaved to the commodity character in an industrialized world."[12] In his 1966 manifesto on establishing revolutionary communes in modern metropolises, communard ringleader Dieter Kunzelmann, largely uninterested in aesthetics, drove home the centrality of using "extralegal means" to achieve praxis and action in the commune's "dialectic of reality and possibility."[13] Yet the communards' exclusion of the aesthetic was never absolute. The rubric under which the politics of the West German student movement in general and that of the communards in particular fell frequently attested to this unavoidable contamination of the aesthetic in the political. Writing for the Hamburg weekly *Die Zeit* in late 1967, journalist Gisela Stelly aptly noted that the term *happening* had advanced in public discourse to describe everything from violent street riots between students and police, to Peter Handke's legendary play *Publikumsbeschimpfung,* to absurd fashion shows.[14] The ambivalence surrounding the happening's form and content was anything but value-free. Many a newspaper reporter and commentator embraced the term in order to disparage any and every student demonstration as unintelligible theatrics lacking artistic decorum and political clarity. They also played up the dangerousness of these provocations, especially when their actors directly engaged state violence.[15] Happenings were something between bad art and borderline terrorism. The instability of the term did not escape the communards either. Unquestionably the most rabble-rousing faction within the student movement to embrace the happening, the original Kommune I also used the term sarcastically to describe, for example, the arson-related deaths of roughly three hundred shoppers in a Brussels department store on May 22, 1967.[16] By resignifying a real-life tragedy as a happening, the communards displaced onto others an idea otherwise reserved by the mass media for undercutting the student movement. They also deployed the ambiguity already at work in the happening's intermediacy between politics and the aesthetic as a political force unto itself.

Adorno dismissed, however, the aesthetic moment at work in the communards' happenings entirely. He downgraded their interruption of his Berlin Iphigenia lecture as a stupid and harmless "happening." In his eyes, their ruckus lacked the careful reflection required to recognize the futility of any praxis in an administered society.[17] For contemporary art critic Heinz Ohff, the Kommune's understanding of the happening was a vulgar derivation of an emergent art form prevalent in vanguard European and American circles since the late fifties. And according to the German coinventor of the happening, artist Wolf Vostell, political happenings like those of the communards lacked "artistic visions."[18] Adorno's dismissal and Ohff's and Vostell's demotion of the communards' happenings together paint, however, a far too simplistic picture. These happenings were neither unmitigated action, nor were they wholly unlike Vostell's own art of the happening. For all their animosity toward the avant-garde, the communards were just as indebted to the historical avant-garde as Vostell was. Even though they were loath to admit it themselves, the communards' avant-garde ancestry would soon come to haunt them. Seven days after the communards distributed the flyers and seven days before the Iphigenia incident with Adorno, Berlin's district attorney arraigned Teufel and Langhans. Among the legal opinions their defending attorney collected a month later, all five substantiated the communards' own assertion that their happenings were merely a "satirical expression of desperation" (*FSS*, 266).[19] According to four of the five solicited legal opinions, the handbills written in response to the Brussels fire contained concrete philological links to Italian futurism, Dada, surrealism, the theater of the absurd, Fluxus, pop art, and even Vostell's own happenings. In his 1969 epilogue to the debacle, critic Karl Heinz Bohrer dubbed the incident the West German renaissance of the surrealist quintessence that André Breton had originally captured when he exclaimed that the "simplest surrealist act" was firing a pistol blindly into a crowded street. In Bohrer's mind, both the surrealists and the communards "declare[d] reality as something aesthetic and, reciprocally, they laid bare the reality character in theatrical processes." Both the communard happening and surrealism announced to the world: "What you see is wrong. You construe what you saw incorrectly. You must learn new interpretative techniques and establish other relations. Do not accept this reality."[20] Unlike the communards, Vostell actively acknowledged his avant-garde credentials. In a public lecture held in April 1964 in New York City's Cricket Theater, he anchored his happenings' pedigree in Cologne Dada, its "slander" and "insult," the shock of its obscenities, and, most importantly, its penchant for encouraging audience participation.[21] Following his most publicized happening to date—a work produced in November 1964 for the city theater of Ulm, Germany, and the local art gallery "studio f"—he recognized Italian futurist F. T. Marinetti and Dadaists Marcel Duchamp and Kurt Schwitters as primary points of departure.[22] A decade and a half later, Vostell, reflecting back on his twenty years of "action art," declared his work to be nothing more or less than an extension of the historical avant-garde.[23]

Whether the communards were derivative of Vostell, whether either was more authentically avant-garde than the other, whether they correctly reinvoked the historical avant-garde's irresolvable tension between the aesthetic and the political, whether the one was sufficiently aesthetic or the other more politically viable; these disputes certainly echo central themes in West German debates on cultural politics in the sixties.[24] As lines of critical inquiry, however, they inevitably lead down the same cul-de-sac Peter Bürger mapped out in 1974. "Attempts . . . to continue the tradition of the avant-garde . . . such as the happenings, for example, . . . can no longer attain the protest value of Dadaist manifestations."[25] In other words, far from returning art to the praxis of life, replications merely confirm the death of the historical avant-garde as well as their own ineffectuality. Moving beyond matters of originality and repetition, this chapter throws into relief how the communards' and Vostell's happenings broke away from their avant-garde precursors by refunctionalizing avant-garde forms according to the post-fascist problem of making bare life visible. Unlike the radical futurity common among their forerunners, the happenings by the communards and Vostell were invested in generating knowledge of the past that would bring about an expanded experience of German time after fascism. In the case of the happening, this temporal shift, so endemic to West Germany's post-fascist avant-gardes, revolved around imagining the bare life that, twenty years earlier, Nazi Germany had mass-produced in the camps and whose traumatic effects continued to define, some twenty years later, the postwar German body as the index of sacred full life. What remains to be seen, then, is whether Vostell and the communards come down on the side of Agamben the historian or Agamben the philosopher. Exactly how do their decidedly necrophilic fantasies contain the German past or elevate it as a heuristic for grasping all of modern life? That both the communards and Vostell wished to jump-start a dialogue with dead people is not to suggest, however, that both grasped the limits of redeeming German history, a process that Oskar Negt and Alexander Kluge describe as exchanging one's own one-sided memories for another set trapped within the bodies of the deceased.[26] As will be seen, the visions of past violence conjured by their happenings diverge most clearly according to the degree to which they fragment modern time and urban space and arrange these pieces in critical constellations.

Wolf Vostell: From Dé-Collage to Happening

Born in 1932 in Leverkusen, Germany, Wolf Vostell spent the next twelve years of his life in Czechoslovakia, where he witnessed his first happening. He professed many decades later: "I experienced my first happening when I was eight or nine years old: during an air-raid alarm we all had to run a kilometer from our school into the country and each of us had to hide ourselves under a different tree, and from there I saw airplane battles and bombs fall to the earth like a flock of birds" (*HF*, 403). However, it was not until 1954, four years into his training as a painter, photographer, and lithographer, that Vostell consciously conceived of the happening, albeit under a different name. "Peu après son décollage," Paris's *Le Figaro* reported on September 6, 1954, "un Super-Constellation tombe et s'engloutit dans la rivière Shannon." (Shortly after takeoff, a Super Constellation crashed and sank in the Shannon River.) A chance discovery while on a walk down the Rue de Buci in Paris, the word *dé-collage* jumped out at Vostell as a "dialectical contradiction" that would end up encapsulating his conceptualization and execution of the happening.[27] Beyond just referring to a plane's takeoff, dé-collage also signified the act of peeling or scratching something off. Additionally, the term overlapped with the German slang term *abkratzen,* roughly to "kick the bucket" or "croak" in English. The French *dé-collage* thus captured a semantic plurality that exceeded the watery disaster in Ireland. The term eventually influenced the unique destructive character of Vostell's own work. "An airplane crash after takeoff. A décollage after a décollage" (*HF,* 399). Art historians have done much to point out the novelty of Vostell's use of the term within the larger scope of twentieth-century avant-garde production. Writing in 1968, Sidney Simon noted how Vostell's dé-collage reversed cubism's constructivist technique of collage.[28] Jörn Merkert went further and argued in 1973 that, unlike the Dadaists and futurists who elevated destruction into a technique for mimetically capturing the otherwise unnoticed chaos of reality, Vostell's dé-collage merely extracted from destruction that which had already happened. Dé-collage, Merkert maintained, "make[s] connections clear."[29] Most recently, Claudia Mesch juxtaposed Dada's link between destruction and forgetting with Vostell's very different anthropological concern for remembering "technological destruction," as with his aforementioned childhood memory.[30]

Vostell's innumerable manifestos and declarations about the form and function of dé-collage do corroborate the diagnoses of Simon, Merkert, and Mesch. For example, in a 1965 statement he declared, "HUMANS WERE FORCED INTO DESTRUCTION IN THE WAR. THE BURDEN OF THESE UNMASTERED FACTORS IN THE WORLD VIEW WILL REFLECT THEMSELVES IN THE ART OF OUR TIME AS PRINCIPLE AND CRITIQUE."[31] Yet Vostell's idea of dé-collage entailed much more than unveiling a pervasive present-day inability to mourn the death and destruction from past wars. The contronymic character of the term *dé-collage*—its inherent "dialectical contradiction"—dovetailed with the Frankfurt School's postwar critical engagement with Enlightenment and reason in late capitalism. "The Enlightenment," Horkheimer and Adorno began in their 1947 masterpiece, "has always aimed at liberating human beings from fear and installing them as masters. Yet the wholly enlightened earth is radiant with triumphant calamity."[32] The authors established from the start that the dialectic of Enlightenment is not just a thing of the past but is a condition endemic to both fascism and the cold war. Similarly, Vostell's dé-collage, the incorporation of crashing in taking off, applied just as equally to German and European history as it did to quotidian experience in the postwar present. Even though Horkheimer and Adorno's ideas on the dialectical accommodation of destruction in human liberation do resemble the ongoing constructive and destructive impulses contained within dé-collage, Vostell's idea dovetailed much more closely with Herbert Marcuse's 1964 inquiry into the "rational character of . . . irrationality" in advanced industrial societies.[33] The total integration of the dialectic's thesis and antithesis that Horkheimer and Adorno ascribed to the periods before and after the fall of Nazism was Marcuse's concern as well; however, it was Marcuse who imbued his gloomy assessment of beleaguered critical theory with a utopian élan. Although society showed no sign of letting up its stranglehold on the collapsed dialectic, it nevertheless accommodated "forces and tendencies [that] may break this containment and explode the society" (ODM, xv). Avant-garde literature on a par with Dadaism and surrealism, Marcuse insisted, had once exhibited the power to reinstate states of negativity where dialectical thought could flourish and resistance to one-dimensionality could establish itself. Although Marcuse credited technical progress with successfully absorbing the historical avant-garde, he insisted that this oppositional imagination, though endangered, has migrated to "new grounds . . . outside the democratic process" (ODM, 249, 256). Though certainly not a social outcast like Marcuse's idealized people of color, Vostell undoubtedly counted himself and his work in this migrated substratum invested in intervening in the reigning state of technical progress.

Vostell experimented for several years with his concept of dé-collage before honing it into what would eventually become the happening, his means for unearthing the past and re-dialecticizing knowledge of the present. Apart from applying his dé-collage concept to found objects, printmaking, poetry, and television, Vostell also applied the term in the mid-fifties to the transformation of entire environments. The first of its kind, *Skeleton* from 1954 planned for the altering of well-known spaces in the Westphalian city of Wuppertal. "Without any explanation," the first of nineteen instructions read, "put 100 skeletons of animals and humans, raw meat, and intestines in the Wupper River" (HL, 342).[34] Urban spaces like those targeted in the other eighteen partially realized transformations (apartment buildings, banks, restaurants, city squares, streets, intersections, elevated trains, street cars, trains) remained the primary staging area for many of Vostell's most prominent dé-collage actions. His second dé-collage demonstration, *The Theater Is in the Street* from 1958, took place in the streets of Paris. In *Cityrama 1* from 1961 he designated twenty-six addresses throughout Cologne for his audience to visit and contemplate. Other German cities for which Vostell created dé-collage events in the sixties included Aachen, Ulm, Berlin, and Munich. With the founding of George Maciunas's Fluxus movement in 1962, Vostell officially connected with American artists and was thus able to include New York City and outlying towns in his roster of dé-collaged spaces. Following his first interaction with American painter Allan Kaprow, who in 1959 performed the first of any such event to call itself a "happening," Vostell resolved to subsume his idea of the "dé-collage event" into Kaprow's English coinage and therewith initiate an international movement.[35] Nevertheless, Vostell actively retained the dialectical tensions at work in his original idea of dé-collage and emphasized the essential conceptual differences between his idea of happening and Kaprow's. German historical experience made Vostell's happenings culturally unique.

Vostell created and produced more happenings in the sixties than in any other decade of his career. Of these thirty-one events, the one staged in the small southwestern town of Ulm in November 1964 was a breakthrough both in terms of its form, sociohistorical contextualization, and popular reception. Ironically, it also contributed to the subsequent absorption of the term *happening* into discourses of and about the student movement in the second half of the sixties. Although Ulm was but a fraction of the size of major metropolises like Cologne, Berlin, and Munich or the industrialized corridor surrounding Wuppertal, it was nonetheless not exceptional for it to play host to Vostell's most ambitious project to date. Home to postwar West Germany's first school of design, Ulm had established itself by the mid-fifties as a West German bastion of post-fascist modernist aesthetics.[36] Ulm was home to the successor of the Bauhaus school and was also an early laboratory for the New German Cinema and a showcase for contemporary theater, as well as a player in Germany's vanguard art scene. Initially contacted in January 1963 by dramaturge Claus Bremer from the city's theater, Vostell merited inclusion in a theater program like Ulm's because of his incorporation of the audience into the fiction of the theater. Five years before Bohrer would make the same claim on behalf of the communards, Bremer praised how Vostell dissolved the boundaries between visual and performing arts and, more importantly, theatrical and everyday reality.[37] The happening Vostell composed for the Ulm Theater brought together a wide palette of Ulm's modernist institutions to witness and contribute to its execution on Saturday, November 7, 1964. Professional actors from the city's theater and student actors from the School of Design played an assortment of prescribed roles; Bremer and director Kurt Fried from "studio f" authored and performed an "action lecture" before Vostell shipped his audience off to the first of seven destinations; and students from the film department in the School of Design were on hand to document the spectacle. From there, the happening triggered countless social, cultural, political, and historical convergences in and beyond the city of Ulm.

Bodies in Ulm, Around Ulm, and All Around Ulm

Vostell's happening in Ulm is commonly referred to by its primary title, the German proverb "In Ulm, um Ulm, und um Ulm herum." Vostell's official title, however, included much more than just the spatial reconnaissance denoted by the initial proverb: *A Happening Composed of 24 Blurred Events, or The Survivors of the Naked Price of Purchase.* How these ideas of blurring, survivorship, or consumerism pertained to the event was anything but obvious. A majority of the participants, the popular press, the intelligentsia sympathetic to Vostell's work, and the general public called the meaning of the happening into question. Of the sixty-seven West and East German newspapers to have published reports about the event—from major conservative West German outlets like the *Frankfurter Allgemeine Zeitung* to the East German daily *Neues Deutschland*—over 50 percent panned it on the grounds that it was psychotic. The other half restricted their reportage to mostly objective descriptions of each of the happening's twenty-four scripted events.[38] Far more patient critics like Urs Jenny, who participated in the happening, engaged Vostell's work only to pick apart the discrepancy between its contrived earnestness and the frivolity felt by many participants, its organization and execution, and the genre's overall feasibility.[39] Like Jenny, Ulrich Brecht, the executive director of the Ulm Theater, reminisced how the happening had failed to live up to the promises that Vostell made in person and that he had published in a nineteen-point agenda in the theater's program. Why, Brecht asked two months later, did the happening have no lasting effect? Had Vostell realized even one of his artistic intentions? Why did so many audience members find the event to be both a gag and tedium? Was the event not marred by an overly ambitious libretto that proved unwieldy for an unprecedented audience of 250 people? Did Vostell not overestimate the penetrating effects of his happening and underestimate his audience's powers of perception?[40] Debate about the happening continued well into the following year. While the Bonn Bundestag investigated Vostell's use of military installations and the Ulm mayor audited the city theater's financial affairs, sympathizers close to Vostell like Bremer and author Peter O. Chotjewitz worked to explain the grounds for the widespread negative reception and to rehabilitate the power of the happening.[41]

Almost every published response to *In Ulm, um Ulm, und um Ulm herum*—regardless of its intellectual rigor, its final assessment, or its political affiliation—circled around the fundamental question, what is a happening? In fact, Vostell identified this definitional conundrum as the event's point of departure. Prior to taking their assigned seats in five sightseeing buses, Vostell's audience listened and watched a twenty-minute "action lecture," in which Bremer randomly read aloud excerpts from a six-part script. "Apart from the fact that it is impossible for me, if I tell you beforehand what you are about to experience," he forewarned, "it would contradict the rules of the happening."[42] As if Bremer's oblique preamble did not frustrate listeners enough, Fried then puréed the nine pages in a blender. Under the premise of preparing their audience for this new art form, Bremer and Fried had performed the first of the happening's twenty-four dé-collages. Like the airliner that crashed into the Shannon River shortly after takeoff, Bremer initially framed Vostell's happening as a constructive exercise in cognition. Fried then undermined Bremer's already garbled elucidations by destroying symbolically and literally his chosen vehicle of clarification, language. "Blur," read the eighteenth proposition in Vostell's Ulm manifesto, "in order to see and let see clearly."[43] Blurring with a blender did not arrest sensory perception entirely, however. The pulping of Bremer's lecture did not eradicate his query into the nature of the happening. Rather, the blender intensified the already collaged state of Bremer's pronouncements to the extreme and, more importantly, stressed the inadequacy of descriptive language with the noise of its motor. One can experience a happening as one hears the sound of a blender, yet one cannot apply a priori categories of knowing or experience in order to make sense of the event. Vostell drove this point home with the amplified noise of opening and pouring twenty bottles of carbonated water into drinking glasses. By bringing forth acoustically an otherwise incidental prop usually seen and not heard at a lecture, Vostell inferred that experience in his happening would transpire along other channels, ones that circumvent the noble sense of sight and instead appeal directly to the body.

In keeping with Bremer's initial refusal to explicate the genre, Vostell's happening proceeded without any further clarification of its meaning, form, or mode of address. The audience promptly filed into five buses outfitted with tape decks that played dé-collaged sentence fragments during the trip to a local military airfield. Upon arrival, Vostell charged the participants to "admire the aircraft!" (*HF*, 388).[44] Cordoned off some twenty yards away, they watched and listened while three fighter jets fired their engines for ten minutes. Following this "open-air concert," participants were whisked off by bus to a car wash. Standing behind a vertical screen propped up at its exit, Vostell's audience watched the artist drive a red Citroën through the automated wash only to be doused by pails of yellow paint. After edging forward into a screen upon which a handful of eviscerated animal lungs hung, Vostell backed the automobile through the car wash and repeated the process anew. Another bus ride and the participants found themselves at the entrance of a parking garage where five women wearing gas masks led them to the top floor while pushing baby strollers and carrying auto tires. After yet another bus ride, participants lined up alongside an emptied outdoor swimming pool where they wore white sacks over their heads, hummed melodies, and watched seven actors veiled in white linens writhe along the floor of the pool. At the next location, a decommissioned convent, participants received pieces of wood, which they exchanged for a food voucher after they traversed a narrow pathway around the building. Thirty minutes later, Vostell's troops arrived in total darkness at a field full of votive candles and animal bones. "Wander about the field and tell someone your life story," Vostell requested (*HF*, 391). Because of a wrong turn, the next planned event—a visit to a junkyard where smoke bombs and televisions were to have exploded—never took place. Instead, the participants, already five hours into the happening, proceeded to the final official station of the night, a slaughterhouse. Unlike the previous environments that involved a single direction for the audience to follow, the slaughterhouse entailed multiple events and tasks for the audience to fulfill. To this end, Vostell transformed the space into a gigantic installation full of colored lights, junk, animal carcasses on automated meat hooks, and slide projections of erotic photography and the assassination of John F. Kennedy. In one corner actors were smothered in foam. While participants were to free the actors from the foam, another five sat around a miked table and read aloud excerpts from a mountain of news publications while gorging themselves. Simultaneously, a conveyor belt produced a motley assortment of foodstuffs for the audience to eat according to a lottery system. An hour later, roughly forty-eight people were shuttled by taxi to various locations throughout the city (e.g., restaurants, casinos, the central post office, movie theaters, the city cathedral, and a memorial to Ulm's rabbi abused during Kristallnacht). The remaining participants were locked into four saunas in the slaughterhouse and told to "think about the most beautiful thing in your life" (*HF*, 393). Half of these people were then transported back to the theater and the other half were sent off to witness either a cow giving birth or a Swiss inventor demonstrating his latest invention, a self-propelled tree saw. After seven hours, at ten o'clock at night, the happening was officially disbanded.

In Ulm . . . bombarded its participants to the brink of incomprehension. With neither a single point of view nor any obvious common thread running through the twenty-three visited stations to guide their experiences, the participants and commentators alike failed to see Vostell's happening as anything other than a jumbled mess. At best, later reflections endeavored to make sense of the happening in a piecemeal fashion by speculating on each station's symbolic logic. Airplanes evoked war; the Citroën and raw meat suggested a tragic auto accident; the parking garage signified life in a bunker; the poolside crooning was likened to a Ku Klux Klan rally; the field of votives triggered myriad associations from Christmas to war cemeteries; and portions of the slaughterhouse scene recalled the parable of Lazarus. Certainly the most unambiguous association, the coda in the saunas was frequently cited as a direct reference to the mock showers in which Nazis gassed millions.[45] What exactly all these puzzle pieces assembled together comprised was, however, anybody's guess. Hardly impressed by what he saw as an "anti-rational hoax," Jenny paraphrased what many concluded to be the happening's ultimate purpose, namely to reassign art the task of perceiving the banal anew.[46] According to this reading, *In Ulm . . .* was nothing more than a self-referential exercise in defining the happening as art form. How, Jenny therefore asked, could anyone fulfill Vostell's intentions—point two in Vostell's Ulm manifesto read "life as art work"—when, after seven hours, the participants were "too hungry, too tired, and too frozen"? Furthermore, how were participants to arrive at Vostell's desired new phenomenology if the happening demanded from them an unprofitable mixture of "obedience, patience, and a good dose of indifference"? In the final analysis, Jenny concluded that what Vostell's happening required from its audience was nothing more than their physical presence. "Willing or not, everyone, even I, was, by virtue of [our] mere presence, part of this happening." All posture without any consequence, Vostell's happening struck Jenny as "an event by people lacking fantasy for people lacking fantasy." In spite of all his vitriol, Jenny unknowingly touched upon the unifying principle that tied together each of the happening's twenty-three stations. The primary medium of signification throughout the happening was not its motley assortment of symbolically rich places and things. Rather, the medium Vostell sought to manipulate in his happening was the participants themselves. More precisely, the work of art in question in the happening was their bodies. Not only were bodies the connective tissue within and between the happening's twenty-three stations, but fantasy, too, undergirded these connections.

Vostell made absolutely clear in his Ulm manifesto that his participants' bodies would play a central role in the happening. Point four reads, for example, ". . . allow one's own body to experience." Point five reads, "The self becomes and is allowed to become color, light, time, material, noise; the self becomes and is allowed to become art." And point one equates art with space and life. What is striking about all three of these propositions is the desired transformation of the self into the object status otherwise reserved for works of art. If life was to become art in *In Ulm . . .*, art stood not for its historically recognized potential for mimesis or anti-mimesis but rather for its status as pure object, its opposition to subjectivity. Indeed, bodies and embodiment abounded throughout Vostell's happening. Beginning with the deafening blast of the three jet engines, the happening momentarily disabled the participants' sensory organs in varying degrees and combinations, creating environments where meaning was frustrated and forestalled and where the materiality of being was thrown into relief by blasting sound waves, constrictive gas masks, cold, hunger, and total darkness. All along the way, bodies both acted and were acted upon. They were transported, schlepped, and also marched forward on their own accord. Bodies were repeatedly shrouded or found in various states of undress. And everywhere they served as props. As such, they appeared as either intact entities or fragmented products of violence. While the happening did instantiate the body's fleshiness using animal carcasses and their entrails, the body's flesh, bones, and blood were anything but the exclusive province of nonhumans. In order to bridge this divide between slaughtered animals and human spectators and actors, Vostell called on the fantasy of his audience. *In Ulm . . .* was to create for its participants new modes of perception, heightened states of self-awareness, and opportunities for discerning new relationships between self and surroundings. According to point eleven of the Ulm manifesto, participants were to arrive at new meanings by breaking through old ones. Illogic was to be found in logic. Vostell's nineteenth and final point emphasized that all this was to be accomplished through the active involvement of its participants, the "ausführende und aufführende" (executors and performers). Articulating modes of being with new categories of knowledge was to transpire through the symbolic contexts prepared and choreographed for each station.

Evoking Non-Time and Non-Space: Vostell's Semiotic Square

In order to unpack Vostell's conceptualization and execution of this articulation of being and cognition in *In Ulm . . .* , an exegesis of the artist's semiotics is absolutely essential. This necessitates a momentary leap into the future. Beginning in 1970, Vostell undertook one of his most time-intensive happenings. Every day for an entire year, the Deutsche Bahn (the German state railway) transported a metal footlocker containing heads of lettuce between Cologne and Aachen. Over the course of the year, biologists at the Max Planck Institute in Cologne regularly performed tests on the lettuce, documenting its deterioration. Similarly, chaperones for the lettuce voluntarily subjected themselves to medical examinations. After a year, data from both sets of tests were exhibited at Berlin's Gallery René Block. As part of Vostell's preparations for the happening, he devised a diagram (fig. 14) comprised of two intersecting oppositions, at the center of which he located the experience of the happening as an experience synonymous with life.[47] What Vostell captured in graphic form surpassed in clarity and economy what he had attempted to outline in numerous manifestos like the one drafted for Ulm. According to an incisive gloss that accompanied this programmatic diagram, Vostell's happening *Salad* was intended to precipitate the intrusion of the recognition of reality (*die Eindringlichkeit der Realitätserkenntnis*) so that a logical connection (*Sinnzusammenhang*) between time and space would arise. Vostell conceived this happening, like all others before it, as creating aesthetic experiences within an intermediary zone, a space belonging to reality but nevertheless partially divorced from it. Vostell's diagram of intersecting opposites intimates that the cognitive experience acquired in a happening

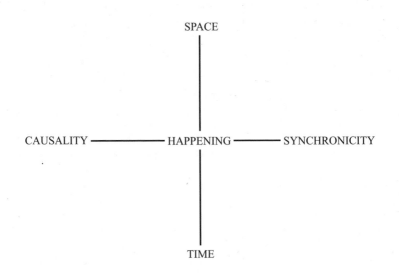

SPACE

CAUSALITY ——————— HAPPENING ——————— SYNCHRONICITY

TIME

Figure 14
Wolf Vostell, diagram for *Salad,* 1970–71.

is made possible by the aesthetic synthesis of opposites, in this case time
and space as well as causality and synchrony. With this in mind, a look
back at the historical origins of Vostell's idea of the happening reframes
dé-collage significantly. Where taking off and crashing comprised an actual "dialectical contradiction," Vostell's dé-collage went one step further.
His happening was to facilitate a dialectical resolution of these opposites
in the minds of its participants. Triggering a deeper consciousness of reality through the juxtaposition of the contraries space and time—core
elements in the constitution of Vostell's Ulm happening—was in fact a
self-reflective process; time and space were also to comprise the content
of their consciousness. However, Vostell's diagram does not tell all. An
overlapping of two interrelated syntheses, it says nothing about the reality
that it sought to unveil.

Fleshing out the contours of the reality inferred by Vostell's diagram
and presumably encompassed by his happenings must proceed piecemeal.
Only after bracketing off the secondary horizontal opposition (causality-
synchronicity) can the spatial and temporal boundaries of this reality
come into view. Yet the binary of space and time comprises only one half
of the perimeter. Logic dictates that this coupling also elicits "invisible"
contradictory terms, in this case non-space and non-time. Following

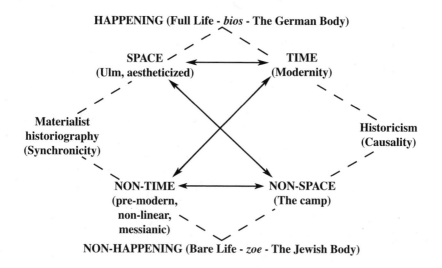

Figure 15

A semiotic square of Wolf Vostell's 1964 happening in Ulm.

Fredric Jameson's lead, plotting these four terms onto a Greimasian semiotic square can help "map . . . the limits of . . . ideological consciousness" endemic to a specific historical reality (see fig. 15). But what these perfunctory categories of non-time and non-space describe is abstruse at best.[48] These mysteries quickly resolve themselves, however, once the contradictory term to the primary synthesis (happening/life) is established. If the political intention of the happening is the production of humane behavior according to Vostell's gloss to *Salad,* then the life with which he equated the happening and the work of art is unquestionably synonymous with what Agamben calls "full life," or *bios.* Although Agamben insists that under modernity both *bios* and its antipode—*zoē,* or bare life—are caught within a zone of indistinction where their opposition is always already a convergence, the two primary quadrants of Vostell's square pull this "aporia" apart for inspection (*HS,* 9). According to the logic of opposites, the dialectical synthesis of these contradictories (non-time and non-space) is bare life (*bios*), or, in Vostell's case, the non-happening. With this piece in place, all four points in the semiotic square hidden within Vostell's original opposites reveal themselves concretely. Most importantly, the lateral, or indexical, syntheses flesh themselves out quite literally as (to cite Jameson once again) the "characterological types, that . . . embody and manifest such contradictions, which otherwise remain abstract and repressed" throughout Vostell's happenings (*PU*, 254).

Returning to the Ulm happening from late 1964, Vostell's semiotic square would read as follows. If the concrete space of the happening entailed the locales in and around the city of Ulm, then the ideological non-space that contradicts it is the Nazi concentration camp, what Agamben calls a "non-place," the "most absolute *conditio inhumana* that has ever existed" (*HS*, 166).[49] A hidden political space, the death camp, Agamben adds, produced bare life as a state of exception that not only existed outside of but also constituted by virtue of its exclusion the normal order of full life (*HS*, 169–71). If the concentration camp was intended to care for the modern nation-state's biological life, the node of time in Vostell's square, which manifested itself in Ulm both in terms of the scripted linear libretto and its grueling duration, also denotes the temporality of modernity, what Walter Benjamin described as "the time of hell."[50] Not coincidentally, Benjamin has much to say about the remaining fourth quadrant of non-time, the node that Jameson labels a Hegelian negation of the original negation (*OM*, xvi). Non-time can be defined as premodern time, what Benjamin calls the "archaic symbol-world of mythology" (*AP*, N2a, 1). It can stand for cyclical time, the "eternal return of the same" that underlies the dreamlike experience of newness under modernity (*AP*, S2, 1). It can also signify messianic time, the redemptive moment associated with Benjamin's angel of history that sees the fullness of the past as a monad beyond its reach. And last, it can represent the temporal consciousness sought by the historical materialist who blasts the homogeneous course of modern time into shards in order to capture within an instance a dialectic of the past and the present as a moment of future possibility.[51] In concurrence with Jameson who identifies this "most critical position" as "open or empty" and "the place of . . . the great deduction," the quadrant of non-space was never just one of these possibilities (*OM*, xvi). In order to yield the synthesis of the happening's opposite, bare life, this fourth term must correspond to the non-time of the camp, the absence of time experienced by the living dead about which Benjamin's chronometry knew nothing. Additionally, for the indexical synthesis of the space and non-time to acquire meaning in the spatial context of Vostell's Ulm happening, the fourth term must vacillate between the destructive modality of Benjamin's cyclical time—the debunking of modern progress—and the constructive modality of his historical materialist method.

If Vostell's original opposition does indeed denote and connote these four interconnected terms, not all were self-evident in the construction or experience of the Ulm happening. Similarly, the square's two lateral syntheses, while discernible now on paper, were not at all apparent during the event itself. The value, therefore, of expounding upon Vostell's original binary lies not just in the revelation of the invisible portion of a distinctly historical reality unique to Germany that his happening sought to imagine. It also illuminates the tensions, oppositions, and historical relations between the network of invisible terms logically evoked by their visible contraries and contradictories. Crisscrossing all four syntheses, the reader thus sees how the dignity of full life on which Vostell's happening constituted itself necessitated structurally the historical existence of bare life that prevailed posthumously within West German post-fascist modernity as a shameful silence. The Holocaust ensured that full life would remain the province of Germans well after the liberation of the camps. The indexical synthesis of modern time (i.e., progress) and the paramount non-place (i.e., the camp) belongs to Benjamin's critique of historicism, the purveyor of a simplistic causality that abets the myth of progress and ensures the ideological divorce between the modern present and the barbaric past of the camps. Directly opposed to this position lies Vostell's utopian synthesis of possibility—the space of Marcuse's oppositional imagination—a position capable of exploding the boundaries of historical consciousness mapped by the square. Within the concrete spaces of Ulm, the historical materialist method would establish what Benjamin called the "secret index . . . between past generations and the present one."[52] As Negt and Kluge point out, the secret this method would seek to unlock is, especially within the post-fascist period, a secret of which only dead bodies know (*GE*, 596). This secret is the secret of bare life that, according to Agamben, "politics has failed to reckon with [as the] foundational moment of modernity" (*HS*, 4). For Vostell, access to and use of this secret index is only possible through the work of fantasy. As outlined in chapter 1, Negt and Kluge impose strict criteria upon fantasy in order for it to contribute successfully to the construction of a redeemed materialist historiography. Rather than fabricating a historical totality, which is the task of the historicist, fantasy mines the fissures between the shards of exploded history and explores possible connections and contexts between disparate pieces that modernity otherwise obscures. The historical materialist in Ulm would therefore see the relationality (i.e., Negt and Kluge's *Zusammenhang*) between the four coordinates in Vostell's semiotic square as well as their four syntheses: the interminable tensions between the now of postwar Ulm and the then of Auschwitz; the delusions of modern linear time and the potentially transformational knowledge won from fantasies that emerged in the fissures in fragmented time; the lasting inscription of bare life within full life; and the diametric opposition between dominant fictions of causality and the historical truths of a synchronous *Realität-serkenntnis* that Benjamin called "telescop[ing] the past through the present" (*AP*, N7a, 3).

With the intricacies of Vostell's semiotics unveiled, the relationality of time, space, bodies, and historical knowledge in the Ulm happening comes into view. Paying particular attention to the emblematic seventh and ninth stations, a close reading attentive to the aforementioned visible and invisible terms along with their syntheses illuminates why the production of a materialist historiography remained locked within the happening's libretto as an unrealizable utopian moment. Following the visit to the airfield and the car wash, Vostell's participants arrived at approximately six in the evening at a three-floor concrete parking garage, where they were instructed to "form a procession. Take a baby carriage, a gas mask, a bicycle, a tire, and follow the cortège." Before they could form the procession themselves, the participants witnessed five women already donning masks emerge with carriages from the garage's nooks. In the course of their march upward, participants were instructed to collect in blankets the twenty lifeless human bodies played by male actors in gas masks (see fig. 16) and drag them, along with the tires and baby carriages, to the top of the garage. Without an inkling of context, participants walked away from the fifteen-minute experience with an unwieldy list of associations. Günther Rühle of the *Frankfurter Allgemeine Zeitung* associated the procession with the apocalyptic visions of the Belgian expressionist painter James Ensor.[53] Writing for Ulm's local newspaper, Erich Kaiser wrote solemnly of macabre memories of war: "Life in the bunker. Sirens. Cavalcades of refugees."[54] In his initial response to the happening, Jenny found the scene in the garage a combination of "pleasures from a children's playground and an air raid exercise."[55] Conversely, Susanne Ulrici wrote of a travesty of Mardi Gras in her widely published reportage.[56] That none of these accounts accurately captured Vostell's inspiration for this segment of the happening is highly illuminating, but not because they misunderstood Vostell's intentions. In fact, grasping his intentions had nothing to do with the happening's overall success. In the fall of 1964, West Germany's Federal Agency for the Protection of the Civilian Population published a thin pamphlet called *Zivilschutzfibel*

Figure 16

Photo from the Ulm happening by Roland Fürst, 1964.

(*Civilian Protection Primer*) intended to inform the general population about measures required for safeguarding themselves against the threat of nuclear, biological, and chemical warfare. The cardinal rule the primer asked its readers to remember was simple. "Stay home!" it advocated. Primarily intended to counter the uncertainty of an imminent World War III, the *Zivilschutzfibel* insisted that it was the government's responsibility to educate its citizens about every possible threat to the German body politic. Crucial for facilitating this fantasy work is a series of photographs portraying misfortune in all shapes and kinds: a weapons array, atomic explosions, gas masks, auto wrecks, natural disasters, wounded limbs,

Figure 17
Federal Agency for the Protection of the Civilian Population,
Zivilschutzfibel, 1964. Page 14.

governmental command centers, bunker life, passports, first-aid kits, and emergency rations. Of particular significance for Vostell's Ulm happening is a photograph of a man and young girl walking hand in hand through what could be a bunker to some, a parking garage to others (see fig. 17). Although this picture that accompanies the chapter titled "You're safest in a bunker!" appears nowhere in previously published materials about the Ulm happening, there is no doubt that this particular image of survival functioned as a springboard for Vostell's parking garage scene.[57] In effect a realization of a cold war fantasy—"The effects of a nuclear war are unimaginable," the primer's authors claim—that mobilized the public sphere through an ideology of fear, Vostell's parade through the parking garage was firmly anchored in geopolitical fantasies of the West German present.[58] True to the complexities of the semiotic square, this station in the happening played out cold war fantasies of a nuclear holocaust. Lurking underneath its choreographed fantasies is the historical dimension of postwar German bodies as the bearers of *bios.* So when the primer insists that "good civilian protection can save many human lives," the life in question is politically consecrated life *and* bare life, the physical body that nuclear radiation and biological and chemical agents threaten to destroy and that Vostell's participants had to drag up the parking garage. This imagined threat to bare life was, however, a threat to the historical transformation of the bare substrate that Germans had disavowed some twenty years earlier within and without their own bodies in order to achieve their own full life. The long-standing placeholder of bare life that facilitated this displacement was the Jew, and the camp was the place where Germans had undertaken this transformation, the result of which came under threat two decades later. In other words, fantasies of nuclear war imperiled the lingering postwar results of Nazi biopolitics.

Just as Vostell's participants failed to see the present within the historical associations in the garage procession, their reaction to the ensuing environment at a public swimming pool only mined the present at the expense of ignoring the past. "Put a bag over your head," Vostell instructed his participants. "Hum softly the first song that comes to mind. Stand around the swimming pool." As before, seven actors emerged from the crowd covered in white sheets. After crawling into the empty pool surrounded by floodlights, they slithered around and on top of one another. After screaming for five minutes, they punctured plastic sacks of dyed water and bags of feathers. A smaller adjoining pool was then set on fire. Public reactions to this station were unanimous. Vostell was out to simulate his own Ku Klux Klan rally. While the visual associations with American white supremacists were apparently unmistakable, not a single report cared to explain how uncanny the hooded spectators' song was. Hans Baumann's 1932 "Es zittern die morschen Knochen" ("The Rotting Bones Tremble") developed during the Third Reich as a canonical Nazi anthem propagandizing anti-communist warmongering and the German claim to lebensraum. A purely arbitrary choice on the part of the participants, Baumann's tabooed song did not even warrant comparison in the press to the Klan's involvement in the internationally publicized assassinations of three civil rights activists in Philadelphia, Mississippi, in June 1964. Once again, Vostell set his sights on a much larger target in this portion of the happening. Clues were to be found back in America. In conjunction with his aforementioned lecture at New York City's Cricket Theater, Vostell and his audience performed the libretto to his happening *YOU*. Held at a private residence in Long Island, *YOU* revolved around an empty swimming pool. Bused in from Manhattan, the audience was eventually asked to "go into the white swimming pool please." "Lay down and build a massengrab or shoot the mountain of people" with a toy gun (*HL,* 261). In the eyes of Fluxus member and participant Al Hansen, *YOU* was unquestionably referencing the camp with its industrial executions and mass graves (*Massengrab*). "It has such a strong concentration camp, Nazi feeling," Hansen wrote in 1965. He also recorded another participant who took "umbrage that a person [like Vostell] would do something like this that seemed so full of fun."[59] Within the discrepancy between the homologous features of *YOU* and the ninth station in *In Ulm . . .* and the opposing reactions of participants—Germans fantasized about contemporary American racism and Americans imagined memories of bygone German racism—lay dormant the explosive potential of these body spectacles. The point for Vostell was that "the Germans had [camps] and there are people now . . . that have them."[60] Only the space between these two reactions could be said to capture the fullness of these twin environments, a fantastic space that neither the Germans in Ulm nor the Americans in Long Island managed to perceive simultaneously, a space that in Ulm would have exposed the interminable role of the camp in German life after fascism. In the dialectical spirit of dé-collage, stations seven and nine, along with the rest of the Ulm happening, sought to momentarily arrest the forward march of modern time by unveiling the presence of the past in the present and, conversely, the breaks between the present and the past. Furthermore, *In Ulm . . .* constructed its individual scenarios around the camp as the definitive historical space of bare life within modern post-fascist German life. That so many on both sides of the Atlantic found in Vostell's happenings more cause for pleasure than critical reflection might very well speak to the faulty construction of his librettos. (Vostell intentionally altered subsequent happenings in order to avoid, for example, further charges of creating entertaining sightseeing tours.) Be this as it may, the entertainment factor was equally, if not more, attributable to the constitutive absence of those historical parameters of reality that Vostell's happening in Ulm sought to make visible, a twenty-year absence for which no single happening could compensate.

From Vietnam to Berlin and Back to Auschwitz Again

Vostell was quite aware of the representational and political limits of his happenings. While the happening proved to be well suited to tackle Germany's unmastered problems with its fascist past, the political turmoil of the mid-sixties both at home and abroad necessitated different media. This was especially the case with respect to the Vietnam War, which had become a pivotal event for the mobilization of West Germany's student movement. Immediately after the happening in Ulm, Vostell returned to painting in a vein that many have described as derivative of Robert Rauschenberg's pop aesthetic. In large-format works from 1964 like *1 km Autobahn* and

Wir waren so eine Art Museumsstück (*We Were a Kind of Museum Piece*), Vostell incorporated photographs and newspaper clippings related to the ongoing Auschwitz trials. With each passing year, however, explicit references to the Holocaust faded and in their place Vostell featured icons from the present. Starting in 1966, iconography from the Vietnam War began to consume entire canvases. Although Vostell did realize one happening in 1967 intended to "UNCOVER FACTS AND TRUTHS" about the Vietnam War, painting—photographic emulsions and silkscreen prints in particular—advanced as Vostell's medium of choice for dealing with "BRUTAL AND MILITARISTIC IMAGES" depicting the production of bare life in Southeast Asia.[61] The grounds for this shift arose because of the inapplicability of the spatial and temporal categories in Vostell's semiotic square to the image politics of this widely televised war. Unlike the Ulm happening, in which fantasy could flesh out invisible spatial and temporal links between the present and Germany's genocidal past, German television's coverage of the Vietnam War—a far more brutal set of images than what American networks allowed—frustrated the underlying processes of fragmentation and differentiation at work in the happening.[62] Once engendered in between times and places and their invisible contradictories, fantasy now bled into the manifest portions of the semiotic square so that space and non-space appeared coterminous. How could a happening trace the contours of contemporary biopolitics if the space of the reincarnated camp was the Vietnam on television screens in German living rooms? This dilemma—what Jameson describes as the postmodern suppression of distance—was largely technical in origin.[63] Yet television's implosion of spatial differences had crucial ramifications on the dialectical contradictions and sublimations so central to Vostell's dé-collage. His painting *Kaum hatte er sich an das zweite Herz gewöhnt—da bekam er schon das dritte* (*Hardly Had He Adjusted to His Second Heart When He Received His Third*) from 1968 (fig. 18) illustrates perfectly his response to the postmodern compression of space. Composed of two layers, the painting's foundation is an aerial photograph of the city of Cologne and the Rhine transferred onto canvas. Atop a layer of white paint slathered over the city's downtown, Vostell applied a silkscreen print of a traffic jam. Secured on top of this is a second layer of Plexiglas, on which Vostell reproduced a screen print of photojournalist Eddie Adam's iconic image of a South Vietnamese general executing a captured Vietcong. Together both layers produce a composite image suggesting that modern urban life in Cologne and the production of bare life in Vietnam were merely a river's width

Caption and copyright by Vostell Family, Malpartida de Cáceres.

Figure 18

Wolf Vostell, *Kaum hatte er sich an das zweite Herz gewöhnt—da bekam er schon das dritte*, 1968. Silkscreen and photo emulsion on canvas and Plexiglas. 49 × 79 inches.

apart. In other words, although it did not appear within Cologne proper, Vietnam was purportedly somewhere inside Germany. Considered cross-sectionally, however, Vostell's canvas shows this postmodern perception of Vietnam infolded into Germany to be an illusion. In spite of this mirage of proximity, Vietnam never actually intersects the plane of Cologne. Most importantly, Vostell's painting makes utterly clear the dangerous collapse of space so central to Vostell's dialectical method. Postmodernity forced Vostell's dialectics to fragment and differentiate within a framework only a few millimeters deep.

The implosion of space and the accompanying illusions it engendered did not pass over the Kommune 1. Their set of four handbills read like a satire of the postmodern space that reactionary organs like Berlin's daily *Bild-Zeitung* propagandized as being real. Particularly outrageous to the communards was the newspaper's coverage of the 1967 department store fire in Brussels, a tragedy that its manager attributed to extremist antiwar protestors. Adding insult to injury, the paper substantiated the rumor that a protester against the Vietnam War had threatened to explode a bomb in the department store. The communards were highly skeptical. Pacifist through and through at that point, Europe's New Left was not the sort to wield violence, they thought.[64] Their handbills sought to expose this fiction of violence by exaggerating the postmodern compression of space tangentially inferred in the original news report. In their minds, no objector to the Vietnam War would ever seek to replicate it at home. A spoof on the journalistic style of the *Bild-Zeitung*, the first flyer described the tragedy as a "huge happening" orchestrated by pro-Chinese Belgian students who felt that a firebombing was the best way to convey the horrific conditions of the unjust Vietnam War in a European society lulled by media manipulation. The second handbill—a parody of student accusations against American imperialist propaganda—attributed the events in Brussels to the latest in American marketing techniques: "Yet another new gag in the variegated history of American marketing methods, an American week has just opened in Brussels . . . A burning department store full of burning people conveys for the first time in a European metropolis that crackling Vietnam feeling (to be right there in the action and burn along with it) that we have been missing for so long in Berlin." The third handbill described the events abroad as a prescription for German objectors to the Vietnam War to jump-start their own protest at home: "No longer must any of us shed tears on the morning newspaper on account of the poor Vietnamese people. As of today he goes in the confection department at KaDeWe, Hertie, Woolworth, Bilka or Neckermann and discreetly lights a cigarette in the dressing room." The flyer concluded with the proclamation, "Brussels has given us the sole answer to [American imperialism]: burn, warehouse, burn!" Coiled like a snake, the fourth and final broadside was a mishmash of advertising copy for dishwashing liquid, newspaper propaganda, pro-American boosterism, and the Marxist rhetoric prevalent within much of the student movement:

REVOLUTION IN PINK REVOLUTION IN RED ☆ furs fly into the street through flaming red ☆ a mink for every housewife in Brussels ☆ L'Innovation's pink-red invasion ☆ The completely new revolutionary feeling ☆ a bottle of propane gas and you can experience the same thing ☆ the most developed propaganda for Johnson's Vietnam policy ☆ American cultural goods ☆ fluttered about by pink and gray clouds ☆ you can experience the apocalypse in Brussels yourself ☆ through a revolution in pink ☆ propane gas in red ☆ at Kepa and Ka-De-Weh ♦[65]

A culmination of the three preceding texts, this handwritten handbill spiraled like a corkscrew toward the center of the page only to end with what looks like a drop. Common to all four handbills was a grotesque sarcasm that inferred that terrorist violence could collapse gargantuan geographic distances and make real that to which Germans had otherwise been oblivious. The handbills' piecemeal construction out of various styles and concomitant ideologies as well as their sarcasm escaped Berlin's Sixth District Court entirely. "The handbills take the department store fire that took place on May 22, 1967, in Brussels," Berlin's prosecuting attorney insisted, "as an occasion to inspire arson in Berlin's department stores, in order to impart a realistic presentation [*Vorstellung*] of the battles in Vietnam." Their purpose, he suggested, was "to denounce American action in Vietnam."[66] The crux of the state's case was a willful and immoral slippage from the power to imagine (*vorstellen*) to the need to make present (*vorstellen*). In other words, the communards were accused of attempting to perpetrate the very collapse of space they lampooned. Quoting the communard Kunzelmann, who once insisted that Germany's antiwar movement must make its ideas (*Vorstellungen*) concrete through action, the prosecution saw nothing less than a pro-communist putsch intent on dismantling the democratic foundations of postwar West Germany. Any academic attempt to read these pamphlets as harmless surrealist documents, as the defense had done, ignores the fact that the flyers reached an audience of students utterly incapable of such an expert exegesis.

Kommune 1 did not formulate their own explicit theory of the happening, nor did they compose like Vostell a substantial body of intricate and costly librettos that became works of art.[67] According to the defendant Langhans, however, the communards' notion of a happening did share essential features with Vostell's. First, their demonstration in front of the Free University's cafeteria, where they distributed a set of four leaflets, relied on the participation of any and all passersby who read their flyers. Second, their happening was intent on wrenching everyone away from what Langhans decried in court as the "obstinate marching formation" of everyday life (*KM*, n.p.). In other words, like Vostell, the communards sought to expand the boundaries of their own revolutionary praxis—a revolution enclosed within the domestic space of communal living—by provoking outsiders. Third and most important, Langhans insisted that this interface between the commune and passersby was predicated on activating fantasy. In the court proceedings on July 6 and 7, 1967, Langhans illustrated this imaginary dimension by asking the lawyers to "just imagine if [Berlin mayor] Albertz stood here." "You could throw something at him," he continued, "even you would have fun with that." "You mean a poster?" replied the prosecution. "No, a real beautiful figure," Langhans insisted (*KM*, n.p.). Not unlike the position of the ideal historical materialist in Vostell's semiotic square, the fantastic dimension in the communards' happening was elusive. Fixated on establishing criminal intent, Berlin's lawyers failed to see that the communards did not seek to assault the mayor. Instead, their intention was merely to trigger visions of violence and, using grotesque parody, divulge the inappropriateness of both such an action within a court of law and a mayor who had just played host to an oppressive tyrant, the shah of Iran. In fact, the most concentrated imaginative work to emerge out of the handbill happening was the two-day hearing itself. The trial against Langhans and Teufel, commonly referred to as a soap opera, resulted because the dominant order of reality, the court, conceived the communards' fantasies of terrorism as belonging entirely within the space and time of the real. "And what if," the prosecution hypothesized in conjunction with the fourth leaflet, "someone had happened upon the idea to try out what is in the handbills and light a cigarette in the changing room of a department store?" "I must say," replied Teufel, "none of us thought that anyone would do that—except for Mr. Prosecuting Attorney. But he didn't do it either. Instead, he wrote an indictment" (*KM*, n.p.). In other words, the "Moabit soap opera" was fantasy, too, but solely the fantasy of the state, the mass media, and the public sphere. Together they insisted on making fantasy into something very real with potentially dire consequences for everyone involved.

The communards' own fantasies within the handbills markedly differed from those of the court insofar as they inferred this collapse of space—the imaginary transformation of Berlin into Brussels and therefore Hanoi—to be implausible. And yet this implausibility was not as steadfast as the handbills themselves insinuated. In fact, the communards' fantasy soon betrayed the very boundaries that their sarcasm sought to reinforce. On the communards' authorial intentions, Langhans admitted in court, "We tried to depict things in the form of fiction using mocking language." The prosecution retorted, "But it was we elders who experienced burning houses." In the face of the Allies' scarcely discussed air war on German cities, the communards' fiction of a burning KaDeWe in the heart of West Berlin had purportedly evoked images from the past that reframed Germans as victims. Whether pretense or not, the threat of arson reverberated in the minds of the prosecution as the return of the repressed. Even though the handbills did not evoke German victimhood explicitly, German victimhood was precisely that which lurked latently in the fantasies of both the prosecution *and* the defense. When asked against what he and his comrades were protesting, Teufel added to his list the Vietnam War and the Germans' postwar smugness and complacency. Asked to elaborate, he said, "Let me reformulate that differently. Germans are a democratic, peaceful, hardworking little folk. True, they killed a bunch of Jews, but for that Arabs are now being killed with German weapons. It's a kind of reparations. It's true, however, that if the more Blacks or Yellows kick the bucket down there, the better it is for us" (*KM*, n.p.). "You don't seriously mean that?" the prosecution inquired in disbelief. "Oh yes, very much so," he insisted. Underneath all the sarcasm, Teufel was indeed earnest. Within the fantastic space of the handbills, he and his coauthors imagined a number of spaces and times colliding. From the present in Hanoi and Brussels to the past in Auschwitz and back again to the present in Berlin, the communards implicated Germany in this fantastic time-space travel as playing a central role in the continued production of bare life in the twentieth century. No longer Jews, but Asians and Africans were now the people out of whom bare life was manufactured and, as with the Holocaust, Germany had blood on its hands. The prosecution's attempt to pathologize the communards illuminated Teufel's own place within this historical map of bare and full life. "If our anti-authoritarian position," Teufel asked, "is a characteristic of a constitutionally determined abnormality, are authoritarian behavior and National Socialism then a consequence of the healthy normality of the Germanic race?" (*KM*, n.p.). Implicit in Teufel's question was his own willed exclusion from a tradition of German normality that was steeped in racism and predicated on the biopoliticization of German bodies at the expense of other undesirable bodies (*HS*, 171).

Teufel was not alone when he interpolated German history into the fantastic dimensions of his commune's Vietnam happening. In fact, while Teufel was sitting in jail awaiting trial, his cohorts foreshadowed his declaration of victimhood with their own imagined identification with bare life. In a protest pamphlet distributed roughly two weeks before the hearing, fellow communards authored and distributed their first brochure, a twenty-three-page collection of "authoritative writings and miscellanea" intended to illustrate how the state and the mass media inflated them into "monsters, subhumans, pure evil, eradicable people, detriments to humanity, unworthy life" (*JK*, 160). Featured prominently on the front page was the now-iconic photograph of seven naked communards and a child leaning with their hands against a wall. The accompanying caption read, "Naked [*kahle*] Maoists against a bare [*kahlen*] wall." According to Rudi

Dutschke, a former communard cohort and the figurehead of West Germany's student movement, the image was an unmistakable allusion to the Nazi concentration camp. "The photo of the naked commune members," he explained on July 10, 1967, "appears to me to . . . reproduce . . . the gas chamber milieu of the Third Reich. Behind this exhibitionism hides helplessness, fear, and horror. The commune members conceive themselves as the oppressed and expelled people of this society."[68] In light of Dutschke's analysis, Adorno's indictment from a month earlier—"The students have taken up a bit of the role of the Jews"—was remarkably prescient. Posing as if they were subject to a police raid and strip search, the communards also framed their own bodies as if to say that they were the heirs to bare life in post-fascist Germany. In this respect, the homonym in the caption (*kahl*) evoked both the synchronic as well as the diachronic dimensions of bare life. The bestialization of man was, the communards inferred, as much an essential element for qualifying full life in fascist Germany as it was in a post-fascist Germany that called itself a democracy.

Psychoanalytic assessments of this legendary photograph contend that the communards unconsciously identified themselves with the victims of their Nazi parents.[69] A Freudian heuristic that insists on an unconscious reactionary Oedipal conflict fails to mine, however, the overt critical dimensions of the photograph. Furthermore, it dismisses altogether the photograph's causal link to the preceding handbills. Similarly, Negt and Kluge's definition of oppositional fantasy as that realm of social consciousness that refutes the dictates of reality falls short of explaining the consequences of a fantasy that splits itself into one part text and one part image (*GE,* 512).[70] Even Vostell's semiotic square cannot adequately explain the relationship between the string of times and places articulated in the handbills and the photograph. The disjuncture between defiant visual fantasies of a modern-day Auschwitz and the literary fantasies of simulating napalm bombings in Brussels and Berlin was a function of the communards' need not to demarcate but rather to articulate together different times and spaces. Both Teufel and his fellow communards made this clear in their fantastic amalgam of word *and* image. This composite insisted that Germany did belong to their subversive fantasies of Vietnam, or more precisely, that the crimes against humanity committed in Vietnam did run to the core of Germany's Nazi past. Admittedly, this articulation was not entirely unique. In a 1967 letter to Adorno, Marcuse aptly insisted that the fact that "the concentration camps, murders, and tortures take place outside of metropolises (and usually left to the henchmen of other nations) changes nothing of its essence" (*FSS*, 262; *HS*, 180). The war in Southeast Asia signaled a new global relations of the production of bare life. The maintenance of full life in the West was now predicated on outsourcing the manufacture of bare life to the Third World. The communards' all-consuming fantasy of a transhistorical network of bare life was, in many respects, a precursor to Agamben's own transhistorical philosophy. Nevertheless, by inferring a causal relationship between Auschwitz and Vietnam as well as an equivalency between Jewish victims of the Holocaust, Vietcong, and themselves, the communards collapsed into a single point both the visible and invisible perimeters of reality that Vostell had so carefully dissociated in Ulm. The contradictories space/non-space and time/non-time imploded in the communards' happening entirely. In their imagination the camp and the city were synonymous and modern time reigned supreme over its revolutionary antipode, fragmented time. For all the communards' talk about the creation of another and better future by collectively imagining the past against the grain, their happening did not so much fail to arrive at the historical materialist position in Vostell's happening as it demolished the very structural preconditions necessary for this dialectic.[71] As much as the sarcasm in the flyers scoffed at the idea that Brussels and Berlin could never become Hanoi, the photograph nevertheless announced that twenty years after the liberation of Auschwitz the camp had migrated back into the German metropolis. Accordingly, propane gas was hardly necessary to re-create "that crackling Vietnam feeling" of being burned alive. According to the commune's fantasy, being the unworthy life that is worthy of eradication was a transhistorical German tradition once reserved for Jews and now bestowed upon the long-haired and bare dissidents of the state.

Failure compromised both Vostell's and the commune's happenings. These failures were, however, remarkably productive in their own right. If failure for Vostell arose from the near-impossible task of bringing others to imagine themselves vis-à-vis the invisible non-spaces and non-times that constituted their collective place within the postwar present, then the communards compounded this challenge by incorporating into this reality the very real hall of mirrors that impinged on everyday experience in the sixties like never before. Entirely absent from Vostell's happening, the communards' unconscious acknowledgment of their place within the society of the spectacle—Guy Debord's 1967 designation for the transformation of direct lived experience into mere representation—illuminated how the social imagination had shifted toward total convergence.

Geographic distance was reduced to spectacular separation.[72] Irreversible time, history, and memory became paralyzed. In their place, the spectacle advanced "false memor[ies] of the unmemorable," mirages of linear time that obfuscated the dominant order of cyclical time of the commodified image.[73] As the medial divide between the communards' handbills and self-portrait illustrates, the convergences at work in their fantasy of bare life were not a purely photographic phenomenon. This spectacularization of bare life was a function of the transformation under late capitalism of every imaginative faculty, be it linguistic or visual, whereby the latent and invisible categories of non-space and non-time were taken to be manifest attributes of everyday experience. This spectacular inversion of reality into unreality, truth into falsehood, life into non-life is remarkably similar to Marcuse's 1964 diagnosis of one-dimensional society in which the belief in technical progress canceled the gap between the imagination and reason. Like Debord, too, Marcuse insisted that this absolute reification of fantasy was, in theory, breakable. Call it the society of the spectacle or one-dimensional society, the collapse of time and space contains within it potentialities to rematerialize the dialectic and therewith the space of revolutionary fantasy. For Debord this meant embracing an insurrectional style steeped in plagiarism, and for Marcuse it meant practicing civil disobedience. Indeed, the communards embraced both of these tactics in the disparate parts of their amorphous happening. And yet the entire expanse of their vision ended up not breaking apart but rather affirming the compression of times and places already so prevalent in the everyday spectacles on German television and in German newspapers. Because of its fundamental incursion into the patterns and structures of everyday life, the happening proved to be an ideal means for the communards to translate their revolutionary theory into a potentially transformative practice.

The communards' desired social transformation never materialized. The trials against Teufel and Langhans took a toll on Kommune 1 and its investment in the happening as a symbolic form. In the wake of the "Moabit soap opera," the cohesiveness of the commune began to crumble. For its most radical member, Dieter Kunzelmann, the only way to salvage the commune's desire to realize political praxis was through physical violence. His involvement in the attempted bombing of the West Berlin synagogue on November 9, 1969, was in this respect a logical upshot of the commune's original expropriation of Jewish suffering in the name of conflating German and Vietnamese suffering. Others like Teufel and Langhans resettled in Munich, where they established new communes that, at least in the mind of Kunzelmann, either deluded themselves by embracing undergound cultures or only halfheartedly flirted with the promise of material violence.[74] In comparison with the communards, Vostell's happenings were certainly more complex and their execution exceedingly obscure. Yet Vostell could not subsume under the happening his intentions to both uncover the truths of bare life and explain the spectacular logic of the mass mediation of brutal images. Within the decade after the sudden rise and fall of the West German student movement, his own allegiance to the happening practically vanished. As for his original problem of visualizing the politicization of bare life, neither an audience's imagination (as ideally activated in a happening) nor representation (à la a pop aesthetic) proved capable of reversing the collapse of the dialectic. While the spectacle professed to divulge the political unconsciousness of modern life, it actually dissimulated—much like Agamben's trans-historicizing philosophy—the interlocking distinctions between past, present, and new future possibilities so crucial for historical materialism. In hindsight, Adorno's bizarre dream of mass executions with an automated guillotine was prescient in terms not only of its content but also of its form. Only in that entirely involuntary world of preposterous images devoid of any claim to rational experience—the dream—might it have been possible to evoke what the conscious subject otherwise could not succeed at putting into language, capturing on camera, or even choreographing in the street.[75] Given the fundamental assimilation of fantasy into reality that emerged in the West German sixties, reclaiming the negativity necessary for reanimating the dialectic became the post-fascist avant-garde's primary hurdle to defusing the dominion of modern and postmodern time. Without this negativity, evoking the abominations of the fascist past would show little promise of ever inducing a redemptive future beyond the interminable present of the spectacle.

Still, what is nazism if not also the worst moment in the history
of technology?
—Avital Ronell, *The Telephone Book: Technology, Schizophrenia,
Electric Speech*

Resistance begins with the capacity for silence.
—Rolf Dieter Brinkmann, *Der Film in Worten: Prosa, Erzählungen, Essays, Hörspiele, Fotos, Collagen 1965–1974*

It is no longer possible to tell a story, but the form of the novel
requires narration.
—Theodor Adorno, *Notes to Literature*

5. Technologies of Fascism and the
Poetics of Silence and Light

Women on the Line

Roughly three years after renouncing his prior successes as a new realist novelist and underground pop poet, writer Rolf Dieter Brinkmann
began making home audio recordings using equipment furnished by the
Westdeutschen Rundfunk (West German Broadcasting Service). Among
the 657 minutes of recorded material he made from October to December
1973, a nineteen-minute string of over forty calls made on his rotary telephone stands out. In addition to the whirring of the dial on his phone, the
busy signals, and the ringing on the line, Brinkmann's recording captures
a myriad of disembodied voices. Some were live, some prerecorded, but almost all—as Brinkmann whispered into the microphone midway through
his audio experiment—belonged to women:

"This number is no longer in service."
"Herzberg residence."
"Tokyo 324.06, Zurich 335.9, Milan 115.36 . . . "
"At the next tone the time is twenty hours nineteen minutes and ten
seconds."
". . . amburg. Via Dusburg-Essen main train station: Bochum Dort-
mund Münster . . . "
"Add the cubes of meat with dried mushrooms to the sauce."

Women's voices everywhere. Women's voices everywhere.
"The Cinema, phone number 218182, is showing *Non-Stop Sex Show.*
Starting times at 10 A.M., 12 P.M. except Sundays . . . "
"Hello. Hello? Heello? Hey! Heelllooo? Heellllooooo?"
"Solters residence. Hello. Hello?"
"This number is no longer in service."[1]

Hardly a prank caller, Brinkmann used his telephone like a radar, bouncing phatic signals off of various receivers in order to hear who was on the line. And then he promptly hung up, only to dial yet another number. Regardless of whether he called a disconnected or wrong number, a private residence or city office, or an automated phone line with stock exchange information or movie times, the voice on the line was that of a woman. Brinkmann's sole enunciation—*Women's voices everywhere. Women's voices everywhere*—leaves little doubt of his contempt for the ubiquity of women on the line. The acoustic space blown open by telephony had become the exclusive province of the feminine. Brinkmann's discovery was nothing new. Women operators have "manned" switchboards and answered calls since the dawn of mass telecommunications. This gendered labor was hardly coincidental, Avital Ronell notes. With "softer voices, more patience, and nimble fingers," women afforded the medium faster connectivity and, more importantly, maternalized the message and elevated it to the status of superego.[2] The telephone cord doubled as an umbilical cord insofar as it reeled the receiver back into the other, obligating him to fulfill the incoming call's "hearing assignment." In other words, "a woman's voice is perfectly suited to perform phallic penetration," to captivate the caller and reel him back in to the symbolic system of reality (*TB*, 28, 201–2). The ontology of the telephone does not stop with gender matters, however. Telephony is as historically monumental as it is fundamentally political, for its genderized voice comprises but a fraction of the ways in which technology in general, and its synecdoches, signed a deadly pact with National Socialism, a pact that still haunts the post-fascist present. Telephone lines are "never wholly spliced off from the barbed wires circumscribing the space of devastation," Ronell writes, returning to the camp (*TB*, 6–7). The long-distance call always already enables a deadly violence on the part of the caller.

It would be hasty at this point to map the trouble with telephony onto Brinkmann's telephone recordings. In fact, Brinkmann's experiment departs from Ronell's own primary texts in profound ways. Unlike Ronell's prime suspect (Martin Heidegger, who in 1933 answered a telephone call that resulted in his affiliation with Hitler's regime), Brinkmann placed each of those forty-some calls himself. No one ever called him. In effect, Brinkmann ventriloquized the female caller who haunts every phone call, by dialing up people and answering machines and obligating them to answer his call. Yet unlike the call to Heidegger made in 1933 that implicated his philosophy in the criminal ideology of fascism, Brinkmann's calls conveyed nothing other than structural relations inherent in the medium itself. Without saying a word, he placed the call only long enough to ascertain who or what was on the line and then promptly hung up. If there was any violence at work in his recorded experiment, then it was a structural violence underlying all telephonic communication. The violence in Brinkmann's calls was thus committed in the name of both an epistemological and ontological inquiry into the nature of telephony and the effects of interfacing with communication technologies. Placing a telephone call feminizes, Brinkmann suggests, because everyone who and everything that answers the call possesses a woman's voice. In this respect, his recording infers an indistinguishability between a living woman and the answering machine. If live telephony and the automated operator have become synonymous, Brinkmann refrains here from elucidating how, why, or when modern communication technologies have called the surety of a humanist ontology in question. Indeed, Brinkmann's recording raises more questions than it answers. Above all, it begs the question whether anything can be done to counter the telephone's ability to emasculate and dehumanize. Certain, however, is the sliver of a critical space that Brinkmann opened with a telephone and a tape recorder.

According to American Beat writer William Burroughs, who wielded much influence on Brinkmann's aesthetics of the seventies, the tape recorder has the potential not just to critique but also to alter perception and experience. Much more than just a means for recording and playing back sounds, the tape recorder can "bring you a liberation from old association locks" by dubbing over, mixing up, and playing out of context the normative soundtracks that permanently accompany everyday experience. Astute listeners familiar with Burroughs's guidelines will notice in Brinkmann's telephone recording how it lives up to Burroughs's prescription for capturing an audio "cut up on tape."[3] In opposition to the emancipatory possibilities of the tape recorder stood "control machines" like the television, commercial mass media that Burroughs saw as being full of "the ugliest stupidest most vulgar and degraded" of sounds ("IG,"

215). In order to defuse their power, the renegade recorder must "isolate and cut association lines of the control machine," which is precisely what Brinkmann did ("IG," 217). Yet Brinkmann's recording is neither arbitrary nor extemporaneous in its construction and execution. At both the beginning and ending of the track, Brinkmann dialed rapidly, as if to generate random numbers without any forethought. Toward the middle of the recording, the sound of the winding and uncoiling dial slows, suggesting a more careful approach, as if he concentrated on dialing specific numbers chosen in advance. Unlike the incomplete calls at the beginning and end of the recording, those dialed toward the middle all produced prerecorded messages from automated phone lines. In addition to hearing the invisible script underlying his sequence of calls, the most careful of listeners will discern how Brinkmann not only hung up the phone abruptly but also stopped the recording intermittently, as if to splice each phone call together as closely as possible. In accordance with Burroughs's recommendations, Brinkmann also altered the recording speed in the final minutes to give the impression that the dialing and ringing accelerated into a reckless frenzy. All these clues suggest that Brinkmann conceptualized his experiment as a coherent whole, a carefully planned musical composition with an identifiable overture, climax, and finale. Unlike Burroughs's call for chance, exposing the ontology of mass media necessitated the most methodological of approaches for Brinkmann.

Unmasking the nature of one mass medium (like the telephone) and its address to a single sensory organ (like the ear) reveals just how far the media intrude into every other modality of sensory perception. Burroughs actually intended his instructions for renegade audio recording as a means of regaining a purchase on visual experience. "What we see," he began his tutorial, "is largely determined to a large extent by what we hear" ("IG," 205). In other words, tape recorders are tools for undoing the spectacles in movie theaters and on television that invariably enforce superficial ways of visualizing the world without ever really seeing it. According to Ronell, this media-induced blindness is a hallmark of telephony. In contradistinction to Marshall McLuhan, who labeled the phone cold because of the absence of the visual and hence the need for high participation on the part of the listener, she attributes this denigration of sight to a telephonic way of seeing the world from a distance.[4] Telephony arrests seeing, perturbs it, reduces it to a more rudimentary form of vision entirely incapable of making sense of what the eye registers. In addition to indicting philosophers-who-telephone like Heidegger and Maurice Blanchot who indulged in this visual impairment, Ronell turns to Sigmund Freud, the champion of the talking cure.[5] Visual apprehension, Freud remarked in his proceedings on hysterical blindness, shuts down when the voice reprimands it for scopic transgressions like peeping. Seen from this vantage point, the telephone has elevated the debilitating Oedipal effects of the (maternal) voice to a structural principle. While Burroughs and Ronell together lend considerable credence to an inverse relationship between the technical transmission of sound and the shrinking human ability to see, Brinkmann's telephone recording says little, if anything, about vision or the image world.

Tracing Brinkmann's audio experiment from late 1973 backward to his incomplete second novel—a time span of only a few months from when he abandoned the 156-page manuscript—fills in this omission. In fact, Brinkmann's posthumously published novel fragment, *SCHNITTE* (*Cuts*), not only attests to the centrality of this coupling—hearing and seeing—in his battle against the mass-mediated world of the seventies; his novel also locates a solution for seeing again in acoustics, that sensory dimension that he discovered as having become entirely the province of disembodied women's voices. If telephony emblematized the aural means through which technology covertly interpellated, controlled, and blinded subjects, then silence marked the possibility of unfettered seeing, acting, and experiencing. In this respect, Brinkmann's avant-garde program from the seventies could not be any more different than his earlier adoration of the cinematographic eye as delineated in chapter 3; once thought to be a means to fortify the self from problems of the past, technology became the problem itself. Apropos his newfound regard for the absence of recorded sound and vision, Brinkmann explained in a programmatic essay from 1974 that "silence [*Stille*] is not saying nothing [*Schweigen*]." Instead, silence corresponds to fleeting instants of time, entirely devoid of words, that unwilling media consumers create for themselves. Silence is a "fantastic moment [*Augenblick*]" when reality is not only unmasked as a deceptive construction of mass media but also taken off-line temporarily.[6] In the context of making a phone call, silence meant for Brinkmann avoiding the medium altogether. "Telephone conversations obviously serve sheer business just as much as they do the transmission of unresolved problems," he informed his wife in a letter from October 1972.[7] Instead of phoning, Brinkmann wrote letters, pasted together autobiographical tracts, hammered out radio plays, and composed essays and reviews, all while conceptualizing, framing, and executing in part his plans for *SCHNITTE*. Silence was entirely a function of writing. Brinkmann was thoroughly disenchanted with the West German institution of literature's delusional investment in conveying realistic narratives, and according to him, the novel had but one remaining function in a world saturated by electronic media; literature in late 1973 was only valid in terms of its ability to afford writers the chance to wage war against the omnipresent effects of the mass media.[8] Accordingly, Brinkmann's novel shows what cannot be seen amidst the blinding noise of everyday life. *SCHNITTE* thus stages a space of silence. Therein it exhibits the media's spectacles as having immediate effects on the viewers and readers, and it unveils those effects as both violent and lethal. As with his telephone recording, *SCHNITTE* identifies woman as playing a primary role in the mass media's phallic penetration of the subject, a heroic subject, in fact, whom the novel can only evoke as being male, heterosexual, and defiant. And just like Ronell's deconstruction of the telephone, *SCHNITTE* casts the terror in all media as a temporal phenomenon rooted in National Socialism and responsible for the paralysis of modern irreversible time. Brinkmann's articulation of the media with fascism was, however, not entirely new for West Germany. Only five years earlier, the student movement had identified the mass media as the single most dangerous threat to West German democracy after fascism.

Manipulation Theories circa 1968

The detrimental effects of the mass media were never a chief intellectual or practical concern among West Germany's rebellious students until West Berlin police officer Karl-Heinz Kurras shot point-blank one-time student protestor Benno Ohnesorg on June 2, 1967. While the political organ SDS (Socialist German Students' Federation) did respond to the infamous police raid on the editorial offices of *Der Spiegel* on October 26, 1962, the issue at hand was not the abuses of the media but rather the freedom of the press from state violence and censorship.[9] The debates around the imminent emergency laws, including the SDS-organized symposium "Democracy Before the Emergency" held in May 1965, helped sustain student interest in the sanctity of Article 5 of the Basic Law forbidding the censorship of the press. However, prior to June 1967, the central organ of the SDS, the journal *neue kritik,* hardly paid attention to the possible consequences of mogul Axel Springer's media empire.[10] This is not to say that a discussion of Springer's questionable business ethics was of no concern at all in the Federal Republic. In an article published in early 1965, the newsmagazine *Der Spiegel* was one of the first major media outlets to lay bare Springer's monopoly. Other far more oppositional publications like *Sozialistische Politik* and *Marxistische Blätter*, which were unaffiliated with the SDS, followed suit in the ensuing year.[11] Students were certainly exposed to this burgeoning criticism. Writer Reinhard Lettau ensured this assertion in a speech titled "On the Servility of the Press," which he delivered on April 19, 1967, at a Vietnam teach-in in West Berlin's Free University.[12] But only after the fateful street riot on the night of June 2, 1967, did students experience their disenfranchisement from the means of self-representation through the mass media.

At the heart of the SDS's newfound campaign against the Springer media empire lay its conviction of the media's ability to manipulate public opinion. Manipulation was, however, not a new idea in the discourse on media in the Federal Republic of Germany. In his widely influential post-doctoral thesis, *The Structural Transformation of the Public Sphere* from 1962, Jürgen Habermas contended that as a result of the commercialization of the press at the end of the liberal era circa 1870, the mass media betrayed the interests of a public sphere concerned with exposing political domination. Instead, the mass media re-circuited the public sphere in order to manufacture an ideological consensus in the name of consumption and profit. Manipulation, as Habermas defined it, is "the socio-psychologically calculated offers that appeal to unconscious inclinations and call forth predictable reactions without on the other hand placing any obligation whatever on the very persons who in this fashion secure plebiscitary agreement."[13] Although Habermas was not the first to advance the idea of the psychosocial manipulation of the media—credit is due in large part to Max Horkheimer and Theodor Adorno—he remained, in spite of his early fall from grace with the SDS, a vocal custodian in the campaign against media manipulation.[14] Once the student opposition experienced firsthand the ramifications of their exclusion from the means of mass communication, Habermas's Freudian-Marxist language on media manipulation became ubiquitous.

By the fall of 1967, expropriating Springer became a central theme within the SDS and among many other kindred student organizations like the Republican Club, Liberal Student League of Germany, and the Social Democratic University Union. Conferences, university seminars, and student periodicals all focused attention on the problem of media monopolies and manipulation. In some cases the problem with the mass media rose in status to become the bête noire of the entire extra-parliamentary opposition. In preparation for a "Springer Hearing" planned for February 1968, to which Habermas was invited, student activist Peter Schneider authored a manifesto in October 1967 maintaining that Springer's *Bild-Zeitung* manipulated the material needs of its readers by concealing those class differences that, if exposed, would destabilize capitalism's class hierarchy.[15] Schneider defined the power of the *Bild-Zeitung* primarily in terms of its ability to mobilize working-class opinion by exciting and thereby harnessing the emotions of its readers in order to fortify the interests of a ruling economic class. Accordingly, the newspaper manipulated not by repressing the material needs of the masses, but rather by carefully displacing them at just the right moment so that their articulation did not threaten the status quo. In other words, the Springer press intentionally excited its readership when it best suited Springer. In addition, the newspaper orchestrated the fulfillment of class needs only within the mind of the individual reader. The possibility of belonging to a constituency and asserting class interests in concert was perpetually forestalled. The *Bild-Zeitung* also manipulated readers' libidinal investments by diluting the specificity of the class struggle that shaped the readers' immediate world into a universal struggle of good versus bad, strong versus weak, male versus female. Schneider never fully explicated the mechanics of media manipulation. Instead, he emphasized the importance of acknowledging its effects and forming a solidarity between students and the working class for an effective battle against Springer.

By the time the battle against Springer reached its apex in the spring and summer of 1968, the SDS's analysis of manipulation had reached new levels of sophistication. In an article published immediately after the assassination attempt on Dutschke, Heiner Schäfer called upon Herbert Marcuse's idea of the one-dimensional society as well as Springer's own marketing directives in order to advance his own Freudian reading that the *Bild-Zeitung* stunted the psychic maturation of individuals. "One of the essential prerequisites for the development of a strong ego," he explained, "is the establishment of an identity in concert with other people with whom libidinal attachments can be made. Identification with the *Bild-Zeitung* and with those persons who appear in its pages do not allow for satisfying cathexis. It is merely superficial and labile."[16] The newspaper intervened in healthy processes of identification by establishing itself as an authoritative proxy that usurped the familial ego ideal. Before the ego had a chance to constitute itself as an autonomous subject in relation to others, Springer's newspaper regularly inserted itself into the individual's mental life as the superego that instantiated acceptable and unacceptable modes of social behavior. Unlike Schneider, who posited a simple communicative model based on the idea that every manipulated input brings about a commensurate output, Schäfer contended that the genesis of mass rage against the student movement resulted from the transient nature of any libidinal binding to a commercial good. "Constant excitation without the possibility for satisfaction releases instinctual energies that can prove to be destructive. . . . Released aggressions could only be directed at people who do not conform to the demands of the superego of the *Bild-Zeitung*, those who are the enemy of the system."[17] What separates Schäfer's from Schneider's idea of manipulation was the former's understanding of the origins of media effects. While Schneider merely emphasized the power of maligned content over class consciousness, Schäfer traced the problem back to a pandemic psychological pathology brought about by the commercial replacement of the familial authoritative personality under late capitalism. In this respect, Schäfer's analysis was in large part a homage to the various psychoanalytic explanations of fascism developed by such luminaries as Theodor Adorno, Wilhelm Reich, and Erich Fromm.

Lodged somewhere between Marx and Freud, the reigning theories of media manipulation in the student movement were not without their shortcomings. For one, they left the opposition impotent. Sociologist Oskar Negt sympathized with the plight of the students in an interview with *Die Zeit* from April 26, 1968, exclaiming that they lacked access to mass media capable of broadcasting their message. "Their public sphere," he elucidated, "is that of the street, open urban spaces, lecture halls, churches, everywhere where a large number of people is within reach."[18] This flight from the mass media to more immediate forms of communication implied that with the decisive means of production in the hands of the enemy, alternative venues were ineffectual from the start.[19] According to Hans Magnus Enzensberger's 1970 essay on the media, Negt skirted the deeper problem of manipulation theories, insofar as he cast students as victims with little resolve. For Enzensberger, the opposition's focus on attacking existing property relations—Springer's media monopoly—refused to acknowledge its unrealistic insistence on the possibility of a pure, unmanipulated truth, just as it refused to entertain the manipulative practices in its own messages and to envision how the media should function after the expropriation of Springer. More importantly, the New Left never considered drafting its own Marxist strategy for the media. Enzensberger maintained that because the use of media was inherently and unavoidably manipulative, a revolutionary plan for the mass media, one that rested on the conviction that "new media are egalitarian in structure," would effectively transform every manipulated individual into a potential manipulator.[20] Far from suggesting a battle between countless amateur and professional journalists, Enzensberger asserted that an effective realignment of the media's potential power lay in the reintroduction of individuals to regional communities in which the local use of amateur media existed as a collective concern.

Enzensberger charged the student movement with overemphasizing the legacies of Horkheimer and Adorno at the price of obscuring the revelations in Walter Benjamin's "Work of Art" essay. This was, however, not the only deficiency among the students' theoretical preoccupation with the psychology of manipulation. They never addressed contemporary claims that the media exerted violence on the consumer. Accounts like Schneider's invoked the idea of violence in order to underscore the severity of the press's intrusions in the mental life of its readers; according to this approach, manipulation was not especially violent.[21] For Habermas, manipulation involved a hegemonic exchange that transpired on both a material and psychological level. Enzensberger contended that manipulation simply referred to the "technical encroachment in a given material with a particular goal in mind."[22] Marxist scholar Wolfgang Fritz Haug explicitly defined the term as the "non-terrorist control of the consciousness and behavior of the masses through linguistic and aesthetic means."[23] And Schäfer implied that manipulation itself was not violent even though its side effects were. In contrast to these theoretical disputations, a great deal of spontaneous dialogue about manipulation immediately after the shootings of Ohnesorg and Dutschke insisted that the media were indeed violent. Student protesters chanted on the evening of the May 1968 Easter riots: "Axel Cäsar Springer! He shot, too!!" and "Bild shot too!" SDS member Hartmut Barsnick exclaimed following the clashes between students and police on April 11 in Mainz: "A tendentious headline in the Bild-Zeitung is more violent than throwing a rock at the head of a police officer."[24] In similar fashion, Berlin Bishop Scharf asserted the day after the Dutschke shooting that "murder begins with evil words about fellow human beings. . . . A denunciatory evil word about another is already an assault on his life."[25] SDS spokesman Hans-Jürgen Krahl claimed a month later in a speech against the impending emergency laws: "violence, that is the incitement to hatred and violence against the German population by the Bild-Zeitung."[26] Knut Nevermann, chairman of the Student

Council at West Berlin's Free University, summarized the upshot of this diffuse, undertheorized conviction of media violence as an invitation to students to exercise their own counter-violence:

> We had no other choice. We had no means of counter-manipulation. We had no counter-means of communication. We had to make clear to the rest of the world that the existing means of manipulation had to be destroyed for the organized use of violence to come to an end. For this reason we had to resort to counter-violence. . . . Our future actions will not depart from this principle. We will, however, not wield violence against people.[27]

The student opposition's legitimization of violence against objects but not against other human beings certainly reflected its Marxist conviction in the unequal distribution of the means of production. It also attested to the students' belief in their ability to differentiate their progressive brand of violence from the reactionary violence of media monopolies and the state.[28]

The Novel *SCHNITTE* and the Phantasmic Present

There exist significant points of contact between the varying conceptions of media effects in and around the student movement and the aesthetic-political program that Brinkmann conceived in the wake of the failed revolts. Above all, they both concurred that the mass media exerted power over media consumers and robbed them of their agency. Furthermore, they regarded the media, albeit using distinctly divergent explanations, as inherently violent. Consequently, they insisted that the inequitable distribution of the means to broadcast warranted the adoption of counter-violence. Just as students regarded "Springer journalism [as] pogrom journalism," Brinkmann, too, pinpointed the roots of media effects in the technological reanimation of the German past in the present.[29] Opposing the power of the media was for both camps a matter of staving off the return of fascism. In spite of these similarities, *SCHNITTE* rests on a markedly different understanding of media effects, one neither romanced by street violence nor intent on establishing alternative media outlets like West Berlin's unprecedented *die tageszeitung*.[30] Unlike the emphases of Habermas, Schneider, and Schäfer on the cognitive impact of the media, *SCHNITTE* insists that the media bombard the mind *and* the body. The threat of fascism redux in the seventies was thus not as the students would have it, namely the proliferation of a

reactionary ideology or a collectively metastasized pathology. Far from po-
larizing society into willing executioners and pitiless victims, *SCHNITTE*
identifies all of Western civilization as the object of media violence. For
the novel's nameless protagonist, whose resemblance to Brinkmann be-
stows the book with an irrefutable autobiographical character, this violence is, however, entirely that of the modern-day concentration camp. The
gamut of media—from printed word to electric speech to televisual spectacle—transformed the world of mass-mediated culture into an inescapable realm where the politicization of biological life continued to transpire
well after the Holocaust. In effect, the camps were never really liberated
in 1945. The media subsumed them to engulf the whole of modern life.

Following the publication of his scandalous first novel, *Keiner weiß
mehr* (*No One Knows More*) from 1968 along with a string of pop poetry
collections and translations of American underground texts into German, Brinkmann rescinded his ties to the literary establishment. In spite
of this self-imposed isolation, writing remained a staple of his everyday
life, and his plan for a follow-up to his wildly successful first novel consumed his diary-like sketchbooks. An early draft for the novel's opening
from October 1971 cast its crux as a quest for self-orientation. "Tattered
and yanked around and pretty shaken up after 31 years I found myself
again,and that was in the present,stuttering somewhat and babbling and
still clumsy, but healthy and all right and standing on my own feet."[31] His
subsequent attempts foreshadowed crucial themes of querying the self,
contempt for a hopeless world, and the dissolution of the body.[32] Gradu-
ally, these false starts gave way to more conceptual ruminations on what
the novel should be: ": about the novel,My novel,as I imagine it:as a kind
of development novel [*Entwicklungsroman*],with trips,places,people,situa-
tions,a delirium,jumbled up scenes from 1940 to 1970" (*EP,* 250). A quasi-
autobiographical genre written in the first person, the developmental novel
Brinkmann envisioned would impose upon the chaotic world not only a
narrative teleology, but also a self-reflective subject capable of mastering
his environment.[33] Later in his journals, Brinkmann planned on shaping
the novel around a figure who "(:go[es] out into the world, into the elec-
trified, controlled diurnal and nocturnal world laid out like an artificial
labyrinth by persistent unwavering impulses!)" (*EP,* 285). This protagonist
was to begin as a character without a coherent sense of self. "I are many
and thus I went through the many I's and noticed how devastated this
place is." In keeping with the heroic trajectory of the development novel,
Brinkmann's protagonist would, by novel's end, remedy the shattering of

his self and arrive at a "self-conscious clarity before things, people, among things,people,places" (*EP,* 281). In spite of his exhaustive plans and mountains of preliminary sketches, Brinkmann's second novel never came to fruition within his lifetime. Even in the later planning phases, he began to doubt the feasibility of writing such a novel in the tradition of Goethe's *Wilhelm Meister's Apprenticeship* or even Karl Philip Moritz's more ambivalent *Anton Reiser.* Full of despair, he wrote in early November 1971, "stuck actually in the middle of approaches to the novel, without characters, without a beginning, am hanging in mid air, too many pieces that I cannot fit together, too many plans and incursions/(but no person! 'I' cracks)" (*EP,* 205). A year later, Brinkmann reached an impasse. Convinced that he could not make a coherent whole out of the countless fragments compiled over the last two years, he considered incinerating everything (*RB,* 385). Brinkmann's inability to develop the novel's culmination—the constitution of a unified subject—did not end in defeatism or despair. Although he waffled later on whether the development novel was still viable, he nevertheless continued with his intention of writing such a novel.[34]

There exists to date no critical consensus about the literary status of *SCHNITTE.* Brinkmann's widow first established in 1987 the existence of a folder titled "SCHNITTE" in her husband's estate and called it a diary (*EP,* 412). In her editorial notes to *SCHNITTE* published a year later, she redesignated *SCHNITTE,* using ample supporting evidence, as the second collage novel he had intended to write all along. In her 1989 monograph on Brinkmann's entire literary oeuvre, however, Sibylle Späth shed doubt that *SCHNITTE* represented the planned novel. Merely a condensed version of his two preceding diaries, *SCHNITTE* only stood out insofar as it represented the highest form of the author's imbrication of collage with text.[35] Similarly, Thomas Gross categorized *SCHNITTE* as the subordinate third in Brinkmann's triumvirate of collaged texts from the seventies, especially since it recycled so much of the author's earlier work.[36] Späth's and Gross's insistence on the work's derivative character is not unfounded. Repeated allusions in *SCHNITTE* to Brinkmann's childhood home of Vechta, his travels in Rome (October 1972 to January 1973), and mentions of his wife Maleen and his disabled son Robert, as well as photographs of himself, suggest that *SCHNITTE* is more autobiographical than a fictional novel would allow. Taking Brinkmann's executrix at her word, Michael Strauch in 1998 rolled back these suspicions of the work's pure autobiographical character by establishing its status as a novel philologically.[37] Intent on elucidating the work's genesis, intertextuality, construction, and major themes, Strauch pulled apart and catalogued its messy mass of words and images for close inspection. According to Strauch, reading the novel boiled down to deciphering its semiotics, a task heedful of both sign and technique. Yet what makes *SCHNITTE* a novel escaped Strauch's analysis entirely in spite of his initial assertions. Still unresolved is the question of why Brinkmann was so wedded to writing a development novel in the first place. Why be beholden to a genre that the young Georg Lukács had exposed almost six decades earlier as a paramount expression of modern alienation, especially when it was the alienated condition that Brinkmann sought to dispel? A perfect inversion of Lukács' position in *Theory of the Novel*, Brinkmann's adherence to the development novel was, in fact, the logical consequence of his diagnosis of the world around him. Whereas Lukács lamented the modern novel's escapist turn inward to the consciousness, Brinkmann saw his novel as the means by which to ward off what Enzensberger early on called the mass media's consciousness industry.[38] The subjective illusions of the modern novel had become collective reality in the postmodern society of the spectacle. Lukács' golden age had rematerialized as hell on earth and only the novel, with its drive to create a compensatory sense of wholeness, could embrace the "unrestricted, uninterrupted flow of time."[39] *SCHNITTE* does not tell a story per se but rather embodies its deployment as a linguistic-visual means by which to differentiate modern time following its paralysis by the mass media.[40]

From the outset of *SCHNITTE,* it is apparent that the piles of words and images are an inventory of media signals that besiege the protagonist. The novel's first chapter, "Control," begins much like Brinkmann's earlier false starts for the novel: ":came upon an intersection."[41] This opening scenario of a nameless man, who rarely invokes the first-person singular pronoun and who wanders through Rome, jumps randomly from each of the typewritten snippets arranged around eleven collage images (see fig. 19). Text and image together suggest that the urban landscape the figure negotiates—the focal point of the two-page layout—is comprised of torn images of female bodies, idyllic natural landscapes, construction sites, and technology. In contrast to the idyllic postcard of an Italian urban intersection, the collage includes in the lower right-hand corner a photograph of a dingy small town with two silhouettes, a foreshadowing of dystopias yet to come. Called a "phantom present" by the protagonist, this urban reality is said to feel like a hallucination in which "every minute ugly image from the past" resurfaces in the present (*S,* 8). Early on the narrative voice clarifies that this enfolding of the past into the present is largely attributable to the

Figure 19

Pages 6–7 of *SCHNITTE*, by Rolf Dieter Brinkmann, 1988.

empire of the cinematic imagination; the unreal present is the product of tattered and abandoned sets from old Hollywood films lingering in everyone's consciousness. Referring to those invisible few in control of this unreality, the protagonist exclaims "they were everywhere shooting the dirtiest film of all time according to a lost screenplay" (*S*, 8, 13; see fig. 20). The protagonist indicts not just the image world but also the building blocks of all communication, language. In particular, the German language is shackled with the dubious honor of smuggling the past into the present. Nowhere does the protagonist make this clearer than when he poses the question, "(Do you speak German?)" and produces the answer that "'German I learned in a KZ/(state)'" (*S*, 96). Not only are state ideological apparatuses like schools equated with concentration camps (KZ), but language, too, emerges as a corporeal violence that subjects learn to embrace.

The temporal conundrum that befalls the protagonist is, however, not just a case of the infringement of the past on the present. The future, too, has encroached on the here and the now. As before, the protagonist cites language as the primary culprit: "in order-to constructions, the future tense,that devour every single moment,the compulsion toward a future" (*S*, 127). Because of the interminable past's intercession in the present and

Technologies of Fascism and the Poetics of Silence and Light 177

Figure 20
Page 13 of *SCHNITTE*, by Rolf Dieter Brinkmann, 1988.

the present's obsession with the future, the protagonist concludes that the present itself is nearly extinct, a ghost of what it could be. The symptom but not the cause of the phantasmic present, the erasure of the present emerges already at the outset of the novel as the hero's quest: "How the devil do I safely get out of this hostile territory? turn back the clock" (*S,* 9). Just as Brinkmann had concluded in his diaries that "the flip side of memory is hallucination," so, too, does the protagonist of *SCHNITTE* turn to his own memories as a bulwark against a vanishing present (*EP,* 41). He confesses, for example, ":a disorienting feeling of placelessness befell me, and I wanted to turn back to a past impression" (*S,* 38). In effect, remembering bygone impressions blocks the past's own intrusion into the present. It affirms the protagonist as an agent capable of determining which

Figure 21

Page 5 (cover page) of *SCHNITTE*, by Rolf Dieter Brinkmann, 1988.

memory to recall and when to do so. And it differentiates the present from the past, insofar as the latter is evoked as a personal lived experience privy only to the protagonist. Two forms of memory consume the protagonist. On the one hand, his minutely detailed chronicle about daily life in Rome is recorded in the simple past. On the other hand, he interlaces these more recently transpired events and impressions with a handful of fleeting childhood memories in war-torn West Germany as well as recollections of his son and wife living in Cologne. As already announced on the book's cover page, the protagonist intends to remove himself with this twofold memory work from the empire of phantasmic time signified by the title of the American newsmagazine *Time* (see fig. 21). Ripping himself—"ME

MAGAZINE"—out of the commercial "TIME [Sub]SCRIPTION SER-
VICE" encapsulates perfectly the protagonist's approach to interceding in
the false present (*S,* 5).

Pornography and the Docile Body

Memories, the protagonist soon realizes, offer no lasting solution. "But
as soon as I concentrated on a scene from my own past," he explains in
the second chapter, "I saw therein only the contemporary decay" (*S,* 38).
Chronicling the temporal difference between the present and the past invariably fails because of culture. Words, sounds, and images continually
bombard the protagonist and undermine any and all distinctions that his
mnemonic chronometry can possibly generate. The protagonist is quite
literal when he insists that the media soften and drain bodies (*S,* 55, 13),
smolder and paste over human flesh (*S,* 17, 21), block the brainstem (*S,* 21),
infect the senses like a virus (*S,* 116), paralyze consciousness (*S,* 25), and
transform humans into larvae and anaerobic bacteria (*S,* 33, 41). The upshot
of excessive being in the past leads to the transformation of bodies into
ghosts that float through the phantom present. The protagonist's belief in
the somatic effects of language stems primarily from Burroughs. First captured in his review of the German translation of Burroughs's novel *Nova
Express,* Brinkmann's interest in a physiological model of unconscious
communication and memory intensified during his preparations for his
second novel ("IG," 205). Brinkmann later invoked not just Burroughs
but also a phalanx of unorthodox authors and scientists to substantiate
his claims for the material effects of words, sounds, and images. General semanticist Alfred Korzybski's *Manhood of Humanity,* psychoanalyst
Wilhelm Reich's interviews on Freud, and novelist Colin Wilson's *The
Mind Parasites,* as well as media theorist Marshall McLuhan's *Understanding Media* all surface in Brinkmann's preparatory notes that precipitated
SCHNITTE.[42] What bound this motley crew in Brinkmann's mind was
their common conviction of the otherwise-ignored active involvement of
the body in verbal-visual communication. Literally a concoction of science
and fiction, Brinkmann's engrammatic theory boiled down to a seemingly fantastic notion that words, sounds, and images behave as viruses
and cause physical transformations in the human brain and body. "Every
event," he exclaimed, "transpires on a nonverbal level and is absorbed on a
nonverbal level" ("NB," 277).

As outlandish as Brinkmann's biophysical model of media effects may appear to twenty-first-century readers, the essence of his position is actually not that alien. Ultimately, Brinkmann sought a model of media effects that parted ways with the student opposition's (failed) theory of manipulation. Primarily intent on pinning the genesis of manipulation on a few capitalists like Axel Springer, the students adhered to nineteenth-century models of hierarchical power wedded to a Cartesian conceptualization of embodiment.[43] According to this approach, media moguls single-handedly repress the masses by virtue of their control of both the means of production and the distribution of ideologies that warp minds from on high. With the help of Burroughs, Korzybski, Reich, Wilson, and McLuhan, Brinkmann advanced antithetical notions of media power and its relationship to the body. Media power for Brinkmann derived in large part from the productive energies of consumers themselves: "They project for themselves the sleaziest pictures of people over again, carry them out into the streets, schlep them around the whole day" ("NB," 280). In addition to this egalitarian power to subordinate oneself by recirculating media spectacles, Brinkmann maintained that this power presided over bodies as well. Just a few years before Michel Foucault sharpened his grim theses on biopolitics and the modern administration of bodies, Brinkmann inferred the existence of discourse, its propagation through the public consumption of mass media, and its investment in disciplining bodies. In other words, the fanciful amalgam of thinkers that Brinkmann adopted for his theory of media effects overshot by virtue of their wild heterogeneity not only French post-structuralism's concept of decentralized power but also its post-humanist, post-Cartesian idea of embodiment. Together they point to the very same discursive construction of material bodies that Foucault unveiled in *The History of Sexuality*. That Foucault and Brinkmann both identified sex as the paragon of biopower corroborates another common thread in their projects. For Foucault, the historically evolving discourse of sex was one of the most important technologies of power over a population; it produced docile bodies, enforced normative guidelines for their health, and ensured their compliance with economic progress. Of the strategies by which the politics of sex achieved the regulation of human populations, Foucault cited the hysterization of woman and the medicalization of her sexuality as particularly important since the late eighteenth century. For Brinkmann, the predominant late twentieth-century institution that exercised power over women's and men's bodies was pornography.

SCHNITTE is first and foremost a picture book. Readers infuriated by the protagonist's nonlinear, nonnarrative typewritten voice will invariably resort to flipping through the book's myriad eye-catching images. Pornography in every guise—from light erotica to hard-core fetishes—consumes a majority of the novel's visual space. Similarly, pornography litters the urban landscapes through which the protagonist passes. "A torn tit," he notes of a ripped pornographic photo in the street "blown by the wind" (S, 12). In fact, the entire city of Rome is described as inundated with pornography. In the first chapter alone he writes of men ejaculating in public (S, 13), anal erotic pictures plastered all over urban decay (S, 15), and bars full of pornography (S, 16). Pornography does not just plague Rome. He recalls adult bookstores in his hometown of Cologne (S, 132). He sees it racing by his train window while traveling to Rome (S, 131). And he finds it firmly installed in culture industries both big and small, from Hollywood's film studios to Italian popular culture. Together, the protagonist's acknowledgment of porn's ubiquity and the excessive reproduction of actual pornography—from amateur black-and-white to professional color photographs—reproduce mimetically the inescapable labyrinth of naked female spectacles that determines his urban experience. The pornographic images reproduced in SCHNITTE do more, however, than just mirror the pornification of Western visual experience. First, pornography divulges, in concert with the novel's other representations, how pornography is homologous with physical violence to women. Second, pornography implicates both the text and the reader into the physical effects of words and images; porn epitomizes the biophysical force of mass media to which not even SCHNITTE is impervious. Violence against women already figures prominently on the novel's cover page (fig. 21). Triangulated by the large-print words "TIME," "Totenbuch," and "MAGIC AND REALITY," a black-and-white photograph of two women assaulted by two men from behind infers that the quandary of men subduing women lies at the heart of Brinkmann's novel, a book of the dead about the erasure of the present and the transformation of reality into magic.[44] Examples of related images that follow in the book include a vampire sucking a woman's neck (S, 13; see fig. 20); the iconic still of a man slicing a woman's eye in Luis Buñuel's film Un chien andalou (S, 72); a comic strip of a woman slitting her wrists (S, 89); a montage of a woman in flames (S, 123); a police officer apprehending a semi-nude woman (S, 142); and most graphic of all, a pile of female corpses (S, 155). More often than not, violent images like these stand alongside pornographic images. Side by side, they continually dialogue with one another; violence against women is porn and porn is violence against women. The signifying logic of the collage in *SCHNITTE* thus conveys the ideological incompatibility of these paired images. Only when juxtaposed does the homologous relationship between violence and sex come to light.

The enlightening work afforded through collage clears, however, no unincorporated space untouched by porn. The novel regularly gives way to full-spread reproductions of pornography with little or no commentary by the protagonist. In such cases, hard-core pornography speaks unencumbered within the space of the nonnarrative. Two women perform same-sex acts (*S*, 16). A man grabs a woman's breasts (*S*, 49). Women pose nude for the camera (*S*, 63–65, 70). Female models spread their legs to reveal their genitals (*S*, 11, 18, 78, 85, 147). A woman ejaculates a man (*S*, 83). Whether or not the novel succeeds in exuding the erotic force of the pornographic spectacle onto the heterosexual male voyeur, these images stand alone. Their status as porn goes unquestioned. The voice of the novel disappears and *SCHNITTE* becomes pornographic. Not only do these moments of indistinguishability between the interiority of the novel and the outside reality infer the irrepressible nature of pornography, but they also suggest that in spite of its critique of porn, *SCHNITTE* cannot detach itself from the pornographic reality it wishes to withstand. Implicated in the pornographic spectacle, *SCHNITTE* does exactly what the protagonist credits William S. Burroughs as having unmasked, namely eliciting a behaviorist response to pornography: " 'a Roman cunt shows her ass and the cocks at the bar pulsate,' (WSB)" (*S*, 13; see fig. 20). Ultimately, sex reduces humans to body parts that act and react autonomously. Vaginas arouse penises. Conversely, men interpellate women into their roles as sources of anal eroticism. The narrator is not above this. In a variant of the novel's opening, the narrator repeats again and again how his body's autonomic response to pornography accompanies a saunter through Rome: "came upon a rotten picket fence in pulsating jerks shot sperm out of the body" (*S*, 31). What elicits this unpredicted orgasm presumably remains a mystery. " 'Turn around,' " he tells an Italian prostitute, who responds "no capito signore." He then adds "but she understood From Behind" (*S*, 22). Presumably married with child, he infers that monogamy exerts no means for resisting the pornographic exchange between bodies. " 'Turn around,' " he commands the prostitute again, "/she turned her ass around / . . . &/ : with a few thrusts it was over / ejaculated & had paid in advance, is good manners/" (*S*, 22). Willing or not, he, too, submits to the power of pornography, for which prostitution counts as a verification of its success.

Although pornography most obviously sets its sights on conquering, enslaving, and annihilating women's bodies, men's bodies bear the brunt of this violence as well. Beginning in chapter 2 ("A LETTER FROM Death market"), the novel incorporates images of murdered men. Next to the handful of photos of street riots, the most potent and double-edged instantiation of violence against men is that of the gangster, more often than not bound, shot, and left for dead (*S*, 61, 69, 70, 94, 107). The novel's inclusion of the gangster is highly symbolic, to be sure.[45] According to Robert Warshow, the classic gangster seeks out opportunities in the city for surviving as an individual. He operates outside the normative bounds of society in his effort to conquer new territories. Invariably, his efforts are destined to failure. The gangster is also a lonely and melancholy type "because he has put himself in a position where everybody wants to kill him and eventually somebody will."[46] In the gangster drama, the city always wins. If the allusions to the character of the gangster in *SCHNITTE* confer upon the novel's protagonist a heroic outsider status, then this status is nevertheless conflicted. Just as cinema's gangster exerts violence, he, too, eventually becomes the object of this violence. *SCHNITTE* drives this point home lucidly with a photograph taken by the author that visualizes the aforementioned fence against which he ejaculates (*S*, 44). At the base of a cobblestone alley, the viewer sees a white fence bordering a street. On the other side stands a billboard for the Italian version of director Jean-Claude Roy's 1973 heist film *L'Insolent*. With a gun pointed practically at the viewer, the poster of actor Henry Silva's gangster persona suggests that what brings the protagonist to climax at the fence is not the pornographic spectacle but rather the referent lurking beneath all sex, namely the violence that the gangster himself commits. The protagonist's orgasm thus stems from the panic of an impending self-annihilating violence (*S*, 41).

While the metaphor of the gangster frames the tragic dimensions of the protagonist's own drama, the gangster's paradigmatic demise applies neither to the physical violence experienced by the protagonist nor his ultimate fate. The protagonist clarifies at the outset of the novel, for example, how media signals split apart his sensorium: "I was completely torn apart . . . for I heard something other than what I saw, and I smelt something other than what I sensed, and I thought something other than what I felt, and I felt something other than what I saw" (*S*, 8). Due to the onslaught of words that jam his throat and fill his intestines, he declares, "I can no longer speak" (*S*, 8). In the third chapter he asks, "Can you feel the words like a tattooing on the naked skin?" (*S*, 75). Jukeboxes in restaurants are identified as "Juck:kasten," literally itching boxes, that emit melodies that "itch out what needs to be itched out" (*S*, 16). Opening up a newspaper is compared to walking into a silent war zone (*S*, 74–75). Regardless of whether his eyes are open or closed, spectacles encountered on the street bring about "a vague, diffuse exhaustion" (*S*, 119–20). Words and images cause "choking/twitching in the throat/stiffened back" (*S*, 105). Similarly, the frequent phonetic spelling of German, Italian, and English words—citing the lyrics to a rock song, he writes, " 'you ßink juur ziviehleist? : kloos juur eis!' "—denotes the primarily auditory character of language that literally bombards the body (*S*, 130). The visual equivalent of all these verbal descriptions culminates in four self-portraits of the author as protagonist (*S*, 41, 122, 130, 155). Recognizable in only one, Brinkmann's likeness barely exceeds that of a silhouette at the close of the novel (see fig. 22). A phantom caught within a phantasmic present, the author as protagonist thus pictures his own body as never surmounting the plight in which he finds himself. Like all the other violated bodies that litter *SCHNITTE*, his, too, is sucked dry. For all their hopelessness, these photographs nevertheless are ambivalent. On the one hand, the negative space of the protagonist's body signifies the erasure of his detailed features that he credits to the words, images, and sounds around him. On the other hand, the silhouettes represent the perpetual baseline of his material existence in the media storm of the present, a condition he nevertheless fights to improve.

Cuts, Noise, Silence

As dire as the visual evidence of the protagonist's fate seems at the close of *SCHNITTE*, his ending is not that of cinema's gangster. Similarly, Brinkmann's conceptual proximity to Foucault's largely pessimistic theory of discourse and the disciplining of bodies refuses to settle for hopelessness. While the novel's title unquestionably refers to both the cuts that the media administer to bodies as well as the fragmentary nature of postmodern experience in the early seventies, cuts also denote the protagonist's last remaining form of agency. He makes no secret of his intentions. "How the hell will I get safely out of this enemy territory?" he asks using cut-up pieces from an English article. His reply, "I CUT OUT," not only affirms his conviction in the possibility of excising himself from the phantom present but also that he can indeed occupy that state of temporal alterity already announced on the title page (*S*, 81; see fig. 21). According to the novel's superficial appearance, the innumerable cuts suggest a phenomeno-logical violence at work that is intent on laying waste to the outside world. As is especially apparent in the novel's incorporation of visual material, cutting and juxtaposing create antipodes that negate one another. Yet the art of collage—the cutting, arranging, and pasting of words and images onto the page—is not an ultimate solution unto itself. For one, cutting does not produce closure, nor does it lead him out of the labyrinth of control. As the novel's recurring motif of "Cut:Continuation/" suggests, every cut requires a step forward toward another cut (*S*, 14). Indeed, the novel's pile of words and images makes clear that the protagonist knows collage to be a survival tactic useful only when adopted as a full-time preoccupation. Second and more fundamentally, the agency of cutting comes undone if inserted into the larger inventory of avant-garde collage. As Peter Bürger points out, the nonorganicism of collage once affirmed the heterogeneity of reality, a state of affairs that bourgeois organicism strategically whitewashed.[47] However, this enlightenment of nonorganic mimesis—the affirmation of fragmented reality—undercuts Brinkmann's rationale for the development novel and its commitment to assembling a sense of totality. The protagonist admits as much when commenting on his efforts to expand the present through a precise chronicling of reality's fragments. "As soon as I pursued an impression here in the present," he says, "I fell into a barren,shattered place,that incessantly consisted of frac-tures" (*S*, 116). Above all, the aesthetic product of cutting says nothing outright about its ability to remedy the debilitation of the protagonist's body, for if *SCHNITTE* is indeed a development novel, then the trajec-tory it seeks to traverse concludes with constituting a coherent, embodied protagonist who is impervious to the effects of the media.

In his posthumously published final essay on poetics, Brinkmann clari-fied once and for all the corporeal utility of cuts. Cutting aids the cutter with regaining mastery over his own body. It is the key to materializing what Brinkmann himself saw at the very end of his life to be the contempo-rary relevance of Romantic poet Ludwig Tieck's poetic program, namely "to give the shadows their bodies back" ("UN," 246).[48] The present, the protagonist declares at the outset of *SCHNITTE,* amounts to nothing more than a "dirty reality film from yesterday" (*S*, 9). Although he does not spare television, radio, or newspapers and magazines from his wrath, cinema remains in the protagonist's mind as the one single medium with the most comprehensive influence on life in the present. Brinkmann, too, asked rhetorically, "Is the present a gangster film?" ("UN," 231). Trapped within the cinema without a way out, Brinkmann concluded that if the screen is indeed inescapable, then the viewer can prevent the spectacle from absorbing his body entirely. Unlike the technical cuts in cinema that magically congeal into a totality, the cuts exercised by the cinema-goer open up a space of difference between himself and the screen. More importantly, they ensure that the body remains the purview of the viewer and not the spectacle. Brinkmann best illustrated his idea for cutting one-self out of the present using an example from inside the movie theater:

> I go to the movies and watch a film / unscrupulously people talk about cuts in film, without paying attention to what the experience is that is denoted by cuts / Cut actually means that the movement of a body is truncated, a sequence of movement, the rambling look across a city square / I lean back in the darkness of the theater, I squint an eye, there-with cut myself out of the content & and hold up an index finger at some distance in front of me against the movement to and fro on the screen / I concentrate on my fingertip with the other eye opened. I have broken through the confinement by the substantive order of events in the film, and while I concentrate on my fingertip, I experience a cut / from the hefty jolt, that runs through my body, as soon as a cut happens, a scene is cut, jolting light. ("NB," 286)

Cutting first begins with the insertion of one's own body in front of the spectacle and then the vigilant maintenance of one's attention on oneself through movement. Brinkmann's sober prescription tells readers that they cannot block the spectacle completely. Always present, the spectacle will continue to radiate the body. Cutting nevertheless ensures, at most, a less-ening of those effects and, at least, a bodily awareness of being caught in the slipstream of cinematic reality. Brinkmann also noted that the goal resides in heightening the sense of embodiment in the present and thereby exploding the cinematic façade of reality ("UN," 243). Accordingly, cut-ting entails not controlling time, but rather one's experience both in it and of it.

In SCHNITTE, the process of writing approximates Brinkmann's ex-tra-cinematic technique for giving the body back to one's shadow. Writ-ing, or more accurately typing, intercedes in the power of the phantom present over the sensing body. The physics of this agency begins, how-ever, not by focusing the eye on the body, but rather by drowning out the noise of the media. As Brinkmann indicated in his tape recordings from the winter of 1973, silence belongs to writing.[49] Unsurprisingly, the protagonist of *SCHNITTE* finds his environs in Rome drowned out by ubiquitous noise. Human voices sound like barking dogs or grunting apes. The sounds of traffic, police sirens, and automobile accidents regularly flood his ears. The protagonist finds "television noises on every corner" and jukeboxes that emit "rock 'n' roll as a slum-melody" (*S*, 48, 81). Again and again, he calls the Roman capital's urban spaces gas chambers and thereby insists once again that Hitler's final solution has lived on through the invisible transmission of sounds through antennas, amplifiers, and the airwaves. Amidst all this noise, the protagonist nevertheless succeeds in finding moments of silence unspoiled by the noise of the undead past. The virtues of silence are many. For one, silence entails divorcing oneself from the chaos of reality. Silence thus precludes the protagonist's participation in media culture and the exchange value with which it articulates bodies and information (*S*, 136). Second, his memory once and for all takes hold of bygone experiences that encapsulate the physical tenderness that the pornographic spectacle ruins (*S*, 128). And most importantly, silence transpires more often than not inside at his desk, as several photographs of his work space in the novel indicate (*S*, 54, 102, 112, 127). Within this space and under these conditions, the protagonist, who initially lamented the disassociation of his senses, finally begins to see clearly: "& in the silence I could see the pictures of the present ablaze = bursting words) / 'everything is from yesterday' / :broken!" (*S*, 21). In other words, silence affords him the ability to unmask the reality outside his window as phantom and capture its chaos mimetically on the page. But recording reality is only a first step for the protagonist. Silence facilitates new, unincorporated forms of perception beyond the realm of media violence. In the novel's concluding scene, he writes of "light without subject and predicate here in the present time fresh and cool reflected white pages and blinding brightness . . . a living view of quietness, in the room" (*S*, 156). Enveloped in silence, the protagonist finally sees without interference from the spectacle that insists on enforcing violence between subjects and objects. Seeing that verges on blindness allows for the reemergence of "tender feeling" (*S*, 156).

A core element in Brinkmann's design for *SCHNITTE* was the sun. In November 1971, he went so far as to declare enigmatically "/: I WOULD LIKE MY <u>NOVEL</u> TO BE ABOUT THE <u>SUN</u>!!!/" (*EP*, 241). Indeed, *SCHNITTE* concludes with a page comprised of three narrow typewritten columns, the first of which begins with "a ghostly larvae-show of rotating melodies" and the third of which ends with an upward gaze into

Figure 22
Page 155 of *SCHNITTE*, by Rolf Dieter Brinkmann, 1988.

the "high,bright midday sky" (*S*, 156). This course from blinding noise to piercing transcendental light encapsulates the essence of the heroic development that Brinkmann originally sought to capture with his second novel. As isolationist and inward as this conclusion to *SCHNITTE* seems, it is neither disillusioned nor defeatist. On the contrary, the protagonist's retreat into the solitude of his study and his gaze into the sun together comprise an active strategy for turning the technical relations of production and distribution as determined by the mass media on their head. *SCHNITTE* stages this reversal visually on its penultimate page (fig. 22). An arrangement of six images and three text blocks, this page infers through its final image a romantic ending. A still of the closing shot from an unidentified film, the final lower right-hand image shows a shadowy man following a woman walking into the sunset. Pure romantic kitsch, the image is nothing other than cinematic reality's attempt to impose the illusion of closure—the Italian "FINE" announces a fictional ending—through its simulation of blinding light. Diametrically opposed to this false appearance, the novel positions at the top of the page a photograph of a window in a room. Daylight floods the aperture of the window frame while leaving the room entirely dark. Much like the previous illustrations of the protagonist's work space in which typewriters sit before window-sills, this interior room shrouds the camera eye in darkness while never-theless providing a high-definition bird's-eye view of Rome. Nothing less than a life-size camera obscura, the protagonist's retreat indoors affords him with the opportunity to frame and expose bits and pieces from the outside by virtue of the intensity of the sunlight. Simultaneously the di-rector and spectator of his own makeshift film, the protagonist creates a pre-cinematic theater within the nightmarish cinematic reality in which he finds himself trapped. And in contrast to the self-portrait adjacent to the phony ending in which the protagonist appears as a shadow in the world, the indoor photograph indicates that as the active viewer of his own film, he now sees slices of the world—its spectacles now thoroughly overexposed and washed out—and continues writing to tell that he can still see without outside interference.

That the protagonist's triumph culminates in seeing white light does not mean that he embraces blindness. Similarly, Brinkmann's hero is no kindred spirit of Heidegger, the philosopher of technology whom Ronell indicts for indulging once in telephonic vision, a vision that shuts down the eyes in favor of the far-reaching telephonic voice. According to Ronell, Heidegger fell prey at the outset of National Socialism to the seduction of communication technologies that colluded with fascism's "phantasms of unmediated instantaneity, defacement, and historical erasure" (*TB,* 6). Unsurprisingly, telephones are entirely absent in *SCHNITTE.* Similarly, the protagonist of *SCHNITTE* exhibits an acute awareness of not only technology's inexhaustible penetration of everyday life but also the actual mediated character of those fantasies that masquerade as authentic experi-ence by appealing directly to bodily sensation. In direct opposition to Hei-degger, the protagonist of *SCHNITTE* sees the essence of technology—what the later Heidegger called *techne*—not as revealing but rather as con-cealing truths about its own ontology and the ontology of human being within a technologized world.[50] Furthermore, he diagnoses the phantom reality of his mediated present as dangerously desirous, insofar as the sights, sounds, and signs of reality inculcate widespread collaboration with the annihilation of immediate experience. This destruction, he stresses again and again, transpires on and within the material body before consciousness ever registers it, if it does at all. His search for silence and light therefore emanates from an underlying conviction in the individual's inherent ability to switch off the otherwise inescapable violence of technological mediation. An antithesis to Heidegger's *poiesis* of technology, the poetics of silence and blinding white light that closes *SCHNITTE* corresponds to an alternative form of mediation made possible by first staring into the sun. Far from promoting a retreat into an expressionist-like primitivism that exalts a myth of a pre-discursive natural world—the novel's earliest images of nature make clear, in fact, its incorporation into the spectacle (see fig. 19)—the protagonist cites the immediate experience of being blinded by the sun as a physiological precursor for writing. Light flushes the senses by drowning out the rest of the media garbage that clogs the eyes, deafens the ears, jams the throat, and deadens the nerves. The light of the sun, he writes, is reflected in the white pages that eventually become his novel about a present moment that is neither the spectral past nor the escapist future. The development novel facilitates, therefore, the subject's wish to clear space for the eclipsed present as a moment of possibility.

The Historical Origins of Psychic and Corporeal Mutilation

SCHNITTE is, in large part, a novel about the recalibration of modern irreversible time after technology's promise of immediacy turned out to be a sham. The protagonist repeatedly reiterates his need to establish his own ontological certainty, his presence in the present. "I am present in the room," he writes in a moment of silence at his work space, and then adds "now" and another "now" and yet another (*S*, 136). This repetitive emphasis on the now attests to the inherently elusive and paradoxical nature of capturing the presence of the present using a medium only capable of recording traces of its expiration.[51] The seriality of the protagonist's references to the present—as with his recurrent cuts and his intermittent respites of achieved silence—makes clear that the novel's optimistic development is contingent on the interminability of writing the present. The novel *SCHNITTE* is therefore not an end unto itself, a final product of time regained. Instead, it is the medium through which the writer's poetics of silence enable him to close in on an authentic and tender feeling of being in the present that is not infected by phantoms from the past.

Brinkmann himself testified to the transitional importance of silence in his tape recordings; silence precedes the reintroduction of the acoustic world. "I like to listen to silence most of all," he confessed to his wife in a home interview, "and in this silence particular noises, and after these particular noises comes music, and the music is Soft Machine."[52] A British underground psychedelic rock band from the late sixties, Soft Machine, the protagonist's favorite rock band, surfaces regularly in the final third of *SCHNITTE*. His allusions to Soft Machine throughout *SCHNITTE* do not signal, however, any solutions or finality. In keeping with Burroughs's idea of controlling the soundtrack that determines vision, the protagonist replays the music of Soft Machine in his head in order to promote visions of tenderness (*S*, 128). Recalibrating modern time therefore entails achieving and maintaining favorable conditions conducive for maximizing bodily feeling free of media influence; the occasional breakthrough of good rock music—clearly a subjective category—signals the emergence of individual agency over seeing. Contrary to the protagonist's earliest convictions, recalibration must neither turn the clock backward nor arrest it altogether. On the contrary, irreversible time makes possible the additive process through which the protagonist staves off media effects and momentarily gains control over his own body, hence the rationale for the development novel. Anything but solipsistic, the writer's task of opening up a space for feeling in the present aims at transforming the present into a moment of possibility precisely because the onslaught of the past and the commercial push into the future have been held at bay. Making present bodily feeling in the present affords the individual opportunities to differentiate time: to reflect on what was the past; to shape an alternative present in opposition to it; and to pilot this present toward a future unlike the one promised by the mass media.

As much as *SCHNITTE* brokers the protagonist's purchase on regaining presence in the present, the novel has as much, if not more, to say about the body's place in the course of time. In fact, there is more to Brinkmann's attention to technology's use of gendered embodiment than just Germany's history of technologized power. While *SCHNITTE* shares with Brinkmann's later telephone experiments a sensitivity to technology's incorporation of woman as seductive sign, neither of these projects clarifies explicitly how their discoveries of the nefarious gender of technology directly address a specifically West German problem with time. While *SCHNITTE* does continually liken reality to National Socialism's concentration camps and equates Zyklon B with commercial pop music, its seemingly hyperbolic insistence on the past's contamination of the present neither looks nor reads particularly fascist in the German sense of the word. In fact, the glut of Italian print materials strewn throughout the novel, which Brinkman collected during his extended stay in Italy from late 1972 to the middle of 1973, suggests that the contaminating past in question is actually Italian. On the contrary, *SCHNITTE* intervenes into a markedly German problem, one bound to the protagonist's German body and linked to the West German student movement that reached its peak some five years earlier. Establishing this vital connection necessitates digging deeper for intertextual links beyond *SCHNITTE* that further erode the fictionality of the protagonist and, conversely, bolster the phantasmic character of reality in which he and Brinkmann found themselves. If *SCHNITTE* does indeed model itself after the development novel, a genre whose heroes were once molded after the lives of their creators or into a fictional fulfillment of their wishes, then Brinkmann's person bears significant import for unlocking the historical foundations of *SCHNITTE*.[53]

Although remembering alone proved for the protagonist to be an ineffectual bulwark against the dedifferentiation of the past and present, memories consume Brinkmann's journals of the same period. Made possible by silence and light, writing memories, while designed to counteract the hallucinations of media reality, also laid claim to an individual past, one that explains the origins of the violence against which Brinkmann, like the protagonist, wage battle. Brinkmann began recording detailed memories from his past in his first diary from late 1971 and continued to do so throughout the remainder of his creative work. Of his innumerable recollections, growing up during and immediately after the Third Reich assumed particular importance. Brinkmann summarized most succinctly not only his own childhood but also those of his entire generation in his audio recordings from late 1973. "The terror under which everyone born around 1940 grew up," he explained, "lasted a long time, up until now." Asked by his wife exactly what he meant, Brinkmann retold his story of growing up amidst air raids entirely from the perspective of bodies. "The first impressions that the body felt were diffuse. A three-year-old body, a four-year-old body, a five-year-old body. And it never had the possibility to ward off with the mind what it had experienced directly."[54] If war had not debilitated these children's consciousness entirely, then their enforced compliance to collective guilt, he added, ensured that their consciousness was not only preprogrammed but also entirely divorced from their own bodies.

Fast-forward roughly twenty-eight years to the era of the tumultuous student movement, when many men and women from Brinkmann's own generation sought to roll back the lingering intrusion of fascism into their lives. Unlike those who wielded neo-Marxism or marched in the streets, Brinkmann aligned himself with those dedicated to liberating themselves from the shackles of post-fascist German society through sex radicalism. Nonmarital sex, historian Dagmar Herzog explains, represented for many so-called sixty-eighters an assault on the postwar German nuclear family and its conservative sexual mores. Sex radicals also identified sexual liberation as a thoroughly anti-fascist endeavor capable of articulating the very bodily pleasures that their parents forbade their children and that had precipitated the horrors of war and genocide.[55] In the second half of the sixties, Brinkmann elevated sex as his most pivotal theme. His novel *Keiner weiß mehr* (*No One Knows More*) incorporates, for example, embellished depictions of marital, extramarital, homosexual, and masturbatory sex in its narrative about a man in search of an ever-elusive bodily feeling of tenderness.[56] Sex, or more precisely, fantasies of sex, drive Brinkmann's first novel forward. Traced on top of the generational problem that Brinkmann would go on to delineate several years later, *Keiner weiß mehr* is as much a story about sex as it is about reclaiming one's own mind and body. Sex promised the corporeal immediacy that fascism extinguished. With *SCHNITTE*, Brinkmann drastically revised these hopes he had once affixed to sex. What he thought to be the immediacy of authentic sex in *Keiner weiß mehr* became in *SCHNITTE* yet another instantiation of power intent on expropriating the mind and body. Moreover, sex is entirely subject to mediation. In addition to remedying the student movement's self-defeating and outdated theory of media manipulation, Brinkmann's *SCHNITTE* maintains that the commercial fantasies of sex that congest everyday experience continue the deadening of bodily feeling and consciousness that began in bomb shelters between the years 1940 and 1945. National Socialism, Brinkmann exclaimed in late 1971, arose from a "perverted German consciousness" that sought with technology to elevate Germans as the chosen people, a distinction that merely led to widespread psychic and corporeal mutilations (*EP,* 213). At the historical juncture in the sixties and early seventies when sexual liberation became not only politically but also commercially viable, *SCHNITTE* professed that the contagion that continued these mutilations well into the present was a legacy of a fascist technology savvy enough to employ fantasies of sexual immediacy.

I have not found as of yet a way how I can film Stalingrad.
— Alexander Kluge[1]

As long as videocassettes look like books, film can relate to this
medium like a dear relative.
— Alexander Kluge, *In Gefahr und größter Not bringt der
Mittelweg den Tod: Texte zu Kino, Film, Politik*

6. Alexander Kluge's Impossible Film

On the Usefulness of Anachronistic Media

In 1985—three years before he abandoned cinema for television—
Alexander Kluge exclaimed, "We are experiencing in recent years . . . the
birth of new media" ("DMB," 104).[2] With a handful of European communication satellites already in orbit, multinational business initiatives
in place, and conservative politicians at work dismantling the legal foundations of West Germany's long-standing public broadcasting service, it
was just a matter of time until private cable television, broadband and
fiber-optic networks, digitization, and microcomputers colonized everyday experience.[3] For Kluge, the promise of new communication technologies was nothing short of a disaster waiting to happen. "On a large scale,"
he continued, "the project involves the industrialization of consciousness,"
a process whereby a society's trust in the substance of mediated consciousness is never called into question ("DMB," 53, 64). Underneath all the
propaganda about the merits of privatization lurked a recipe for precipitating pandemic inattention, mobilizing passivity, and splintering subjectivity. Far more fundamental to Kluge's argument, new media threatened to
collapse the differences between different orders of time at work within
everyday experience. These temporalities, Kluge explained, include, but
are not limited to, "physical time (that a metronome measures), psychological time, production times, daytime, times over the course of one's
life, historical time" ("DMB," 104). All media, Kluge pointed out, are
Zeitkunstwerke, literally "works of art of time." Regardless of their level

of historical and technological sophistication, they have always exhibited a propensity to expropriate time. Above all, psychological time stands to lose the most, for the media are especially adroit at condensing it, assigning it false value, shaping one's relationship to it, and ultimately expropriating the experience of time.[4] Losing a sense of time is, first and foremost, a conundrum for the individual. "Expropriated historical time," Kluge added, "means: I can delete years of my life. I may not regard them as my own. I lose them in relation to my identity" ("DMB," 104). Kluge insisted that if one traces this identity loss onto a society it inevitably leads to nothing less than the dialectic of Enlightenment. New media mobilize collective passivity and divert the public sphere. They absolutize the tyranny of irreversible time (*chronos*) and invite whole societies to forsake the time of agency (*kairos*).[5] And they arrest the political potency of storytelling and block the use value of history and mourning. The pending sea change in West Germany's media landscape heralded the emergence of what Kluge called "ersatz fascism," an empire of distracted individuals indifferent to future oligarchs like the Leo Kirch/Springer group and Bertelsmann that did, in fact, devour Germany's airwaves ("DMB," 54).

At the heart of Kluge's media politics rests a simple observation. There is never enough time, especially when it is needed most. Moreover, the realization of this deficiency always comes too late. Although media privatization has seized time and strangled the public sphere like never before, the conundrum of new media is not a fait accompli. In theory, it should be possible to make more time (*kairos*) than new media consume (*chronos*). With respect to private television, classical media (music, theater, film, newspapers, literature, the sciences) can facilitate utopian thought. This claim resides in classical media's ability to ignite and organize a public's imagination and its collective energies. Reviving classical media can make it possible to discover "that there could still exist something beyond the insufficient and fleeting present" in which people live.[6] It is, however, not efficacious merely to recycle the films of the Lumière brothers or Georges Méliès or to insist upon the analog origins of modern-day digital cinema.[7] There exist fundamental corporeal, experiential, and political differences between classical and new media, differences that must be accounted for. Above all, the experience of watching a film in the theater is neither physiologically nor phenomenologically identical to watching that same film on a television screen. These differences, Kluge insists, are locked within the media's materiality. The logic of infusing new media with the material differences of classical media lies in the latter's ability to compensate for the former's expropriation of time. Within their historical contexts, classical media (like the cinema of the historical avant-garde) achieved this restitution by virtue of the innumerable gaps and breaks—Kluge calls them "unseen pictures" in the viewer's head—characteristic of celluloid projection and cinematic montage ("DMB," 106). New media, the television being a prime example for Kluge, afford the eye no such reprieve. With its high-resolution screen and unremitting pixels, the television obligates the human eye to read indefinitely. Worse, "it fills and destroys all gaps," the interstices in filmic montage that Kluge calls "time niches." Television proves therefore particularly well equipped to annihilate the classical medium's "formal space [*Formenwelt*] for reflection" ("DMB," 66).[8]

The television's place in Kluge's media typology is, however, not a straightforward matter. In spite of its all too frequent alliance with new media's twin penchants for the fleeting and repetitious, television is in fact a hybrid medium. As long as it deliberately fails to enforce the dictates of commercial television programming, it can live up to classical media and bring *kairos* into being ("DMB," 73). Although television does away with cinema's structural gaps—the subliminal sequence of tiny blackouts in the projection—television can be made to compensate for this loss through the radical juxtaposition of heterogeneous material. Stringing wildly heterogeneous materials approximates the formal gaps between individual frames of celluloid film. And with the development of computerized post-production technologies, television can enfold montage within the frame, oftentimes updating the special effects first developed by cinematography's earliest wizards. This refunctionalization of new media with the intention of producing temporal spaces is politically urgent, says Kluge. While private capital has certainly colonized the public sphere, it nevertheless provides an unparalleled interface with spectators in numbers which the New German Cinema's auteurs dreamt of a decade earlier. Kluge's rationale for folding film into television is not delusional, for he has never intended to unseat the dominance of commercial television's aesthetics of distraction. Instead, the importance of cinematizing television rests on its exceptional status vis-à-vis the wasteland of the mainstream, its ability to question the dominant medium's professed truths, and its demonstration of television's untapped possibilities. Equipped with both partial ownership of West Germany's first private channel and his theory of classical cinema's compensatory potential within new media, Kluge first ventured into the fray of television production in early 1985. Though he was already active in the seventies with brokering ties between filmmakers and public television, his transition from filmmaking to television programming was nevertheless an entirely new and time-consuming endeavor. In his first year alone he broadcast more material than all his full-length films (1965–86) combined.[9] Kluge nevertheless mastered the peculiarities of the form, and by 1987 he had perfected his signature twenty-four-minute "cultural window" that has continued to air into the new millennium in spite of attempts to put him out of business.[10]

Making Time for History

In spite of the political urgency informing Kluge's move to television, it would be erroneous to designate television as the culmination of his diverse creative career, one that began with a short film in 1960, quickly veered into fiction, and years later made its first of three forays into theory. With his recent publication of several anthologies of stories, Kluge's insistence on being an author foremost calls attention to the formal and substantive relationship among his many media outlets.[11] In fact, scholarship has regularly contemplated the logic underlying the multitude of Kluge's media. Prior to Kluge's entry into television, Rainer Lewandowski maintained, for example, that literature and film—Kluge's first two primary staples—were always complementary and therefore inseparable forms even in his earliest literary and cinematographic work.[12] Over a decade later when Kluge was well ensconced in television, Georg Stanitzek proffered the thesis that Kluge was always at the mercy of the technological limitations of each individual medium; with the advent of the personal computer and the Internet in the nineties, technology finally caught up with Kluge's original multimedia project.[13] Mindful of Kluge's fundamental investment in utopian thinking, Matthias Uecker insisted most recently that debate over Kluge's yearning for multimediality misses the point; regardless of the medium in question, all of Kluge's work shares a common concern for activating the consciousness of its audience.[14] Uecker's resulting petition for intermediality does explain the productive function of the interstices between Kluge's media. (Kluge regularly produces media gaps with the publication of printed volumes to accompany his films and television interviews.) However, the concept of intermediality does not clarify an interminable blind spot in his film and video. None of his audiovisual productions comprehensively engages his first and most important novel. Initially published in 1964 under the title *Schlachtbeschreibung*—literally "Battle Description," though a 1967 translation reduced it to *The Battle*—Kluge's novel about the fall of Hitler's Sixth Army in Stalingrad in 1943 has undergone a total of seven different editions over the course of thirty-six years.[15] Some minor, others extensive, Kluge's revisions together affirm not only his intense and lifelong interest in representing the Battle of Stalingrad but also a long-term inability to find an audiovisual medium capable of rendering this disaster. Admittedly, Kluge's cinematic and televisual work has incorporated bits and pieces of Stalingrad.[16] (In January 1972, Kluge's remake of Stalingrad as science fiction fantasy—*Willi Tobler und der Untergang der 6. Flotte* [Willi Tobler and the Wreck of the Sixth Fleet]—debuted on public television. In February 1989 he broadcast a thirty-minute television program titled "Das ferne Stalingrad" [The Distant Stalingrad].) Nevertheless, this crucial turning point in the fate of National Socialism has persisted for Kluge as a topos that only literature can mine extensively, though never exhaustively. With respect to Stalingrad, it would appear that neither multimediality nor intermediality sufficiently describe the essential literariness of Kluge's repeated engagement with this dark chapter in Germany's fascist past. With Stalingrad, Kluge's media politics as a politics of time mushrooms into a patently German problem in history.

Readers of the last two substantial editions of *Schlachtbeschreibung* from 1978 and 2000 immediately notice how these redactions exhibit a media shift. Although Kluge did retain the core of the original work's material, the new editions are stocked with illustrations of every variety. Over the course of time, *Schlachtbeschreibung* assumed an increasingly extraliterary character. Additionally, each edition significantly expanded the original work's temporal scope; the 1978 edition folded in the recent fallout of domestic German terrorism from the year before, and the 2000 edition referenced German reunification. This self-referentiality makes clear that *Schlachtbeschreibung* is as much about the historical moments in which these editions were written as it is about the events that transpired between late 1942 and early 1943. It is not enough, however, to explain these formal and substantive changes to *Schlachtbeschreibung* in terms of Kluge's increasingly intensive investment in film and television before and after 1978. Similarly, while historical events in 1977 and 1989 certainly precipitated, in part, the substantive transformation and reemergence of Kluge's only novel, they can neither account for these changes in toto, nor can they illuminate why it is the Battle of Stalingrad that repeatedly resurfaces in Kluge's oeuvre only as text. Situating the various editions of *Schlachtbeschreibung* in a chronological bio-bibliographical timeline invariably overlooks how his experimentation with what he calls forms—what most others call media (literature, film, and television), Kluge describes as people's experiences, wishes, and fantasies—always emanates from literature.[17] Literature is for Kluge the preeminent time machine, for what it tells always requires less than the time it spends smoldering in the reader's head. In the foreword to the eponymous book that accompanied his seminal 1979 film *Die Patriotin* (*The Patriot*)—a project contemporaneous with the 1978 edition of *Schlachtbeschreibung*—Kluge explains, for example, that "in order to shoot a book of this kind one would have to produce 600 hours of film."[18] According to this logic, the surplus time that one of Kluge's twenty-four-minute television shows creates is considerably less than the time the film *Die Patriotin* generates. The book that accompanies the film is even more industrious. But this time for thinking in the present comprises only half of the task at hand; the object of this thought is supremely historical. As the various editions of *Schlachtbeschreibung* insist, the causes for the disaster on the Eastern Front date back to either the Thirty Years' War (1618–48) or the crowning of Frederick I as Holy Roman emperor in 1155. Given this backlog of history, only literature can begin to approach the volume of time required to throw this enormous historical catalogue into relief.[19] The innumerable hours required for thinking about the mistakes made at Stalingrad—in other words, the catastrophic culmination of modern German history—reflect not a demand for the epic novel, but rather the depth of reflection needed to jump-start the mourning process that Kluge claims Germans have failed to undertake in spite of the ample opportunities in 1989, 1977, 1968, 1945, 1918, 1871, and so on ("DMB," 66).[20] This reconstructive process must account for why modern German history, ever since its earliest beginnings, always resulted in disaster. To do so, literature must generate not only ample *kairos* but also a body of knowledge about past mistakes in order to shed light on the future possibility of the past's return.

The breadth of literature's appeal to the mind is, however, marred by what Kluge identified in 1985 as classical media's one deficiency: not everyone can acquire it ("DMB," 59). Herein lies the contradiction on which Kluge's reliance on the so-called mass media rests. Because literature is a solitary pursuit, only forms like cinema and television can create the communal experiences capable of organizing the necessary collective reflection and mourning that would, above all, steer an entire society's present and future away from the interminable return of its disastrous past. The periodic reemergence of *Schlachtbeschreibung* throughout Kluge's long career is therefore not a function of the feasibility or ethical questionability of reifying this particular chapter of German history, but rather of offsetting the temporal limitations of Kluge's cinematic and televisual work with the reservoir of time and the breadth of thinking afforded by literature. The relationship between Kluge's forms extends well beyond literature's unparalleled capacity to compensate for new media's expropriation of time. Kluge's novel about the Battle of Stalingrad provides his intervention into television with a formal technique for overcoming the commercial restrictions placed on his misuse of the medium. Conversely, Kluge's television functions as a powerful heuristic for unlocking the countervailing politics of time in his Stalingrad novel that otherwise gets lost in the enormity of his montage. Establishing this reciprocal relationship between television and the novel requires traveling backward through Kluge's oeuvre, from his beginnings in television in 1988 to the debut of his Stalingrad novel in 1964. This time travel must then journey back into the future to that point when Kluge's prose (in conjunction with his philosophy) insists that the restoration of psychological time can only succeed if physical time—the time of clocks, mechanical, biological, or otherwise—has a voice. Above all, the time for cognition can only make a difference when measured up against, amended, and augmented by the historical experiences of the material body. "The [body's] cells know everything under the stars," Kluge declared in 1981 with his collaborator Oskar Negt, "the head never experienced such a thing or simply forgot it" (*GE*, 151). At the threshold to the eighties, Kluge's renewed engagement with Stalingrad undertakes this mediation between mind and body by communing with dead soldiers. The novel practices necromancy through the art of telling stories. Kluge's revision of *Schlachtbeschreibung* from 1978 thus represents both a formal and substantive innovation that sheds light on the underlying narrative drive of his television programs.

1988: Heidegger on Television

On December 19, 1988, Kluge concluded his first year of producing twenty-four-minute cultural television magazines for Germany's private channel RTL with a program titled "Zeitenwechsel (rasch)" ("Changing Time [quickly]").[21] The program begins with two time-lapse shots. The first captures a candle burning alongside the face of a superimposed clock (see fig. 23). The clock's hands whirl away. In the second shot, a bird's-eye view of city traffic at night replaces the candle and the clock face now

Figure 23

Alexander Kluge, still from "Zeitenwechsel (rasch)," 1988.

appears tilted. In the first seventeen seconds of the program, twenty-two hours have passed. These first two sequences out of a total of roughly eighty encapsulate the two countervailing forces at work in Kluge's program: television's rapid compression of time versus the manufacture of surplus time within the timelessness of television. As if to explode the depth of the program's topic a thousandfold, Kluge then introduces the first of two intertitles. The first establishes the topic of this installation of his series *10 till 11:* Martin Heidegger's tome on transcendental ontology, *Being and Time.* The second announces the title of the program. The rapid succession of ensuing images and sounds leaves little time for the viewer to stop and reflect on the significance of Heidegger's complex thought. According to the intertitles, *Being and Time* has something to do with simulated fireworks displays at New Year's celebrations, Kluge's reoccurring heroine Gabi Teichert, Friedrich Schiller's "Ode to Joy," the corresponding movement in Ludwig van Beethoven's Symphony no. 9, astronomy, Vladimir Lenin's funeral, everyday city life in the Weimar Republic, the headlines to a 1918 edition of Berlin's brand-new communist newspaper, Ernst Lubitsch's *Carmen,* Hitler at a performance of his favorite operetta (Franz Lehár's *The Merry Widow*), the Allied firebombings of German cities, the score to Richard Wagner's *The Valkyrie,* and Fritz Lang's *Metropolis.* What is clear, however, is a series of photographic images and intertitles: Heidegger as a young man, his Jewish lover Hannah Arendt around 1928, Arendt's American passport issued after her naturalization in 1950, Heidegger as an older man, and the third of four quotations from

Being and Time. The onslaught of material invites the viewer to piece together Kluge's vexing puzzle. Jumping straight into the minutiae would ignore, however, a far bigger question: what is Heidegger doing in a Kluge television program?

Of the many intellectual giants who inspired Kluge since his creative beginnings in the early sixties, Heidegger is not one of them. An avowed follower of critical theory in general and a disciple of Theodor Adorno in particular, Kluge (together with Negt) never explicitly contend with Heidegger in their own philosophical work. Heidegger's absence, along with Kluge's allegiance to Adorno—Heidegger's most outspoken archenemy—should make viewers pause before hastily categorizing "Zeitenwechsel (rasch)" as an unusual video essay illuminating *Being and Time* or a veiled biopic about Heidegger's problematic biography as a Nazi sympathizer. Situating Kluge's television program requires viewers to consider how the program speaks to its own historical context, a context for which its sounds and images provide few direct clues. The view outside Kluge's cultural window on December 19, 1988, that eludes unsuspecting viewers today was a heated international debate over Heidegger's intellectual legacy. In October 1987, Victor Farias's *Heidegger and Nazism* triggered a firestorm of controversy in France. Farias's thesis was as simple as it was damning. Heidegger, the forefather of French post-structuralism, had been a devoted Nazi and everything he wrote is permeated by this personal conviction. In spite of its suspect hyperbole and the questionable execution of its argument, Farias's book put the French intelligentsia on the spot for its unreflecting reliance on a Nazi philosopher. Soon France's leading Heideggerians, Jacques Derrida and Philippe Lacoue-Labarthe among others, reckoned with Farias's charges, providing the theretofore missing philosophical acumen needed to substantiate the political contamination of Heidegger's thought. As Richard Wolin keenly discerned in the autumn of 1988, Derrida's and Lacoue-Labarthe's individual confirmations of Farias's contentions amounted to nothing more than strategies of denial.[22] Their book-length analyses published in 1987 (*Of Spirit: Heidegger and the Question* and *Heidegger, Art, and Politics: The Fiction of the Political,* respectively) perform rescue operations intent on containing a salvageable core of Heideggerian post-humanism. For Lacoue-Labarthe, this remainder is to be found in Heidegger's work after 1935, the point in time when Heidegger rooted out, once and for all, the metaphysical and proto-fascist contagion in his earlier crusade against metaphysics. For Derrida, the early Heidegger of *Being and Time* merited clemency on the grounds that he avoided the metaphysically suspect idea of spirit so crucial for his later pro-fascist rhetoric around 1933. In spite of their differences over which Heidegger to rescue, both men ventured to secure a Heideggerian anchor for their own post-metaphysical projects.

Though the Heidegger debate in France dealt a shock to post-structuralism, Farias's book caused little reaction in West Germany. From Wolin's North American perspective in late 1988, German intellectuals had yet to formulate a response to this case against Heidegger.[23] In January of that same year, the former Heidegger student Hans-Georg Gadamer differed sharply. Writing for the Parisian periodical *Le Nouvel Observateur,* he expressed astonishment at the hoopla. "In German-speaking lands," he explained, "almost all of what Farias reports has long been known." Gadamer went so far as to insist that Farias's book was "wholly superficial and long outdated," and had generated such a brouhaha because the French apparently knew very little about the Third Reich.[24] Far more systematic in his containment of Farias's assault, Jürgen Habermas concurred in large part with Gadamer in his foreword to the 1989 translation of Farias's book into German. While a long string of German philosophers and historians have brought to light Heidegger's biographical and conceptual links to National Socialism, none, however, generated the public attention that Farias had. Like Gadamer, Lacoue-Labarthe, Derrida, and others before him, Habermas fashioned his introduction as a user's manual for German readers, warning them to avoid making the mistake of dismissing Heidegger's thought altogether. "It is simply foolish," he argued, "to think that the substance of [*Being and Time*] could be discredited, more than five decades later, by political assessments of Heidegger's fascist commitments."[25] The value of Heidegger's contributions to existentialist, phenomenological, hermeneutic, and post-structural thinking inside and outside of Germany is immeasurable. In contrast to the French debates that ended with efforts to separate the wheat from the chaff in Heidegger's philosophy, Habermas conceded the inextricability of Heidegger's entire philosophical corpus—from *Being and Time* to his ideological turn in 1929, from his disillusionment in 1935 to his retreat into quietism after 1945—from Heidegger's political underbelly. Accordingly, the occasion of Farias's publication in Germany was nevertheless useful. For one, it exposed how Heidegger exemplified a pervasive West German weltanschauung of denial and revisionism. These specters continued to haunt Germans well into the eighties with conservative attempts to relativize the Holocaust in the infamous Historians' Dispute that began in 1986.

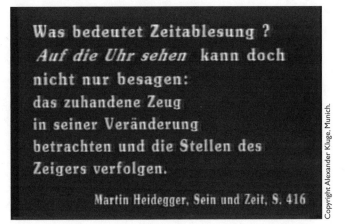

Figure 24

Alexander Kluge, still from "Zeitenwechsel (rasch)," 1988.

Second, it reminded all of Heidegger's acolytes to track down the traces of denial in Heidegger's thinking and, consequently, bestow their appropriations of his work with only the greatest of suspicions. When appropriated wisely—in a historically cognizant and ethical fashion—Heidegger's legacy can attain its originally intended revolutionary potential.

Although Kluge's television program preceded the German publication of Farias's biography and Habermas's essay, it shares much with the latter's call for wrenching Heidegger's philosophy out of its historical and political context. Establishing the context into which Kluge's program inserts *Being and Time* necessitates filling in several gaps and striking omissions. The most glaring of these lacunae is the program's paltry and lopsided use of *Being and Time*. All four quotes originate from the final chapter of Division Two of the book. All relate to Heidegger's interest in establishing the unspoken existential subtext to the everyday, resolutely historical experience of telling time. Listed in order of their appearance in Kluge's television program, the four passages are as follows. (See also fig. 24.)

What does "reading off the time" signify? "Looking at the clock" does indeed amount to more than observing the changes in some item of equipment which is ready-to-hand, and following the positions of a pointer.[26]

The horizon for the retaining which expresses itself in the "on that former occasion" is the "*earlier*"; the horizon for the "then" is the "*later on*" ("that which is to come"); the horizon for the "now" is the "*today.*" (*BT,* 459)

When we use a clock in ascertaining what o'clock it is, *we say*—whether explicitly or not—"It is *now* such and such an hour and so many minutes; *now* is the time for . . ." or "there is still time enough *now* until . . ." (*BT,* 469)

"In time the point thus has reality." (*BT,* 482) [27]

Given the enormity of *Being and Time,* these excerpts can only convey a sliver of Heidegger's argument. It should suffice to say that the common thread in these first three quotations is his case for an underlying existential temporality of being that precedes and therefore makes possible the measurement of everyday time. The fourth quotation is his summary of G. W. F. Hegel's dialectical interpretation of time. Heidegger invokes Hegel in his finale as a foil against which to accentuate the uniqueness of his own existential-ontological approach. Whereas time is secondary for Hegel's notion of spirit, being for Heidegger is always already temporalized, even in the most quotidian of contexts. Regardless of whether one lives in a primitive society or an industrial one, tools for telling time prevail because of being's inherent temporality. Heidegger's case for understanding the homologous relationship between "primitive" being and "advanced" being reverberates throughout Kluge's program (*BT,* 468). A series of four animated photographs begin the cultural window, each portraying a skyline filled with fireworks and stars. Intertitles attribute each image to a New Year celebration. The first has yet to take place (December 31, 1988) and the remaining three are attributed to the years 1923, 1908, and 1812. Although the intertitles insist that these New Year celebrations span almost two hundred years, nothing about the fireworks themselves conveys the passing of time other than making present the *now,* as Heidegger would argue. Like Heidegger, Kluge calls attention to the modern signification of time, or what Heidegger calls time's datability (*BT,* 459). Kluge's inquiry grows out of his initial two time-lapse shots; measuring time according to the movement of heavenly bodies is akin to both the distance a candle burns and the rotations of a clock's hands. By replacing the "primitive" technology of the candle with the lights of nighttime traffic, Kluge echoes Heidegger's contention that modernity's technological

Copyright Alexander Kluge, Munich.

Figure 25
Alexander Kluge, still from "Zeitenwechsel (rasch)," 1988.

advances, although independent of the rhythms of the sun and the moon, remain tethered to the existential time of being.

Faint allusions to Heidegger's thoughts on time abound in "Zeitenwechsel (rasch)." Potential links lurk in an excerpt from Ernst Herbeck's poem "Wintertage" ("Winter Days"); a photograph of a jailed man looking out his prison window into the sun; shots of Cologne at night and animated diagrams of solar systems; the lengthy footage of Lenin's funeral; documentary sequences of everyday life in the twenties; and the digitally modified excerpt from *Metropolis* (fig. 25). As much as Kluge lends credence to Heidegger's argument through his disparate imagery, his cultural window parts ways with Heidegger's query of being. Traces of this departure are to be found in Kluge's citations; none say anything about Heidegger's key concept: being. From its title alone, Kluge's program makes clear that its topic is a matter of knowledge—a query of the speed at which time changes—and not the existence of time or the time of being. And whereas *Being and Time* underscores the historicality (*Geschichtlichkeit*) of being as an existential temporality that precedes all history, "Zeitenwechsel (rasch)" neither designates nor reserves a privileged designation for such originary time. Not only does Kluge's program jumble various kinds of temporalities (e.g., compressed time, mechanical time, astrological time, daytime) in a non-hierarchical pastiche, but it also prominently features signs of historical time. Certainly the most pronounced manifestation of Kluge's difference is the sequence about Gabi Teichert taken from the final portion of Kluge's 1979 film *Die Patriotin* (*The Patriot*).[28] Teichert, Kluge's voice-over explains, "explores the wording of the third verse to the song 'Ode to Joy.'" A history teacher disillusioned by the negative outcome of German history and the negativity in German history lessons, Teichert takes up literary analysis in her quest to right German history and unearth supporting evidence. Unlike her colleagues who sing along to a recording of the ode, Teichert studies the text word for word. She seeks concrete clues about the identity of the lyrical subject and the circumstances behind what the libretto calls the reconciliation of the world's registry of guilt.[29] Although the television program's employment of Teichert says nothing about her turn in the film to archaeology, medicine, the natural sciences, and philology, this quotation from Kluge's own work nevertheless establishes the program's primary focus on the political use of history. Building on Teichert the schoolteacher's need to materialize history, "Zeitenwechsel (rasch)" repeatedly produces concrete historical references that balance out any and all allusions to Heidegger's transcendental historicality. An intertitle stating "Air raid, no New Year— (Christmas trees)" interrupts the sequence of indistinguishable New Year celebrations. Another intertitle, "New Year 1935/36," places Hitler's visit to the opera alongside these other dates. And yet another intertitle, "Young Wagnerian rehearses the words of the master in the late morning of New Year's Eve 1914," conjoins New Year with Wagner's *Ring* cycle. Moreover, it inserts both of these elements into the imagined historical context of a Wilhelmine Germany still euphoric at the prospect of national rejuvenation through world war. Above all, Kluge's brief series of photographs of Arendt and Heidegger infers their love affair by citing their lives before and after National Socialism. Although the sequence says nothing about Heidegger's ideological turn to fascism or fascism's role in Arendt's move to the United States, the in-between gaps nonetheless convey an ineluctable connection between the passing of historical time and these two figures' very different fates due to anti-Semitism.

A conceptual tension presides over "Zeitenwechsel (rasch)." On the one hand, the program establishes a link between the modern clock and a far more primitive temporality reminiscent of Heidegger's existential idea of historicality. On the other hand, it forecloses Heidegger's insistence on historicality's a priori character and its status as an ideal state of whole, authentic being. Modern time, primitive time, and modern German history all appear side by side in "Zeitenwechsel (rasch)" as having equal value. If, however, National Socialism represented for Heidegger the moment when German being reclaimed its right to authentic historicality, then the representations of Nazi history in Kluge's program (air war, Hitler at the opera, firebombings) also represent this time of nationalistic becoming as mere history.[30] In this respect, Kluge also catalogues Heidegger's thought and biography as being firmly anchored in history—what Heidegger himself calls *weltgeschichtliches Geschehen* (world-historical happening)—and not above or below it (*BT,* 41). This countervailing move in Kluge's program echoes, in part, his mentor's own censure of Heideggerian time. For Adorno, Heideggerian historicality jettisons social history and deifies it at the same time. Heidegger's ontologization of time dismisses the sociohistorical conditions of experience as negligible and, at the same time, opportunistically elevates them "as though [they] were commanded by Being itself."[31] By asserting the place of historicality within history, "Zeitenwechsel (rasch)" puts the ontological thrust of *Being and Time* in context. In so doing, Kluge's program implies that the fascist transformation of Heidegger's original idea of being—in particular the German being to be inherited by the *Volk* and that sent Arendt into exile—was not transcendental but rather ideological, resolutely historical, and unquestionably violent. Yet Kluge neither trashes Heidegger's philosophy nor naively wishes to revert back to thought before Heidegger. On the contrary, Kluge's program shares Heidegger's underlying interest in laying bare other temporalities hidden by the dominance of modern irreversible time and the clock. Instead of revealing the existential time of German being, Kluge sets his sights on throwing into relief the place of this existential time in German history *and* making time in the present necessary for this historical consciousness to happen. What Kluge exhumes from Heidegger is the central ideal around which the first three aforementioned quotations orbit: the present. Just as Heidegger identifies the present as the hub of temporalities past and future, Kluge anchors the present of this television program—that point in 1988 when the French Heidegger debate started to leak into the Federal Republic—as the starting point for an abbreviated excavation of Germany's past to which *Being and Time* belongs. The commotion that Farias's publication generated about Heidegger is, however, a mere springboard for another far more politically pressing present. Unlike classical media that enveloped spectators in a timeless illusory space where the ticking clock hovered above their line of sight (see fig. 26), Kluge's program pushes the time of the present into the foreground by using his unorthodox form of television programming. In this respect, Kluge's allegiance to the dialectics of critical theory comes to the fore.

Figure 26

Alexander Kluge, still from "Zeitenwechsel (rasch)," 1988.

Writing some three years earlier on time in the media, Kluge maintained that "the present [is] a convention." "There exists," he continued, "a seam [*Nahtstelle*] between 'just now' and 'right now' . . . that represents the present."[32] "Zeitenwechsel (rasch)" is flush with these momentary blank gaps—or more accurately, radical juxtapositions—of present time. They prevail as the glue that is supposed to hold together in the minds of its viewers the program's myriad and vexing montage fragments. Unlike Hegel, who bestowed the weight of reality on the point in time, Kluge defined these seams as purely fantastic. Present time is not what television portrays or what the spectator sees. It arises entirely in the hours of dialectical work the imagination spends to fill in television's approximation of these interstices. On the occasion of the nascent Heidegger debate, Kluge's program thus aims at triggering and molding a collective opportunity to imagine German history as always emanating from these gaps in the present. However, the conditions for fantasizing about history are not restricted to registering Germany's involvement in the monumental catastrophes of the twentieth century. At its core, this fantasy work relates to fantasizing about the present as the *kairos* that Germans continually fail to exploit. Again and again, Kluge's program evokes the New Year as the archetypical benchmark of forward-marching time devoid of consequence. Two intertitles at the end of the program sum up this German problem perfectly; together they spell out a recurring case of misplaced affect: "On New Year's Eve, December 31, 1899, we were excited about tomorrow, January 1, 1900." As Kluge explained elsewhere, this centurial turn was

Figure 27

Alexander Kluge, still from "Zeitenwechsel (rasch)," 1988.

illusionary, without historical significance, and devoid of experience (*Erfahrung*) insofar as it unreflectingly ushered more of the nineteenth into the twentieth century.[33] Dates may have changed, but the experience of irreversible time had not. This lost chance applies also to the majority of other New Years denoted and connoted in Kluge's program: 1988, 1978, 1935, 1923, 1914, 1908, and 1812. New Year's Eve 1918, Kluge added, was a different story. This turning point after the Great War represented a potential moment of *kairos* when Germany could have taken up an entirely different path, one that did not lead to world war and mass murder. This opportunity, too, was squandered at the movies, "Zeitenwechsel (rasch)" suggests. Lubitsch's *Carmen* won out over the German Communist Party founded on December 30, 1918. Far from holding Lubitsch accountable for the firebombing of Hamburg (see fig. 27), Kluge nevertheless illustrates by logic of association a relation between cinema's fantasies and Germany's neglected opportunities to pilot the flow of time away from disaster. For this, the Germany of 1918, like the West Germany of 1988, would require a public sphere capable of accommodating forms (i.e., media) that facilitate historical reflection and mourning ("DMB," 66). Like Heidegger's existential temporality of being, commercial television paralyzes the historical dimensions necessary for this fantastic labor. In the case of Kluge's cultural window from December 1988, introducing Heidegger to television, networking fragments of his work and person with a larger web of historical shards from Germany's past, and, most importantly, laying ample enigmatic "seams" throughout combined to form an interface. For viewers willing to tune in, this broadcast represented a means of making time to imagine German history as a case of forsaking *kairos.*

1964: Benn, Brecht, and Heidegger in Stalingrad

Since the private television station RTL allotted Kluge less than a half hour of airtime for each of his broadcasts, many of his cultural windows have been exercises in using montage to compress as much fantasy in as little time as possible. The initial time-lapse images in "Zeitenwechsel (rasch)" of burning candles, spinning clocks, and whizzing traffic, in which twenty-two hours pass in seventeen seconds, convey simultaneously the swath of time expropriated by commercial television and the time ideally produced by Kluge's program. The crucial difference lies in how the form is used. As of late 1988, Kluge's idea for misusing commercial television effectively in the minimal time afforded to him was roughly twenty-four years old. Kluge's televisual interpretation of his earlier cinematic technique for producing time through montage goes back to when *Schlachtbeschreibung* was first published in 1964. In an excerpt published prior to the novel's release, Kluge appended his work with an explanatory footnote. Gottfried Benn's postwar poetics had functioned as a blueprint for his conceptualization of the novel. "It deals with an attempt to represent in kaleidoscopic fashion the Battle of Stalingrad from the various perspectives of the people who contributed to the event militarily or by using acts of thought [*Denkakten*]. In so doing, it approaches a technique that Gottfried Benn, with reference to the early attempts by André Gide, defined in his *Roman des Phänotyp* [Novel of the Phenotype] and that served as a model for the absolute prose he had in mind."[34] What Kluge described as kaleidoscopic, Benn referred to as his orange style. "An orange," Benn explained in 1949, "consists of numerous sectors. The individual pieces of fruit, the divisions, [are] all the same, all side by side, equivalent. . . . None extend outward, into space. They tend toward the middle, toward the tough white root that we remove when taking the fruit apart." The phenotype of the orange, the root, provides the only connection (*Zusammenhang*) for all the other pieces.[35] Like *Schlachtbeschreibung,* Kluge's television program from late 1988 takes Benn's orange style as its model. Although seemingly disparate in terms of their individual themes, each sequence in "Zeitenwechsel (rasch)" points inward toward an absent core, that thing that the German nation continually disregards: the idea of *kairos.* The television program's individual sequences throw their nucleus into relief only when assembled together. To conclude, however, that an equivalency prevails between the late Benn, the early literary Kluge, and the later Kluge on television would be shortsighted. Benn's existential interest in materializing "art as art for itself" is antithetical to Kluge's preeminently political interest in producing knowledge about time and history.[36]

From the start, Kluge appropriated Benn for purely formal purposes. Kluge's interest in the orange style has always revolved around practicing a kind of objective realism that Benn rejected outright. To Benn's idea of the orange style Kluge wedded Bertolt Brecht's recipe for activating a consciousness of the functional infrastructures that undergird reality. Writing in 1980 on the role of montage in his films, Kluge explained, for example, that "when shooting films I always stand before the problem that what I can see does not actually contain the context." "The central problem with realism," Kluge clarified with Brecht's guidance, is the fact that "most real relations have slipped into the functional."[37] Instead of attempting to render reality objectively—an endeavor dangerously close to reproducing the false appearances of reigning ideologies—Kluge's cinematic realism produces favorable conditions for knowing these invisible structural connections. In order to represent the unrepresentable, it devises codes comprised of at least two contrasting shots. Montage, Kluge's tool for producing time in the heads of television viewers, also makes conceivable the influential abstractions lurking beneath the façades of concrete reality. In other words, montage pieces together the relationality that previously went missing in historical experience, that could have made a difference in the past, and that could ideally make a difference in the present. In the case of "Zeitenwechsel (rasch)," this abstraction, when read formally, is television's expropriation of present time, and, when read substantively, is the misguided notion of historicality that underlies the disasters of modern German history. These two dimensions comprise the recto and verso of Kluge's televisual project. Since the present functions for Kluge as a moment for revealing the common ground shared by otherwise disparate times and histories, neither can exist without the other. Of the many pieces that comprise the orange-like composition of Kluge's program, Heidegger plays a crucial role in the relationality of this television program. The ethos of *Being and Time* in Heidegger's biography lends the seemingly random array of temporalities an unmistakably German instantiation of time. In light of its reach back to 1812 (when Napoleon unsuccessfully invaded Russia), "Zeitenwechsel (rasch)" infers that German time is not limited to the history of the Third Reich or its reactionary harbingers from the Weimar Republic. According to the logic of Kluge's program, bits of Heidegger's concept of German time lurk in both the most and least suspected places in German history; *Being and Time* does not foreshadow Nazism but rather represents the intellectual culmination of modern German history that continued to plague German thought even at the threshold to reunification. The functional revelations of Kluge's montage thus unveil the nationalistic illusions of temporal totality and wholeness that comprised Heidegger's political philosophy and that guided German history. Moreover, they expose the very real fragmentation endemic to modern temporal experience that precipitated the catastrophes of the twentieth century. And lastly, this fragmentation functions as a strategic incursion into the time of the present. What "Zeitenwechsel (rasch)" encourages readers of Kluge's first edition of *Schlachtbeschreibung* to unearth is the place and function of Heideggerian time in the Battle of Stalingrad.

Kluge's account of the Battle of Stalingrad tells no single story.[38] Readers learn nothing of the enormity of the event, neither the staggering number of dead and casualties nor the battle's significance in World War II. The book establishes no lines of identification with its horde of characters. The political circumstances behind Hitler's campaign in the Caucasus are never explicated. The geography of the battlefield remains unclear. The innumerable variables contributing to Germany's defeat—the Russian winter, General Paulus's obedience, Hitler's indifference, insufficient military supplies, inadequate military support, the impossibility of mutiny—receive none of the attention a war historian would expect. The fate of some 100,000 captured German soldiers—a centerpiece of West German-Soviet arbitration that fueled popular postwar discourse on German victimhood—remains a mystery.[39] And given the absence of a narrator throughout the book, a clear political agenda like anti-fascism, pacifism, or even nationalism prevalent among other Stalingrad novels never materializes. To borrow the language of cinema, Kluge's account of Stalingrad delivers a dizzying series of close-up shots, jump cuts, point of view shots, reverse angles, accelerated montages, and stock shots of the battle from shortly before the Soviets encircled Paulus's troops (November 19, 1942) to when the Germans finally capitulated (February 2, 1943). Kluge organizes his account of the battle according to ten main divisions, each comprised of what Benn called "suites," or slices of an orange. The themes of these enigmatically titled chapters are listed in order of appearance:

1. News reports of the battle
2. Governmental memoranda for acceptable reportage on the battle
3. Official guidelines for winter warfare
4. Clerical sermons written on occasion of the battle
5. Interviews with officers
6. Interviews with medical officers
7. A diary of the battle
8. A genealogy of the disaster beginning with the Peasants' Revolts in 1524
9. An abbreviated dramatis personae
10. A tripartite appendix: a brief military history (1872 to New Year's Eve 1942), a war lexicon (Kant to Hitler), and a section entitled "World of Forms"

In spite of the book's seemingly esoteric and scattershot approach to historiography, *Schlachtbeschreibung* is not addressed to the professional historian. In fact, numerous reviews that appeared after its original debut described it as being neither historically accurate nor poetically satisfying.[40] Entirely indifferent to presenting the events in Stalingrad coherently, Kluge's book denaturalizes its subject matter. In one of several unfavorable reviews that appeared in 1964, one critic asserted that "as a whole, the book never congeals, it is like a matching game, a mosaic whose shape mutates minute by minute, a puzzle for which one either loses the solution, or refrains from saying that one does not exist."[41] What this and other critics failed to discern is how the orange-like composition of the chapters traces the contours of the book's encoded functional root about the time of war.

Heidegger begins Division Two of *Being and Time* by insisting that "Dasein reaches it wholeness in death" (*BT,* 281). This fulfillment of being presents a conundrum, for in death being-there (*Dasein*) transcends the realm of experience, both for the deceased and for those who survive. Heidegger mounts therefore a string of propositions that brings him to an "existential-ontological" exegesis of death. Accordingly, the possibility of death in everyday being—what Heidegger calls Being-toward-death—represents the futurity of primordial totality in the present. This time of death as a moment of becoming whole permeates the outset of *Schlachtbeschreibung.* In chapter 1, the spirited reports from the front concede on February 3, 1943, that the battle is over. Although the enemy was superior, the

Sixth Army "died so that Germany might live" (*SB* 1964, 31). The death of hundreds of thousands of German soldiers is thus chalked up to the nation's becoming, a moment in the future when their example will continue to shine. The state propaganda apparatus embellishes this ideology in chapter 2. News reports of the defeat of the Sixth Army are instructed to convey the "immortal heroism of the men of St." as a "guarantee [of] the victory which the German nation is now, more fanatically than ever before, determined to achieve" (*SB* 1964, 46). If, as some commentators argue, Heidegger's existentialism is, in fact, a Christian theology-cum-science, then the ecumenical responses to the downfall in chapter 4 further illustrate the pervasiveness of this thanato-chronometry on the home front.[42] For example, Pastor J. from Hamburg implores his congregation to "learn to say 'Yes' to the war and all its suffering, to its 'destiny' as being sent by God" (*SB* 1964, 80). Pastor N. from Breslau assures his own parishioners that this war, death, and suffering precludes "the resurrection of the dead and eternal life"; "How much better off we are!" he exclaims (*SB* 1964, 73–74.). Wedged in between these fervent propagandistic spins on death, *Schlachtbeschreibung* lodges a seemingly unrelated excerpt from a soldiers' manual. This third chapter begins with descriptions of the natural rhythms of winter in the Caucasus: the onset of subzero winter, the duration of winter daylight, and the shifts in weather over time. Cast as a deadly place, southern Russia is also characterized as a primitive place where German superiority prevails. While the manual credits this assured victory to a "will to power," its emphasis on the lethal qualities of Russian time and space comes closest to materializing the quotidian experience of Heidegger's Being-toward-death.

Decades after *Schlachtbeschreibung* first appeared, Kluge declared (along with Negt) that German identity has always been in deficit. War, they asserted, has been nothing less than the mass mobilization of collective labor organized around a sought-after realization of an imagined Germany, a totality that exists only as a "collective preconception with attached institutional apparatuses" (*GE*, 391, 798). Negt and Kluge contended that natural defenses do exist against the dictates of nationalistic identitarian politics. If, in *Schlachtbeschriebung*, Heideggerian time and the imminence of German being stand for this "inorganic whole," then the form of Kluge's novel articulates the unorganized, organic feelings of protest—non-identitarian counter-fantasies—that resist this identity work and its rhetoric of death (*GE*, 363). Of the six modalities, to which the functional belongs and with which individual subjects concretize historical relationalities that withstand identitarian imperatives, the novel deploys the vertical.[43] Far less abstract than the functional, the vertical corresponds to the comprehension of mediated experience, historical thinking being a prime example. The most obvious manifestation of the vertical is found in the novel's diachrony of the battle. Due to their journal-like construction, chapters 1, 2, and 7 slowly march forward day by day, beginning around the time of the encirclement of the Sixth Army and ending with its defeat and capitulation. Time in these sections corresponds to what Kluge calls physical time (as measured by the calendar) and production time (the time required to produce a disaster). The excerpt from the soldiers' manual in chapter 3 introduces future time in the form of ideology; soldiers mentally prepared for the harshness of winter warfare "not only can defend themselves against [the primitive, native Russian] but can also destroy him in attack" (*SB* 1964, 55). Similarly, chapter 4 stands out because of its theology of transcendental time. Comprised of thirty-six postwar interviews with survivors, chapters 5 and 6 feature biographical time. The temporality that dominates these testimonies is the imperfect tense; these stories are quickly told. Chapters 8 and 10 capture historical time. Whereas one suite condenses four hundred years of German military history into a list, another recounts, for example, Hitler's involvement between the years 1941 and 1943 in the demise of the Sixth Army. Readers who take Kluge's recommendation in the 1978 edition to read the book "against the grain" will discover that the vertical also encompasses a synchronic axis (*SB* 1983, 7). The focus of attention on Saturday, January 30, 1943—the eve of Paulus's surrender—is particularly revealing in this respect. According to the firsthand account in chapter 1, readers learn little if anything at all. "In St. the situation is unchanged. The courage of the defenders is unbroken" (*SB* 1964, 29). According to media censors from that same day, newspapers were instructed to distract their readers with vague reports about a speech by Reichsmarschall Hermann Göring (*SB* 1964, 44). From the perspective of one of Paulus's officers, January 30 marked the tenth anniversary of National Socialism. Nearly triumphant, the Soviets pulverized German morale by sending an armada of warplanes to fly over Stalingrad's Red Square (*SB* 1964, 99). From the perspective of a medic, the last days of January were spent euthanizing German casualties before imminent imprisonment (*SB* 1964, 138). The diary entry in chapter 7 reports that Paulus considers suicide while his officers celebrate his promotion to field marshal (*SB* 1964, 239). Most significantly, it details the unconditional surrender between the German command and Russian truce officers. Chapters 1 and 8 establish that, concurrent with Paulus's capitulation, efforts were underway that same day to reincarnate the Sixth Army.

Far from whipping up the battle's myriad temporalities into an epic panorama, *Schlachtbeschreibung* vivisects history diachronically and synchronically in order to lay bare both the temporal continuities and fissures that contributed to the "organizational buildup of a disaster" (*SB* 1964, 7). The novel's diachrony accredits the kingdom of Prussia with installing the principles of the Enlightenment as the foundation for a renewed militaristic society after Napoleon (*SB* 1964, 251). This destructive tradition—nothing less than the dialectic of Enlightenment—sealed the Sixth Army's fate almost a century and a half later. Compared to this long-term reach into the past, the short-term, day-by-day accounts of the battle seem inconsequential. Beginning either shortly before or immediately after the encirclement of the Sixth Army, these accounts' diachrony tells us nothing about causality or last-minute opportunity; adequate time for that had long since passed. Rather, they reflect the making of Heideggerian time in Russia's southern steppes. Other diachronic accounts like the biographies of officers and soldiers in chapter 5 clarify the actual disjointedness of historical experience in and after Stalingrad. Instead of facilitating a totality of Being, war fragments it. Soldiers neither possess a total sensorium on the battlefield, nor can they grasp the grand historical continuum in which they act. This dissociation is so pervasive that each war experience is severed from every other one. The underlying synchrony in *Schlachtbeschreibung* represents, however, the culmination of this splintering. At any given moment, no individual experience overlaps with that of another. The mass mobilization of hundreds of thousands of men in the name of the idea of Germany, while conceptually coherent, culminates in what Negt and Kluge call the "anarchic organizational form" of all modern wars (*GE,* 842). These diachronic and synchronic disjunctures unveiled by vertical concretion all lead back to the novel's functional core. If, as Negt and Kluge argue, the functional divulges the imperceptible abstractions of history, the unveiled abstractions in Stalingrad correspond to this atomization of time that both fuels war for an idea and guarantees disaster because of this idea. As the dramatis personae in chapter 9 suggests, this atomization envelops the entire German military, from Hitler at its apex to the lowest of enlisted men at its base. This structuralist deconstruction of the battle into diachronic and synchronic planes does more, however, than just flesh out the enigmas of historical experience. Slicing up Stalingrad into cross-sections and genealogical timelines arrests historical time. Neither diachrony nor synchrony corresponds to the lived temporal experience of war.[44] Instead, they are analytic tools that engender time in the present (*kairos*) for the text and stimulate analytic thought about the temporal constellations that have propelled German history toward disaster (*chronos*). This is the time for undercutting the façade of whole Heideggerian time with the incongruity of the time of war, a time hardly unique to German modernity. Stalingrad was yet another modern factory that no photograph or film could ever sufficiently describe.[45]

1978: Fiction and Fantasies of Living Labor Lost

The rationale behind Kluge's significantly revised edition of *Schlacht-beschreibung* from 1978 remains disputed. For Stefanie Carp, the intro-duction of new and lengthier stories, explanatory footnotes, and sundry images compromised the mimetic abstractions of the original edition.[46] Other scholars have ruled in favor of the text's status as a work in progress, its resolve to reposition itself vis-à-vis the changing West German present, and its new multimedial character.[47] Indeed, Kluge endowed this revi-sion with substantial additions. While some portions from the original are truncated and the original chapter titles and sequence are altered—the majority of the 1964 edition does reappear in 1978—the most radical transformation involves the interpolation of entire chapters taken from publications and films Kluge had produced earlier that decade.[48] Because of these supplements, the 1978 edition undergoes a significant theoretical shift away from the purely structuralist approach of 1964 with its penchant for dissecting history along diachronic and synchronic axes. This edition is a different beast. Whereas previous editions do produce functional knowl-edge that no phenomenology could produce, the reinvention of the work in 1978 prompts a phenomenology that no sensorium is capable of perceiv-ing. This edition of *Schlachtbeschreibung* counterbalances its forerunner's exclusively epistemological focus by introducing another line of defense against the interminable idea of Germany. What previous editions lack and what the 1978 edition introduces is a crucial bodily relationship to the past. Though certainly not an elaboration on Heidegger's ontology and its underdeveloped relation to the body, Kluge's corporeal turn is also not a reception of French post-structuralism's interest in disciplined, organ-less, or deconstructed bodies. On the contrary, his inspiration for revising his novel stemmed, in large part, from a suggestion by neo-Marxist Karl Korsch. A footnote in the 1978 edition explains: "Korsch [writes] in an unpublished note, Boston 1942, the political economy of labor would have to be written, that is its entire history in Germany" (*SB* 1983, 311). As Negt and Kluge explicate in their 1981 magnum opus *Geschichte und Eigensinn*, Korsch's proposed economy, which they themselves elaborate, is the flip side to Marx's political economy of capital (*GE*, 88). Querying German history as a history of its political economy of labor entails accounting for the ways in which bodies labor either for or against the illusion of a total Germany. Such a historiography must thus account for the labor and time expropriated for the production of Heideggerian time. And it must also reckon with the scant remainder of labor power that—unbeknownst to the laborers' consciousness—could have produced other, less disastrous outcomes under different circumstances. As this latter inconsequential labor resides within the material body, the mode of concretion required is what Negt and Kluge call the horizontal. It "is that with which the five senses primarily deal" (*GE*, 513). Along with the vertical, it comprises the foundation for the public sphere, experience, reflection, and mourning. However, the bodies in question belong to the dead: the Third Reich's fallen or frozen soldiers in Stalingrad. Establishing sensory contact requires nothing less than magic.

Because the body lacks the training and capacity for such long-range perception into the past, Kluge exchanges the powers of fantasy for horizontal concretion (*GE*, 597). For Negt and Kluge, fantasy arises out of "feelings of protest" that emerge when people are alienated from their bodies, as in wartime, for example. Such feelings, Kluge insisted, "reside in bodies."[49] In the most extreme cases, it is the feeling of unbearable pain and the concomitant need to protect the body's welfare from imminent death. In less drastic scenarios, fantastic thoughts arise. A form of unincorporated living labor, fantasy emerges from alienated bodies and yet is never chronicled in the annals of history.[50] For Negt and Kluge a moment of political resistance, fantasy—regardless of whether it is a body in pain or fanciful flights—represents the inverted basis for an organized critique of alienated reality and its expropriation of time. In theory, engendering fantasy through literature has the potential for turning these feelings inside out and producing an organized formal space (*Formenwelt*) conducive to manufacturing much-needed psychological time in the present to feel emotions from the past. Fantasy thus binds at any given moment current impressions, bygone wishes, and the fulfillment of future wishes. These wishes are simple. "No one wants to die without ever having lived" (*SB* 1983, 304). Fantastic labor expended in the present thus functions like a time machine that travels into the past and future. Yet Kluge's extensive revision of *Schlachtbeschreibung* makes clear that whatever past fantasies readers take away from the book, these are no more or less historically authentic than the fictional stories that comprise a majority of the novel's new chapters. "There is not a single person in Germany," the novel insists in one of these appended chapters, "who feels, sees, or thinks like any of the affected parties in 1942" (*SB* 1983, 298). No book or fantastic labor will change this fact. The aesthetic and political task at hand therefore entails linking up the readers' capacity to fantasize with the fantasies in both new and old portions of the text. Although the original novel was comprised of materials culled from archives, interviews, surveys, radio broadcasts, and sundry other records, the history they convey is purely phantasmic. Far from barring access to all of history, Kluge makes the crucial distinction that embodied feelings cannot be passed directly down through the generations, let alone from one person to another. Kluge announces the centrality of this phantasmic communion in the new novel's afterword: "The book, like every fiction (including those that consist of documentary material), contains a grid on which the fantasy of the reader can cling to when it moves in the direction of Stalingrad" (*SB* 1983, 368). And in the foreword, he instructs readers to harbor a "tenacious interest, as anti-realistic as the wishes and the certainty, that realities are wicked fictions that yield Stalingrad." "That I persevere with Stalingrad," he continued, "is grounds for protest that the absence of memory is unreal" (*SB* 1983, 7). Fantasy and fiction thus verge on the territory of Negt and Kluge's irrational modality of concretion, the domain of protest. This irrational dimension emphatically stands in opposition to the alleged rationality of reality, be it in Stalingrad in 1942 or in the Federal Republic of Germany in 1978. In other words, speaking with the dead is politically explosive.

All the theoretical sophistication undergirding the new *Schlachtbeschreibung* aside, its decisive transformation boils down to a problem of communication. As one new chapter describes "Stalingrad as message," the 1978 edition is intent on transmitting news from the battle into the present (*SB* 1983, 297). In his prefatory note, Kluge makes clear that this is difficult at best: "A message, e.g., is: 'A boy does not cry.' That is a message about the sense of reality" (*SB* 1983, 7). A footnote from the same page defines "the encirclement in Stalingrad as non-message." And another new chapter explains that the news blackout of February 1943 was not the result of a single political decision. All in all, these passages underscore a collective unconscious tradition of staving off feeling after the battle. Messages are rational and therefore stymie the expression of feeling. In spite of this predicament, the new edition introduces a cast of historians intent on rectifying this communication blockage. By far the most explicit case is that of a nameless scholar at Frankfurt's Institute for Social Research. Five years old when his father died, the scholar wishes to develop a historical perspective that would provide him access to what is otherwise barred historical experience. The past in question is that of his father, Bertram. Having volunteered in 1923 for the Seventh Prussian Mounted Regiment in Breslau-Kleineburg, Bertram is credited with carrying on a military tradition dating back to Friedrich Wilhelm, the elector of Brandenburg (1620–88). "Precise" and "realistic," this tradition is dubbed Bertram's "feeling for proportion" (*SB* 1983, 284). Anything but a feeling of protest, Bertram's "feeling of proportion" accompanies him in the steppes of southern Russia. He retains it during his harrowing escape from the Battle of Stalingrad. And it shapes his Weltanschauung as a new member of the 116th Panzer Division stationed near Rome. Bertram's feelings are proportional insofar as they indiscriminately fuel him to commit the very same acts of destruction in Rome as he had in Stalingrad.[51] In spite of surviving the encirclement, Bertram is fatally wounded by an air raid and all his possessions go up in flames. Because of this, his son grows up knowing nothing of his father's feelings or memories. Such feelings are not mental, the story's narrator explains. While they are indeed corporeal, they "however do not perish with the body." Although Bertram the person is gone, "a feeling like this cannot vanish" (*SB* 1983, 288). Bertram's son believes this as well. In effect, what Bertram seeks is twofold: the lethal feeling of proportion in his father's consciousness and the wish not to die embedded in his father's body. In defiance of a colleague's rebukes and misunderstandings, the son continues to seek a materialist perspective with which to access both.

In stark contrast to the son's nebulous idea of materialist historiography, another new chapter zeros in on the most concrete example of communing with the dead. Russian pathologist Dr. W. performs before his colleagues an autopsy on the frozen corpse of a German lieutenant, who presumably succumbed in the battle. After opening the rib cage, excising the shriveled heart, and probing the desiccated gut, the pathologist concludes that starvation was the cause of death (but withholds the information for ideological reasons). When asked whether " 'wishes,' 'information about earlier generations,' or the 'protest set in motion after Stalingrad' are contained in the lost fatty tissue" of the lieutenant, the doctor answers in the negative (*SB* 1983, 302). An illustration of a "vulgar materialist perspective," the Russian autopsy is clearly not the method that Bertram's son pursues in the Institute for Social Research. In contrast to the autopsy, other more plausible historiographic methods emerge. There is historian Fred Pratschke's long-term approach that requires him to search for the earliest root of Stalingrad, "at least a thousand years ago" (*SB* 1983, 297). And there is Professor Zöberlein, presumably the fictional child of actual Nazi author and SS Werewolf member Hans Zöberlein. Zöberlein the younger is a "structural researcher" who also is committed to a long-term perspective with a radical interdisciplinary flair. Zöberlein funnels an East African skullcap from 60,000 BC, East Galician genealogies from 1820, an Italian story from 806 AD, and Celtic ruins along the Donau River into his "generous historical operations" (*SB* 1983, 293). Gabi Teichert, too, shares Pratschke's and Zöberlein's galactic sensibility. Millions of people, she insists, would have known that the causes that led to Stalingrad live on well into the present. "In a certain opposition to the aforementioned scholars," the narrator clarifies, however, "[these millions] 'knew' nothing in the strictest sense." Yet they were gravely earnest about Stalingrad. Regardless of whether Teichert is referring to the casualties of the battle or their survivors' grandchildren, her contribution to fleshing out the materialist approach to history that Bertram's son left unfinished is significant insofar as she maintains its egalitarian character. Knowing Stalingrad is not a measure of professional historical knowledge but a feeling, and anyone can feel Stalingrad lingering in the present. "A message," the narrator explains, "was buried in" the millions of people that Teichert mentions (*SB* 1983, 294). That message is the feeling for which Bertram had no time and that young boys are told not to feel. For this to happen, however, an irrational predisposition is crucial. Teichert, for example, "opposes all accounts [of Stalingrad] that mention strategic mistakes of the generals, the high army command, or Hitler" (*SB* 1983, 294). In addition to her instinctual rejection of an ostensibly rational historicist explanation of the battle, the focus of her method revolves around the absence of this very sensibility in Stalingrad. "How then could 300,000 men . . . have been hindered from pulling out of the trap?" she asks of the troops encircled in Stalingrad. Such an inexplicable hampering force, she added, was entirely absent in Hamburg shortly before Germany capitulated, when nine thousand women and children pilfered coal from a freight train under police surveillance. At face value an irrelevant story, Teichert's Hamburg story is relevant for understanding Stalingrad inasmuch as it proves that Germans in the Third Reich did act according to their own irrational sensibility. Stealing coal was a matter of rejecting the reality principle—the threat of being shot—and seizing *kairos,* a chance for survival. But why was this feeling of protest absent in Stalingrad?

Neither the aforementioned scholars nor Teichert explicate Bertram's feeling of being inside or outside Stalingrad. The story of Bertram accomplishes this task on its own. To his last fiber a German soldier, Bertram's precise and realistic feelings cloud his awareness of the multitudes of time, the narrator explains. Instead of finding time for "experience [*Erfahrung*], knowledge, the feeling of protest . . . the conscience of forefathers"— elements of his "total personality" that would have conflicted with his deadly feeling for proportion—he whiles away his time either waiting for or waging war (*SB* 1983, 284). Bertram has no sense of psychological or historical time. He is only disposed to the production times of death and destruction. Bertram is an exemplary Heideggerian who has no time for the dimension of the irrational. The reasons for this are to be found in the orange-like casing surrounding these addenda in the new edition. "Can the formal space [*Formenwelt*] carry out a putsch?" the original edition asks toward its close (*SB* 1964, 358). The answer is a resounding no for reasons to be found within the novel's original exploration of the vertical and functional. In *Geschichte und Eigensinn,* Negt and Kluge invoke Carl von Clausewitz in order to propose that war is merely a continuation of the bourgeois public sphere by other means (*GE,* 829). If the public sphere does represent a formal space where time is either expropriated or produced, then the absence of Bertram's capacity for irrational consciousness arises from the complete and total alienation of his labor capacity. That Bertram's story leaves no evidence of feelings of protest even at the cellular level explains the new edition's inclusion of fantastic narratives. Only fiction can throw into relief the deficit of living labor in such a monumental catastrophe. Although Teichert does link up with minor instances of affective protest in German history (like the one in Hamburg), feelings in Stalingrad—even when they manage to escape the encirclement, as is the case with Bertram—are forever lost to her, for there exists no correspondence between her feelings of protest in the present and those of devotional compliance among soldiers dead and gone. This is a case of radical incongruence between Teichert's quest for *kairos* and Bertram's embrace of *chronos.*[52] The sole repository where someone like Teichert can begin to explore these feelings lies in stories. In a footnote, *Schlachtbeschreibung* cites Korsch as saying that only fairy tales can explain an enigma like

Germany (*SB* 1983, 311n2). Taking Korsch at his word, the new edition accompanies the story of Bertram with a Grimm's fairy tale and a medieval epic poem. If storytelling, as Walter Benjamin argues, "creates a chain of tradition which transmits an event from generation to generation," then all of these stories participate in passing down the memory of feelings involved in the organizational buildup of disaster.[53] And all stand in contrast to the mantra, "No one wants to die without ever having lived." As for Bertram's body—his "eyes, legs, brain, ribs . . . skin" that were marched into Stalingrad because of an idea—there emerges no message of protest at all (*SB* 1983, 301). For this, Kluge later invents in his film *Die Patriotin* the specter of a dead soldier's fragmented body. What it, a wandering knee, utters mirrors exactly Gabi Teichert's own feeling of protest: "We are full of protest and energy. Who wants to die already?"[54]

2000: Heidegger and Benjamin in the Crimea

Stories are not thematic, Kluge exclaimed in 1989. They are instead short pictures, flashes.[55] Characteristic of both his prose and his television programs, this brevity has perplexed scholars of late. Above all, the succinctness of Kluge's storytelling presumably undermines his theoretical conviction in unearthing and awaking resistant, affective sensibilities. Eric Santner, for example, identifies in Kluge a frigidity lacking any and all affect necessary for Germans to mourn the loss of the other and master the atrocities of their national past.[56] What Santner misses in his censure of Kluge's aesthetic is an adherence to Benjamin's characterization of epic storytelling. A thousand-year-old vehicle for transmitting history into the present, stories adhere to a "chaste compactness which precludes psychological analysis."[57] The less narrative explication there is, the more a story grafts itself into the memory of listeners in the present. For Benjamin, the compactness of storytelling performs a radically different function than the historicism symptomatic of modernity and the modern novel. Instead of rooting out historical narratives of causality, storytelling makes present the fullness of the past by spinning both major and minor events into one epic weave. In keeping with Benjamin's idea of historical materialism, the story is not invested in practicing historicity, either. Because it bears the imprint of each and every storyteller, the story mediates memories of the past—Benjamin writes of images that flash up—in order to crack open its "secret index" for the present age.[58] Writing shortly before his own demise, Benjamin described this index as the secret to redemption that oppressed classes could deploy in their struggles. Benjamin saw knowledge of this redemption as materializing only outside of time. Instead of adhering to Benjamin's messianism, Kluge seeks this index through the anthropology of laboring bodies.[59] This index is the wish of dead bodies, dragged into war because of the idea of Germany, not to die. And it is also the wish of unorthodox historians like Bertram's son, Dr. Zöberlein, Fred Pratschke, and Gabi Teichert to appropriate these wishes for the present. To be sure, these dimensions of protest—the protest of obstinate bodies and historians—transpire within lived time. Yet the transmission of these feelings is never the undertaking of the story itself. Reading and listening are designed to be deeply interactive, insofar as Kluge's audience is supposed to engage in this affective labor. Kluge's work is merely a form in and through which reflection and mourning are to transpire. In this respect, his television programs beginning in the eighties represent an intensification of his storytelling. These stories are compressed into literal images that flash on the screen. They gather up myriad memories of the past. They obligate the viewer to assume the irrational position of the historical materialist. Above all, the television format allows for a community (of viewers) that storytelling has long since missed. For all its strengths, however, his television walks a fine line between guarding the grammar of historical time and emulating the very Heideggerian time that propelled the Sixth Army to defeat. In light of television's unavoidable threat to psychological time, Kluge's grandiose return to prose in 2000 was only logical.

Kluge was not finished with Heidegger after his television program "Zeitenwechsel (rasch)" from late 1988. With the publication of *Chronik der Gefühle* (*The Chronicle of Feeling*), Heidegger reemerged again in an unparalleled fantasy. The story "Heidegger auf der Krim" ("Heidegger in the Crimea") narrates Heidegger's fictional foray to the Eastern Front. "In the zeal of the fall of 1941, the army high command planned to have a group of university professors (archaeologists, Goth researchers, experts on settlements, philosophers) flown in to the front directly after the seizure of the Crimea. They are supposed to secure and investigate the remains of a Greek colony and seek traces of the eastern empire of the Goths."[60] The core of Kluge's story revolves around December 13, 1941, when the story's fictionalized Heidegger witnessed an actual historical event; on that day commanding officer Otto Ohlendorf and his Einsatzgruppe D liquidated approximately 14,300 residents from the city of Simferopol. The lineup of unsuspecting victims awaiting registration and deportation to a mass grave is momentarily thrown into chaos because of an oncoming motorcade. Standing off to the side, Heidegger suddenly finds himself mixed up among the undesirables. Once order is regained, the army's philosopher feels something different. "I sense a touch in my hand. I close my hand and have a hand in my grasp. A small dark-eyed woman placed a child's hand in mine and I took hold of it" ("HK," 242). Instead of delivering the child to certain death, Heidegger asks to keep the child. Ohlendorf gives in and Heidegger recites from his 1935 Freiburg lecture "The Origin of the Work of Art": "To hold originally means to take into protective heed."[61] Heidegger quickly faces the conundrum of providing for and protecting a presumably Jewish child that he cannot escort back to the fatherland. Ohlendorf finally confronts Heidegger on account of his foolishness. "You must, dear Heidegger, be able to say then: Even if she is a Jewess, I will put my existence on the line (i.e., not only with my life, but also with my prize body). Do you want to say that? You mean something private. You are following a private feeling. And that is something impossible under the conditions of an EMERGENCY." Heidegger's response is as simple as it is recalcitrant. "Then the emergency is nothing real" ("HK," 428).

Kluge's story ventriloquizes Benjamin's voice through Heidegger. "The tradition of the oppressed," Benjamin wrote in 1940, "teaches us that the 'state of emergency' in which we live is not the exception but the rule."[62] The fictionalized Heidegger's rejection of the reality principle (the state of emergency) stems not, however, from the flash of a past image à la Benjamin or from communing with the dead à la Kluge. Rather, his anti-realist feeling of protest arises from the touch of a living person, a child. In spite of the persistence of his loveless language—he commonly refers to the girl as a living being (*Lebewesen*)—Heidegger's feelings intensify to the point that he refuses to leave the Crimea, even as Soviet troops pose an imminent threat. Negt and Kluge propose that this "clinging-onto-the-skin-of-another-living-being" resists the dominion of the mind. The skin demarcates an "eigentümliche . . . Grenze"—a peculiar border *and* property line—between subject and object, conscious and unconscious, materialism and idealism, interiority and exteriority, safety and danger (*GE*, 288). This touch of the skin and Heidegger's passionate defense of the child encapsulate Kluge's mediation of both Heideggerian and Benjaminian thought in his lifelong engagement with Stalingrad. In a moment when the horizontal axis of consciousness interrupts, Heidegger turns on his own existential ontology reserved for German being. The abstractions of being fall away and the concretion of individual bodily contact presides (*GE*, 1162). The body unseats the tyranny of the mind and in a flash Heidegger stands down, amidst the killing fields of southern Russia, from his presumed cynical position on genocide.[63] This clearing, to use Heidegger's terminology, is theoretically significant insofar as his haptic protest is an utterly Benjaminian moment whereby he rejects the ideology of fascist progress. That this anti-realism transpires through his body is symbolic as well. Whereas Benjamin sought to realize his historical materialism in the flash of the dialectical image—that monadic constellation of past memories that shock consciousness—Kluge's Heidegger sidesteps the deadly course of German history because of a touch to his hand. He refuses to hand over the child to the executioners. In effect, Heidegger's own embodied being becomes a force of resistance in spite of his own unwavering thought. This melding of Benjamin's shock and Heidegger's being encapsulates Kluge's revision of critical theory. Instead of designating a story, film, or philosophy as the messenger of shock (as Benjamin or Adorno would have had it), Kluge's story advances the body as *the* ideal site through which a politics of time transpires. By misappropriating Heidegger's category of being in the form of his own body, Kluge maintains that the body not only comprises the center of all temporalities but that it can also unconsciously alter its relationship to the multitude of times. Alas, Kluge's story of Heidegger in the Crimea is a fantasy of touching that neither his novels about Stalingrad nor his television show about Heidegger approximate. Their form and content necessitate other, more circuitous lines of defense against history, nation, identity, and the disappearance of time. They nevertheless all share a common investment in making more time in the present before it is too late in the future.

> The separation of fantasy and reality, a relation of degree.
> —Oskar Negt and Alexander Kluge, *Massverhältnisse des Politischen*

> An aesthetic of cognitive mapping . . . will have to hold to the truth of postmodernism, that is to say, to its fundamental object—the world space of multinational capital—at the same time at which it achieves a breakthrough.
> —Fredric Jameson, *Postmodernism, or The Cultural Logic of Late Capitalism*

7. Phantasmagorias of Normalcy
Avant-Gardes After Unification

Technology and Fantasy at the Millennium

Fantasies of bodies torn asunder fueled a great many German avant-gardes after fascism. Common among all of the corporeal fantasies examined in *Visions of Violence* is the link between bodies imagined from the past and the potential influence these phantoms have on changing the course of present time. In the first three case studies, these bodies belong to core participants in the disasters and crimes of German fascism. Peter Weiss envisioned the exilic body as having been smashed to pieces; through painting, literature, collage, and film, he sought to regain a sense of wholeness that turned out to be itself a phantasm. The young Rolf Dieter Brinkmann wrestled with specters of the Nazi male body that haunted the youthful rites of passage in a reconstructed West Germany; intended as a disavowal of *Heimat* (home), his imperfect adaptation of French avant-garde prose animated illusions of fascist embodiment that only de-territorialization could remedy. Wolf Vostell orchestrated spaces conducive for imagining the destruction of the Jewish body; in keeping with the concentration camp's historical status as non-space, this phantasmic body could only be located when triangulated with respect to German bodies and spaces in the postwar present. By the end of the sixties, when the fabric of postwar modernity began shifting toward the postmodern, avant-garde fantasy retained its ethical imperative but began outgrowing the spatial and historical boundaries that had once inscribed it. Case in point: Berlin's communards fell prey to the spatial and temporal compressions endemic to postmodernity by equating the Vietnam War with the Holocaust and tracing these victims' identities directly onto their German bodies. In spite of this slippage, German avant-gardes prevailed after the student movement but underwent a shift from the aesthetic mediation of corporeal fantasies to an aesthetic intervention into technology's reanimation of fascist violence. For Weiss, Brinkmann, and Vostell, imagining specific bodies was always a function of technology and technique. For the late Brinkmann and Alexander Kluge, the mass media exhibited a propensity to exert the very same effects on bodies that fascism had at the middle of the century. While Brinkmann identified mass media fantasies as evidence of a fascist dialectic of reality, Kluge contended that fantastic labor could advance forms of resistance against technology's effects. As new media penetrated everyday life more and more, avant-gardes turned from fantasies of bodies to fantasies of technology's effects on those fantastic bodies. The medium eventually replaced the body's message with a techno-massage.

One of many possible narratives about the history of German avant-gardes after 1945, the story that *Visions of Violence* tells insists that fantasies of fascist violence comprise the fulcrum around which each and every avant-garde episode turns. Historical junctures like the founding of the Federal Republic of Germany in 1949, the student riots in the "hot summer" of 1968, and the terrorist spectacles in the "German Autumn" of 1977 played only a secondary role, if that, in the constitution of the avant-gardes presented here. Political, social, and cultural events never eclipsed the primacy of the fascist past in avant-garde politics of the present. And yet the fall of the Berlin Wall in late 1989 and the subsequent unification of East and West Germanies have shaken the German imagination to the core. While some avant-gardes after 1989 have followed in the tradition of their predecessors, others have brought to light fascism's fall from prominence. Evidence of this is certainly not limited to the domain of the avant-garde. In fact, some of Germany's most visible public intellectuals and cultural figureheads have called for a paradigm shift in German historical thought. In his reviled 1993 essay "Anschwellender Bocksgesang" ("Swelling Cry of the Billy Goat"), writer Botho Strauß, for example, charged the postwar intelligentsia and mass media with promoting German self-hatred. Strauß avers that their needless harping on the spectral return of history irrevocably stunted the mind-set of entire generations.[1] In a 1998 acceptance speech, writer Martin Walser—reiterating Strauß—indicted the mass media with instrumentalizing German guilt, and cudgeling Germans with obligatory acts of conscience.[2] Most recently, philosopher Peter Sloterdijk recycled the Nazi language of racial purity and the Final Solution in his 1999 speech "Regeln für den Menschenpark" ("Rules for the Human Park"); in light of unprecedented life-altering technologies like bioengineering, postwar West German codes for acceptable historiographies of fascism were no longer valid.[3] In each of these instances, technology and history converge as grounds for reappraisal. For Strauß and Walser, this union disfigured historical consciousness in much the same way that the late Brinkmann had portrayed twenty years earlier, hence their grounds for lambasting the mass media. For Sloterdijk, technology signaled a possibility of social progress but only on the grounds that it be carefully managed. In this respect, his optimism is not unlike Kluge's sanguine misappropriation of new media. Whether they intended to or not, these thinkers erected their case for moving beyond the ethics of German history on the corpse of a divided Germany. Unification signaled a caesura, a decisive break from the bleak past and a move toward a brighter future. In this respect, the fact that all three thinkers encountered similar charges of flirting with the specter of fascism hardly comes as a surprise.

There is nothing new to breaking postwar taboos by relativizing the Holocaust and fascism. Years prior to unification, German academics and public intellectuals had already battled over the ethics of moderating memory of the fascist past. Nevertheless, normalizing Germany's history after unification has assumed an entirely new guise in which technology and fantasy have conjoined in the most unparalleled of ways. Where Strauß, Walser, and Sloterdijk only called for a sea change in the relationship between past and present, work was well underway to reconfigure the spatial logic of German history. In addition to the unprecedented architectural transformation of Berlin into the new capital, this remapping has thoroughly pervaded the imaginary spaces of contemporary German culture as well. However, not all spaces are equal. As is the case with Berlin's Potsdamer Platz, the filling of divided Berlin's voids with neoliberal signs of political power and commercial profit has ushered in landscapes of renewal at the price of paving over traces of the past.[4] In other instances, like the renovated Reichstag and the Jewish Museum, this push to rebuild has thoughtfully incorporated these voids and traces into the city's monumental façades. Other prominent commercially driven sites have elevated the past as consumer spectacle with delirious consequences; instances of the past are reified and flattened into spaces belonging to the present.[5] Within the imaginary spaces of unified Germany's cultural artifacts, a surfeit of memory has dominated. Like the heterotopias of Berlin's cityscape, these spaces are anything but identical. What a great many do share, however, is an excess of memory. Much recent popular cinema and literature has been intent on serving up nostalgic impressions of East and West Germany's postwar pasts.[6] These fantastic spaces have also reached back to the era of the Third Reich. In a great many of these cases, the effects are strikingly reminiscent of the compressions that emerged in quasi-avant-garde quarters from the late sixties: differences between past and present, history and memory, self and other, fantasy and reality implode into the black hole of the present.[7] In effect, the postmodernity that first reared its head around the time of the student riots became the matrix of unified Germany.

Of the many new technologies held accountable for this acceleration, compression, displacement, and global transmission of memories of the twentieth-century German past, it is the human-computer interface that scholars have singled out the most. New media like computers and the Internet advance both amnesia and a hypertrophy of prosthetic memories. Virtualization and simulation create asocial urban spaces while promoting alluring illusions of total immersion and immediacy. Digitization advances the false premise that the space of the user interface allows anyone to sculpt memories into history of their own choosing. Warning against the lure of high-tech phantasmagorias, Lutz Koepnick has even proffered the thesis that the visual excess of hyperreality actually "numbs the senses and denies the body as a private site of experience."[8] If technology does indeed occupy a central place in the spatial and temporal remapping of the fascist past in unified Germany, which tools are suitable for cracking open, if not breaking through, the fantastic totalities of neoliberalism undergirding much of hyperreality? Is there any room for the violent fantasies of postwar Germany's post-fascist avant-gardes in a national culture in which the power of a technologically choreographed fantasy fuels dominant narratives of normalization? Andreas Huyssen has petitioned that neither the austerity of Theodor Adorno's critique of the culture industry nor the optimism of Walter Benjamin's faith in the progressive character of cinema adequately mine the formal and substantive dynamics of this millennial dialectic of memory.[9] German avant-gardes after unification seem to concur. Although an unadulterated Frankfurt School proves unprofitable for the following last two case studies, critical thinking is nevertheless indispensable in their incursions into the vertigo of the virtual.

Far from tracing avant-garde praxis onto theoretical master documents that are better suited for wrestling with postmodernity, these illustrations reproduce the very structures and symptoms they wish to topple. Implicit and external in the first example and explicit and internal in the second, theory's place is always secondary in these avant-garde spectacles. This relationship between theory and avant-garde praxis is significant insofar as it subordinates the work of the mind to the primacy of bodily experience. In contradistinction, then, to Koepnick's concern for new media's paralysis of the body, experience, and history, these avant-gardes demonstrate how bodies continue to serve as agents in the reclamation and defense of an ethical relationship to Germany's past in spite of normalizing forces after unification. In the face of technologies that presumably derealize and dematerialize the temporal and spatial differences so crucial for avant-gardes before unification, these examples insist on the resilience of the body's materiality, its function as a placeholder between fantasy and reality, and its ability to crack open a critical space between past and present. For these avant-gardes, bodies still prove powerful enough to pierce the phantasmagorias of unification.

The idea of the phantasmagoria originally applied to ghost shows of the late eighteenth and early nineteenth centuries. A combination of technology and spectacle, the phantasmagoria was quite often a primitive light show in which the audience's loved ones would purportedly return from the dead. As the border between the rational and irrational vanished, pandemonium ensued. Over the course of a century, the idea of the phantasmagoria shifted.[10] While it had first applied to public spectacles, the concept morphed to describe the irrational fancies within the modern mind. With these final two examples of German avant-gardes after unification, the phantasmagoria regains its original meaning and form. Both of these examples deploy human-computer interfaces as technologies capable of conjuring up ghosts that must be dispelled. In the first illustration, by the German filmmaker turned artist Christoph Schlingensief, the phantasmagoria in question is comprised of a complexly orchestrated constellation of old and new media: a proto-cinematic peep show, computers, the Internet, television, and cell phones.[11] In the second illustration, a play by René Pollesch, the phantasmagoria assumes the form of an imagined private residence fully networked to the Internet.[12] Where Schlingensief's phantasmagoria projects fascism's ghosts into city streets, Pollesch unveils the space of the phantasmagoria as a private sphere that technology haunts. In both cases, the ocular primacy of the original phantasmagoria is retained.

In keeping with his beginnings in underground filmmaking from the middle of the eighties, Schlingensief creates a cinematic spectacle intent on empowering and undercutting the spectator's gaze. For Pollesch, who has directed well over thirty of his own plays since his theatrical debut in 1999, the gaze is transformed into the power flow of technology pouring into the home; the traditional spectator of the phantasmagoria assumes the new role of prisoner in the virtual panopticon. This optical distinction between Schlingensief and Pollesch reveals a fundamental conceptual divide that shapes their relationship to German avant-gardes before unification. Given its investment in preserving and protecting the historical difference between victims and perpetrators for the present, Schlingensief's work harks back to the identitarian politics of Weiss, the early Brinkmann, and Vostell. In Pollesch's play, such differences struggle to exist. While suggestive of the late Brinkmann and Kluge and their battles against the technological apparatus, Pollesch's work—because of its emphasis on an unparalleled technological transformation of the world—wanders into the (post)modern dystopias described by post-structuralist theory further than any of his predecessors. In the realm of the high-tech panopticon, identity (like the bodies, histories, and spaces to which it belongs) becomes immaterial. In this respect, Pollesch picks up the story of German avant-gardes after fascism where Berlin's communards left off. Whether his theater signals the endgame of Germany's post-fascist avant-gardes or merely the severest of challenges to their continuation remains to be determined.

Peep Show Politics: Christoph Schlingensief's Austrian Container

On February 4, 2000, Wolfgang Schüssel was sworn in as Austria's newest chancellor and promptly formed a coalition government between his conservative party, the Austrian People's Party (ÖVP), and the Freedom Party of Austria (FPÖ), a right-wing nationalist party committed to stopping undesirable foreigners from immigrating to Austria.[13] Vienna exploded with street demonstrations, and the European Union's other fourteen members promptly enforced a cordon sanitaire around the country. In conjunction with the annual Vienna Festival, Christoph Schlingensief crafted his action *Bitte liebt Österreich* (*Please Love Austria*) as a direct response to this surprising turn in Austrian politics, history, and culture. In a televised interview aired during the action, Schlingensief likened the project to that of a film studio. "We erected a film village," he noted. "We're producing images that simply take FPÖ leader Jörg Haider and his slogans at their word."[14] To this end, Schlingensief erected alongside the city's Staatsoper (State Opera) a container compound comprised of two layers: an interior complex of steel containers and a courtyard, and a shrouded construction fence blocking the Viennese public from gazing freely inside. Within this 200-square-foot complex of containers he interned twelve asylum seekers from Africa, Asia, and Eastern Europe for seven consecutive days, from 9:00 P.M. on June 11 to 9:00 P.M. on June 17, 2000. Conceived in part as a reworking of the German version of the then widely popular reality show *Big Brother* broadcast on the German television station RTL-2, *Bitte liebt Österreich* invited the Austrian public to eliminate via phone or internet (www.webfreetv.com) all but one of the foreigners from the game by voting for their deportation from the country. The last remaining contestant won thirty-five thousand schillings and a chance to acquire Austrian citizenship through an arranged marriage. Schlingensief's action galvanized the Austrian media, the public, and—above all—everyone who came in direct contact with it. Spontaneous and unscripted public debate erupted in front of the container in the first twenty-four hours after the asylum seekers arrived. Not everyone was willing, however, to just debate the implications of the action. At the close of the third day, two people broke into the compound but were promptly chased off by security personnel. A third protester was hauled away by police. On the fourth day, a coalition of concerned citizens erected a billboard stating, "This is not reality. This is a game, a dangerous game of emotions. Direct your complaints to: Mayor M. Häupl . . . " That evening, another trespasser failed in his attempts to set the container's sleeping quarters on fire. Day five witnessed a butyric acid attack on the compound. On the evening of day six a storm of protesters climbed atop the highest container and vandalized a banner exclaiming "Foreigners Out." On the final day, Schlingensief was charged by police with engaging in public demagogy.

Unlike the asylum seekers who saw the action as a promise of personal gain, spectators were hard-pressed not to view the action as a political provocation aimed at Austrian citizens and Austrian national politics, as well as Austria's unmastered fascist past. For some Viennese, Schlingensief's action swindled city funds in the name of pseudo-art, threatened to unleash violence in Vienna's streets, polluted the city's cultural landscape, and sullied the nation's international reputation.[15] Conversely, veteran sixty-eighter Daniel Cohn-Bendit exemplified the opinions of many proponents when he publicly exclaimed that the dream of the historical avant-garde had been resurrected in the name of a democratic, multicultural society: "Art is once again central in the political process," he told a crowd assembled before the container (*SAR,* 212). Yet Cohn-Bendit's blessing, his implication that after a long hiatus aesthetics had once again interceded successfully in the political economy of the real, grossly oversimplified and even mischaracterized the history of the avant-garde after fascism and the intention and effects of Schlingensief's action, as well as the historical and cultural context in which it unraveled. Indeed, the public debates around Vienna's "container city" unknowingly slogged through the critical vocabulary of the historical avant-garde: the action's status as a work of art; its relationship to the hegemonic institution of art; and the degree of its political intervention in everyday life. But in the end, it was Sloterdijk who convincingly declared that any and all allusions to the historical avant-garde and its principal parts were misguided. "The epoch is over in which an avant-garde could work with surprises or with direct attacks on an unprepared nervous system. Immunologically speaking . . . we are thoroughly immunized" (*SAR,* 226). While the mechanics of the historical avant-garde may very well be extinct, Schlingensief was nevertheless convinced that his action had achieved avant-garde effects. Referring to Breton's second surrealist manifesto from 1929, he explained in an interview after the action, "The true surrealist act is to shoot into a crowd. . . . Even though you heard no shot, you still saw a lot of seriously injured people who staggered around or screamed in pain or suddenly started hollering." [16] Whether these effects signaled actual success remains to be seen. Certain, however, was the way in which *Bitte liebt Österreich* played out new media's deactivation of the classical public sphere in order to turn new media against themselves.

In spite of all his overt allusions to the television program *Big Brother,* Schlingensief insisted that his action was most indebted to the silver screen. In an interview with Kluge, he explained, "Vienna is for me . . . a film studio" (*SAR,* 142). Upon closer inspection, however, his action's status as film was not definitive, for it actually fluctuated between cinema and television, as well as theater and performance art. It was, above all, the action's explicit incorporation of reality television that mesmerized a majority of spectators and commentators alike. Nevertheless, little consensus emerged as to what exactly the container made real. The author Elfriede Jelenek hypothesized with Jean Baudrillard's postmodern philosophy in mind that *Bitte liebt Österreich* was a medial reflection of reality's simulations. [17] Daniel Cohn-Bendit insisted that via reality TV Schlingensief had succeeded in fulfilling Haider's xenophobic promises as well as the racist predilections of all Austrians. The more theoretically minded critic Diedrich Diederichsen contended that the action collapsed theatricality and reality and as a result revealed the current public sphere as nothing more than a staged performance.[18] All over the map, these and other assertions all presumed that reality television—transplanted into the body of presumably socially engaged art—transcended the base realm of the cultural industry and succeeded in demystifying by making transparent the abstractions that otherwise cloud and confuse the true nature of social relations. In other words, if reality TV ultimately serves the commercial interests of its producers, then Vienna's "container city" indubitably furthered Schlingensief's presumed interest in laying bare the "true" deplorable nature of Austrian multiculturalism. What makes these and other suppositions so problematic is their assumption that both reality television shows like *Big Brother* and Schlingensief's container succeed in cutting through the veil of mediation and accessing an obscured truth.

If the promise of total visibility in reality programming is nothing but a ruse, what then of Schlingensief's appropriation of the format?[19] Reality television, especially in the guise of the *Big Brother* series, concocted, according to media scholar Mark Andrejevic, an amalgam of comprehensive, round-the-clock surveillance and online interactivity. This invasive network of technology promised to denaturalize and demystify the otherwise invisible production processes responsible for the artificial form and content of prime-time television (*RTV,* 120–30). Jettisoning the artifice of the frame, reality television purportedly served up authentic interpersonal conflict among its houseguests whose "realness" was a function of their willingness to just "be" themselves. Armed with Slavoj Žižek's political philosophy, Andrejevic contends, however, that the dedifferentiating move of eradicating, or pretending to eradicate, the frame—nothing more than an assault on representation, mediation, master narratives, and by extension the symbolic order—engenders just the opposite, namely a totalization of the frame through the disavowal of the borders that once separated it from reality.[20] Speaking in terms of Lacan's linguistic orders, Andrejevic insists that "getting real" now entails in this postmodern condition "a short circuit between the imaginary ([i.e.,] imagined alternatives to the given reality) and the real that results from the impasse of the symbolic order" (*RTV,* 202). Said differently, in the viewer's mind representation's previous incongruence with lived experience—the abstract nature of mediation—is resolved so that representation now becomes all of real experience. As this sense of incongruence infiltrates everything, experience must nevertheless be debunked as patently false yet inescapable. Andrejevic writes that "the promise of reality TV is not that of access to unmediated reality . . . so much as it is the promise of access to the reality of mediation" (*RTV,* 215). In light of this assessment of ubiquitous mediation as the conceptual linchpin of reality television's cultural politics, it becomes clear that Cohn-Bendit, Jelinek, Diederichsen, and others underestimated the complexities at work in the model on which Schlingensief based his own reality game.

Keeping Andrejevic's illumination of reality television in mind, it is arguable that this "reality of mediation" comprises one substantial strand of Schlingensief's aesthetic politics, and furthermore, that the action's promise of access to and agency over that which its spectators think they see replicates what Andrejevic and Žižek cite as the postmodern denigration/proliferation of the symbolic. Just as reality TV strives to convince viewers that it has cast off what is believed to be its material ideological apparatus, so too did Schlingensief's action strive to undo its presumed status as a scripted art event masterminded by a notorious provocateur and performed in conjunction with an arts festival.[21] Take, for example, Schlingensief's exchange with Jelinek: "'It is not art, what I do,' he says. I say, 'On the contrary. . . .'" Schlingensief's exchange with bystanders is similar: "They asked me why 'Foreigners Out!' is hanging there. I said because this is a theatrical work. 'Is there also a text for it?' they wanted to know."[22] Debates like these over the site's status as a legitimate artwork make obvious that the container action, by flirting with and simultaneously refusing the institution of art, destabilized the work's intermediary position as signifier. Hardwired to relinquish any and all influence over the course of events inside and outside the container, *Bitte liebt Österreich* pushed to complete the postmodern short circuit between the imaginary and (a false) reality by accommodating interactive participation and the promise of a populist experience. Accordingly, the public actively sidestepped the symbolic order, otherwise perceived as residing at the level of mediation, with imaginary ideals that in the end expanded the boundary of experience to include spectators.[23] However, "getting real" with the container was anything but singular for those who came in contact with it. For resolute right-wing sympathizers of Haider's isolationist nationalism who voted night after night for (and thus against) asylum seekers, getting real entailed fulfilling Haider's promise by dialing in or logging on. For the anti-fascist "Indianer," who on day four assaulted the container, defaced its "Ausländer raus" sign and temporarily "liberated" its inhabitants, reality was equally accessible and malleable according to their anti-racist vision. But the agency these social actors attained, their dismissal of the container as theatrical representation, did not in any way denote their belief in the dissolution of art as an intermediary or conversely in the realness of the reality that their actions engendered. The keystone of Andrejevic's argument—the persistence of the symbolic order in spite of its abolition—very much applies to *Bitte liebt Österreich;* throughout their engagement with the action, spectators remained fully aware of the constructed nature of the reality on display in the Herbert-von-Karajan Platz. In fact, the conservative *Kronen Zeitung* punctuated both the artifice of the action and its pointlessness in seeking out an authentic reality; in a headline published on the last day of the event—"Container-Show kostet Millionen"—it was reiterated that the container was just entertainment, a costly show that wasted taxpayers' money (*RTV,* 6–7). In this respect, it would seem that Schlingensief was entirely correct when he declared that from the start there was no success to be had for either side in his elimination game; *Bitte liebt Österreich* was nothing more than a twenty-first-century manifestation of *l'art pour l'art,* art that made no claim to altering social reality whatsoever.[24]

Reality TV's promise of direct access to the real manifests itself in the primacy of sight. Comprehensive surveillance and the promise of total transparency, along with the involvement of a commercial public sphere, Andrejevic notes, are the building blocks of television's reproduction of postmodern society's phantasmagoria of authenticity, transparency, and agency. Clearly, *Bitte liebt Österreich* borrowed reality TV's camera technology along with its sealed digital enclosure; vision, though central to experiencing the container, was not as transparent as many thought. Advertised in the Kärntner Straße with a sandwich board announcing an "Asylum Seeker Peep Show," the container complex enclosed and concealed its contents with the express purpose of constraining its consumption as mass spectacle. A peep show was originally a box punctured with an aperture that rewarded paying spectators with titillating pictures of freakish humans often demonstrating extraordinary feats. This show presented viewers with three access points into the inner workings of the container: a low-lying, narrow slit in the outlying wooden fence; a live video feed composed of round-the-clock footage from eight surveillance cameras accessible to outsiders via closed-circuit television; and streaming video via available through a web browser.[25] Clearly not a function of technological limitations as was the case with the kinetoscope of the mid-1890s, Schlingensief's apparatus employed the limited scopic vectors of the peep show as a counterpoint to the irresistible, bombastic spectacle announced by the stacked containers, the agitprop banners that adorned it, and the public commotion on top of and around it. Furthermore, Schlingensief's peep show departed from its precursors' penchant for featuring extravagant characters like vaudevillian strongmen, exotic dancers, and contortionists. While ironically billed by Schlingensief as "the square of heavenly execution" where Haider's undesirable outsiders were to be detained and executed, this peep show was not only boring but provided little if any information with which to cast a vote.[26] The banality of this peep show's "secrets" along with its restrictive aperture undercut the ocularcentric thrust of the project. Seeing failed to produce either a collective experience or any relevant knowledge required to vote an asylum seeker out of Austria. In the words of the action's most incisive reader, Georg Seeßlen, the container deflects the look back at the spectator entirely.[27]

It is arguable that in spite of these allusions to cinema's prehistory, the container's rehabilitation of the pre-cinematic gaze was actually a duplication of reality TV. The deployment of the scopic drive in shows like *Big Brother* and their exposure of spectators as "impotent masters" who frame the spectacle does certainly apply to *Bitte liebt Österreich*. Nevertheless, the reach of reality television only partially penetrated into the architecture and outcome of Schlingensief's action. The relevance of the pre-cinematic apparatus must not be underestimated when reckoning with the political potency of the container project.[28] In spite of their many similarities, *Bitte liebt Österreich* neither replicates it entirely, nor does it abandon its spectators to a state of blissful complicity, in which the dominion of "the reality of mediation" makes racism in contemporary Austria that country's unalterable fate. On the contrary, Schlingensief's container folds the scopic mechanics, spatial dimensions, and the social relations characteristic of early cinema into the action's high-tech surface in order to make counter-publicities possible that sidestep the vertigo endemic to the search for a more real reality. The degree to which such alternative public spheres actually materialized is, in hindsight, statistically unclear, but it is undeniable that the container made their very existence conceivable thanks to the experiences—in the Frankfurt School sense of the word—that its aesthetic composition made possible.[29] To borrow from Miriam Hansen's reading of early cinema's production of counter-public spheres, Schlingensief's peep show—unlike classical cinema with its invisible gazes—rehabilitated the conscious exhibitionism and voyeurism typical of early cinema and theater that reminded viewers of their participation in the spectacle (*BB*, 36). Second, the social relationship between the public spaces of Kärtner Straße and Herbert-von-Karajan Platz and the enclosed space of representation behind the container's viewfinders was neither abstract nor severed; both constituted together "a social horizon of experience" that punctuated the invisible exclusionary logic of Austria's dominant public opinion (*BB*, 12). Third, the container and the events that transpired in and around it culminated in a discursive experience capable of mediating "individual perception with social meaning, conscious with unconscious processes, [and a] loss of self with self-reflexivity" (*BB*, 12–13).

These connections are not limited to the temporal confines of the present. The production of this alternative experience in *Bitte liebt Österreich* took on historical dimensions, insofar as it invited the juxtaposition of racially motivated nationalism from the Nazi past with its pending return in the Austrian present. The event insisted on such temporal connections through its incongruities; by designating the container as a concentration camp, recycling Waffen SS slogans like "Unsere Ehre heisst Treue" ("Our Honor Is Loyalty"), or accusing bystanders of being closeted Nazis, Schlingensief trafficked in anachronisms while nevertheless drawing attention to potential legacies from Austria's fascist past. Most importantly, *Bitte liebt Österreich* remained, in spite of its more exclusive forms of technological participation, a thoroughly public event that anyone and everyone could engage communicatively. Indeed, countless spectators sparred with one another and with the action in their efforts to make sense of the disparate discursive connections that it conjured up. Similarly, Schlingensief accounted for the de-territorialized and fractured state of the dominant industrial-commercial public and accordingly deployed his container action as a space and process whereby competing counter-publics (e.g., the left-wing liberationists, liberal intellectuals, Austria's minorities) and partial publics (e.g., the FPÖ's constituency, *Kronen Zeitung* subscribers, Internet users) congregated, collided, and together exposed the potential power in unveiling the otherwise obscured relationality underlying all experience. Ultimately, Schlingensief's project acknowledged not only the unavoidable "reality of mediation" that impairs contemporary vision's purchase on epistemological certainties, but also the irrevocably mediated quality of postmodern publicity.[30] And lastly, it was not in spite of but rather because of this pervasive mediation in Schlingensief's action that any contestation of hegemonic mechanisms and forces of exclusion from below was divulged as being inextricably complicitous in those very same mechanisms and forces.

For all its visual bombast, then, *Bitte liebt Österreich* was one big spectacular ruse. The action's lessons in mediation called upon the eye only to pass it over for the body. Yet it was not some singular ideal body that Schlingensief's action addressed. On the contrary, *Bitte liebt Österreich* incorporated a plenitude of bodies, among which crucial distinctions exist. On the one hand, foreign bodies inhabited the interior spaces of the container as virtual bait. The preordained objects of the gaze, these bodies were, however, mere signifiers of the symbolic order, flickering signs scripted, performed, and perceived as being alien. If their status as image did not forcefully underscore the virtuality of their bodies in the interactive spectacle, their costumes (sunglasses, head scarves, garishly colored wigs) certainly did convey the performative and thus discursive character of their (largely feminized) role in both the container action and Austria's right-wing politics. Looking from the outside in, these foreign bodies became fleshy only at that point in the event when, disqualified by the public, security guards whisked them out of the container and into cars waiting to escort them out of Austria. Read through the lens of philosopher Giorgio Agamben, the material body of the other emerged in *Bitte liebt Österreich* at precisely that point where the polis jettisoned from its sphere of qualified good life what it deemed to be simple biological life, bare life.[31] As Agamben deftly points out, this exclusion not only marks a cornerstone of modernity, which has lived on in both totalitarian regimes and twenty-first-century democracies, but was also the crux of biopolitics under National Socialism. Playing a game of exclusion in the streets of Vienna thus made palpable not only the contemporary politics of exclusion touted by Haider, but also its historical precedent: the culmination of modern biopolitics. In this respect, the obfuscating architecture of the container coded the technological virtualization of the material body as a precondition for the execution of biopolitics both past and present.

On the other hand, indigenous bodies populated the environs around the container as agents contracted to fulfill the task of seeing. Visitors to the container lined up, filed through queues, ducked down to see the tightly cropped body parts of the asylum seekers through peepholes, huddled around closed-circuit television monitors, charged the container and vandalized it, rushed back to their computers, or dialed up the appropriate telephone numbers to vote their least favorite foreigners out of Austria. Not unlike the pre-cinematic devices that bound the visual with the haptic,

Schlingensief's peep show was a thoroughly mobile, multisensory experience reliant on people doing things with their bodies. As some scholars of new media argue, digitization has transformed the analog image from a thing to see into a phenomenological process whereby bodies are called on to bestow form upon the information swirling around them.[32] Similarly, Schlingensief emplaced this constitutive role played by the multitude of spectators before his container within an ongoing historical drama about bare life that was hardly limited to Austria's right-wing FPÖ. In *Bitte liebt Österreich,* the interactivity of classical media invented before the advent of cinema not only obligated spectators to move their bodies in order to construct and perceive the frame but also facilitated dialogues about the structural and historical conditions for political power, the gaze, and the making of citizenship. Enframing with one's body came at the price of excluding other bodies. Yet the body's involvement was also the very thing that drew attention to and stirred public debate around Haider's promise to undertake a draconian biopolitics in contemporary Austrian society.

By unmasking postmodernity's unfettered access to reality as deception, *Bitte liebt Österreich* turned reality television on its head. Schlingensief exposed television programming's latest promise—to convene individuals in a social matrix where new forms of experience emerged—as yet another instance of administered culture's propensity to hawk cheap time-consuming events to ready and willing consumers. The flip side of this revelation was a conviction that exploding the medium and its myths created the conditions for actualizing a space where ethical and collective experiences could unfold. In this respect, Schlingensief was following in the footsteps of Alexander Kluge and Oskar Negt, who maintained in *The Public Sphere and Experience* from 1972 that both emancipatory critique and proletarian experience cannot transpire on the television screen. On the contrary, they can only emerge out of qualitative situations, collective fantasies of social diversity, and material contact with the body politic.[33] Schlingensief concocted his own recipe for such a counter-publicity by choreographing a symbolic, fantastic, and material engagement with the technological mediation of televisual experience within the spaces of the affirmative public sphere. In order to unseat the fantasies of reality television, Schlingensief gleaned from media archaeology those cinematic forerunners capable of disrupting the passivity underlying the voyeurism and exhibitionism that reality programming nurture. Unlike commercial television, the action's incorporation of cinema's precursors obligated spectators to become the spectacle using their own bodies. While encouraging their complicity in the promotion of right-wing xenophobia, it also allowed for the possibility of critical distance, the perception of a reconfigured aura, the reciprocity between social actors and the spectacle, and above all, a sense of sympathy toward the other. Sloterdijk's appraisal, the theoretical confirmation summoned only after the conclusion of the action, confirmed this. If, as Sloterdijk proposed, Schlingensief's action did indeed bring to life, albeit momentarily, a politically efficacious event, then this politics is measurable not in the degree to which it aided and abetted progressive or right-wing ideals. Instead, the politics of Schlingensief's deployment of classical and new media alike emerged in its potential for invigorating counter-publicities wedded to the conviction that embodied experience is always already historical.

The Digital Panopticon: René Pollesch's Theater of Orientation

When questioned whether Schlingensief's action would have had any effect in Germany, Sloterdijk responded enthusiastically: "Oh yes, absolutely. I'm entirely convinced that it would have had an even bigger resonance in Germany than in Austria." The deportation of asylum seekers would have exuded, Sloterdijk added, a much higher "reality bonus" for Schlingenseif's action. In light of deadly outbreaks of neo-Nazi violence against foreigners in unified Germany, a German version of *Bitte liebt Österreich* would have been the apotheosis of hyperreality. Far more interesting for Sloterdijk, however, would have been the national debate about the state of the avant-garde at the millennium that such an event would have triggered. He explained, "One would have surely reacted in Germany much harder against certain artists who stand in the tradition of the avant-garde who claim to have found a way to continue avant-gardism."[34] That Sloterdijk staged his action in Vienna was without question a case of being in the right place at the right time. *Bitte liebt Österreich* did play off of distinctly Austrian political and cultural conditions that might have been overshadowed by a German equivalent. Yet the action was never so much the fulfillment of a fantasy within the borders of a single nation-state, as it was an exploration of the transnational techniques and technologies of new media within that portion of German-speaking central Europe haunted by the fascist past and affected by global migration. The second more intriguing question Sloterdijk entertained—the missing German debate over the state of the avant-garde—is one for which playwright

René Pollesch might have had little time or interest. His mentor Hans-Thies Lehmann explained in his 1999 manifesto-cum-encyclopedia for postdramatic theater that the historical concept of the avant-garde connoted a far too martial, dogmatic, and unilinear program for it to apply accurately to artworks today. Postdramatic theater like Pollesch's is far too deconstructive and discursive, heterogeneous and multimedial, nonnarrative and self-reflective for it to rightfully join the ranks of the historical avant-garde.[35] Neither wedded to just the afterwardness of the postmodern nor nostalgically loyal to the modern, the postdramatic theater, Lehmann maintains, seeks Brechtian ends by other post-Brechtian means.[36]

If by "Brechtian" Lehmann means epic theater and its penchant for provoking spectators to think critically, then Pollesch's theater could be called, in part, excessively epic. In fact, the humor in much of Pollesch's work is so inundated with critical theoretical discourse that only experts initiated into the intricacies of contemporary cultural theory catch on. Pollesch has said much about his relationship to theory. "I am hardly a theoretician," he explained in an interview from 2003.[37] Other people's theory, he insists, is merely a point of departure for the production of his texts. Theoretical models lurk everywhere in his plays. With respect to the hugely influential theoretical tract *Stadt als Beute* (*The City as Booty*) penned by a sociologist, a political scientist, and an urban planner in 1999, Pollesch admitted that what inspired him to appropriate the book and what influenced him to pen his own *Stadt als Beute* was its unique phenomenology. "Therein the city is discussed differently . . . than what one is normally accustomed to. . . . The exciting thing for me is finding a language that does not yet predominate in the theater."[38] Pollesch wears his admiration for theory's unfamiliar and de-familiarizing language on his sleeve. "Spaces and territories play only a subordinate role for global players," actress Astrid Meyerfeldt declares in Pollesch's own *Stadt als Beute*. "In the course of the 'international division of labor,' entire corporate divisions are shut down and strewn across the globe."[39] The theoretical blueprint of the same name that inspired Pollesch's text reads almost verbatim.[40] Yet Pollesch has made it clear that his intentions have never been to cut and mix, even though theatrical texts like Pollesch's *Stadt als Beute* do read at times like emulations of a disc jockey's work. Cultural theories invested in unveiling the neoliberal instrumentalization of postmodern imploded space, for example, are only starting points.[41] Theory initiates for Pollesch and his actors subjective associations and opportunities to articulate abstract propositions with their own lived experience. Instead of conceiving theory as a finished product, a script with which to instantiate objective reality, Pollesch deploys theory as the kernel of a self-reflective process for himself as well as his actors. Rehearsing for a performance entails, therefore, making sense of theory, trimming its claims according to the specific context and consequences of acting and directing today, and developing performative techniques that preserve and convey the egalitarian character of this process. If, as Pollesch claims, the most important development in his work is the unveiling of theory's suitability for everyday life, the life in question is undoubtedly that of the creative and intellectual classes.[42]

Lest anyone unfamiliar with Pollesch think his work is nothing more than academic pyrotechnics outfitted for the stage, a closer look at *Smarthouse* [®]*1+2* reveals the multiplicity of contradictory and conflicting voices and bodies that coexist alongside theory. Commissioned by the State Theater of Stuttgart and performed with a cast of amateur actors on November 23 and 24, 2001, the script to *Smarthouse* [®] *1+2* has never been published.[43] Although the original actors performed "pirated copies" of the work on stages in Berlin (2002) and Hamburg (2003), the singularity of the piece runs to the core of Pollesch's politics of theater. Pollesch's scripts are never just textual blueprints to be shipped off indiscriminately to any troupe or playhouse. Instead Pollesch binds his work to his own person as well as his actors, whose personal and professional lives are the life of his texts. As the original labor expended in rehearsals is unique to all involved parties, and as the labor spent on stage is never a final product but rather the continuation of that original labor, Pollesch remains resolved to restrict the redistribution of his and their work. To borrow the language of Negt and Kluge, Pollesch retains the possibility of protecting unalienated labor in spite of the fact that the labor of the theater in the present era, in which culture is capital, is always alienated work.[44] In this respect, it is not far-fetched to conceive of Pollesch and his regular stable of actors as a cottage industry. As for the actual execution of *Smarthouse* [®] *1+2,* the performance took place on a makeshift illuminated disco dance floor (roughly six feet by eighteen feet) erected atop seats in the theater's parquet. Hanging well behind this stage and high above the stage proper, a screen displayed sundry images, including live video footage of the play itself, projected from a data projector. The cast's production crew—including an indispensable prompter—occupied the first of the last nine rows of the theater; the rest were allotted to the audience. On stage, four actors outfitted with wigs and retro attire from the seventies plopped themselves on beanbags, cushions, and an equestrian saddle. In between rounds of rapid-fire dialogues and monologues, the play would cut to what Pollesch calls "clips," musical interludes during which actors performed choreographed stunts, paused to refresh themselves while images flickered by on the screen behind them, and prepared the stage for the next round of script. With its mise-en-scène entirely exposed for all to see, *Smarthouse* ®*1+2* dispensed with all theatrical illusion.

In this two-part production, Pollesch recycled characters, forms, language, and themes developed in previous productions since 1998.[45] As with Pollesch's *world wide web-slums* from the previous year, the Internet dominates the script's themes. Even the names of the four characters resonate like outlandish aliases characteristic of online chat rooms: Frank Olyphant, Gong Scheinpflugova, Bambi Sickafosse, and Turm Garten. All four live together in Frank's "smarthouse." Frank, a passionate on-line shopper, lives happily in his high-tech home, in which the heating and cooling system is connected to his refrigerator, computer, television, telephone, home security system, and, of course, the Internet. Frank's enthusiasm for his biometric-sensitive home fades, however, at precisely that moment when the voice of conscience surfaces in the form of theory. Such a shift transpires discursively in the form of a single word or concept like "social practices." "But with which social practices," Frank asks, "is a home supposed to be produced?" And from that point, he, Gong, Bambi, and Turm bandy about theoretical jargon—the heterosexual means of production, the gendered division of labor, the character of commodities, the fantasy of capital, everyday subjectivity versus objective reality—in order to expose the humanistic liberties that Frank's home extinguishes. In their attempt to make sense of what is missing in Frank's smarthouse, the characters arrive at a point where these keywords no longer address what he lacks. Instead, they describe affirmatively the conditions under which he lives. "Capital makes your utopias come true," Bambi later exclaims. She then sloganeers, "Shop around in the utopias of the revolutionary corporations out there!" At this point, Marxism fully morphs into postindustrial managerial-speak.[46] Critique collapses into affirmation. Alterity becomes interiority. This slippage of cultural critique—its susceptibility *and* instability—recalls the flexible flows of neoliberalism, that theory of dominant economic, political, and social discourses responsible in the last thirty-five years for advancing the liberalized marketplace as the basis of a new social ethics.[47] In the case of *Smarthouse* ®*1+2*, the world of cultural theory is just another commodity, one perfectly well suited for democratic advocacy groups and neoliberal managers alike. Not only the characters in Pollesch's play but also Pollesch himself are keenly aware that the language of cultural critique has become freely exchangeable cultural capital.

The constellation of recurring themes in *Smarthouse* ® *1+2*—the networking of the private sphere, the reach of digital technology, and the power of global commerce—does more than just deflate the language of critical thought. According to cultural theorists like David Harvey, every aspect of daily human life has taken on a host of new and decidedly anti-democratic symptoms since the emergence of neoliberalism in the seventies.[48] In addition to harnessing critique for cultural capital, neoliberal economic policies and political programs have opened new global markets, privatized the public sector and dismantled the welfare state, commodified biological life, affirmed hetero-patriarchal relations as the locus of state and capitalist power, and even transformed the citizen into biological capital.[49] For the characters of *Smarthouse* ® *1+2,* information technologies—their abilities to accumulate, store, and process hordes of data run to the core of neoliberalism's advancement of the marketplace—trump Frank's initial worry over vanquished social movements like those that West Germany's New Left produced after the student movement.[50] Worst of all, neoliberalism topples the humanist subject. Frank's smarthouse invites global capital to burrow itself into the bodies of its inhabitants. Subjects are reduced to biological matter programmed to consume. Software enforces hetero-normative identities and sexualities. Lived history is flattened into a clickable list of sites visited on the Internet. In spite of the severity of the subjects' condition, their state of complicity to neoliberalism's "cannibalization of the subject" is anything but passive. The aforementioned assimilation of critical discourses—theory's fall into consumerism—repeatedly reverts back into two opposing forces. This occurs especially in instances when a subject's consciousness reasserts itself. "No," Frank shouts, "I can't live in this shit any longer." Conversely, the reconstitution of the arsenal of keywords used by Michel Foucault, Michael Hardt and Antonio Negri, Giorgio Agamben, or any other theoretician repeatedly fails to gain enough momentum to make a lasting difference. In the end, the tug of war between theory and technology makes an ambivalent impression. While audiences find the discursive whirlwind humorous and thus presumably entertaining, critics like Diederichsen have pondered whether the ineffectual theory fetishism of the play parodies a very real theory fetishism that befell Germany's younger educated class after 1989.[51] But according to Pollesch, his use of theory is anything but parodic. By virtue of its abstractions, theory can break though the illusions of reality by providing orientation. "Place," Pollesch clarified in 2001, "is the problem. And in this respect orientation becomes a task."[52] "[Theory]," he explained in 2002, "is the language with which the actor-personalities attempt to orientate themselves."[53] And in 2004 he explained that only theory can help solve the "problem of orientation" that has arisen now that concepts as basic as love float freely apart from their referents.[54]

There exists much more to *Smarthouse* ®*1+2* than this never-ending cat-and-mouse chase between theory and capital. Orientation is indeed at work, but it involves much more than theory. Another look at the play is necessary, one that goes beyond the play's script and instead attends to the dialogue's delivery. If theory and capital comprise the two primary antagonistic voices of the play, then the scream counts as a third voice, what Negt and Kluge would label the "enclosed third." The following excerpt is taken from the third scene of the first installment of the play. Capitalized words signify screamed dialogue.

TURM GARTEN. I thought we lived in a commune. I thought that this here
    was a commune, that this social movement HERE was a commune!
GONG SCHEINFLUGOVA. But this isn't . . . AHHHHH [*Gong looks at
    the prompter*]. But this isn't a commune here. In here the service-
    provider commune from outside just comes in and goes out. There
    is no social movement in this house. There is only a movement of
    SERVICE PROVIDERS!
TURM GARTEN. The Internet in your home is everywhere. Your REFRIG-
    ERATOR supports your lifestyle . . .
BAMBI SICKAFOSSE. . . . which is individual and social, cozy and complex,
    functional and entertaining.
TURM GARTEN. The network in this house . . .
GONG SCHEINFLUGOVA. . . . refrigerators that surf the Net . . .
FRANK OLYPHANT. That's what you wanted in the commune HERE. Liv-
    ing individually in opposition to mass consumerism, and capital re-
    alized this utopia.
BAMBI SICKAFOSSE. Capital makes your utopias come true.
GONG SCHEINFLUGOVA. And you can go shopping and go FUCKING
    SHOPPING in your utopias.

BAMBI SICKAFOSSE. Shop around in the utopias of the revolution . . . Shop
. . . AHHHHH Shop in the utopias of the revolutionary corpora
. . . AHHHHH [*Bambi looks at the prompter. The audience begins to
laugh.*] Shop in the utopias of the revolutionary corporations OUT
THERE!

There are two modalities of screaming in this excerpt. A long-standing
staple of Pollesch's theater, the first variant involves the actor distancing
her body from the conflict at hand.[55] When Gong, Bambi, Turm, and
Frank shriek keywords like *home, here, out there, service provider,* and *shopping,* their bodies convulse and stiffen. The result of an affective surplus
that language cannot capture, screaming sets off a chain reaction that
interrupts the corporeal effects of Frank's smarthouse. Frank's home is
not so much a roof over his head and those of his friends as it is a vehicle
for excising capital directly from their bodies. In opposition to this neoliberal commodification of the body, the shrieking and jerking establish
embodiment as both the target of global capital and the material basis of
a resistance against this affront. Pollesch himself has equated this kind
of outburst with the cinematic cut, a necessary rupture in the otherwise
unstoppable flow of narrative.[56] The second modality of screaming results from the debilitating effects of theory overload. The rapid-fire script
in *Smarthouse* repeatedly pushes the actors (Bambi in particular) to the
brink of breakdown, at which point they all scream and flail, and await
the prompter to guide them back into the torrent of cultural theory and
advertising copy. As with the purposefully scripted screaming, these un-
predictable screams involve the body asserting its presence. Yet unlike the
first order of screaming that identifies the body as the victim of the smarthouse, this second order reveals how theoretical discourse has aided and
abetted this cannibalization by divorcing itself from the body. "When it
comes to one's belongings [*Eigentum*]," Negt and Kluge explain, "the path
to annulling the alienation of the self travels through a third term" (*GE,*
42). In the case of these four characters, the possessions in question are
their bodies. The only remotely effective antidote emanates in brief fits
and starts from their voices and bodies.

If the scream affirms the importance of the obstinate body in Pollesch's
theater, and if it also confirms theory's effectuality against (if not its complicity in) the body's transformation into just another piece of hardware in
the smarthouse, the orientation generated through screaming never cul-

minates in a final escape. It appears, therefore, that Pollesch has happened upon the very same postmodern conundrum that Negt and Kluge did in *Geschichte und Eigensinn*. "What do we do," they pondered, "when we possess no fixed points of reference that . . . fulfill the need for concrete social orientation?" (*GE*, 1006). Indeed, navigational points of reference are seemingly absent in the smarthouse. Digital technology has facilitated the complete integration of inside and outside, such that the resulting erasure of boundaries and borders leaves one screaming in desperation. Orientation—what Negt and Kluge call the "prototype of theoretical work"—is incapacitated (*GE*, 1002). Interestingly enough, Pollesch does not resign himself to this dead end. Rather, he follows precisely the solution that Negt and Kluge propose in such moments of vertigo. They insist that people can "orientate themselves practically, when they otherwise have nothing, according to what they know historically" (*GE*, 1006). Indeed, history plays an irrefutably crucial role in all of Pollesch's theater. Historical personae like Angela Davis, Mae West, or John Wayne operate in some works as historical foils for Pollesch's characters caught in the present. In other works, cultural artifacts like films by Rainer Werner Fassbinder, John Cassavetes, Fritz Lang, or even Kluge serve as a heuristic for measuring the historical dimension of the digital age when experience has otherwise collapsed the past into the present. In *Smarthouse* ®*1+2*, the contours of history are thrown into relief primarily through the uniquely German cultural history of the house itself. Specifically, this cultural history began with the theory and practice of communal living that emerged in the second half of the West German sixties and concluded with the squatting scene in the seventies and eighties that spilled over into urban guerrilla violence and terrorism. So when Turm confesses, "I thought we lived in a commune" and Gong replies, "In here the service-provider commune from outside just comes in and goes out," both are engaging a thirty-five-year-old assertion by the founding member of Berlin's legendary Kommune 1. According to the mastermind of West Germany's original commune, Dieter Kunzelmann, socially transformative praxis hinges on the possibility of demarcating between the outside world and the interiority of the commune.[57] When all four characters sing karaoke-style to the "Rauch-Haus-Song"—Ton Steine Scherben's 1972 rock anthem to Berlin's squatter scene—they make utterly clear their wish to reactivate this battle cry for their own twenty-first-century squatters' battle. Above all, when Frank suggests they jump-start a social movement by throwing Molotov cocktails into his smarthouse, and that they all then ingest gasoline and immolate themselves like suicide bombers, Pollesch's characters radicalize further what Bommi Baumann had begun within the proto-terrorist faction of the Movement 2 June. In effect, the past's importance for Pollesch lies in establishing a patently German historical basis for orientation.

Alas, historical consciousness is not a panacea. In each of these aforementioned instances, reconstituting revolutionary wishes from the past produces a new round of failures in the present. This is especially obvious when all four characters rematerialize on stage after projecting themselves as Molotov cocktails into the audience. Not even the symbolic destruction of one's own body can halt the smarthouse's animation of its occupants. Nevertheless, the history of praxis does make a difference, for it operates in tandem with the knowledge of theory and the affective intensities of screaming to establish what Negt and Kluge call relationality. In Pollesch's work, relationality entails unveiling the otherwise obscured historical context of the present; exposing the postmodern transformation of the private into the public; disclosing the post-humanization of the white, straight, male, liberal subject; and establishing cultural theory's proneness to lapse into theoretical culture. Just as Negt and Kluge warn, Pollesch refrains from mechanically translating theory into praxis. "Theory," they insist, "has its practical dimension . . . in that which praxis is not capable of achieving on its own" (GE, 484). What praxis cannot deliver is orientation. Negt and Kluge contend that Eigensinn—that underdeveloped sixth sense called obstinacy, autonomy, or self-will in English—is the seed of revolution that bears fruit when the body no longer yields to the dictates of power.[58] The orientation needed to harvest this obstinacy in actual revolution exceeds the means of theory, however. Orientation, they insist, lies "not only in the feelings, not only in reason, and not only in the external chain of events," but rather in liminal social spaces where all three intersect and where that juncture becomes publicly perceptible (GE, 84). In spite of the fact that Pollesch equates the interior space of the theater with the exterior realities of the simulacrum, his work nevertheless does succeed in generating epistemological and ontological differentials between inside and outside with which to fulfill, in part, his desire for orientation. That Pollesch's work falls short of harnessing the gargantuan quota of orientation throughout society necessary for triggering revolution should certainly come as no surprise. Pollesch makes clear that a romantic notion of reconstituting politically potent grand narratives—Marxism, feminism, postcolonialism—against the hegemony of neoliberalism will not amount to change. Theory is only one piece of a larger puzzle in which both historical experience and the body play equally decisive roles.

Impossible Returns and Uncertain Futures

With Pollesch's *Smarthouse* ®*1+2,* the story of *Visions of Violence* comes full circle. Peter Weiss's paintings, prose, and films of the thirties, forties, and fifties were inundated with images of travelers and the desire to return home. Homecomings turned out to be impossible for these exiled characters. It is arguable that the exilic condition is also relevant for Pollesch's play about the Internet and its infiltration of the domestic sphere. Technology's rampant and inexorable influence has alienated an entire class from their homes and their bodies. In stark contrast to the private spaces of Berlin's communes from the late sixties, the borders between private and public have crumbled entirely. The very thing that Weiss sought, the idea of home, is now engulfed. Exile emerges as the only viable option for escaping the smarthouse. But unlike the traveler in Brinkmann's early prose who is continually on the move, Pollesch's characters are never at liberty to seize a line of flight out of their predicament. There is no question that the origins and conditions that led to exile in Weiss's work and those that engendered alienation in Pollesch's play are radically different. Above all, Pollesch's work can only reference German fascism obliquely through an allusion to Berlin's communards who reinvented the private sphere in the name of practicing anti-fascism. That this tie to the National Socialist past goes unmentioned would seem to suggest that the only historical divide which *Smarthouse* ®*1+2* traverses invariably leads back to the history of the Federal Republic of Germany. Nowhere in Pollesch's oeuvre does the preceding chapter of twentieth-century German history—the era of the Third Reich—present itself as a reference point for mapping the present. Neither Schlingensief nor any of the other representatives of West Germany's post-fascist avant-gardes presented in *Visions of Violence* would have made such an inference. In spite of these impressions of Pollesch's superficiality versus the gravitas of Weiss's lifelong expulsion, the world of the smarthouse does border structurally on what Agamben calls a non-place. In contrast to Vostell, however, who invoked the Nazi concentration camp as a fantastic space from the past that continues to haunt the present, Pollesch infers that technology transforms the present into a non-place that threatens to collapse the past altogether. Any line tracing the camp of virtual reality back to the death camp that Weiss believed would be his end is suspect at best. If the historical incompatibility of these two opposites illuminates anything, then it is certainly the great distances that German avant-gardes have traversed in such a short period of time.

Like all of the individual narratives of post-fascist avant-gardism told in *Visions of Violence,* Pollesch does not resort, though, to nihilism and defeat. Substantively, his theater does stage a protest by articulating the enunciation of history with the mind and body. Formally, it strives to protect the living labor of its actors and, conversely, lessen the alienating effects it puts on display through strict proprietary restrictions on performance and publication rights. Once again, the body emerges as a site of vulnerability and possible resistance. Of all the more recent practitioners of German avant-gardes prior to unification discussed in *Visions of Violence,* the late Brinkmann and Kluge are Pollesch's closest kin. Well before the Wall fell, both credited new media with an unparalleled power to hijack consciousness, impede bodily sensation, and blot out the past. This menace notwithstanding, both also evinced varying degrees of optimism about the possibility of holding one's ground and dispelling the illusory phantasmagorias that obfuscate time and space. Brinkmann and Kluge pass on this hope not just to Pollesch but to Schlingensief as well. Yet for all their shared hope to quell the phantasmagorias of normalcy at the millennium using fantasies of the German past, Schlingensief and Pollesch could not be any more different. While both do extensively incorporate the Internet into the architecture of their work, and while both also infer the detriments of this technology, only Schlingensief retains the ethical imperative to unmask these effects specifically in terms of their dangerous incursion into German and Austrian memory. Far from operating like the "moral cudgel" that Walser abhorred in 1998 for its knee-jerk invocation of Auschwitz, Schlingensief erected his own version of the high-tech concentration camp at a cultural-political juncture when the past did seem to rise from the dead. What was thought to be the spectacle, however, ended up reflecting the spectators' complicity in Schlingensief's fantastic concoction of right-wing populism and interactive technology. While a political transformation of the Austrian public sphere never emerged out of *Bitte liebt Österreich,* a space for critical reflection on time and politics did. This virtual camp was but a means to unmask the unreal hauntings at work in the present. With Pollesch, a shift transpires from fantasies of the past to fantasies of the present. Although certainly an actual artifact of the twenty-first century, the smarthouse of Pollesch's play prevails as a dystopian fantasy in which the past conveys little if any ethical import. The utility of the past resides in its ability to throw the timeless present into historical relief. Since the German past in question encompasses a time and space that only knew the cold war, the predicament of thoroughly integrated living is left detached from the epicenter of postwar German identity politics. In this respect, the scraps of West German history incorporated into *Smarthouse* ®*1+2* function like identitarian pillars upon which Pollesch affirms the end of identity. It is indeed too premature to elevate Pollesch's work as the sign of all future avant-gardes in Germany. His example nevertheless calls attention to a possible sea change in the historical consciousness of future German avant-gardes.

At the outset this book, I maintained that avant-gardes in Germany acquired an entirely new purpose after fascism. That purpose involved coming to terms with the ramifications of fascist violence for the forward march of time after the downfall of the Thousand Year Reich. Contrary to a great many charges leveled at West Germans for avoiding memories of the past, *Visions of Violence* contends that a tradition persisted in both the Bonn and Berlin Republics that was intent on inflecting the unacceptably unhistorical state of the present with sharp doses of the fascist past. Far from dredging up actual artifacts or spinning simple causal relationships between past and present, these avant-gardes produced fantasies of the past that at least stood in direct opposition to the course of present time. At stake in all of these case studies is the promise of a future unlike the one promised by the present, one either unblemished by fascism or mindful of how to prevent the immanent threat of fascism's return. These avant-gardes undertake precisely what Benjamin meant in his theses on the philosophy of history when he wrote, "The past can be seized only as an image that flashes up at the moment of its recognizability." [59] In all of the avant-gardes discussed here, it is the body that both triggers this moment of recognizability and comprises the flashing image, a fantasy of an embodied past. The fact that all of these fantasies involve bodies—exiled bodies, German bodies, Jewish bodies, male and female bodies of those born after fascism—attests to the importance these avant-gardes placed on circumventing the memories of the mind. Bodies tell histories about which consciousness has little interest or knowledge. Although purely phantasmic, these bodies had always conveyed the weight of real, material history. Over the course of time this authority waned, for the materiality of the body and the concreteness of history were no longer certain. Fantasies of the past were overtaken by fantasies of the present. Whether this dematerialization will continue to silence the body's claim to Germany's past is a question that only future German avant-gardes can tackle. The legacy of post-fascist German avant-gardes leaves these indeterminate heirs a testimony to both the phantasmic *and* material bodies' incontrovertible roles in any politics of time.

Notes

Unless otherwise noted, all translations from German into English are those of the author.

Introduction

1. Alexander Kluge, "On New German Cinema, Art, Enlightenment, and the Public Sphere: An Interview with Alexander Kluge," interview with Stuart Liebman, *October* 46 (Fall 1988): 57.

2. F. T. Marinetti, "The Founding and Manifesto of Futurism," in *Marinetti: Selected Writings,* ed. R. W. Flint, trans. R. W. Flint and Arthur A. Coppotelli (New York: Farrar, Straus and Giroux, 1972), 43.

3. André Breton, *Manifestoes of Surrealism,* trans. Richard Seaver and Helen R. Lane (Ann Arbor: University of Michigan Press, 1972), 47, 32.

4. For a detailed discussion of German militaristic cults of violence and world war and futurism's and expressionism's involvement in these, see Michael Geyer, "The Stigma of Violence, Nationalism, and War in Twentieth-Century Germany," *German Studies Review* 15 (1992): 76–80.

5. Recent scholarship that grounds both Dada and surrealism in the violent aftermath of World War I includes Amy Lyford, "The Aesthetics of Dismemberment: Surrealism and the Musée du Val-de-Grâce in 1917," *Cultural Critique* 46 (Fall 2000): 45–79; and Bridget Doherty, "'See: We Are All Neurasthenics!' or, The Trauma of Dada Montage," *Critical Inquiry* 24 (Autumn 1997): 82–132.

6. The primary texts from the expressionism debates can be found in Ernst Bloch et al., *Aesthetics and Politics* (London: Verso, 1980).

7. Vincent Kaufmann, "Life by the Letter," trans. Caren Litherland, *October* 64 (Spring 1993): 95–96.

8. John Clute, "Fantasy," in *The Encyclopedia of Fantasy,* ed. John Clute and John Grant (New York: St. Martin's Press, 1997), 338.

9. This instrumentalization of fantasy as violence meted out onto reality follows Kathryn Hume's important contention that fantasy and mimesis are neither antithetical nor inherently countervailing. See her *Fantasy and Mimesis: Responses to Reality in Western Literature* (New York: Methuen, 1984), 21.

10. Breton, *Manifestoes of Surrealism,* 125.

11. Theodor W. Adorno, "Looking Back on Surrealism," in *Notes to Literature,* vol. 1, ed. Rolf Tiedemann, trans. Shierry Weber Nicholsen (New York: Columbia University Press, 1991), 87.

12. Renato Poggioli, *The Theory of the Avant-Garde,* trans. Gerald Fitzgerald (Cambridge, Mass.: Belknap Press, 1968), 25–26.

13. Helmut Heißenbüttel, "Zur Geschichte des visuellen Gedichts im 20. Jahrhundert," in *Über Literatur* (1963; Stuttgart: Klett-Cotta, 1995), 81, 89.

14. Greil Marcus, *Lipstick Traces: A Secret History of the Twentieth Century* (Cambridge, Mass.: Harvard University Press, 1989), 18.

15. Yvonne Spielmann, *Eine Pfütze in bezug aufs Mehr: Avant-Garde* (Frankfurt am Main: Peter Lang, 1991), 35.

16. Bettina Clausen and Karsten Singelmann, "Avantgarde heute?" in *Gegenwartsliteratur seit 1968*, ed. Klaus Briegleb and Sigrid Weigel (Munich: Deutscher Taschenbuch, 1992), 463.

17. Kristine Stiles, "Never Enough Is *Something Else:* Feminist Performance Art, Avant-Gardes, and Probity," in *Contours of the Theatrical Avant-Garde: Performance and Textuality,* ed. James M. Harding (Ann Arbor: University of Michigan Press, 2000), 265–76.

18. Peter Bürger, *Theory of the Avant-Garde,* trans. Michael Shaw (Minneapolis: University of Minnesota Press, 1984), 83 (hereafter cited parenthetically in text as *TAG*).

19. While Bürger in his concluding sentences does link "post-avant-gardiste art" with the excessive irrationality of late capitalism, only in subsequent essays does he firmly establish a link to the postmodern (*Theory of the Avant-Garde,* 94). See Peter Bürger, "Aporias of Modern Aesthetics," *New Left Review* 184 (November–December 1990): 56.

20. Examples of these respective positions can be found in Jost Hermand, "Das Konzept 'Avantgarde,'" in *Faschismus und Avantgarde,* ed. Reinhold Grimm and Jost Hermand (Königstein: Athenäum, 1980), 14; Miklós Szabolcsi, "Avant-Garde, Neo-Avant-Garde, Modernism: Questions and Suggestions," *New Literary History* 3, no. 1 (1971): 64–65; Matei Calinescu, "Avant-Garde, Neo-Avant-Garde, Post Modernism: The Culture of Crisis," *Clio* 4, no. 3 (1975): 334; Benjamin Buchloh, "The Primary Colors for the Second Time: A Paradigm of Repetition of the Neo-Avant-Garde," *October* 37 (Summer 1986): 52; and Charles Russell, *Poets, Prophets and Revolutionaries: The Literary Avant-Garde from Rimbaud Through Postmodernism* (New York: Oxford University Press, 1985), 243.

21. See Benjamin Buchloh, "Theorizing the Avant-Garde," *Art in America* 72, no. 10 (November 1984): 19, 21; and Buchloh, "Primary Colors," 43. Hals Foster elaborates further on Buchloh's critique of Bürger's idea of repetition in *The Return of the Real: The Avant-Garde at the End of the Century* (Cambridge, Mass.: MIT Press, 1996), 21.

22. Of the many postwar appraisals of the avant-garde, Hans Magnus Enzensberger's scathing essay "The Aporias of the Avant-Garde" (1962) best exemplifies the simplistic conflation of avant-garde violence with fascist violence (see the discussion of Enzensberger in chapter 1). Concentrating on the legacies of avant-garde violence for the American art scene of the 1960s, James M. Harding's essay "The Simplest Surrealist Act: Valerie Solanas and the (Re)Assertion of Avantgarde

Priorities" begins to infer the different registers of violence in the avant-garde before and after World War II. His essay can be found in *Drama Review* 45, no. 4 (December 2001): 142–62.

23. Benjamin Buchloh, introduction to *Neo-Avantgarde and Culture Industry: Essays on European and American Art from 1955 to 1975* (Cambridge, Mass.: MIT Press, 2000), xviii.

24. Given its state-sanctioned embrace of socialist realism, the dominant conceptualization as well as the underground recuperation of the avant-garde in the East followed an ideological dynamic that merits its own investigation. For a thumbnail sketch of the avant-garde discourse in the German Democratic Republic and other Soviet bloc countries, see Hermand, "Das Konzept 'Avantgarde,'" 8–11.

25. Geyer, "Stigma of Violence," 102.

26. Hans Magnus Enzensberger, "Am I German?" *Encounter* 22, no. 4 (April 1964): 17. For a closer reading of the extirpation of the national in postwar German culture, see my "Roll over Beethoven, Chuck Berry, Mick Jagger, etc.: Rock, Identity and the Illusion of Progress in the West German Literary Imagination," in *Sound Matters: Essays on the Acoustics of German Culture,* ed. Nora M. Alter and Lutz Koepnick (London: Berghahn, 2004), 183–96.

27. Hermand, "Das Konzept 'Avantgarde,'" 12.

28. See Andreas Huyssen, "The Search for Tradition: Avantgarde and Postmodernism in the 1970s," in *After the Great Divide: Modernism, Mass Culture, Postmodernism* (Bloomington: Indiana University Press, 1986), 164–65 (hereafter cited parenthetically in text as "ST"). Huyssen writes that Fiedler "was really attacking modernism, and he himself embodied the ethos of the classical avant-garde."

29. Hermand, "Das Konzept 'Avantgarde,'" 9; see also Wolfgang Welsch, "Modernity and Postmodernity in Postwar Germany (1945–1995)," in *Culture in the Federal Republic of Germany, 1945–1995,* ed. Reiner Pommerin (Oxford: Berg, 1996), 110–13.

30. Martin Walser, "Über die Neuste Stimmung im Westen," *Kursbuch* 20 (March 1970): 36.

31. Roman Luckscheiter, *Der postmoderne Impuls: Die Krise der Literatur um 1968 und ihre Überwindung* (Berlin: Duncker und Humblot, 2001), 37–42.

32. The comment is attributed to poet Hilde Domin and is reprinted in *Protest! Literatur um 1968,* ed. Ralf Bentz et al. (Marbach am Neckar: Deutsche Schillergesellschaft, 1998), 384.

33. Three West German treatises on the idea of the avant-garde that attest to the longevity and variability of the idea of the postwar avant-garde include Alfred Andersch, ed., *Europäische Avantgarde* (Frankfurt am Main: Frankfurter Hefte, 1949), 5–11; Helmut Krapp and Karl Markus Michel, "Dichtung als Ärgernis: Noten zum Avandgardismus," *Akzente* 5 (October 1955): 399–407; and Hans Egon Holthusen, "Kunst und Revolution," in *Avantgarde: Geschichte und Krise einer*

Idee, ed. Bayerische Akademie der schönen Künste (Munich: R. Oldenbourg, 1966), 7–44.

34. Welsch, "Modernity and Postmodernity," 199, 124.

35. Manfred Frank, *What Is Neostructuralism?* trans. Sabine Wilke and Richard Gray (Minneapolis: University of Minnesota Press, 1989), 342. See also Jürgen Habermas, "Modernity—An Incomplete Project," trans. Seyla Ben-Habib, in *The Anti-Aesthetic: Essays on Postmodern Culture,* ed. Hal Foster (Seattle: Bay, 1983), 3–15.

36. Hanns-Josef Ortheil, "Was ist postmoderne Literatur?" *Die Zeit* (17 April 1987): 21. Reprinted in *Roman oder Leben: Postmoderne in der deutschen Literatur,* ed. Uwe Wittstock (Leipzig: Reclam, 1994), 126.

37. Geyer, "Stigma of Violence," 102.

38. For more on the historical debates and ambiguous definition of this term, see Werner Wertgen, *Vergangenheitsbewältigung: Interpretation und Verantwortung, Ein ethischer Beitrag zu ihrer theoretischen Grundlegung* (Paderborn: Ferdinand Schöningh, 2001), 14–26.

39. Robert G. Moeller illuminates this selective remembering in "War Stories: The Search for a Usable Past in the Federal Republic of Germany," *American Historical Review* 101 (October 1996): 1008–48.

40. Theodor W. Adorno, "The Meaning of Working Through the Past," trans. Henry W. Pickford, in *Critical Models: Interventions and Catchwords* (New York: Columbia University Press, 2005), 92.

41. Alexander Mitscherlich, *Gesammelte Schriften,* ed. Helga Hasse, vol. 4 (Frankfurt am Main: Suhrkamp, 1983), 14.

42. See Andreas Huyssen, "The Politics of Identification: 'Holocaust' and West German Drama," in *After the Great Divide,* 97–100.

43. Eric Santner, "The Trouble with Hitler: Postwar German Aesthetics and the Legacy of Fascism," *New German Critique* 57 (Fall 1992): 23. Santner is referring to Kiefer's series of self-portraits as a saluting Hitler titled *Besetzungen* as reproduced in Mark Rosenthal, *Anselm Kiefer* (Chicago: Art Institute of Chicago, 1987).

44. See Eric Santner, *Stranded Objects: Mourning, Memory, and Film in Postwar Germany* (Ithaca: Cornell University Press, 1990).

45. See Michael Geyer and Miriam Hansen, "German-Jewish Memory and National Consciousness," in *Holocaust Remembrance: The Shapes of Memory,* ed. Geoffery H. Hartman (Oxford: Blackwell, 1994), 185.

46. Sigrid Weigel also makes this point in *Bilder des kulturellen Gedächtnisses: Beiträge zur Gegenwartsliteratur* (Dülmen-Hiddingsel: tende, 1994), 11. For a theoretical overview of this Cartesian schism and feminism's response, see Elizabeth Grosz, "Bodies and Knowledges: Feminism and the Crisis of Reason," in *Space, Time, and Perversion: Essays on the Politics of Bodies* (New York: Routledge, 1995), 25–43.

47. Leslie Adelson, *Making Bodies, Making History: Feminism and German Identity* (Lincoln: University of Nebraska Press, 1993), 32–33.

48. Richard Huelsenbeck, "En Avant Dada: A History of Dadaism," trans. Ralph Manheim, in *The Dada Painters and Poets: An Anthology,* ed. Robert Motherwell (Cambridge, Mass.: Belknap, 1988), 40.

49. See Hermand, "Das Konzept 'Avantgarde,'" 9ff.; and Michel, "Dichtung als Ärgernis," 401.

Chapter 1

1. It must be made clear that the leading question of this chapter is the nature of the avant-garde's politics, not its anti-aesthetic characteristics per se. While seminal arguments about the avant-garde (like Peter Bürger's) have established the irrefutability of their interdependence, this coupling of politics and anti-aesthetic intent has served as the primary means with which to repudiate the avant-garde's viability in the second half of the twentieth century. For example, Bürger claims that "neo-avant-gardiste art is autonomous art." As will be made clear over the course of this volume, deploying this argument overlooks the ways in which many avant-gardes after 1945 move beyond their forebearers' problematization of the status of the work of art. By focusing on the avant-garde's temporal politics, this first chapter paves the way for subsequent case studies, in which questions of avant-garde form cannot be limited to an adherence to montage, which Bürger calls the "fundamental principle of avant-garde art." Nevertheless, traditional avant-garde aesthetic practices like montage do continue to prevail after fascism, and while many fashion themselves as embodying an anti-aesthetic that is intent on deposing the category of the work of art, they are equally if not more invested in deploying the avant-garde's politics of time in the German context. For Bürger's position, see his *Theory of the Avant-Garde,* 58, 72.

2. Poggioli, *Theory of the Avant-Garde,* 73. Poggioli defines the avant-garde as an extreme form of what Reinhart Koselleck would later call modernity's decoupling of the horizon of expectation (the future in the present) from the space of experience (the past in the present). See Reinhart Koselleck, *Vergangene Zukunft: Zur Semantik geschichtlicher Zeit* (Frankfurt am Main: Suhrkamp, 1989), 354–55, 359.

3. Hans Magnus Enzensberger, "The Aporias of the Avant-Garde," in *Zig Zag: The Politics of Culture and Vice Versa* (New York: New Press, 1997), 259 (hereafter cited parenthetically in text as "AAG").

4. Enzensberger alludes to modernity's state of exhaustion at the close of his "Aporias" essay. The place of the past in the matrix of the modern is more fully developed in Enzensberger's "Weltsprache der modernen Poesie," in *Einzelheiten II: Poesie und Politik* (Frankfurt am Main: Suhrkamp, 1984), 10–11 (here-

after cited parenthetically in text as "WMP"). It should be noted that there is little doubt that the early Enzensberger stands on the side of modernists and not postmodernists. "Let others," he writes in his "Aporias" essay, "harbor hopes for the end of modernity" (264).

5. With respect to Adorno's own pronouncement of the avant-garde's post-apocalyptic passing, see, for example, his "Looking Back on Surrealism," 86–90.

6. Susan Buck-Morss, *Dialectics of Seeing: Walter Benjamin and the Arcades Project* (Cambridge, Mass.: MIT Press, 1989), 273.

7. Walter Benjamin, *The Arcades Project,* trans. Howard Eiland and Kevin McLaughlin (Cambridge, Mass.: Belknap, 1999), 458. Hereafter cited parenthetically in text as *AP* along with the alphanumerical index shared by both the German original and the English translation. This citation corresponds to N1, 9.

8. For more on Benjamin's appropriation of surrealist temporality, see Peter Osborne's succinct yet rich essay "Small-Scale Victories, Large-Scale Defeats: Walter Benjamin's Politics of Time," in *Walter Benjamin's Philosophy: Destruction and Experience,* ed. Andrew Benjamin and Peter Osborne (London: Routledge, 1994), 59–109. See also Buck-Morss, *Dialectics of Seeing,* 253–86; and Peter Osborne, *The Politics of Time: Modernity and Avant-Garde* (London: Verso, 1998), 138–59, 175–96.

9. Walter Benjamin, "Surrealism: The Last Snapshot of the European Intelligentsia," in *Selected Writings, Vol. 2: 1927–1934,* ed. Michael W. Jennings et al. (Cambridge, Mass.: Belknap, 1999), 208 (hereafter cited parenthetically in text as "SLS").

10. See Osborne, "Small-Scale Victories," 63.

11. See Buck-Morss, *Dialectics of Seeing,* 272. The editors of Benjamin's selected works have parceled the term *Eingedenken* into its components (the preposition *eingedenk* and the verb *gedenken*) in order to render it translatable. They define it as an active form of memory that merges with commemoration. See Walter Benjamin, "On Some Motifs in Baudelaire," in *Selected Writings, Vol. 4: 1938–1940,* ed. Howard Eiland and Michael Jennings (Cambridge, Mass.: Belknap, 2003), 345n12 (hereafter cited parenthetically in text as "MB").

12. Osborne, "Small-Scale Victories," 84–85.

13. See Walter Benjamin, "On the Concept of History," in *Selected Writings, Vol. 4: 1938–1940,* 394 (hereafter cited parenthetically in text as "CH").

14. Walter Benjamin, "Paralipomena to 'On the Concept of History,'" in *Selected Writings, Vol. 4: 1938–1940,* 407 (hereafter cited parenthetically in text as "PCH").

15. Benjamin had already established his concept of the messianic in *The Origins of German Tragic Drama* (1925). For further information on the messianic, its origins in Jewish mysticism, its career among secular Marxists, and Benjamin's appropriation of the concept, see Buck-Morss, *Dialectics of Seeing,* 230–31, 242–48.

See also Richard Wolin, *Walter Benjamin: An Aesthetic of Redemption* (Berkeley: University of California Press, 1994), 31–63.

16. Osborne, *Politics of Time*, 152–53.

17. Benjamin insists in Convolute N that his anthropological materialism is "not that what is past casts its light on what is present, or what is present its light on what is past" (*Arcades Project*, N2a, 3). Enzensberger's prescription for a post-war modernism involves precisely these temporal trajectories: "Every backward glance at an avant-garde whose future is known has an easy time of it. . . . It is . . . our duty to draw conclusions from its downfall" ("Aporias of the Avant-Garde," 263).

18. Irving Wohlfarht, "Re-fusing Theology: Some First Responses to Walter Benjamin's Arcades Project," *New German Critique* 39 (Autumn 1986): 16–17.

19. Wolin, *Walter Benjamin*, 163–212; Susan Buck-Morss, *The Origin of Negative Dialectics: Theodor W. Adorno, Walter Benjamin, and the Frankfurt Institute* (New York: Free Press, 1977), 136–63. The core of Adorno's rebukes can be found in Bloch et al., *Aesthetics and Politics*, 110–33.

20. Theodor Adorno, *Minima Moralia: Reflections on a Damaged Life*, trans. E. F. N. Jephcott (London: Verso, 1974), 151 (hereafter cited parenthetically in text as *MM*). See also Theses VII and VIII (Benjamin, "Concept of History," 391–92).

21. For a discussion of Adorno's more favorable and much less discussed estimations of surrealism (especially in his *Aesthetic Theory*), see Richard Wolin, "Benjamin, Adorno, Surrealism," in *The Semblance of Subjectivity: Essays in Adorno's Aesthetic Theory*, ed. Tom Huhn and Lambert Zuidervaart (Cambridge, Mass.: MIT Press, 1997), 114–19.

22. The formulation "discover the new anew" is borrowed from Osborne ("Small-Scale Victories," 91, 108n132), who lifted it from Buck-Morss, *Dialectics of Seeing*, 274.

23. Adorno's equivalency of return (*Rückkehr*), traumatic neurosis, and eternal sameness (*Immergleichheit*) eclipses the revisionist processes that Freud located in the work of repetition. According to Jean Laplanche and J.-B. Pontalis's composite of "traumatic neurosis," it begins with an emotional shock that, after a period of remission, returns in the form of inhibiting symptoms. This delay between cause and effect, a period Freud calls *Nachträglichkeit*, allows the unconscious to endow the return with new meaning and effectiveness. See Jean Laplanche and J.-B. Pontalis, *The Language of Psychoanalysis*, trans. Donald Nicholson-Smith (New York: W. W. Norton, 1973), 470, 111.

24. In his seminar "On the Network of Signifiers," Jacques Lacan insists that Freud's concepts of return (*Wiederkehr*) and repetition (*Wiederholen*) should not be confused or conflated. Adorno does exactly that in *Minima Moralia*. Freud's idea of the return, Lacan notes, is grounded in the constitution of consciousness as influenced by the symbolic order. Referring to Freud's seminal essay "Remembering, Repeating and Working-Through," Lacan associates repetition with remem-

bering missed encounters with the real or *tuché* (i.e., a traumatic event). Adorno's apparent confusion of the structural nature of returning with the historical character of repeating is deliberate and is ultimately a symptom of his negative dialectics. See Lacan's *The Four Fundamental Concepts of Psychoanalysis,* ed. Jacques-Alain Miller, trans. Alan Sheridan (New York: W. W. Norton, 1978), 47–55.

25. Theodor W. Adorno, *Negative Dialectic,* trans. E. B. Ashton (New York: Continuum, 1973), 3 (hereafter cited parenthetically in text as *ND*).

26. Fredric Jameson, *Late Marxism: Adorno, or The Persistence of the Dialectic* (London: Verso, 1996), 113.

27. Sigrid Weigel, "Non-Philosophical Amazement—Writing in Amazement: Benjamin's Position in the Aftermath of the Holocaust," in *Body- and Image-Space: Re-Reading Walter Benjamin,* trans. Georgina Paul et al. (London: Routledge, 1996), 166–67.

28. Theodor W. Adorno, "Cultural Criticism and Society," in *Prisms,* trans. Samuel Weber and Shierry Weber (Cambridge, Mass.: MIT Press, 1983), 34. For a detailed reception history of Adorno's thinking on the temporal space of "after Auschwitz," see Stefan Krankenhagen, *Auschwitz darstellen: Ästhetische Positionen zwischen Adorno, Spielberg und Walser* (Cologne: Böhlau, 2001), 87–96.

29. Adorno, "Cultural Criticism," 34. In addition to Krankenhagen, see Michael Rothberg's essay on the conceptual development of Adorno's "Auschwitz" theorem in which he contextualizes the 1951 essay: *Traumatic Realism: The Demands of Holocaust Representation* (Minneapolis: University of Minnesota Press, 2000), 34–58.

30. Adorno, "Working Through the Past," 98.

31. See Rothberg, *Traumatic Realism,* 38.

32. Dominick LaCapra, "Reflections on Trauma, Absence, and Loss," in *Whose Freud? The Place of Psychoanalysis in Contemporary Culture,* ed. Peter Brooks and Alex Woloch (New Haven: Yale University Press, 2000), 179 (hereafter cited parenthetically in text as "RT").

33. Benjamin's notion of "other systems" of psychic experience in the "Work of Art" essay is taken directly from the fourth section of Freud's *Beyond the Pleasure Principle* (1920). Buck-Morss points out that because of Adorno's criticisms of the original version of this essay, "The Paris of the Second Empire in Baudelaire" (1938), Benjamin turned against his own much more affirmative concept of traumatic shock as developed in the "Work of Art" essay from a year earlier (Buck-Morss, *Origin of Negative Dialectics,* 160–61). Benjamin's tone, particularly at the outset of the second Baudelaire essay, does not fail to reiterate his belief in deploying shock in the name of recovering *Erfahrung.*

34. Ruth Leys, *Trauma: A Genealogy* (Chicago: University of Chicago Press, 2000), 10–11, 18–40.

35. Dominick LaCapra, "History, Psychoanalysis, Critical Theory," in *History in Transit: Experience, Identity, Critical Theory* (Ithaca: Cornell University Press,

2004), 86–87. LaCapra is more or less reiterating his long-standing contention that working-through must be integrated more fully into theories of trauma, a factor that Leys and countless others overlook. For the basis of LaCapra's argument, see his *Representing the Holocaust: History, Theory, Trauma* (Ithaca: Cornell University Press, 1994), 206–23. In a way, LaCapra, though he is wont to overlook his engagement with trauma, invokes Benjamin to counteract Leys's more Adornean position.

36. This list of tensions, which are conceived here not as binaries but rather as absolute moments within a field of varying degrees, is limitless and could easily be expanded to include additional tensions, many of which resurface in later chapters; they include interiority versus exteriority, homogeneity versus heterogeneity, present time versus past time, narrativity versus abstraction, body versus mind, male versus female, victim versus perpetrator, and human versus machine.

37. *Geschichte und Eigensinn* has posed challenges to English-language commentators, for the second half of its title resists easy translation. It has been captured as "obstinacy," "autonomy," "willful meaning," and "self-will." The German literally means "own-sense" or "own-meaning."

38. For more on Negt and Kluge's temporal disjuncture as well as their theoretical allegiances and divisions with the first and second generations of the Frankfurt School and French post-structuralism, see Stefanie Carp, *Kriegsgeschichten: Zum Werk Alexander Kluges* (Munich: Wilhelm Fink, 1987), 13–42; Winfried Menninghaus, "Geschichte und Eigensinn: Zu Hermeneutik-Kritik und Poetik Alexander Kluges," in *Geschichte als Literatur: Formen und Grenzen der Repräsentation von Vergangenheit*, ed. Harmut Eggert et al. (Stuttgart: J. B. Metzlersche, 1990), 258; Christopher Pavsek, "History and Obstinacy: Negt and Kluge's Redemption of Labor," *New German Critique* 68 (Spring–Summer, 1996): 139, 143–44; and Christian Schulte and Rainer Stollmann, ed., *Der Maulwurf kennt kein System: Beiträge zur gemeinsamen Philosphie von Oskar Negt und Alexander Kluge* (Bielefeld: transcript, 2005).

39. Fredric Jameson, "On Negt and Kluge," *October* 46 (Fall 1988): 152.

40. Oskar Negt and Alexander Kluge, *Geschichte und Eigensinn*, vol. 2, *Der unterschätzte Mensch: Gemeinsame Philosophie in zwei Bänden* (Frankfurt am Main: Zweitausendeins, 2001), 16 (hereafter cited parenthetically in text as *GE*).

41. See "Die Geschichte der lebendigen Arbeitskraft: Diskussionen mit Oskar Negt und Alexander Kluge," *Ästhetik und Kommunikation* 13, no. 48 (June 1982): 100.

42. On the resemblance between profane illumination and Negt and Kluge's idea of protective spheres, see Carp, *Kriegsgeschichten*, 28, 34–42. Like Benjamin, Negt and Kluge employ a host of synonyms to describe a couple of core temporal ideas. They name the temporal manifestation of this sphere a "time sluice" and a moment of "incubation time," or *Inkubationszeit* (*Geschichte und Eigensinn*, 212). The spatial equivalent of this sphere is an "Archimedean point," "a pole of qui-

etude" (*Ruhepol*), and "an abaric point," the threshold between two gravitational fields where a body is momentarily free (*Geschichte und Eigensinn*, 280, 787–90).

43. Also noteworthy is Negt and Kluge's insistence on the synchronicity of multiple orders of time (*Geschichte und Eigensinn*, 280); the roles of acceleration and speed in the experience of historical time (276); the multiple histories a country like Germany has ignored (517); and the decentralized generators that produce different histories using the same forces (252).

44. On sidestepping eschatology, Negt and Kluge write, for example, "There must be a way out. And not only in theology" (*Geschichte und Eigensinn*, 368). In one of the first English reviews of *Geschichte und Eigensinn*, Andrew Bowie drew attention to this categorical difference between *erlösen* (to redeem in the sense of atonement) and *einlösen* (to redeem in the sense of compensation); see his review of *Geschichte und Eigensinn* in *Telos* 66 (1985–86): 187.

45. See Pavsek, "History and Obstinacy," 146–47.

46. These and all subsequent typographical emphases are original to Negt and Kluge's text.

47. Adorno originally wrote in his first censure of Benjamin's preliminary 1935 exposé of the Arcades Project titled "Paris, the Capital of the Nineteenth Century": "If you transpose the dialectical image into consciousness . . . you not only take the magic out of the concept . . . but you also deprive it of that objective liberating power." See Bloch et al., *Aesthetics and Politics*, 111.

48. Oskar Negt and Alexander Kluge, *Öffentlichkeit und Erfahrung*, vol. 1, *Der unterschätzte Mensch: Gemeinsame Philosophie in zwei Bänden* (Frankfurt am Main: Zweitausendeins, 2001), 378.

49. Negt and Kluge enumerate in *Geschichte und Eigensinn* a total of six coordinates of social consciousness. Jameson rightly notes that the first three (the horizontal, the vertical, and the Brechtian functional) correspond to empirical experience ensconced firmly in historical time. Of the latter three that reside within the realm of fantasy—the irrational, the imaginary, and the revolutionary—Negt and Kluge cite the second, imaginary, realm as being responsible for the disasters of German history. See Jameson, "On Negt and Kluge," 173–74; and Negt and Kluge, *Geschichte und Eigensinn*, 511–15.

50. See Jameson, "On Negt and Kluge," 174.

51. Klaus Eder and Alexander Kluge, ed., *Ulmer Dramaturgien: Reibungsverluste* (Munich: Carl Hanser, 1980), 64. Kluge makes an important qualification, insofar as he distances "surprise" from Benjamin's idea of shock. "It would be wrong to say that one should be shocked by film," he writes. "The viewer's independence and powers of perception would be robbed."

52. Jameson, "On Negt and Kluge," 176.

53. See Lisa Yun Lee, *Dialectics of the Body: Corporeality in the Philosophy of T. W. Adorno* (New York: Routledge, 2005), 4.

54. Julia Kristeva defines the abject as any phantasmic substance that is either

foreign or intrinsic to the subject that must be expelled in order to preserve its psychic integrity. The term *abjection* designates this process of self-preservation. On their relationship to Auschwitz, she writes: "The abjection of Nazi crime reaches its apex when death . . . interferes with what . . . is supposed to save me from death." See Julia Kristeva, *The Powers of Horror: An Essay on Abjection*, trans. Leon S. Roudiez (New York: Columbia University Press, 1982), 4.

55. Negt explains in an interview: "Whoever sees only capital, commodity production, and advertising at work wherever they go, they will perceive very little of the actual life-contexts in different countries, and above all they will overlook entirely how resistance movements constitute themselves." See "Die Geschichte der lebendigen Arbeitskraft," 86.

Chapter 2

1. Walter Benjamin, "The Destructive Character," in *Selected Writings, Vol. 2: 1927–1934*, 543.

2. See Walter Benjamin, "Dream Kitsch Gloss on Surrealism," in *Selected Writings, Vol. 2: 1927–1934*, 3–5.

3. Benjamin, "Destructive Character," 541; Benjamin, "Surrealism: The Last Snapshot," 217. See also Irving Wohlfahrt, "No-Man's-Land: On Walter Benjamin's 'Destructive Character,'" in *Walter Benjamin's Philosophy: Destruction and Experience*, 168.

4. Wohlfahrt, "No-Man's-Land," 164.

5. Benjamin, "Destructive Character," 542.

6. Hans Egon Holthusen, "Naturlyrik und Surrealismus," in *Über Karl Krolow*, ed. Walter Helmut Fritz (Frankfurt am Main: Suhrkamp, 1972), 36, 35–38. Holthusen uses the word *kombiniert* (combined). See also Neil H. Donahue, *Karl Krolow and the Poetics of Amnesia in Postwar Germany* (Rochester: Camden House, 2002), 40, 74.

7. This quote stems from the sole report of this initial meeting in Bannwaldsee as reproduced in Reinhard Lettau, ed., *Die Gruppe 47: Bericht Kritik Polemik* (Neuwied: Luchterhand, 1967), 23.

8. Ilse Schneider-Lengyel, "Jean Paul Sartre: Der Surrealismus und die Antisartristen," *Der Skorpion* 1 (1948): 47. See also Gerhard Köpf, "Eine Asphodele: Über Ilse Schneider-Lengyel," in *Die Vorzüge der Windhunde: Essays gegen das Vergessen* (Tübingen: Klöpfer und Meyer, 2004), 119–20.

9. Alfred Andersch, *Deutsche Literatur in der Entscheidung: Ein Beitrag zur Analyse der literarischen Situation* (Karlsruhe: Volk und Zeit, 1948), 25.

10. Johannes Hübner, "Der Begriff Freiheit existentialistisch und surrealistisch," *Athena* 2, no. 5 (1948): 41.

11. Scant scholarship has illuminated the postwar surrealist landscape in war-

torn Germany. In addition to Schneider-Lengyel, Hübner, and others mentioned below, such a microscopic literary history might begin by considering the surrealist cabaret Die Badewanne in Berlin (1949–50); the surrealist sensibilities in paintings by Hans Thiemann, Heinz Trökes, Mac Zimmermann, and Karl Otto Götz; the influence of journals like *Athena, Das Lot,* and *META;* the creative energies fostered by local institutions like Galerie Rosen in Berlin and Zimmergalerie in Frankfurt am Main; and poetry by Anneliese Hager, Lothar Klünner, and Friedrich Umbran.

12. Szabolcsi, "Avant-Garde, Neo-Avant-Garde, Modernism," 64; and Hal Foster, *The Return of the Real: The Avant-Garde at the End of the Century* (Cambridge, Mass.: MIT Press, 1996), 5, 21.

13. Little has been written about these contemporaries, both of whom published small journals (Gerhardt's *fragmente* [1948–54] and Riegel's *Zwischen den Kriegen* [1952–56]) that targeted dominant poetics in the Western sectors.

14. Wolfdietrich Schnurre, "Theater der Zeit," *Der Skorpion* 1 (January 1948): 50.

15. Jost Hermand, "Das Konzept 'Avantgarde,'" 9.

16. Franz Mon, "Meine 50er Jahre," in *Gesammelte Texte: Essays,* vol. 1 (Berlin: Gerhard Wolf Janus, 1994), 14.

17. Mon, "Meine 50er Jahre," 17–18.

18. Poets and scholars have insisted on the presence of a destructive impulse in concrete poetry. In a programmatic editorial published in 1955 in his journal for concrete poetry, *Augenblick,* Max Bense exclaimed, for example: "Experiments: we deem them necessary when dealing with a new existence. Destruction: we deem it legitimate, but naturally there are conditions in which destruction is no longer worthwhile" (cited in Mon, "Meine 50er Jahre," 11). Reminiscing over his initial confrontation with Eugen Gominger's poetry, Helmut Heißenbüttel writes of "breaking out of a barrier" and "becoming free" to explore an unarticulated poetic space. (See Heißenbüttel's introduction in *Konstellationen, Ideogramme, Stundenbuch,* ed. Eugen Gomringer [Stuttgart: Reclam, 1977], 10, 13.) While this language certainly echoes Benjamin's idea of the destructive character, Bense's own aforementioned comment illustrates the primacy of the experiment itself over any destructive impulse.

19. For a discussion of the avant-garde in exile, see Rainer Rumold, *The Janus Face of the German Avant-Garde: From Expressionism toward Postmodernism* (Evanston: Northwestern University Press, 2002).

20. Dieter Wyss, *Der Surrealismus: Eine Einführung und Deutung surrealistischer Literatur und Malerei* (Heidelberg: Lambert Schneider, 1950), 58. Interestingly enough, Wyss also implied that an exhibition of German surrealist painters in Mannheim in 1948 confirmed its anachronistic return in war-torn Germany, for it evoked the return of the repressed (86).

21. Adorno, "Looking Back on Surrealism," 87.

22. Although he stops short of contextualizing his critique of surrealism with the emergence of French existentialism, Adorno was not short of vitriol for Sartre's political philosophy. See, for example, his essay "Commitment," in *Notes to Literature,* vol. 2, trans. Shierry Weber Nicholsen (New York: Columbia University Press, 1991), 76–94.

23. Andersch, *Deutsche Literatur,* 133.

24. For an overview of the messy convergence of existentialism's many sources as well as its patently German appropriation, see Marieluise Christadler, "Der französische Existentialismus und die deutsche Intellektuellen in der Nachkriegszeit," in *Frankreich: Ein unverstandener Nachbar (1945–1990),* ed. Wolfgang Asholt and Heinz Thoma (Bonn: Romanistischer Verlag, 1990), 224–38.

25. For a general overview of this discursive link, see Henri Paucker, "Exile and Existentialism," in *Exile: The Writer's Experience,* ed. John M. Spalek and Robert F. Bell (Chapel Hill: University of North Carolina Press, 1982), 82–94.

26. At the close of his essay, Andersch quotes liberally from Sartre's foreword to the German edition of *The Flies* in which he wrote: "Today the Germans have the same problem before them" (*Deutsche Literatur,* 30–31). Together Sartre and Andersch blur the difference between cause and effect.

27. See Lukács' *Existentialismus oder Marxismus?* (1951) and Habermas's *Philosophical-Political Profiles* (1983).

28. Jean-Paul Sartre, "What Is Literature?" in *What Is Literature? and Other Essays* (Cambridge, Mass.: Harvard University Press, 1988), 164. The first complete translation into German of this work appeared in 1958. It must be emphasized that the postwar German reception of Sartre transpired largely through secondhand overviews published in newspapers. A pivotal text for German readers, a Swiss translation of *Existentialism and Humanism* appeared in 1947. Already in 1946, excerpts from work by Sartre and Camus were translated into German and published in the literary journal *Sammlung. Being and Nothingness* would first appear in German in 1952. See Christadler, "Der französische Existentialismus," 226–27.

29. Sartre would revise his initial dismissal of surrealism in 1948 in the essay "Black Orpheus," in which he approves of the African appropriation of a surrealist destructive character in the name of battling racism. An extremely provocative and problematic claim, especially in the shadow of the Holocaust, he excludes the Jew from this revitalization of surrealism because he can pass as white. See Michel Beaujour, "Sartre and Surrealism," *Yale French Studies* 30 (1993): 86–95.

30. Peter Weiss, *Fluchtpunkt: Werke in sechs Bänden* (Frankfurt am Main: Suhrkamp, 1991), 2:289–90. Both of Weiss's autobiographical novels, *Abschied der Eltern* and *Fluchtpunkt,* were consolidated into a single volume in their English translation: *Exile,* trans. E. B. Garside et al. (New York: Delacorte, 1968), 239–40.

31. Otto Best's monograph is a perfect example of the convergence of existentialist and surrealist discourses. In his analysis of Weiss's micro-novel *The Shadow*

of the Body of the Coachman (1952–60), for example, Best writes of the work's "neo-surrealist game with image and word associations" in its exploration of Sartrean hell: *Peter Weiss: Vom existentialistischen Drama zum marxistischen Welttheater* (Bern: Francke, 1971), 53. The most recent and extensive reading of the surrealist thread throughout Weiss's oeuvre is Silvia Kienberger, *Poesie, Revolte und Revolution: Peter Weiss und die Surrealisten* (Opladen: Westdeutscher Verlag, 1994). As with earlier studies, hers overlooks the primary texts in question in this chapter.

32. Alfons Söllner, *Peter Weiss und die Deutschen: Die Entstehung einer politischen Ästhetik wider die Verdrängung* (Opladen: Westdeutscher Verlag, 1988), 90. Söllner's study, it should be noted, is by far the most theoretically sophisticated and thorough defense of what he calls Weiss's surrealist "dialectic of aesthetic modernity." Like Best and others, his language nevertheless slips at times between existentialism and surrealism.

33. Harun Farocki, "Gespräch mit Peter Weiss," in *Peter Weiss,* ed. Rainer Gerlach (Frankfurt am Main: Suhrkamp, 1984), 121, 125. See also Robert Cohen, *Peter Weiss in seiner Zeit: Leben und Werk* (Stuttgart: J. B. Metzler, 1992), 80–81.

34. Schneider-Lengyel, "Jean Paul Sartre," 47.

35. Peter Roos, "Der Kampf als meine Existenz als Maler," interview with Peter Weiss, in *Der Maler Peter Weiss: Bilder, Ziechnungen, Collagen, Filme,* ed. Peter Spielmann (Berlin: Fröhlich und Kaufmann, 1982), 40.

36. Susan Rubin Suleiman, introduction to *Exile and Creativity: Signposts, Travelers, Outsiders, Backward Glances* (Durham: Duke University Press, 1998), 5.

37. Unless otherwise noted, all images discussed in the following pages are reproduced in Spielmann's catalogue.

38. With its blind man, amputee, and young girl staring directly at the viewing position, *Jahrmarkt am Stadtrand,* a panorama of otherwise countless figures attending an annual fair, must be considered a notable exception to this list. Posthumously published images from this period that continue this theme can also be found in the story "Die Gezeiten: Eine Erzählung aus unseren Tagen" (1938) as well as in his diaries and sketchbooks (Spielmann, *Der Maler Peter Weiss,* 163). See also the reproduced sketches in Peter Weiss, *Briefe an Hermann Levin Goldschmidt und Robert Jungk 1938–1980,* ed. Beat Mazenauer (Leipzig: Reclam, 1992), 31, 57.

39. Peter Weiss, *Notizbücher 1960–1971,* vol. 1 (Frankfurt am Main: Suhrkamp, 1982), 58–59. The quoted entry was written in 1962 while Weiss was traveling in Zurich.

40. Weiss, *Briefe,* 215. According to Beat Mazenauer's annotated footnotes to Weiss's letters to Goldschmidt, the green gate is a reference to Hermann Hesse's novel *Klingsor's Last Summer* (1920); see *Briefe,* 215–16.

41. Weiss, *Briefe,* 63. Weiss's allusion to experiencing reality as if it were a dream is significant with respect to the painting's magic realist style, which is apparent in its painterly technique, composition, and content. Although no concise definition for it exists, magic realism—more or less a style in which the degree of

reality's realness verges on illusion—captures the unreality of exile of which Weiss wrote. This correspondence between experience and representation suggests that far from merely regurgitating bygone modernist idioms arbitrarily, Weiss was all along carefully wedding form with content. See Seymour Menton, *Magic Realism Rediscovered, 1918–1981* (Philadelphia: Art Alliance, 1983), 20–23.

42. Maurice Merleau-Ponty, *The Structure of Behavior,* trans. Alden L. Fisher (Boston: Beacon, 1963), 213.

43. Friedrich Weltzien lists five long-standing painterly techniques with which to unify the body's visible front with its invisible back: the mirror, the twisting of the torso à la the *figura serpentinata* (serpentine line), the Three Graces, the juxtaposition of front and back perspectives as developed in anatomy illustrations, and the self-referencing of the painting subject. See Friedrich Weltzien, "Der Rücken als Ansichtsseite: Zur 'Ganzheit' des geteilten Körpers," in *Körperteile: Eine kulturelle Anatomie,* ed. Claudia Benthien and Christoph Wulf (Reinbek bei Hamburg: Rowohlt, 2001), 450–54.

44. On Weiss's emotional attachment to his sister, the unremitting trauma her violent death produced, and her place in his painting, see Roos, "Der Kampf," 21.

45. Merleau-Ponty would read the stick that the blind man wields as an extension of his tactility "providing a parallel to sight." In this respect, he and the amputee are phenomenally homologous. See Maurice Merleau-Ponty, *Phenomenology of Perception,* trans. Colin Smith (London: Routledge, 2002), 165.

46. Jacques Outin, "Interview Peter Weiss," in *Peter Weiss im Gespräch,* ed. Rainer Gerlach and Matthias Richter (Frankfurt am Main: Suhrkamp, 1986), 301.

47. In his reading of a handful of Weiss's paintings, including *Jüngling am Stadtrand,* Frank Trommler contends that Weiss embraces the alienation produced by exile as a productive force for his art. This chapter's reading of Weiss's depiction of the human body calls such an affirmative reading into question. See Frank Trommler, "Das gelebte und das nicht gelebte Exil des Peter Weiss: Zur Botschaft seiner frühen Bilder," *Exilforschung* 13 (1995): 86.

48. Weiss originally requested Goldschmidt to loan him the painting for the showing. Because the war prevented its safe passage, Goldschmidt supplied Weiss with a photograph instead. See Weiss, *Briefe,* 150–51, 240.

49. Roos, "Der Kampf," 41.

50. Sepp Hiekisch maintains that Weiss's iconography ca. 1946–47 orbited primarily around the theme of the artist as inspired by members of Fyrtiotalisterna. While this can nevertheless be traced back to the predicament of exile, Weiss's depiction of the body departed from the previous focus on the back. "Zwischen surrealistischem Protest und kritischem Engagement: Zu Peter Weiss' früher Prosa," *Text and Kritik: Zeitschrift für Literatur* 37 (May 1982): 22–38.

51. Merleau-Ponty, *Phenomonology of Perception,* 113.

52. Benjamin, "Surrealism: The Last Snapshot," 217.

53. Edward Said, "Reflections on Exile," in *Reflections on Exile and Other Es-*

says (Cambridge, Mass.: Harvard University Press, 2000), 173, 173, 177, and 174 respectively.

54. León Grinberg and Rebeca Grinberg, *Psychoanalytic Perspectives on Migration and Exile,* trans. Nancy Festinger (New Haven: Yale University Press, 1989), 10, 12.

55. Grinberg, *Psychoanalytic Perspectives,* 156–65, 13.

56. Said, "Reflections on Exile," 173, 177.

57. Cathy Caruth, *Unclaimed Experience: Trauma, Narrative, and History* (Baltimore: Johns Hopkins University Press, 1996), 3, 21.

58. See Said's discussion of Lukács and Adorno ("Reflections on Exile," 181–85). See also Adorno, *Minima Moralia,* 18.

59. Readings of trauma in Weiss's later works have been undertaken by Mattias Kontarsky, *Trauma Auschwitz: Zu Verarbeitungen des Nichtverarbeitbaren bei Peter Weiss, Luigi Nono und Paul Dessau* (1999); and Katja Garloff, *Words from Abroad: Trauma and Displacement in Postwar German Jewish Writers* (2005).

60. Söllner, *Peter Weiss und die Deutschen,* 54.

61. Söllner, *Peter Weiss und die Deutschen,* 21, 17. Söllner's use of the term *derealization* of the past stems from Mitscherlich's ruminations in *The Inability to Mourn* on the forestalled melancholy that predominated the postwar German psychic landscape.

62. Söllner, *Peter Weiss und die Deutschen,* 102.

63. Weiss makes this claim in several interviews in Gerlach and Richter, *Peter Weiss im Gespräch,* 29, 35–36, 282. See also Roos, "Der Kampf," 38.

64. Peter Weiss, *The Shadow of the Body of the Coachman,* trans. E. B. Garside, in *Marat/Sade, The Investigation, and The Shadow of the Body of the Coachman,* ed. Robert Cohen (New York: Continuum, 1998), 1 (hereafter cited parenthetically in text as *SBC*).

65. The original German for these four quotations is "[ich] sehe," "ich höre," "[ich] kann [es] mir . . . denken," and "Ich befinde mich jetzt." See Peter Weiss, *Der Schatten des Körpers des Kutschers* (Frankfurt am Main: Suhrkamp, 1978), 7, 9, 12, 13.

66. Drew Leder, *The Absent Body* (Chicago: University of Chicago Press, 1990), 22.

67. Erwin Straus, *The Primary World of the Senses: A Vindication of Sensory Experience,* trans. Jacob Needleman (New York: Free Press of Glencoe, 1963), 363–64.

68. Straus, *Primary World,* 366.

69. Leder calls this focal thematization on the body induced in an unharmonious state "dys-appearance" (*Absent Body,* 87).

70. Weiss, *Schatten des Körpers,* 18. Garside's English translation captures this rather poorly as "bring[ing] up images" (*Shadow of the Body,* 6).

71. Best, *Peter Weiss: Vom existentialistischen Drama,* 52–53; Sepp Hiekisch,

"Zwischen surrealistischem Protest und kritischem Engagement," 30; and Peter Hanenberg, *Peter Weiss: Vom Nutzen und Nachteil der Historie für das Schreiben* (Berlin: E. Schmidt, 1993), 26.

72. Benjamin, "Surrealism: The Last Snapshot," 209. See also Walter Benjamin, "Hashish in Marseilles," in *Selected Writings, Vol. 2: 1927–1934*, 673.

73. André Breton, "Manifesto of Surrealism," in *Manifestoes of Surrealism*, 21–22.

74. The sole investigation of the collages in the micro-novel is Kirsten Gleinig, "Collage als ästhetisches Verfahren in Bild und Sprache: Bild-Text-Beziehung in den frühen Veröffentlichungen von Peter Weiss" (master's thesis, University of Göttingen, 1998). Gleinig concludes that the collages do not supplement the text (44).

75. Peter Weiss, "Laokoon oder Über die Grenzen der Sprache," in *Rapporte* (Frankfurt am Main: Suhrkamp, 1968), 179.

76. See Hanenberg, *Peter Weiss: Vom Nutzen und Nachteil der Historie*, 26.

77. Linda Williams, *Figures of Desire: A Theory and Analysis of Surrealist Film* (Urbana: University of Illinois Press, 1981), 30–45.

78. Lacan, *Four Fundamental Concepts of Psychoanalysis*, 20.

79. The two most recent instances of this are Christine Ivanovic, "Die Sprache der Bilder: Versuch einer Revision von Peter Weiss' *Der Schatten des Körpers des Kutschers*"; and Adam Soboczynski, "Von Schatten oder Schwarz auf Weiß: Überlegungen zu *Der Schatten des Körpers des Kutschers* von Peter Weiss." Both appear in *Peter Weiss Jahrbuch* 8 (1999): 34–67, 68–88.

80. Weiss refers directly to the unification of the shadows of the coachman's and housekeeper's bodies as a visual game (*visuelles Spiel*) in Michael Roloff, "Ein Interview mit Peter Weiss," in Gerlach and Richter, *Peter Weiss im Gespräch*, 36.

81. Weiss, *Schatten des Körpers*, 88.

82. Williams contends that with *Un chien andalou* and *L'Age d'or* surrealist film mastered structurally the cinematic duplication of the imaginary as it is perceived in the dream. Instead of distorting images cinematographically, these films evoke strangeness through "profilmic" effects that do not impede identification but do underscore their uncanny character (*Figures of Desire*, 32, 49).

83. Peter Weiss, *Avantgarde Film*, ed. and trans. Beat Mazenauer (Frankfurt am Main: Suhrkamp, 1995), 7.

84. Weiss, *Avantgarde Film*, 141. All subsequent references to Weiss's own recounting of the film are taken from this same page. See also Harun Farocki, "Gespräch mit Peter Weiss," in Gerlach and Richter, *Peter Weiss im Gespräch*, 255. In this second interview with Farocki from 1980, Weiss describes how the *tableaux vivants* were composed of various appendages from numerous actors such that they culminated into one figure.

85. Farocki, "Gespräch mit Peter Weiss," in Gerlach and Richter, *Peter Weiss im Gespräch*, 121.

86. Weiss, *Avantgarde Film,* 143.

87. Michel Chion, *The Voice in Cinema,* ed. and trans. Claudia Gorbman (New York: Columbia University Press, 1999), 18.

88. This use of Chion's theory of acousmatic sound with Lacanian psychoanalysis is modeled after Slavoj Žižek, "The Real and Its Vicissitudes," in *Looking Awry: An Introduction to Jacques Lacan Through Popular Culture* (Cambridge, Mass.: MIT Press, 1991), 40. It must be noted that the acoustic realm in *Studie II* shares little with its representation in the micro-novel. Although the narrator does rely on his ears to imagine the expansiveness of space beyond the boundaries of the visual, what he "sees" synesthetically with his ears is always transcribed back into the visual (and linguistic) as something knowable. This is not the case in the film.

89. Peter Weiss, "Meine Ortschaft," in *Rapporte,* 124.

90. Fredric Jameson, "Imaginary and Symbolic in Lacan: Marxism, Psychoanalytic Criticism, and the Problem of the Subject," in *Literature and Psychoanalysis: The Question of Reading: Otherwise,* ed. Shoshana Felman (Baltimore: Johns Hopkins University Press, 1982), 384–94.

91. Franz Mon, "perspektive," in *movens: Dokumente und Analysen zur Dichtung, bildenden Kunst, Musik, Architektur,* ed. Franz Mon (Wiesbaden: Limes, 1960), 85. Unsurprisingly, the thematic directory that follows Mon's quasi-manifesto and that catalogues illustrations of Mon's theory skips Weiss's "prosa" (65–74) entirely.

92. Walter Höllerer, "Veränderung," *Akzente* 5–6 (1964): 386–98. See in particular 392–93 and 397–98.

Chapter 3

1. Bürger, *Theory of the Avant-Garde,* 87.

2. These aforementioned positions can be found under the title "Der Schriftsteller vor der Realität," *Akzente* 4 (1956): 303–29. Less comprehensive than the coverage in *Akzente,* the French proceedings were produced in "Le dialogue de Vézelay," *Documents* 7 (July 1956): 725–53.

3. Luc Estang, "Streitgespräch um einen Goldfisch," *Akzente* 4 (1956): 312.

4. Keith Bullivant, *Realism Today: Aspects of the Contemporary West German Novel* (Leamington Spa: Berg, 1987), 17–33. See also Hermand, "Das Konzept 'Avantgarde,'" 9–11.

5. Gottfried Benn, "Lyrik des expressionistischen Jahrzehnts," in *Gesammelte Werke,* ed. Dieter Wellershoff (Frankfurt am Main: Zweitausendeins, 2003), 3:1840–41.

6. See Gottfried Benn, "Probleme der Lyrik," in *Gesammelte Werke,* 2:1064.

7. The year of Benn's death also witnessed continued praise. For an overview

of Benn's hold on postwar poetics, see Friedhelm Kröll, "Anverwandlung der 'Klassischen Moderne,'" in *Literatur in der Bundesrepublik Deutschland bis 1967,* ed. Ludwig Fischer (Munich: Deutscher Taschenbuch, 1986), 250–52.

8. Roland Barthes, "Objective Literature," in *Critical Essays,* trans. Richard Howard (Evanston: Northwestern University Press, 1972), 23 (hereafter cited parenthetically in text as "OL").

9. Brinkmann littered his literary essays from the sixties and seventies with admissions of Benn's importance. In his vita contained in his letters from 1974 to 1975, he pinpointed the peak of his fascination with Benn to the years 1955–56. See Rolf Dieter Brinkmann, *Briefe an Hartmut 1974–1975* (Reinbek bei Hamburg: Rowohlt, 1999), 116 (hereafter cited parenthetically as *BH*).

10. Gottfried Benn, *Der Ptolemäer,* in *Gesammelte Werke,* 2:1384 (hereafter cited parenthetically in text as *DP*).

11. Dieter Wellershoff, "Das Schimmern der Schlagenhaut: Existentielle und formale Aspekte des literarischen Textes," in *Werke,* ed. Keith Bullivant and Manfred Durzak (Cologne: Kiepenheuer und Witsch, 1997), 5:800.

12. For an extensive case for German expressionism's foreshadowing of postmodernism, see Richard Murphy, *Theorizing the Avant-Garde: Modernism, Expressionism, and the Problem of Postmodernity* (Cambridge: Cambridge University Press, 1999), 262–99.

13. Dieter Wellershoff, *Gottfried Benn: Phänotyp dieser Stunde: Eine Studie über den Problemgehalt seines Werkes* (Cologne: Kiepenheuer und Witsch, 1958), 14 (hereafter cited parenthetically in text as *GB*).

14. Gottfried Benn, "Gehirne," in *Gesammelte Werke,* 2:1185–91.

15. Gottfried Benn, "Lebensweg eines Individualisten," in *Gesammelte Werke,* 3:1896. For another reading of shell shock in "Gehirne," see Murphy, *Theorizing the Avant-Garde,* 101.

16. Peter Sloterdijk, *Critique of Cynical Reason,* trans. Michael Eldred (Minneapolis: University of Minnesota Press, 1987), 4.

17. For more on Benn's political transformation after 1934, see Rumold, *Janus Face of the German Avant-Garde,* 157–69. Rumold's reference to Benn's trauma is noteworthy (166), for it infers that fascism dealt a second shock, one that followed on the heels of that initial shock that figuratively pulverized Rönne's forehead. See Benn, "Gehirne," 2:1191.

18. Sloterdijk, *Critique of Cynical Reason,* 8. Sloterdijk associates violence with fascism's cynical dispensation of the right to legitimation, a move most evident in its politics of pure violence (242).

19. Werner Jung, *Im Dunkel des gelebten Augenblicks: Dieter Wellershoff—Erzähler, Medienautor, Essayist* (Berlin: Erich Schmidt, 2000), 132–33.

20. In his Frankfurt Lectures (1962–63) Wellershoff categorizes Benn as indifferent in "Der Gleichgültige: Versuche über Hemingway, Camus, Benn and Beckett." See also Wellershoff's 1977 interview with Jos Hoogeven in Dieter Wel-

lershoff, "Literatur als Erfahrung." Both are reproduced in Wellershoff, *Werke,* 5:57–75 and 5:896, respectively.

21. Dieter Wellershoff, "Während," in *Werke,* 2:477–81. See also Jung, *Im Dunkel des gelebten Augenblicks,* 136.

22. See Helmut Peitsch, "'Kleine Schritte' zum Neuen Realismus: Dieter Wellershoff als Leser und Lektor," in *Dieter Wellershoff: Studien zu seinem Werk,* ed. Manfred Durzak, Hartmut Steinecke, and Keith Bullivant (Cologne: Kiepenheuer und Witsch, 1990), 67–73.

23. Dieter Wellershoff, "Neuer Realismus," in *Werke,* 4:843–44.

24. Dieter Wellershoff, "Fiktion und Praxis," in *Literatur und Veränderung: Versuche zu einer Metakritik der Literatur* (Cologne: Kiepenheuer und Witsch, 1969), 26, 30 (hereafter cited parenthetically in text as "FP").

25. See Bürger, *Theory of the Avant-Garde,* 72. See also Dieter Wellershoff, "Die Instanzen der Abwehr und das totale Environment," in *Literatur und Veränderung,* 58–62.

26. Wellershoff, "Instanzen," 62.

27. Quoted in Hans Bender, "'Vielleicht erinnern Sie sich meiner': Rolf Dieter Brinkmann und die Akzente," in *Rolf Dieter Brinkmann,* ed. Maleen Brinkmann (Reinbek bei Hamburg: Rowohlt, 1995), 29.

28. Pietsch, "'Kleine Schritte,'" 72–73, 75.

29. Dieter Wellershoff, interview, in *Wahrnehmungsstrukturen in Werken des Neuen Realismus: Theorie und Praxis des Neuen Realismus und des nouveau roman—eine Gegenüberstellung,* by Christa Merkes (Frankfurt am Main: Peter Lang, 1982), 243.

30. Rolf Dieter Brinkmann, afterword to *Ein Tag in der Stadt,* in Rolf Dieter Brinkmann, *Erzählungen* (Reinbek bei Hamburg: Rowohlt, 1985), 408–9 (hereafter cited parenthetically in text as *E*). It should be noted that Brinkmann's prose in "In der Grube" is highly paratactic and regularly fragments and disorientates the very little narrative flow conveyed in the text. All English translations retain Brinkmann's lack of punctuation in order to capture this atomization of language and meaning.

31. Alain Robbe-Grillet, "Für einen Realismus des Hierseins," *Akzente* 4 (1956): 316.

32. Brinkmann, afterword, *Erzählungen,* 408.

33. Alain Robbe-Grillet, "Nature, Humanism, Tragedy," in *For a New Novel: Essays on Fiction,* trans. Richard Howard (New York: Grove, 1965), 52.

34. Roland Barthes, "There Is No Robbe-Grillet School," in *Critical Essays,* 92.

35. Robbe-Grillet, "Nature, Humanism, Tragedy," 52–53.

36. See Barthes's principal essays on Robbe-Grillet, all of which appear in *Critical Essays:* "The Last Word on Robbe-Grillet?" 199; "Literal Literature," 55; and "Objective Literature," 17, 19, 20.

37. Genia Schulz was the first to draw attention to the role of metaphors in this

barely studied story by Brinkmann. See her "Brandblasen der Seele: Zur frühen Prosa und späten Lyrik Rolf Dieter Brinkmanns," *Merkur* 441 (1985): 1015–16.

38. Another decisive allusion to the apple blossoms occurs in a memory of a framed picture hanging above the bed of the traveler's parents: "the picture of a Madonna under an apple tree, the tree dark, the apples rosy but, blackness, black heavy leaves, a thicket, the Madonna sat underneath it, the child in her lap" (Brinkmann, *Erzählungen*, 55). With this recollection, the extent of the traveler's signifying chain arrives at ultimate spiritual transcendence, a union with the Virgin Mary.

39. Robbe-Grillet, "Für einen Realismus," 316–17.

40. Gerda Zeltner-Neukomm's *Das Wagnis des französischen Gegenwartromans: Die neue Welterfahrung in der Literatur* (Reinbek bei Hamburg: Rowohlt, 1960) was the first comprehensive German portrayal of the *nouveaux romanciers*, from Sarraute to Simon, as a unified school. Wellershoff was not only familiar with Zeltner-Neukomm's work but also made use of it in his efforts to constitute a German equivalent. See Pietsch, " 'Kleine Schritte,' " 64–65. See also Wellershoff, "Der Gleichgültige," 99.

41. The following discussion of indifference encounters translational difficulties in English. The German *gleichgültig* can apply to affective states as well as objective facts. The following translations use both "indifferent" and "immaterial" in order to resolve this problem. In every instance, the German original is *gleichgültig*.

42. On the superficial nature of his parents' reading habits, the traveler later admits that "at home they had subscribed only to the local paper, the City Gazette, and on Saturdays the radio magazine, not in order to make note of programs, that was only a habit" (Brinkmann, *Erzählungen*, 45).

43. Theodor W. Adorno, "On the Fetish-Character in Music and the Regression of Listening," in *The Essential Frankfurt School Reader*, ed. Andrew Arato and Eike Gebhardt (New York: Continuum, 1997), 294–95.

44. Historian Uta G. Poiger adds historical credibility to this reading in *Jazz, Rock, and Rebels: Cold War Politics and American Culture in a Divided Germany* (Berkeley: University of California Press, 2000). Although jazz had garnered a reputation as being un-German in the first half of the fifties, by the end of the decade commercial culture had incorporated jazz as an acceptable cultural expression.

45. Benn, "Gehirne," 1188.

46. Sloterdijk, *Critique of Cynical Reason*, 103. On the kynical value of shit, Sloterdijk writes, for example, that it "has to be encountered in another way. It is now necessary to rethink the usefulness of the unuseful, the productivity of the unproductive, philosophically speaking: to unlock the positivity of the negative and to recognize our responsibility also for what is unintended" (151). Whether Brinkmann's protagonist recognizes this responsibility remains to be seen.

47. See also Robbe-Grillet, "A Future for the Novel," 21.

48. Kristeva, *Powers of Horror*, 7. See also Elizabeth Gross, "The Body of Signi-

fication," in *Abjection, Melancholia, and Love: The Work of Julia Kristeva,* ed. John Fletcher and Andrew Benjamin (London: Routledge, 1990), 86.

49. Gross, "Body of Signification," 89.

50. Were punctuation included, this passage might read as follows: "*in view of the political situation, urgent, the downfall, I only hope that it soon becomes better, we live in the courtyard to a crematorium.*"

51. It is of little coincidence that this central portion of the story sheds all punctuation. As was the case with Manon in the bicycle shed, the protagonist loses all control over form from within this interiority. Ideas bleed together into a single flow such that the "reader is supposed to be factored into [the] linguistic circular motion" (Brinkmann, *Erzählungen,* 409). The center of the story thus performs mimetically the vertigo experienced by the traveler.

52. Peter Blickle, *Heimat: A Critical Theory of the German Idea of Homeland* (Rochester: Camden House, 2002), 1–2.

53. For an explicit elucidation of this idea of the "production of wishes of the unconscious," the repression of fantasy, and the concomitant disastrous effects, see Klaus Theweleit, *Männerphantasien* (Munich: dtv, 1995), vol. 1, *Frauen, Fluten: Körper, Geschichte,* 231, 434; and vol. 2, *Männerkörper, zur Psychoanalyse des weißen Terrors,* 11.

54. Theweleit, *Männerphantasien,* 2:412. See also Sloterdijk's formulation of shit and the "usefulness of the unuseful."

55. Gilles Deleuze and Félix Guattari, *A Thousand Plateaus: Capitalism and Schizophrenia,* trans. Brian Massumi (Minneapolis: University of Minnesota Press, 1987), 282.

56. Brinkmann does mention the *nouveau roman* and Wellershoff's Neuen Realismus, but he refrains from inserting Robbe-Grillet into his either of his vitas, which is not the case with Benn. See *Briefe an Hartmut 1974–1975,* 107–16.

57. Negt and Kluge, *Geschichte und Eigensinn,* 212.

58. Kristeva, *Powers of Horror,* 8.

59. Fredric Jameson, "Reflections in Conclusion," in *Aesthetics and Politics,* 211. Jameson illustrates this subversion of modernism in the context of the visual arts, namely photorealism and hyperrealism from the seventies. For more on the relationship between realism and the avant-garde, see also Astradur Eysteinsson, *The Concept of Modernism* (Ithaca: Cornell University Press, 1990).

60. Negt and Kluge, *Geschichte und Eigensinn,* 513. See also Jameson, "On Negt and Kluge," 174.

Chapter 4

1. Theodor W. Adorno, *Traumprotokolle,* ed. Christoph Gödde and Henri Lonitz (Frankfurt am Main: Suhrkamp, 2005), 43.

2. Max Horkheimer and Theodor W. Adorno, *Dialectic of Enlightenment: Philosophical Fragments,* ed. Gunzelin Schmid Noerr, trans. Edmund Jephcott (Stanford, Calif.: Stanford University Press, 2002), 195 (hereafter cited parenthetically in text as *DE*).

3. Cited in Wolfgang Kraushaar, ed., *Frankfurter Schule und Studentenbewegung: Von der Flaschenpost zum Molotowcocktail 1946–1995,* vol. 2: *Dokumente* (Frankfurt am Main: Rogner und Bernhard bei Zweitausendeins, 1998), 254 (hereafter cited parenthetically in text as *FSS*).

4. Subversive Aktion printed a handful of quotations from various publications by Adorno along with the following call to action: "If the discrepancy between analysis and action is also unbearable for you, write to . . . " Wrongly credited with publishing the handbill, Adorno sued authors Dieter Kunzelmann and Frank Böckelmann. See Frank Böckelmann and Herbert Nagel, ed., *Subversive Aktion: Der Sinn der Organisation ist ihr Scheitern* (Frankfurt am Main: Verlag Neuer Kritik, 1976), 145–46.

5. Wolfgang Kraushaar, ed., *Frankfurter Schule und Studentenbewegung: Von der Flaschenpost zum Molotowcocktail 1946–1995,* vol. 1: *Chronik* (Frankfurt am Main: Rogner und Bernhard bei Zweitausendeins, 1998), 233. See also Klaus Briegleb, *1968: Literatur in der antiautoritären Bewegung* (Frankfurt am Main: Suhrkamp, 1993), 114–15. A transcription of Adorno's lecture can be found in "Classicism in Goethe's Iphigenia in Taurus," in Adorno, *Notes to Literature,* 2:153–70.

6. Kraushaar, *Frankfurter Schule,* 1:265.

7. Jürgen Habermas coined the term *left-wing fascist* at an ad hoc conference held immediately after the assassination of Ohnesorg. Critical of student ringleader Rudi Dutschke's flirtation with violence, Habermas accused him and members of the student movement of assimilating fascist violence within the arena of Marxist politics. Although Habermas would later regret this coinage, it quickly assumed a life of its own. See Kraushaar, *Frankfurter Schule,* 2:254–55.

8. Giorgio Agamben, *Homo Sacer: Sovereign Power and Bare Life,* trans. Daniel Heller-Roazen (Stanford: Stanford University Press, 1998), 1 (hereafter cited parenthetically in text as *HS*).

9. For an important critique of Agamben's use and abuse of the historical for transhistorical purposes, see Dominick LaCapra, "Approaching Limit Events: Siting Agamben," in *History in Transit: Experience, Identity, Critical Theory* (Ithaca: Cornell University Press, 2004), 162–94.

10. See also Giorgio Agamben, *Remnants of Auschwitz: The Witness and the Archive,* trans. Daniel Heller-Roazen (New York: Zone Books, 1999), 120.

11. Agamben infers fleetingly that because the exile must flee to survive he, too, is determined by the law of exception (*Homo Sacer,* 184).

12. Christofer Baldeney et al., *Unverbindliche Richtlinien 2* (December 1963); reprinted in Böckelmann and Nagel, *Subversive Aktion,* 114.

13. Dieter Kunzelmann, "Notizen zur Gründung revolutionärer Kommunen in den Metropolen," in *Subversive Aktion*, 143. Kunzelmann is citing Marcuse's seminal "Repressive Tolerance" essay from 1965.

14. Gisela Stelly, "Go-in, Love-in, Sit-in, usw.," *Die Zeit* (9 November 1967): n.p.

15. Contemporary examples of the appropriation and use of the term *happening* by the German press are limitless. Two exemplary newspaper articles are "'Schah-Happening' von der Polizei genehmigt," *Hamburger Abentblatt* (20 May 1967): n.p.; and Karl Zawadzky, "Politik als 'Happening?'" *Westfälisches Zeitung Güterloh* (12 September 1967): n.p. Collector and benefactor Hanns Sohm has amassed one of Germany's most extensive archives documenting this discourse in the popular press. His work is held at the Sohm Archive in the Staatsgalerie, Stuttgart.

16. The communards called the arson a "big happening" in their sixth handbill, which they distributed at the Free University in West Berlin on May 24, 1967. All communard handbills can be found in Siegward Lönnendonker et al., ed., *Freie Universität Berlin, 1948–1973: Hochschule im Umbruch,* vol. 4 (Berlin: Pressestelle der FU Berlin, 1975), 441–42.

17. On Adorno's personal response to the communards' intrusion in Berlin, see Kraushaar, *Frankfurter Schule,* 2:271.

18. Vostell cited in Heinz Ohff, "Der große Spaß am Überdruß," *Der Tagesspiegel* (17 September 1967): 33.

19. The first published opinion was from theologian and philosopher Jacob Taubes: "Surrealistische Provokationen," *Merkur* 21, no. 11 (1967): 1069–79. Three more opinions by philologists Eberhard Lämmert, Peter Szondi, and Peter Wapnewski were reproduced in Walter Höllerer, ed., "Flugblätter, Gutachten, Epiloge oder Wie weit sind Stilprobleme—Stilprobleme?" *Sprache im technischen Zeitalter* 28 (1968): 316–45. The last opinion, by writer and literary critic Reinhard Baumgart, can be found in Jürgen Schutte et al., ed., *Dichter und Richter: Die Gruppe 47 und die deutsche Nachkriegsliteratur* (Berlin: Akademie der Künste, 1988), 338. The communards' lawyer collected a total of nineteen legal opinions. For a critical historical overview of the court proceedings, see Briegleb, *1968: Literatur,* 103–11.

20. Karl Heinz Bohrer, "Surrealismus und Terror," *Merkur* 23, no. 10 (1969): 923, 928, 926.

21. Allan Kaprow and Wolf Vostell, "The Art of the Happening," Cricket Theater, New York City, 19 April 1964. An English transcription of Vostell's lecture, held together with Allan Kaprow, can be found in the Sohm Archive, Staatsgalerie, Stuttgart. A German version is available in Jürgen Beck and Wolf Vostell, ed., *Happenings, Fluxus, Pop art, Nouveau réalisme: Eine Dokumentation* (Reinbek bei Hamburg: Rowohlt, 1965), 401–3 (hereafter cited parenthetically in text as *HF*). Claudia Mesch has established that Vostell culled his appreciation for Dada

in general and for the 1920 "Central W/3" exhibition in Cologne in particular from Robert Motherwell's *The Dada Painters and Poets* (1951). See Claudia Mesch, "Vostell's Ruins: Dé-collage and the Mnemotechnic Space of the Postwar City," *Art History* 23, no. 1 (2000): 95, 112n25.

22. See Wolf Vostell, "Happening," *Theater heute* 6, no. 5 (May 1965): 29.

23. Wolf Vostell, "Jeder Mensch ein Kunstwerk!" lecture given at Marburg University, 31 October 1979; Sohm Archive, Staatsgalerie, Stuttgart.

24. For a thorough overview of the aesthetic and political debates in the sixties, see Martin Hubert, *Politisierung der Literatur—Ästhetisierung der Politik: Eine Studie zur literaturgeschichtlichen Bedeutung der 68er-Bewegung in der Bundesrepublik Deutschland* (Frankfurt am Main: Peter Lang, 1992), 9–31.

25. Bürger, *Theory of the Avant-Garde,* 57.

26. Negt and Kluge, *Geschichte und Eigensinn,* 596–97.

27. Vostell's term *dialectical contradiction* stems from a 1977 interview published in *El País*. A German translation can be found in José Antonio Agúndez García, *10 Happenings von Wolf Vostell,* trans. Helmtrud Rumpf (Mérida: Junta de Extremadura, 2002), 44.

28. Sidney Simon, "Wolf Vostell's Action Imagery," *Art International* 12, no. 9 (November 1968): 41.

29. Jörn Merkert, "Pre-Fluxus Vostell," *Art and Artists* 8 (May 1973): 32.

30. Mesch, "Vostell's Ruins," 95–96.

31. Wolf Vostell, *Happening und Leben* (Neuwied: Hermann Luchterhand, 1970), 199 (hereafter cited parenthetically in text as *HL*).

32. Horkheimer and Adorno, *Dialectic of Enlightenment,* 1.

33. Herbert Marcuse, *One-Dimensional Man: Studies in the Ideologies of Advanced Industrial Society* (Boston: Beacon, 1964), 9 (hereafter cited parenthetically in text as *ODM*).

34. For a narrative overview of the history of Vostell's happenings, see García, *10 Happenings,* 43–59.

35. Vostell made this declaration in conjunction with his *TV-Dé-collage* performed in New Brunswick, New Jersey, in May 1963. See Vostell, *Happening und Leben,* 273. For a history of the idea of the happening as it developed within and without Germany, see Rainer Wick, "Zur Theorie des Happenings (1. Teil)," *Kunstforum* 1, no. 8–9 (1973–74): 106–44.

36. For an overview of the school and its commitment to rejuvenating modernism, see Herbert Lindinger, "Ulm: Legend and Living Idea," in *Ulm Design: The Morality of Objects,* ed. Herbert Lindinger, trans. David Britt (Cambridge, Mass.: MIT Press, 1990), 9–13.

37. See Claus Bremer, letter to Wolf Vostell, 14 January 1963; and letter to Wolf Vostell, 13 August 1964, Wolf Vostell Archive, Malpartida de Cáceres, Spain. See also Claus Bremer, "Happening und Theater," *Ulmer Theater* 22 (1964): 4–5.

38. For an overview of the media reaction, see Rainer Wick, *Vostell Soziologisch: Eine Studie* (Bonn: n.p., 1969), 57–61.

39. Urs Jenny, "Pop-Ulk in und um Ulm," *Süddeutsche Zeitung* (10 November 1964): n.p. Reprinted in Beck and Vostell, *Happenings, Fluxus*, 410–11. A slightly revised version can be found in "Erinnerung an Vostells Ulmer Happening," *Theater heute* 6, no. 5 (May 1965): 32.

40. Ulrich Brecht, "Nach dem Happening," *Ulmer Theater* 1 (1965): n.p.

41. See Claus Bremer, "Die Unmoral auf der modernen Szene unter besonderer Berücksichtigung des Ulmer Happenings," *Ulmer Theater* 12 (1965): n.p.; Peter O. Chotjewitz, "Happenings/Vortrag aus Anlaß der Ulmer Ausstellung Vostell," *Ulmer Theater* 14 (1965): n.p.

42. Bremer's lecture is reproduced in Beck and Vostell, *Happenings, Fluxus*, 395.

43. Originally printed in the theater program (*Ulmer Theater* 22 [1964]: 1–2), Vostell's nineteen-point agenda is reproduced most accurately in Jörn Merkert, ed., *Vostell: Retrospektive 1958–1974* (Berlin: Neuer Berliner Kunstverein, 1975), 304.

44. The libretto for the Ulm happening is reprinted in various sources. The first appeared in the May 1965 edition of *Theater heute* cited in note 39. Arguably the most readily available source for English readers is Beck and Vostell, *Happenings, Fluxus*, 386–94. For economy's sake, the following description outlines only the most pronounced elements of each of the happening's twenty-four stations, which Vostell choreographed with much greater precision than conveyed here. Finer details from stations relevant for this close reading are addressed below.

45. For an overview of this vulgar semiotics at work in firsthand observations and newspaper reports, see Claudia Wolf, "Beschreibung, Deutung, und Wertung eines ausgewählten Happenings" (seminar paper, Ludwig Maximilian University, Munich, 1981), 10–15. Wolf's paper is available in the Sohm Archive at the Staatsgalerie, Stuttgart.

46. Jenny, "Erinnerung an Vostells Ulmer Happening," 32. All subsequent citations from Jenny are taken from this final version of his account of *In Ulm . . .*

47. This diagram is the title page to the brochure printed on the occasion of the documentary exhibition "Anatomy of the Happening *Salad*"at the Galerie René Block in West Berlin, which began November 5, 1971. A significantly altered version is reproduced in García, *10 Happenings*, 330.

48. Fredric Jameson, *The Political Unconscious: Narrative as a Socially Symbolic Act* (Ithaca: Cornell University Press, 1981), 47 (hereafter cited parenthetically in text as *PU*). For more on the following appropriation of Algirdas Greimas's semiotic square as well as the relationships between contrary and contradictory opposites therein, see Fredric Jameson, foreword to *On Meaning: Selected Writings in Semiotic Theory*, by Algirdas Julien Greimas, trans. Paul J. Perron and Frank H.

Collins (London: Frances Pinter, 1987), xiv–xxii (hereafter cited parenthetically in text as *OM*).

49. Agamben's use of the term *non-place* can be found in his *Remnants of Auschwitz*, 48–52.

50. Benjamin, *Arcades Project*, S1, 5 and G°, 17.

51. Benjamin, "Concept of History," 396–97.

52. Benjamin, "Concept of History," 390.

53. Günther Rühle, "Vorsicht—ein Happening: Beschreibung einer siebenstündigen Veranstaltung in Ulm," *Frankfurter Allgemeine Zeitung* (10 November 1964): n.p.

54. Erich Kaiser, "24 verwischte Ereignisse in sieben Stunden," *Donauer-Zeitung* (9 November 1964): n.p.

55. Jenny, "Pop-Ulk in und um Ulm," 11.

56. Susanne Ulrici, "Das Theater zog auf den Schlachthof," *Osnabrücker Tagesblatt* (11 November 1964): n.p.

57. Portions of this brochure are reproduced in Beck and Vostell, *Happenings, Fluxus*, 26–29. The entire pamphlet is included in the file for the *In Ulm . . .* happening in the Wolf Vostell Archive, Malpartida de Cáceres, Spain. See also Bundesamt für zivilen Bevölkerungsschutz, ed., *Zivilschutzfibel* (Bad Godesberg: Bundesminister des Innern, 1964), 5.

58. Bundesamt, *Zivilschutzfibel*, 5. In his critical account of the *Zivilschutzfibel*, Arno Klönne debunked the brochure as an instrument of political control. See his "Zivilschutz oder Regierungsschutz? Zur *Zivilschutzfibel* des Bundesinnenministeriums," *Blätter für deutsche und internationale Politik* 10 (1965): 38, 43.

59. Al Hansen, *A Primer of Happenings and Time/Space Art* (New York: Something Else, 1965), 43.

60. Hansen, *Primer of Happenings*, 43.

61. Wolf Vostell, *Miss Vietnam and Texts of Other Happenings*, trans. Carl Weissner (San Francisco: Nova Broadcast, 1968), 21.

62. For more on the differences in television coverage of the Vietnam War in America and the Federal Republic of Germany, see Gerhard Paul, *Bilder des Krieges, Krieg der Bilder: Die Visualisierung des modernen Krieges* (Paderborn: Ferdinand Schöningh, 2004), 321–22.

63. Fredric Jameson, "Cognitive Mapping," in *Marxism and the Interpretation of Culture*, ed. Cary Nelson and Lawrence Grossberg (Urbana: University of Illinois Press, 1988), 351.

64. For a transcript of the news report from the May 23 issue of *Bild-Zeitung* and the commune's reaction, see Ulrich Enzensberger, *Die Jahre der Kommune I: Berlin 1967–1969* (Cologne: Kiepenheuer und Witsch, 2004), 137–38 (hereafter cited parenthetically in text as *JK*).

65. Lönnendonker, *Freie Universität Berlin*, 426–28, 441–43. Leaflet nine ends

with the name of two prominent postwar department stores, Kepa and KaDeWe, shorthand for Kaufhaus des Westens (Department Store of the West). The final syllable, *We,* which stands for the genitive case of *west,* is replaced in the leaflet with the homonym *Weh,* meaning pain, woe, or sorrow. Whether this is a tear of sorrow, crocodile tears, or a drop of spilt blood remained unclear in court. See Briegleb, *1968: Literatur,* 112.

66. The entire proceedings, including the prosecuting attorney's original brief, is reproduced in Rainer Langhans and Fritz Teufel, *Klau mich!* ed. Bernward Vesper (Frankfurt am Main: edition Voltaire, 1968), n.p. (hereafter cited parenthetically in text as *KM*). For the prosecution's use of the word *Vorstellung,* see the "Anklageschrift" that begins the text.

67. For an anecdotal history of the migration of the happening from the art world to the German student movement via Amsterdam's Provos, see Enzensberger, *Die Jahre der Kommune,* 52; and Stelly, "Go-in, Love-in, Sit-in, usw."

68. Rudi Dutschke, "'Wir fordern die Enteignung Axel Springers," *Der Spiegel* (10 July 1967): 33.

69. This is the approach that Reimut Reiche assumes in "Sexuelle Revolution— Erinnerung an einen Mythos," in *Frankfurter Schule und Studentenbewegung: Von der Flaschenpost zim Molotowcocktail 1946–1995,* ed. Wolfgang Kraushaar, vol. 3: *Aufsätze* (Frankfurt am Main: Rogner und Bernhard bei Zweitausendeins, 1998), 163–64. See also Dagmar Herzog, *Sex After Fascism: Memory and Morality in Twentieth-Century Germany* (Princeton: Princeton University Press, 2005), 181.

70. For more on their idea of irrational fantasy, its relationship to the oppositional anti-real, and its role in the post-fascist avant-garde see chapter 1.

71. See note 1 for chapter 1.

72. Guy Debord, *The Society of the Spectacle,* trans. Donald Nicholson-Smith (New York: Zone Books, 1994), 12.

73. Guy Debord, *The Society of the Spectacle,* 114.

74. For another important reading of the commune's shift from poetics to violence as well as the divergent fates of its principal members, see Wolfgang Kraushaar, *Die Bombe im Jüdischen Gemeindehaus* (Hamburg: Hamburger Edition, 2005), 278–81, 69n88, 131. See also Briegleb, *1968: Literatur,* for his reading of Kommune 1 and the extinguishing of its use of satire (62–71).

75. Jan Philipp Reemtsma, afterword to Adorno, *Traumprotokolle,* 107.

Chapter 5

1. An excerpt taken from Brinkmann's sound collage, this transcription compresses his nineteen-minute recording by presenting only a sample of replies from various phone numbers dialed. This list—though true to the recording's chronol-

ogy—conveys accurately neither the actual sequence of Brinkmann's calls nor the prominence of the sounds of dialing and ringing. Rolf Dieter Brinkmann, "Kein Anschluss," *Wörter Sex Schnitt: Originaltonaufnahmen 1973*, CD grün, ed. Herbert Kapfer and Katarina Agathos, intermedium records, 2005.

2. Avital Ronell, *The Telephone Book: Technology, Schizophrenia, Electric Speech* (Lincoln: University of Nebraska Press, 1989), 302 (hereafter cited parenthetically in text as *TB*).

3. William S. Burroughs, "Die unsichtbare Generation," trans. Katja Behrens, in *ACID: Neue amerikanische Szene*, ed. Rolf Dieter Brinkmann and Ralf-Rainer Rygulla (Frankfurt am Main: Zweitausendeins, 1981), 167. The original English cited here and reproduced in German in Brinkmann's anthology *ACID* was taken from William S. Burroughs, "the invisible generation," in *The Ticket That Exploded* (New York: Grove, 1967), 207 (hereafter cited parenthetically in text as "IG").

4. See Marshall McLuhan, *Understanding Media: The Extensions of Man* (Cambridge, Mass.: MIT Press, 1994), 23.

5. See Avital Ronell, *The Telephone Book: Technology, Schizophrenia, Electric Speech*, 21–23, for Ronell's crucial linkage between Heidegger's *What Is Called Thinking?* with Blanchot's essay "The Essential Solitude" from *The Space of Literature*. For more on Blanchot's thought on blindness, see Martin Jay, *Downcast Eyes: The Denigration of Vision in Twentieth-Century French Thought* (Berkeley: University of California Press, 1994), 551–55.

6. Rolf Dieter Brinkmann, "Ein unkontrolliertes Nachwort zu meinen Gedichten," *Literaturmagazin* 5 (1976): 233 (hereafter cited parenthetically in text as "UN"). See also Burroughs, "invisible generation," 205.

7. Rolf Dieter Brinkmann, *Rom, Blicke* (Reinbek bei Hamburg: Rowohlt, 1979), 40 (hereafter cited parenthetically in text as *RB*).

8. Brinkmann articulates his late literary theory most forcefully in "Notizen und Beobachtungen vor dem Schrieben eines zweiten Romans," in *Der Film in Worten: Prosa, Erzählungen, Essays, Hörspiele, Fotos, Collagen 1965–1974* (Reinbek bei Hamburg: Rowohlt, 1982), 287–88 (hereafter cited parenthetically in text as "NB").

9. See Jürgen Seifert, ed., *Die Spiegel-Affäre*, 2 vols. (Olten: Walter, 1966). See also Heinz-Dietrich Fischer, Jürgen Niemann, and Oskar Stodieck, ed., *100 Jahre Medien-Gewalt-Diskussion in Deutschland: Synopse und Bibliographie zu einer zyklischen Entrüstung* (Frankfurt am Main: Institut für Medienentwicklung und Kommunikation, 1996), 193–96.

10. Gerhard Bauß, *Die Studentenbewegung der sechziger Jahre in der Bundesrepublik und Westberlin: Handbuch* (Cologne: Pahl-Rugenstein, 1977), 74–75. The best example of the SDS's indifference toward the Springer media empire is Lothar Hack's article published in *neue kritik* in which he chided the leftist satirical

monthly *pardon* for questioning Axel Springer's intentions. See "Kein Pardon für *pardon,*" *neue kritik* 15 (1963): 18–20; and the special issue of *pardon* 1, no. 2 (1962) titled "Krieg wegen Axel Springer?"

11. "Bild im Bildschirm?" *Der Spiegel* (3 February 1965): 40; *Sozialistische Politik* 4 (April 1966): 4; Peter Christian and Franz Kegel, "Springers Welt-Bild," *Marxistische Blätter* 5 (1966): n.p. Cited in Bauß, *Studentenbewegung der sechziger Jahre,* 75.

12. Lettau ended his talk by saying, "Please excuse me if I convey the result of my analysis of the Berlin press by ripping here and now Berlin newspapers to shreds" (96). See Rainer Lettau, *Täglicher Faschismus: Amerikanische Evidenz aus 6 Monaten* (Munich: Carl Hanser, 1971). A revised version of this talk appeared in September of that year as "Journalismus als Menschenjagd," *Kursbuch* 7 (September 1966): 116–29. See also Briegleb, *1968: Literatur,* 72–75.

13. Jürgen Habermas, *The Structural Transformation of the Public Sphere: An Inquiry into a Category of Bourgeois Society,* trans. Thomas Burger and Frederick Lawrence (Cambridge, Mass.: MIT Press, 1991), 217.

14. Horkheimer and Adorno's essay on the culture industry from *Dialectic of Enlightenment,* as well as Adorno's own work on mass culture, proved fundamental for Habermas's conception of media effects. Habermas remained a liberal authority on media effects throughout the student movement. See Jürgen Habermas, "Werden wir richtig informiert?" *Die Zeit* (31 May 1968): 17.

15. Peter Schneider, "Die '*Bild-Zeitung,*' ein Kampfblatt gegen die Massen," in *Ansprachen: Reden Notizen Gedichte* (Berlin: Klaus Wagenbach, 1970), 15–28.

16. Heiner Schäfer, "Die BILD-Zeitung: Eine Ordnungsmacht im Spätkapitalismus," in *Die Auferstehung der Gewalt: Springerblockade und politische Reaktion in der Bundesrepublik,* ed. Heinz Grossmann and Oskar Negt (Frankfurt am Main: Europäische Verlagsanstalt, 1968), 24. Another influential analysis of media manipulation in the context of the Springer media empire is Sozialistischer Deutscher Studentenverbund, *Der Untergang der Bild-Zeitung* (n.p.: SDS-Autorenkollektiv/Springer Abreitskreis der KU, 1968).

17. Schäfer, "BILD-Zeitung," 26.

18. Oskar Negt, "Strategie der Gegengewalt," *Die Zeit* (26 April 1968): 4.

19. Hans Magnus Enzensberger, "Constituents of a Theory of the Media," trans. Stuart Hood, in *The Consciousness Industry: On Literature, Politics and the Media* (New York: Seabury, 1974), 101.

20. Enzensberger, "Constituents," 105.

21. Schneider maintains that the nightmarish layout of the *Bild-Zeitung,* particularly the formal arrangement of word and image, engages in "psychological acts of violence" (Die '*Bild-Zeitung,*'" 23–24). The crass, cold-blooded juxtaposition of sex crimes and soft porn, for example, and the fetishization of such topics as murder, war, disasters, and misfortune both contribute to the overall intention to shroud class interests.

22. Enzensberger, "Constituents," 166.

23. Wolfgang Fritz Haug, "Zur Kritik der Warenästhetik," *Kursbuch* 20 (March 1970): 140.

24. Quoted in "'Gefahr für uns alle': Studenten gegen Springer," *Der Spiegel* (6 May 1968): 42.

25. Quoted in "'Wir hauen auf den Putz': Thesen zur Gewalt," *Der Spiegel* (13 May 1968): 40.

26. Hans-Jürgen Krahl, "Römerbergrede," in *Konstitution und Klassenkampf* (Frankfurt am Main: Neue Kritik, 1971), 149–54.

27. Statement given by Knut Nevermann, reprinted in "'Wir hauen auf den Putz,'" 40.

28. Oskar Negt explicated the need for delimiting progressive violence from reactionary violence in "Rechtsordnung, Öffentlichkeit und Gewalt," in Grossmann and Negt, *Auferstehung der Gewalt,* 178. Negt based his argument in large part on Herbert Marcuse's legitimization of violence for the liberation of the oppressed in "Repressed Tolerance," in *Critique of Pure Tolerance,* Robert Paul Wolff et al. (Boston: Beacon, 1965), 116–17. Pessimistic about the possibility of such a differentiation, Habermas pleaded already on June 9, 1967, that students should refrain altogether from exercising any and all violence intended to inflict a wound. See Uwe Bergmann, ed., *Bedingungen und Organization des Widerstandes: Der Kongreß in Hannover: Protokolle, Flugblätter, Resolutionen* (Berlin: Voltaire Schriften, 1967), 48.

29. "'Gefahr für uns alle,'" 42. See also Schäfer, "BILD-Zeitung," 27.

30. On the genesis of *die tageszeitung* in 1978, see Sabine von Dirke, *"All Power to the Imagination!" The West German Counterculture from the Student Movement to the Greens* (Lincoln: University of Nebraska Press, 1997), 120–42.

31. Rolf Dieter Brinkmann, *Erkundungen für die Präzisierung des Gefühls für einen Aufstand: Träume Aufstände/Gewalt/Morde REISE ZEIT MAGAZIN Die Story ist schnell erzählt (Tagebuch)* (Reinbek bei Hamburg: Rowohlt, 1987), 69 (hereafter cited parenthetically in text as *EP*). All subsequent translations of Brinkmann's late work preserve the typographical peculiarities of the German original.

32. Four additional exemplary beginnings to his novel include "Who am I/And what?"; "Jesuuss! I was full of hatred"; "Strange how thin and shadowy the people have passed for years through my consciousness"; "The situation became worse and worse" (Brinkmann, *Erkundungen für die Präzisierung,* 145, 165, 168, 233).

33. On the *Entwicklungsroman,* see Eberhard Lämmert, "Der Autor und sein Held im Roman des 19. und 20. Jahrhunderts," *German Quarterly* 66, no. 4 (Autumn 1993): 415–30.

34. In the fourth section of Brinkmann's poem "Chevaux de Trait," the lyrical subject exclaims "Away, to the development novel!" as if it were an attainable destination, but then declares that "The development novel, Cologne, is dead." See

Rolf Dieter Brinkmann, *Westwärts 1&2* (Reinbek bei Hamburg: Rowohlt, 1975), 13–14. Cited, in part, in Michael Strauch, *Rolf Dieter Brinkmann: Studie zur Text-Bild-Montagetechnik* (Tübingen: Stauffenburg, 1998), 94.

35. Sibylle Späth, *Rolf Dieter Brinkmann* (Stuttgart: J. B. Metzler, 1989), 114.

36. Thomas Gross, *Alltagserkundungen: Empirisches Schreiben in der Ästhetik und in den späten Materialbänden Rolf Dieter Brinkmanns* (Stuttgart: J. B. Metzler, 1993), 258. For a detailed account of the text's sources, see Strauch, *Rolf Dieter Brinkmann*, 94–95, 102–10.

37. Strauch, *Rolf Dieter Brinkmann*, 93–114.

38. See Hans Magnus Enzensberger, "The Industrialization of the Mind," in *Consciousness Industry*, 3–15. On Brinkmann's notion of reality as fiction, see Sibylle Späth, "Gehirnströme und Medientext: Zu Rolf Dieter Brinkmanns späten Tagebüchern," *Literaturmagazin* 30 (1992): 110–11.

39. Georg Lukács, *Theory of the Novel: A Historico-Philosophical Essay on the Forms of Great Epic Literature*, trans. Anna Bostock (Cambridge, Mass.: MIT Press, 1971), 125.

40. In this respect, Brinkmann's definition of distorted time is not entirely unlike David Harvey's notion of the postmodern compression of time; see David Harvey, *The Condition of Postmodernity* (Cambridge, U.K.: Blackwell, 1990), 285–307.

41. Rolf Dieter Brinkmann, *SCHNITTE* (Reinbek bei Hamburg: Rowohlt, 1988), 6 (hereafter cited parenthetically in text as *S*).

42. See the respective pages in Brinkmann, *Der Film in Worten*, for references to Burroughs (292), Korzybski (277), Reich (288–90), Wilson (288, 292), and McLuhan (285). See also Strauch, *Rolf Dieter Brinkmann*, 175–204, for specific references.

43. In this respect, Brinkmann's implied critique of manipulation theories verges on Jean Baudrillard's 1971 criticism of Enzensberger and his case for the media as symbolic exchange. See Jean Baudrillard, "Requiem for the Media," in *For a Critique of the Political Economy of the Sign*, trans. Charles Levin (St. Louis: Telos, 1981), 164–84.

44. For more on the novel's allusion to ancient Egyptian books of the dead, see Strauch, *Rolf Dieter Brinkmann*, 99–102.

45. Brinkmann developed a great interest in gangsters in the late sixties and maintained it throughout the seventies. Many of his essays and radio plays include references to Burroughs's own fascination with New York City's legendary Dutch Schulz.

46. Robert Warshow, "Movie Chronicle: The Westerner," in *Film Theory and Criticism*, ed. Gerald Mast et al. (New York: Oxford University Press, 1992), 453–66.

47. Bürger, *Theory of the Avant-Garde*, 78–79.

48. Brinkmann happened upon Tieck's travel poems, in particular "Olevano,"

during his stay in the mountain village of the same name. See Brinkmann, *Rom, Blicke*, 409, 429.

49. Rolf Dieter Brinkmann, "Schreiben ist etwas völlig Anderes," *Wörter Sex Schnitt: Originaltonaufnahmen 1973*, CD gelb, ed. Herbert Kapfer and Katarina Agathos, intermedium records, 2005. "Writing," he says into the microphone while walking down the street, "is something completely different than speaking. . . . Silence belongs to writing. And a slow disassembling of minute moments into their individual components."

50. Martin Heidegger, "The Question Concerning Technology," in *Basic Writings*, ed. David Farrell Krell (New York: HarperCollins, 1993), 318–19. "Technology," Heidegger writes, "comes to presence in the realm where revealing and unconcealment take place, where aletheia, truth, happens" (319). Nothing could be further from the truth for Brinkmann's protagonist.

51. See Eckhard Schumacher, ". . .jetzt, jetzt, jetzt, ad infinitum!" in *Gerade, Eben, Jetzt: Schreibweisen der Gegenwart* (Frankfurt am Main: Suhrkamp, 2003), 86–87.

52. Rolf Dieter Brinkmann, "Das ist aber hier ein tolles Gerät," *Wörter Sex Schnitt: Originaltonaufnahmen 1973*, CD blau, ed. Herbert Kapfer and Katarina Agathos, intermedium records, 2005.

53. See Lämmert, "Der Autor und sein Held," 417.

54. Rolf Dieter Brinkmann, "Kuck mal da der Eisbaum," *Wörter Sex Schnitt: Originaltonaufnahmen 1973*, CD pink, ed. Herbert Kapfer and Katarina Agathos, intermedium records, 2005.

55. Herzog, *Sex After Fascism*, 152–62. See also Dagmar Herzog, "'Pleasure, Sex, and Politics Belong Together': Post-Holocaust Memory and the Sexual Revolution in West Germany," *Critical Inquiry* 24 (Winter 1998): 399–403.

56. For more on Brinkmann's intentionally amplified sex scenes in *Keiner weiß mehr* and its reception as pornography, see Olaf Selg, *Essay, Erzählung, Roman und Hörspiel: Prosaformen bei Rolf Dieter Brinkmann* (Aachen: Shaker, 2001), 226, 255–65.

Chapter 6

1. Alexander Kluge, interview, in *Die Filme von Alexander Kluge*, by Rainer Lewandowski (Hildesheim: Olms, 1980), 57.

2. Alexander Kluge, "Die Macht der Bewußtseinsindustrie und das Schicksal unserer Öffentlichkeit," in *Industrialisierung des Bewußtseins*, ed. Klaus von Bismarck et al. (Munich: Piper, 1985), 104 (hereafter cited parenthetically in text as "DMB"). Kluge published a shorter draft of this essay as "Zum Unterschied von machtbar und gewalttätig: Die Macht der Bewußtseinsindustrie und das Schicksal unserer Öffentlichkeit," *Merkur* 38, no. 3 (1984): 243–53. The 1985 version is

reprinted (without illustrations) in Alexander Kluge, *In Gefahr und größter Not bringt der Mittelweg den Tod: Texte zu Kino, Film, Politik,* ed. Christian Schulte (Berlin: Vorwerk 8, 1999), 165–221.

3. For a historical sketch of the deregulation of public media in the Federal Republic, see Peter Humphreys, "Germany's 'Dual' Broadcasting System: Recipe for Pluralism in the Age of Multi-Channel Broadcasting?" *New German Critique* 78 (Autumn 1999): 26–39.

4. Kluge derived his notion of experience directly from Walter Benjamin, who spells out a twin concept of experience (*Erfahrung* and *Erlebnis*) in "On Some Motifs in Baudelaire, 313–55. Therein Benjamin casts *Erfahrung* as singular, temporally expansive, and communal and *Erlebnis* as repetitive, fleeting, and individual (314–18). For an explication of *Erfahrung* in Kluge's work, see Miriam Hansen, "Unstable Mixtures, Dilated Spheres: Negt and Kluge's *The Public Sphere and Experience,* Twenty Years Later," *Public Culture* 5, no. 2 (Winter 1993): 187–90.

5. Kluge explained the crucial distinction between *chronos* and *kairos* as follows:

For the Greeks, Chronos stood for time that leads to death, time that consumes itself. Chronos is a gigantic god who devours his own children. His antipode in the Greek pantheon is Kairos, "the fortunate moment." Kairos is a very small, dwarf-like god with a bald head. But on his forehead he has a tuft (of dense hair). If you catch the tuft, you're lucky. If you are just a moment too late, your grip on his bald head will slip and you won't be able to hold on to him. This character, Kairos, is the "happy time" that is hidden in the time of people's lives, in their working time, in everything they might do. He is an object of aesthetic activity. With Chronos on the other hand, you can only become a watchmaker.

Alexander Kluge, interview with Hans Ulrich Obrist, trans. Olav Westphalen, *Art Orbit* (January 1998), http://artnode.se/artorbit/issue2/f_arkipelagtv/f_arkipelagtv.html.

6. Utopian thinking characterized Kluge's theory of cinema at the outset of his filmmaking career. His first formulation of film's commitment to utopia is "Die Utopie Film," *Merkur* 13, no. 12 (December 1964): 1135–46. This quotation is taken from page 1144.

7. This latter approach can be found in Lev Manovich, *The Language of New Media* (Cambridge, Mass.: MIT Press, 2001).

8. On the structural gap in cinematography, Kluge writes "the cinematic projection is based on an exposure of 1/48 of a second, which is followed by a dark phase of 1/48 of a second, the so-called transport phase. On average one half of the time in the movie theater is spent in the dark" ("Die Macht der Bewußtseinsindustrie," 105).

9. For an overview of Kluge's television aesthetics and his legal and political negotiations, as well as a historical account of his earliest television productions, see Peter C. Lutze, *Alexander Kluge: The Last Modernist* (Detroit: Wayne State University Press, 1998), 193–98, 180–85. See also Lutze's videography of Kluge's first television series from 1985, "Stunde der Filmemacher: Filmgeschichten" (253–54).

10. In addition to Lutze's videography in *Alexander Kluge: The Last Modernist,* see the exhaustive catalogue in Christian Schulte, ed., *Die Schrift an der Wand: Alexander Kluge—Rohstoffe und Materialien* (Osnabrück: Universitätsverlag Rasch, 2000), 403–38.

11. A monumental shift from his television work, Kluge's two-volume *Chronik der Gefühle* (2000)—a compendium of his previous prose and new work written after German reunification—first confirmed the ineluctable literary core of Kluge's efforts. On Kluge's self-description as author, see Edgar Reitz, interview with Alexander Kluge, in *Bilder in Bewegung: Essays, Gespräche zum Kino* (Reinbek bei Hamburg: Rowohlt, 1995), 79.

12. Rainer Lewandowski, "Literatur und Film bei Alexander Kluge," in *Alexander Kluge,* ed. Thomas Böhm-Christl (Frankfurt am Main: Suhrkamp, 1983), 242.

13. Georg Stanitzek, "Autorität im Hypertext: 'Der Kommentar ist die Grundform der Texte' (Alexander Kluge)," *Internationales Archiv für Sozialgeschichte der deutschen Literatur* 23, no. 2 (1998): 6.

14. Matthias Uecker, "Rohstoffe und Intermedialität: Überlegungen zu Alexander Kluges Fernsehpraxis," in *Kluges Fernsehen: Alexander Kluges Kulturmagazine,* ed. Christian Schulte and Winfried Siebers (Frankfurt am Main: Suhrkamp, 2002), 84–85, 103–4.

15. The seven editions of *Schlachtbeschreibung* include the original hardcover edition from 1964, a revised paperback edition from 1968, two editions with different titles from 1969, a substantially revised edition from 1978, a reprint of this edition from 1983 including a slight title change, and another considerably altered version published in Alexander Kluge, *Chronik der Gefühle,* 2 vols. (Frankfurt am Main: Suhrkamp, 2000), 1:509–793.

16. See Lewandowski, *Die Filme von Alexander Kluge,* 57.

17. Alexander Kluge, "Rohstoffe, Nachrichten," in *Die Patriotin: Texte/Bilder 1–6* (Frankfurt am Main: Zweitausendeins, 1979), 294.

18. Kluge, *Die Patriotin,* 7.

19. In the 1964 edition, Kluge explains: "The causes date back thirty days or three hundred years." Alexander Kluge, *Schlachtbeschreibung* (Olten: Walter, 1964), 7. This English translation is taken from the unpaginated foreword to Alexander Kluge, *The Battle,* trans. Leila Vennewitz (New York: McGraw-Hill, 1967). Because this English edition modifies the German original drastically, all subsequent translations into the English are those of this author. The 1983 reprint

of the 1978 edition makes a slight revision to the aforementioned quote, with considerable theoretical ramifications to be unfurled in the course of this chapter: "The causes date back 72 days or 800 years." See Alexander Kluge, *Schlachtbeschreibung: Ein Roman* (Frankfurt am Main: Suhrkamp, 1983), 29. German editions are hereafter cited parenthetically in text as *SB* followed by the year of publication.

20. Kluge and his collaborator Oskar Negt explicate this idea of reflection and mourning in greater detail in *Geschichte und Eigensinn*, 361–413, 1145–73.

21. Alexander Kluge, dir., "Zeitenwechsel (rasch)," 19 December 1988, RTL, Electronic Arts Intermix, New York, 1988.

22. Richard Wolin, "The French Heidegger Debate," *New German Critique* 45 (Autumn 1988): 157, 151–58

23. Wolin, "French Heidegger Debate," 137n5.

24. Hans-Georg Gadamer, "Back to Syracuse?" *Critical Inquiry* 15, no. 2 (Winter 1989): 427, 429.

25. Jürgen Habermas, "Work and Weltanschauung: The Heidegger Controversy from a German Perspective," *Critical Inquiry* 15, no. 2 (Winter 1989): 435. In the English translation of Habermas's essay, the author dates the release of the German edition of Farias's book to 1988. It actually appeared the following year.

26. Martin Heidegger, *Being and Time,* trans. John Macquarrie and Edward Robinson (San Francisco: Harper, 1962), 469 (hereafter cited parenthetically in text as *BT*).

27. Translators Macquarrie and Robinson translate *Wirklichkeit* as *actuality.* The English subtitles to Kluge's video translate it as *reality,* a term much more in keeping with Negt and Kluge's own philosophy. This translation accommodates this discrepancy.

28. The sequence lifted from *Die Patriotin* includes not just the black-and-white analysis of "Ode to Joy" but also subsequent shots of Herbeck's poem, the photograph of the inmate, and the three shots of Cologne at night.

29. Teichert focuses the majority of her attention on Schiller's fifth and seventh verses, the second of which begins "Unser Schuldbuch sei vernichtet! / Ausgesöhnt die ganze Welt!" (Our registry of debts be destroyed! / Reconciled the entire world!).

30. While commentators like Lacoue-Labarthe contend that the bond between historicality and the *Volk* always existed in Heidegger's philosophy, his National Socialist assertions became increasingly overt after 1929. See Habermas, "Work and Weltanschauung," 440.

31. Adorno, *Negative Dialectics,* 130.

32. Alexander Kluge, *Der Angriff der Gegenwart auf die übrige Zeit: Abendfüllender Spielfilm, 35mm, Farbe mit s/w-Teilen, Format 1:1,37; Drehbuch* (Frankfurt am Main: Syndikat, 1985), 107. Kluge adds that his thinking about the present as gap derives from the physics of cinematography with its structural gaps of 1/48 of

a second. As established earlier, television's renegade task, according to Kluge, resides in its approximation of these gaps through temporal and spatial montage.

33. Kluge, *Der Angriff der Gegenwart,* 110.

34. Alexander Kluge, "Die Höhere Führung vor St.," *Merkur* 18, no. 5 (May 1964): 445.

35. Scholars translate Kluge and Negt's idea of *Zusammenhang* variously as *context, connection, connection-making, relation, relationship, perspective,* and *relationality.* This polysemy arises from both the conceptual richness of their idea and the divergent contexts to which they put the German original. This instance corresponds to Benn's use of the term. Subsequent translations of Kluge's term shall make use of this expanded catalogue.

36. Gottfried Benn, "Doppelleben," in *Gesammelte Werke,* 3:1998–99. For more differences between Kluge and Benn, see Ulrike Bosse, *Alexander Kluge: Formen literarischer Darstellung von Geschichte* (Frankfurt am Main: Peter Lang, 1989), 116–18.

37. Alexander Kluge, "Montage, Authentizität, Realismus," in *Ulmer Dramaturgien: Reibungsverluste,* ed. Klaus Eder and Alexander Kluge (Munich: Carl Hanser, 1980), 97–98. Kluge cites the following: "A photograph of the Krupp factory or the AEG plant tells us almost nothing about these institutions. The actual reality has transgressed into the functional. The reification of human relationships, for example the factory, means that they are no longer explicit. Something, therefore, must in fact be 'built up,' something 'artificial,' 'posed.' It is necessary as well to create art." See Bertolt Brecht, "Der Dreigroschenprozess: Ein soziologisches Experiment," in *Werke,* vol. 21 (Berlin: Aufbau; Frankfurt am Main: Suhrkamp, 1992), 469. See also Negt and Kluge, *Geschichte und Eigensinn,* 511.

38. Due to both the enormity of *The Battle* and the limited space, readers are encouraged to reference the following narrative accounts of the event, its historiography, mythology, and its depiction in German literature: Antony Beevor, *Stalingrad* (New York: Viking, 1998); Wolfram Wette and Gerd R Ueberschär, ed., *Stalingrad: Mythos und Wirklichkeit einer Schlacht* (Frankfurt am Main: Fischer, 1992); Michael Kumpfmüller, *Die Schlacht von Stalingrad: Metamorphosen eines deutschen Mythos* (Munich: Wilhelm Fink, 1995); and Carp, *Kriegsgeschichten,* 91–104.

39. See Robert Moeller, *War Stories: The Search for a Usable Past in the Federal Republic of Germany* (Berkeley: University of California Press, 2001), 99–105.

40. Günter Blöcker, "Stalingrad als Legespiel," *FAZ* (6 June 1964): n.p.; Marcel Reich-Ranicki, "Autor Klu. scheitert bei St.," *Die Zeit* (12 June 1964): 20.

41. Blöcker, "Stalingrad als Legespiel," n.p.

42. See Osborne, *Politics of Time,* 173.

43. Negt and Kluge write of a triad of protest feelings (the horizontal, the vertical, and the functional) rooted in rational perception and thought (*Geschichte und Eigensinn,* 511, 513). They list an additional three dimensions (the irratio-

nal, the imaginary, and the revolutionary) that verge into what Fredric Jameson calls the realm of the "'libidinal,' or of fantasy" (513–15). As discussed below, the irrational dimension plays an especially pivotal role in the 1978 edition of *Schlachtbeschreibung*. As Jameson cautions, Negt and Kluge define the irrational and imaginary differently than do philosophy and psychoanalysis. See Jameson, "On Negt and Kluge," 173–75.

44. Osborne, *Politics of Time*, 27–28.

45. Kluge references Brecht's explication of the functional directly in his preface to the sixth revised edition of *Schlachtbeschreibung* from 1978/1983. "This is the organized buildup of a disaster. It builds itself up somewhat along the lines of a factory, in the form of the institution of the state" (Kluge, *Schlachtbeschreibung* 1983, 8).

46. Carp, *Kriegsgeschichten*, 134.

47. See Winfried Siebers, "Was zwei Augen nicht sehen können: Wahrnehmungsweisen, Möglichkeitssinn und dokumentarisches Schreiben in Alexander Kluges *Schlachtbeschreibung*," in Schulte, *Die Schrift an der Wand*, 158; Kumpfmüller, *Die Schlacht von Stalingrad*, 249; and Ludger Vogt, "Die montierte Realität: Text und Bild in Alexander Kluges Schlachtbeschreibung," *KultuRRevolution* 23 (1990): 80–83.

48. The works, from which this edition borrows excerpts, include the two anthologies *Lernprozesse mit tödlichem Ausgang* (1972) and *Neue Geschichten: Hefte 1–18, 'Unheimlichkeit der Zeit'* (1977) and portions of the film *Die Patriotin* (1978).

49. Alexander Kluge, "Die Macht der Gefühle: Geschichten, Gespräche und Materialien," *Ästhetik und Kommunikation* 53–54 (December 1983): 178.

50. Negt and Kluge, *Öffentlichkeit und Erfahrung*, 378–79.

51. On the role of the ruin in Bertram's feeling of proportion, see Wolfgang Klimbacher, "'Dem Gleich fehlt die Trauer': Die *Schlachtbeschreibung* und Hölderlin," *Sprachkunst* 22 (1991): 27–28. This feeling of proportion also fuels the substantial excerpt taken from Kluge's *Lernprozesse mit tödlichem Ausgang* that begins the bulk of the additions in the 1978 edition. For economy's sake, this story is not discussed here. For a relevant analysis of this story, see Rainer Stollmann, "Schwarzer Krieg, endlos: Erfahrung und Selbsterhaltung in Alexander Kluges *Lernprozesse mit tödlichem Ausgang*," *Text und Kontext* 12, no. 2 (1984): 349–69.

52. This explains why the 1978 edition proposes an equivalency between Stalingrad and the mayhem generated by the Red Army Faction in the fall of 1977 (Kluge, *Schlachtbeschreibung* 1983, 297–98). The only Germans in the West German present who could have communed with such deadly feelings in Stalingrad were the terrorists, who also perished because of their unwavering devotion to making Germany. They, too, had no time for *kairos*. And like Bertram, they never lived to tell their feelings.

53. Walter Benjamin, "The Storyteller: Observations on the Works of Nikolai

Leskov," in *Selected Writings, Vol. 3: 1935–1938*, ed. Michael W. Jennings et al. (Cambridge, Mass.: Belknap, 2002), 154.

54. Kluge, *Die Patriotin*, 58. The body part in question is a knee that belonged to corporal Wieland, who fell in Stalingrad on January 29, 1943. Wieland's vita is included in *Schlachtbeschreibung;* however, the story of his knee is exclusive to the film (*Schlachtbeschreibung* 1983, 301–2).

55. Alexander Kluge, "Zeitenwechsel (rasch)," in *Zwischenbetrachtungen im Prozeß der Aufklärung: Jürgen Habermas zum 60. Geburtstag,* ed. Alex Honneth et al. (Frankfurt am Main: Suhrkamp, 1989), 813.

56. Santner, *Stranded Objects,* 153–55.

57. Benjamin, "The Storyteller," 149.

58. See Benjamin, "Concept of History," 390.

59. See Jameson, "On Negt and Kluge," 159.

60. Alexander Kluge, "Heidegger auf der Krim," in *Chronik der Gefühle,* 1:418–19 (hereafter cited parenthetically in text as "HK").

61. Kluge, "Heidegger auf der Krim," 425. See also Martin Heidegger, "The Origin of the Work of Art," trans. Albert Hofstadter, in *Basic Writings: From Being and Time (1927) to The Task of Thinking (1964),* ed. David Farrell Krell (San Francisco: Harper, 1993), 181.

62. Benjamin, "Concept of History," 392.

63. Wolin calls attention to Heidegger's 1949 claim that agricultural technology is no different than "the manufacture of corpses in gas chambers and extermination camps" (Wolin, "French Heidegger Debate," 158).

Chapter 7

1. Botho Strauß, "Anschwellender Bocksgesang," *Der Spiegel* (8 February 1993): 202–7.

2. Martin Walser, *Erfahrungen beim Verfassen einer Sonntagsrede: Friedenspreis des Deutschen Buchhandels* (Frankfurt am Main: Suhrkamp, 1998), 9–28.

3. Peter Sloterdijk, *Regeln für den Menschenpark: Ein Antwortschreiben zu Heideggers Brief über den Humanismus* (Frankfurt am Main: Suhrkamp, 1999).

4. Andreas Huyssen, "The Voids of Berlin," in *Present Pasts: Urban Palimpsests and the Politics of Memory* (Stanford: Stanford University Press, 2003), 63.

5. Lutz Koepnick, "Forget Berlin," *German Quarterly* 74, no. 4 (Autumn 2001): 343.

6. Julia Hell and Johannes von Moltke, "Unification Effects: Imaginary Landscapes of the Berlin Republic," *Germanic Review* 80, no. 1 (Winter 2005): 81–87.

7. Lutz Koepnick, "Reframing the Past: Heritage Cinema and Holocaust in the 1990s," *New German Critique* 87 (Autumn 2002): 78. See also the analysis of Kommune 1 at the conclusion of chapter 4.

8. Koepnick,. "Forget Berlin," 350.

9. Andreas Huyssen, "Present Pasts: Media, Politics, Amnesia," in *Present Pasts*, 22.

10. Terry Castle, "Phantasmagoria: Spectral Technology and the Metaphorics of Modern Reverie," *Critical Inquiry* 15, no. 1 (1998): 26–29.

11. A thorough overview in English of Schlingensief's post-cinematic work from the nineties can be found in Mark W. Rectanus, "Populism, Performance, and Postmodern Aesthetics: Christoph Schlingensief's Politics of Social Intervention," *Gegenwartsliteratur: Ein germanistisches Jahrbuch* 3 (2004): 225–49. See also Georg Seeßlen, "Vom barbarischen Film zur nomadischen Politik," in *Schlingensief! Notruf für Deutschland*, ed. Julia Lochte and Wilfried Schulz (Hamburg: Rotbuch, 1998), 40–78.

12. For an introduction to Pollesch, see Birgit Lengers, "Ein PS im Medienzeitalter: Mediale Mittel, Masken und Metaphern im Theater René Polleschs," *Text und Kritik* 11 (2004): 143–55.

13. See Reinhold Gärtner, "The FPÖ, Foreigners, and Racism in the Haider Era," in *The Haider Phenomenon in Austria*, ed. Ruth Wodak and Anton Pelinka (New Brunswick: Transaction, 2002), 17–31.

14. For a transcript of the interview, see Matthias Lilienthal and Claus Philipp, ed., *Schlingensiefs AUSLÄNDER RAUS* (Frankfurt am Main: Suhrkamp, 2000), 99 (hereafter cited parenthetically in text as *SAR*). The documentary film of Schlingenseif's action is Paul Poet, dir., *Ausländer Raus! Schlingensiefs Container*, Monitorpop Entertainment, 2005.

15. For a sample of the popular criticisms of Schlingensief and his contribution to the Vienna Festival, see the various letters of protest in Lilienthal and Philipp, *Schlingensiefs AUSLÄNDER RAUS*, 12, 48, 86–88, 92, 98–110, 119, 130, 133, 209, 232–33.

16. Poet, dir., *Ausländer Raus! Schlingensiefs Container*.

17. Elfriede Jelinek, "Der Raum im Raum," in Lilienthal and Philipp, *Schlingensiefs AUSLÄNDER RAUS*, 159. In her reckoning with the question of the container's revelations, Jelinek argues that the action neither seeks to unveil the fascist or empathetic humanist lurking within the individual, nor does it confront the spectator's relationship with entertainment.

18. Dietrich Diederichsen, "Das Gespenst der Freiheit," in Lilienthal and Philipp, *Schlingensiefs AUSLÄNDER RAUS*, 183.

19. Mark Andrejevic, *Reality TV: The Work of Being Watched* (Lanham: Rowman and Littlefield, 2004), 216 (hereafter cited parenthetically in text as *RTV*).

20. See Andrejevic, *Reality TV*, 200: "In a world in which change is still possible, not only must the symbolic order be irreducible to given experience, but experience must likewise be irreducible to the symbolic order. . . . It is this gap or inconsistency—perceived as a disturbing inadequacy—that becomes the tar-

get of postmodern savviness, which seeks to eliminate it by ruling out anything external to the symbolic order itself (and thereby erasing its internal limit)." Andrejevic is overwhelmingly indebted here to Slavoj Žižek's *The Ticklish Subject: The Absent Center of Political Ontology* (1999).

21. Like reality TV, *Bitte liebt Österreich* entailed an extensive and detailed script that Schlingensief drafted as a guideline for the possible sequencing of events to take place inside and outside the container. See Andrejevic, *Reality TV,* 18–19, 22–23, 26–27. This reference to "ideological apparatuses" is not an allusion to Louis Althusser's notion of a materialized ideology, but rather a reference to Jacques Lacan's and Žižek's notion of the "big Other" as presupposed by the subject.

22. Elfriede Jelinek, "Interferenzen im E-Werk," in Lilienthal and Philipp, *Schlingensiefs AUSLÄNDER RAUS,* 164; Christoph Schlingensief, "Containerreport," *Frankfurter Allgemeine Zeitung* (16 June 2000): 210, reprinted in Lilienthal and Philipp, *Schlingensiefs AUSLÄNDER RAUS,* 216. This insistence by spectators on a textual blueprint is particularly telling because the symbolic, according to Lacan, resides in language. As if the presence of a text would reassure the legitimacy of a symbolic order in the artwork and therefore the work's separation from reality, this suspicion that no text exists underscores the action's effective play with postmodernity's erasure of the symbolic.

23. See Andrejevic for more on this idea of the expansion of the boundary of media experience in the context of "Big Brother" (*Reality TV,* 159–68).

24. See Schlingensief's transcribed interview with Kluge in which he remarks, "The single great revolutionary act is *l'art pour l'art.* This art is highly political" (Lilienthal and Philipp, *Schlingensiefs AUSLÄNDER RAUS,* 146–47).

25. For a catalogue of the usual content of early peep shows from 1893, see David Robinson, *From Peep Show to Palace: The Birth of American Film* (New York: Columbia University Press, 1996), 41–45.

26. Schlingensief spent a portion of each day with a bullhorn agitating pedestrians with ironic declarations that identified *Bitte liebt Österreich* as a neo-fascist project supported by the FPÖ, the *Kronen Zeitung,* and above all the citizens themselves. This allusion to concentration camps, one that surfaced in the earliest planning phases of the project, was announced on day two of the action. See the DVD that accompanies the first edition of the reader to the action: Paul Poet, dir., *Bitte liebt Österreich: Die Container CD,* webfreetv.com, 2000.

27. Seeßlen's essay "Der Populist, der Provokateur, der fremde Blick und das eigene Bild, oder die ersten Sätze des letzten Kapitals der Geschichte Österreichs" concludes Lilienthal and Philipp's volume. Seeßlen writes "The cultural event is no longer the peculiar attraction that draws looks toward itself. On the contrary, it throws the look back entirely" (Lilienthal and Philipp, *Schlingensiefs AUSLÄNDER RAUS,* 251).

28. Andrejevic dedicates an entire chapter to reading Žižek's idea of the "pure gaze" that transforms the voyeur into the exhibitionist into reality television. See, in particular, Andrejevic, *Reality TV,* 179–83.

29. For an overview of the idea of *Erfahrung* as first developed by Kracauer and then expanded by Benjamin, Adorno, and Negt and Kluge, see Miriam Hansen, *Babel and Babylon: Spectatorship in American Silent Film* (Cambridge, Mass.: Harvard University Press, 1991), 12–13 (hereafter cited parenthetically in text as *BB*). Hansen erects her notion of early cinema's counter-public spheres on Alexander Kluge and Oskar Negt's *The Public Sphere and Experience.*

30. In this respect, Schlingensief's project is very much in keeping with *The Public Sphere and Experience.* For an account of the applicability of Negt and Kluge's concept in the postmodern context, see Hansen, "Unstable Mixtures, Dilated Spheres," 179–212.

31. Agamben, *Homo Sacer,* 1–2.

32. See Mark B. N. Hansen, *New Philosophy for New Media* (Cambridge, Mass.: MIT Press, 2004), 10.

33. Negt and Kluge, *Öffentlichkeit und Erfahrung,* 493–94.

34. "Gespräch zwischen Sloterdijk und Schlingensief zur Wienaktion," transcript, 17 June 2000, http://www.schlingensief.com/downloads/schlinge_sloterdijk_wien.pdf.

35. Hans-Thies Lehmann, *Postdramatisches Theater* (Frankfurt am Main: Verlag der Autoren, 1999), 27.

36. Lehmann, *Postdramatisches Theater,* 31.

37. Romano Pocai, Martin Saar, and Ruth Sonderegger, "'Entschlüsselt mich!': Ein Interview mit René Pollesch," *Texte zur Kunst* 13, no. 49 (March 2003): 122.

38. "Das Material fragt zurück," interview with René Pollesch, in *Wohnfront 2001–2002: Volksbühne im Prater Dokumentationen der Spielzeit 2001–2002,* ed. Bettina Masuch (Berlin: Alexander, 2002), 221, 226.

39. René Pollesch, "Stadt als Beute," in *Wohnfront 2001–2002,* 5.

40. See Klaus Ronneberger, Stephan Lanz, and Walther Jahn, *Die Stadt als Beute* (Bonn: J. H. W. Dietz Nachfolger, 1999), 12–13: "The reconstruction of cities takes place in the context of the new international division of labor" (12). "Currently the view prevails for the reason that geographical spaces and territories only play a secondary role for 'global players'" (13).

41. Pocai, Saar, and Sonderegger, "'Entschlüsselt mich!'" 122.

42. "Wir sind ja oft so glücklich, wenn wir überhaupt Reaktionen bekommen," interview with René Pollesch, in *Zeltsaga: René Polleschs Theater 2003/2004,* ed. Lenore Blievernicht (Berlin: Synwolt, 2004), 185–86.

43. The following discussion is based on this production: René Pollesch, dir. *Smarthouse ® 1+2,* Staatstheater, Stuttgart, 23 and 24 November 2001. The author transcribed all subsequent dialogue from a video recording of this performance.

44. Negt and Kluge, *Geschichte und Eigensinn,* 98–102.

45. The one precursor that closely resembles *Smarthouse* ® *1+2* and that is in print and wide distribution is René Pollesch, "world wide web-slums," in *world wide web-slums,* ed. Corinna Brocher (Reinbek bei Hamburg: Rowohlt Taschenbuch, 2003), 103–328. The first series of this ten-part work was originally performed at the Deutsches Schauspielhaus in Hamburg on November 8, 2000.

46. Pollesch is citing the German translation of Gary Hamel's *Leading the Revolution* (*Das revolutionäre Unternehmen* [2001]), a handbook for mobile business strategies for the twenty-first century.

47. David Harvey, *A Brief History of Neoliberalism* (New York: Oxford University Press, 2005).

48. Harvey, *Neoliberalism,* 3.

49. See David Harvey. See also Chandan Reddy, "Asian Diasporas, Neoliberalism, and Family: Reviewing the Case for Homosexual Asylum in the Context of Family Rights," *Social Text* 23, no. 3–4 (Fall–Winter 2005): 103–8.

50. Harvey, *Neoliberalism,* 3.

51. Diedrich Diederichsen, "Denn sie wissen, was sie nicht leben wollen: Das kulturtheoretische Theater des René Pollesch," *Theaterheute* 3 (March 2003): 61.

52. "Verkaufe dein Subjekt!: René Pollesch im Gespräch," interview with René Pollesch, in *world wide web-slums,* 331.

53. "Das Material fragt zurück," 226.

54. "Wir sind ja so oft glücklich," 186.

55. "Verkaufe dein Subjekt!" 342.

56. Pocai, Saar, and Sonderegger, "'Entschlüsselt mich!'" 117.

57. See Kunzelmann, "Notizen zur Gründung," 143.

58. On the semantic plurality of *Eigensinn,* see Jameson, "On Negt and Kluge," 158.

59. Benjamin, "Concept of History," 390.

Index

Page numbers in italics refer to figures.

and avant-garde resistance, 136, 137; on bare life, 159–60; on dialectic, 136, 161, 170

Marinetti, F. T., 5, 133

Marx, Karl, 171; in *Geschichte und Eigensinn*, 44, 45, 46, 47, 48, 54, 220

Marxism: existentialist, 62; and Habermas, 169, 252; and Kommune I, 155; in media theory, 171–72; Negt and Kluge on, 43; neo-, 194, 219; post-, 43; in smarthouse, 247; and student movement, 173, 279n7

Marxistische Blätter, 169

McLuhan, Marshall, 166, 180, 181

media: and avant-garde, 18, 20; and bodies, 173, 180–81, 185, 191–92, 230, 243; boundaries, 7; and existentialism, 63; and German guilt, 230–31; Habermas on, 286n14; Kluge on, 195–201, 209–11; manipulation of, 168–72; power of, 22, 132, 165–74, 176–89, 230; violence, 172–74; West German mass, 44, 128, 155, 157–58, 181, 194. *See also* new media

mediation: of bare life, 130; between life and death, 201; and mass media, 162; in painting, 67; and postmodernity, 230, 237; and public sphere, 241–43; reality of, 238, 240; and sex, 194; technological, 18, 191

Meidner, Ludwig, 5

Méliès, Georges, 196

memory, 6, 29, 254; Adorno on, 38; Benjamin on, 30, 39, 262n11; in Brinkmann, 111, 116, 178–80, 188, 277n38; dialectic of, 232; Freud on, 35; Kluge on, 221, 225; and mourning, 15, 16, 17; Negt and Kluge on, 46–49, 54; Simon on, 112; in Vostell, 135, 161; in Weiss, 95. *See*

also history; mourning; *Vergangenheitsbewältigung* (coming to terms with the past)

Merkert, Jörn, 135

Merleau-Ponty, Maurice, 67, 73, 93, 271n45

Mesch, Claudia, 135, 280n21

metaphor, 98; and avant-garde, 26; Benjamin on, 29; in Brinkmann, 110–11, 116, 117–18, 122, 184, 277n38; Negt and Kluge on, 44; and Robbe-Grillet, 108, 109; surrealist, 57, 59; in Weiss, 68, 83

metonymy, 77, 79, 81, 84. *See also* misrecognition

Metz, Christian, 85

mimesis, 5–6, 106, 219, 257n9; in Brinkmann, 182, 186, 188, 278n51; and collage, 83; and historical avant-garde, 135; in Kluge, 219; and realism, 97; and reality, 106; and Vostell, 142

misrecognition, 83–84, 86

Mitscherlich, Alexander, 15, 49, 272n61. See also *Vergangenheitsbewältigung* (coming to terms with the past)

modernism: and avant-garde, 3, 12, 24, 62, 259n28, 263n17; postwar, 10–14, 59–60, 95, 105; versus realism, 107, 125–26, 278n59. *See also* postmodernism

modernity, 23, 34, 39, 41, 100; and Auschwitz, 38, 47; and bare life, 131, 145, 242; and bodies, 52; cynical, 104; dialectic of, 129, 270n32; end of, 229; Enzensberger on, 26in4; fragmentation of, 147; German, 219, 225; postwar, 10–13, 14, 19, 99, 128; and reality, 19; and time, 26–32, 36, 109, 146, 206, 261n2. *See also* postmodernity

Mon, Franz, 59, 95, 274n91

montage, 3, 5, 7, 18, 51, 135, 201, 245; in Brinkmann, 175–78, 181–83, 185–86, 187, 284n1; Bürger on, 261n1; cinematic, 182, 197; Kluge on, 102, 210, 212, 213–14, 293n37; literary, 39; in Vostell, 139; in Weiss, 76, 81–84, 95; in Wellershoff, 106. *See also* fragmentation; Vostell, Wolf: and décollage

Moritz, Karl Philip, 175

mourning, 49, 53, 54, 196; Kluge on, 200, 211, 226; and melancholy, 15, 16, 41; Negt and Kluge on, 220. See also *Vergangenheitsbewältigung* (coming to terms with the past)

movement, 253; in Brinkmann, 111, 112, 114–16, 118, 122, 126, 187; as deterritorialization, 122, 229, 241; in Kluge, 206; in Schlingensief, 243; in Weiss, 67, 78, 79, 81

national identity. *See* identity: national

National Socialism, 21, 24, 61, 123, 130, 192, 199, 217, 242, 253; and Benn, 103–4; and exile, 60; and Heidegger, 190, 204, 208, 292n30; and historians' debate, 15; specters of, 12, 158, 194; and technology, 164, 168; and violence, 25, 57. *See also* bare life; fascism; Holocaust

Negri, Antonio: and Michael Hardt, 248

Negt, Oskar

—and Alexander Kluge: and Benjamin, 265n42; on bodies, 46–48, 50–52, 54, 201, 220; on dreaming, 44–45; on fantasy, 50–53, 147, 159, 266n49; on fragmentation, 44–45; and Heidegger, 203; on history, 43–51,

134, 216, 218; on labor, 246; on memory, 46–49, 54, 134; on mourning, 220; on orientation, 251–52; in Pollesch, 250–52; on realism, 54; and Schlingensief, 243, 298n30; on screams, 249; on space, 45, 124, 134; on time, 43–55, 124, 265n42, 266n43, 266n49, 267n55; on totality, 44–45; on trauma, 54; on utopia, 51, 54. *See also* Kluge, Alexander

—works with Kluge:
Geschichte und Eigensinn, 44–52, 54, 220, 221, 224, 227, 251–52, 265n37, 265n42, 266n43, 266n44, 266n49, 292n20, 293n43
Massverhältnisse des Politischen, 229
The Public Sphere and Experience, 44, 243, 298n29, 298n30

Nemes, Endre, 60

neo-avant-garde, 8, 9, 10, 14, 28, 261n1. *See also* avant-garde

neoliberalism, 232, 245, 247, 248, 252

neue kritik, 168, 185n10

Neues Deutschland, 138

Nevermann, Knut, 172

New German Cinema, 137, 197

new media, 195–98, 230–33, 236, 242–44, 254. *See also* media

New Objectivity, 60

Nietzsche, Friedrich, 12, 103

normalization, 22, 232

nouveau roman, 22, 99, 105–12, 115, 119, 122, 125–26, 277n40, 278n56. *See also* realism: new

Le Nouvel Observateur, 204

novel, the: and Adorno, 37, 75; development, 174–75, 176, 186, 192–93, 287n34; and exile, 62; Lukács on,

Strauß, Botho, 230–31
structuralism, 218, 219. *See also* fantasy: Negt and Kluge on
student movement, 162; and Adorno, 128; avant-gardes after, 230; Brinkmann and, 168, 193–94; Habermas on, 279n7, 286n14; and happening, 131–32, 137; and Marxism, 155; on media, 169–73; and Negt and Kluge, 44; social movement after, 248; and Vietnam, 152
studio f, 138
Subversive Aktion, 128, 131, 279n4
Suleiman, Susan Rubin, 65
surrealism, 4–5, 9, 22, 133, 136; Adorno on, 6, 29, 61; Benjamin on, 29–33, 56, 73–74; and bodies, 96; death of, 6, 61; dreams in, 59, 81; and exile, 60–63; and fascism, 57, 60, 63, 96; film (*see* film: surrealist); and Kommune 1, 156; and literature, 39, 57–59; manifesto of, 236; metaphor in, 57, 59; and painting, 268n11; postwar, 57–59, 60–61, 96, 267n11, 268n20; relationship to existentialism, 58, 61–63, 269n31; and space, 30, 56. *See also* Weiss, Peter: and surrealism
Syberberg, Hans Jürgen, 15

technology, 8; and bodies, 73, 181, 192, 230–31, 233, 242; in Brinkmann, 176, 192, 194; and fantasy, 230–32; and fascism, 163–67, 190, 194, 230; Heidegger and, 190–91, 206, 289n50, 295n63; Kluge on, 195–98, 206; media, 196; and mediation of historical violence, 18, 22, 135, 173, 191, 231–33; and modernity, 13; and phantasmagoria, 233–34; in Pollesch, 247–54; and postmodernity, 101, 234; and realism, 97;

in Schlingensief, 237–44. *See also* media
telephone, 163–68, 190, 192, 242, 247
television: Brinkmann on, 186, 188; Burroughs on, 165, 166; in happening, 136, 140; Kluge on, 195–203, 205, 208–13, 225–26, 228; in Pollesch, 247; RTL, 201, 212; RTL-2, 235; in Schlingensief, 233; as spectacle, 161; Vietnam War on, 153. *See also* reality television
Tel Zatar, 49
terrorism, 44, 132, 157, 199, 251, 294n52
Teufel, Fritz, 129, 132, 157–59, 161
theory: and Adorno, 128; aesthetic, 23; and Benjamin, 33, 45; Brinkmann's, 180–81; confrontation with the avant-garde, 25; and Foucault, 185; and Holocaust, 25; and Kluge, 197–98, 203, 209, 228, 290n6; and Lacan, 83; and Marcuse, 138; and new media, 233; in Pollesch, 245–52; postmodern, 101; poststructuralist, 234; and praxis, 48, 54, 56, 161, 233; and trauma, 40. *See also* avant-garde: theory of; Frankfurt School; Negt, Oskar: works with Kluge, *Geschichte und Eigensinn;* orientation
Theweleit, Klaus, 121–22
Tieck, Ludwig, 186, 288n48
time: and abject, 124; Adorno on, 33–47; of agency (*kairos*), 196–97, 200, 210–12, 219, 224, 290n5, 294n52; and avant-garde, 4, 13–14, 23–28, 32–44, 53–54, 59, 109; of awakening, 29; Benjamin on, 29–33, 53–54, 146, 226, 263n17, 290n4; in Benn, 102; biographical, 217; and bodies, 20, 25, 39, 228; in Brinkmann, 109, 111, 124, 176–77, 180, 185, 192–93; and communards,

About the Author

Richard Langston is an assistant professor of Germanic languages and literatures at the University of North Carolina at Chapel Hill.

Avant-Garde & Modernism Studies

General Editors
Marjorie Perloff
Rainer Rumold

Consulting Editors
Peter Fenves
Stephen Foster
Christine Froula
Françoise Lionnet
Robert von Hallberg

Avant-Garde & Modernism Collection

General Editors
Rainer Rumold
Marjorie Perloff